TAKE CHARGE!

E IMPROVE YOUR SSAYS

Doug Emory
Chairman/Instructor, Developmental Education Division
Pierce College, Tacoma, Washington

GLENCOE
McGraw-Hill

New York, New York   Columbus, Ohio   Mission Hills, California   Peoria, Illinois

Thomas Hart Benton (1889-1975) is the creator of the cover art, *The Arts of Life in America and The Arts of the West,* a mural housed in the library of the Whitney Museum of American Art. Benton was born in Neosho, Missouri, to a family active in state politics. He began his education at the Art Institute of Chicago and continued his art studies at the Académie Julian and the Collarossi Studio in Paris. His first major exhibition in New York City was the Forum Exhibition of 1916. He is best known for his work employing abstract forms of pure color and his more realistic murals derived from sketching tours of the American midwest.

PHOTO CREDITS: Cover, detail from the collection of the New Britain Museum of American Art, Connecticut, Harriet Russell Stanley Fund, photo by E. Irving Blomstrann; 2-3, Elena Rooraid/PhotoEdit; 36-37, Jim Pickerell/Tony Stone Images; 82-83, Arvand Garg/Photo Researchers; 114-115, Robert Brenner; 162-163, Jeff Greenburg/Omni-Photo Communications; 206-207, Paul Conklin/Monkmeyer Press Photo Service; 234-235, Michael Newman/PhotoEdit; 264-265, Mimi Forsyth/Monkmeyer Press Photo Service; 292-293, Michael Kagan/Monkmeyer Press Photo Service; 320-321, Reuters/Bettmann; 348-349, David Young-Wolff/PhotoEdit; 380-381, Michael Newman/PhotoEdit; 408-409, Arlene Collins/Monkmeyer Press Photo Service; 436-437, Richard Hackett/Omni-Photo Communications

Send all inquiries to:
Glencoe/McGraw-Hill
936 Eastwind Drive
Westerville, OH 43081

ISBN 0-02-802033-2

Printed in the United States of America.

00 99 98 97 96 95 94   HESS-HESS   9 8 7 6 5 4 3 2 1

TABLE OF CONTENTS

Appendix

Improve Your Essays provides a holistic plan for developing essay-writing skills at the college level. The holistic approach is integrated, developing and combining writing skills and knowledge in the comprehensive manner in which they must be used during any writing process. The holistic approach also makes use of students' valuable prior knowledge and skills and uses this experience as the basis for introducing and developing essential writing skills. Drawing from materials used successfully with many classes, *Improve Your Essays* helps students develop skill in expressing and developing their ideas in logically organized essays. The text is highly interactive, requiring students to respond continually to the concepts and examples through both group activities and independent writing. Skills are presented as strategies or sequential steps rather than as rote memorization, enabling students to obtain a deep understanding that fosters mastery. In a wide variety of activities and assignments, students practice new skills by applying what they've learned to write about real-life issues.

ORGANIZATION OF *IMPROVE YOUR ESSAYS*

In working through the four sections and fourteen chapters of this text, students will find informative content and user-friendly features that will help them develop essay-writing skills and increase their confidence in their writing. By the end of the text, they will be ready to apply their essay-writing skills to specialized forms of writing.

- **Section 1. The Writing Process.**   This section focuses on the steps of the writing process: prewriting, writing a first draft, revising and editing drafts, and proofreading and preparing a final copy.

- **Section 2. The Elements of Essays.**   This section explores the four basic purposes for writing: to describe, to narrate, to persuade, and to inform. In addition, this section examines the five key elements of writing—purpose, content, structure, audience, and tone and presents strategies for developing essay content and methods of organizing information.

- **Section 3. Writing to Describe and to Narrate.**   The chapters in this section examine in more depth the two most common writing purposes—to describe and to narrate. Each chapter demonstrates how to accomplish one of those purposes effectively.

- **Section 4. Writing to Inform and to Persuade.**   Each chapter in this section explores a strategy that can be used to develop essay content effectively: example, process, cause/effect, comparison/contrast, classification, definition, and argument.

The Appendix to *Improve Your Essays* includes five enrichment chapters that explore special essay applications: essay tests, summaries, reports, résumés and application letters, and research papers. The Appendix also contains additional grammar-related activities as well as a Writer's Guide—an easy-reference handbook of grammar and style.

FEATURES OF THE STUDENT EDITION

Each chapter of *Improve Your Essays* includes these special features:

- **Chapter Opener.**   The chapter opener includes the chapter title, objectives, focusing question, brief introductory paragraphs, and a picture. The chapter opener engages the students' interest, builds on current knowledge, and describes the focus of the chapter.

- **Getting Started.**   This feature helps students identify what they already know about the content of the chapter. *Getting Started* includes checklists, inventories, and questionnaires that help students assess their prior knowledge.

- **In Your Journal.**   Each chapter has journal-writing activities that encourage students to identify goals for improvement and to chart their progress toward those goals. Other journal activities invite students to do exploratory writing or to gather ideas for later use.

- **Group Activities.**   The peer group activities guide students' work with classmates. Group work has several advantages: Students share tasks and contribute ideas and skills to the group; they learn to appreciate other people's ideas and skills; they can take pride in both their ability to work with others and the outcome of group efforts.

- **Discovery Activities.** Discovery Activities guide students to use what they already know—both experiences and ideas—as a springboard for learning new concepts and skills.

- **Questions.** Every chapter poses questions that invite students to respond to the material presented. Some questions draw on students' prior knowledge and experience while other questions check students' understanding of the chapter content.

- **Do You Write on a Computer?** Each chapter presents a tip on how students can use the many features of word processing programs.

- **Assignments.** Every chapter includes assignments where students apply what they learn about the writing process to creating essays. There are group and individual assignments. To provide evidence of increasing skills, students are directed to save these assignments in a portfolio.

- **Grammar Gremlins.** The Grammar Gremlins in each chapter presents an explanation of a grammar element, examples, and several practice activities. Additional Grammar Gremlins activities are in the Appendix.

- **Wrapping It Up.** Each chapter concludes with a summary, questions, and a journal activity to help students assess their progress.

- **Writing Tools.** A variety of writing tools in the form of charts, checklists, and guides appear throughout the text. These tools include: *Checklist for Revising and Editing, Checklist for Proofreading, Writing Focus Chart, Writer's Tool Box,* and *Writer's Guide.*

- **Writing Models.** Numerous extracts from published sources are included as models in the text. These extracts reflect a variety of college-level subjects and provide models of professional writing as well as student writing.

- **Reading As a Stimulus for Writing.** In addition to the shorter extracts within the chapters, longer selections by published authors appear in the Appendix. These selections serve as a stimulus for students' writing.

FEATURES OF THE INSTRUCTOR MATERIALS

The Instructor's support materials include the following:

- **The Instructor's Wraparound Edition** of *Improve Your Essays* is a unique teaching guide that includes a comprehensive instructor's manual and reduced student pages. Positioned adjacent to the appropriate student material, teaching solutions and strategies focus on each major concept.

- **The Transparency Package** for *Improve Your Essays* contains color teaching transparencies that reinforce the key concepts.

- **The Test Package** contains reproducible test masters correlated with the chapters, Grammar Gremlins, and the Writer's Guide.

- *Hyper*Graphics® **Software** for the *Take Charge!* system is a multimedia instructional system that allows for group and individual exploration of chapter concepts and instructor assessment of student understanding.

- *Electronic Worksheets* **Software** provides guided practice dealing with grammar, usage, and style.

TAKE CHARGE! SERIES

Glencoe's *Take Charge!* series provides comprehensive support for success in college-level studies. The series of four texts—each supported with an Instructor's Wraparound Edition, a transparency package, a test package, *Hyper*Graphics® Software, and *Electronic Worksheets* Software—includes *Improve Your Essays* and these three texts:

- *Improve Your Reading and Study Skills* helps students learn to manage time and resources and improve such necessary skills as listening and note-taking, studying for and taking tests, and reading for information.

- *Improve Your Sentences* presents a logical and thorough treatment of sentence structure.

- *Improve Your Paragraphs* helps students integrate and develop skills and knowledge in using the writing process to create well-organized paragraphs.

Your decision to use *Improve Your Essays* reflects a commitment to developing your students' writing proficiency to the highest degree possible. The text, used with the comprehensive instructor support materials, will provide a complete and empowering tool enabling students to become skillful, confident writers.

Doug Emory

As you continue to answer the challenge of college-level studies, you will become more aware of the need to express your ideas clearly and effectively. Your success in school as well as your success on the job and in your personal life depends in large measure on how well you communicate. *Improve Your Essays* is designed to help you express ideas and information clearly through carefully written essays. This text will guide you in focusing on the elements of sound writing and developing the skills needed for effective written communication.

As you work toward your academic goals, you'll need to write in many different areas of knowledge. You'll want this writing to be an accurate reflection of the care and thoughtful effort you're putting into your studies. *Improve Your Essays* will help you develop and polish specific skills that will enable you to take charge of your writing. To accomplish this goal, *Improve Your Essays* takes you through the writing process, examines the interrelated elements of writing—purpose, content, structure, audience, and tone—and explores how successfully blending these elements is essential to writing effective essays.

Improve Your Essays also makes use of aspects of your abilities that you may not have associated with writing skills, such as your previous life experience and details you have learned through observation. By combining an exploration of the steps of the writing process with activities that engage your emotions and experiences, *Improve Your Essays* provides an effective program of essential writing skills.

As you work through the four sections and fourteen chapters of this text, you'll find informative content and user-friendly features that will help you develop your essay-writing skills and increase your confidence in your writing. By the end of the text, you'll be ready to apply your essay-writing skills to specialized forms of writing such as essay tests, summaries, reports, résumés and application letters, and research papers.

- **Section 1. The Writing Process.**   This section focuses on the steps of the writing process: prewriting, writing a first draft, revising and editing drafts, and proofreading and preparing a final copy.

- **Section 2. The Elements of Essays.** This section explores the four basic purposes for writing: to describe, to narrate, to persuade, and to inform. In addition, this section examines the five key elements of writing—purpose, content, structure, audience, and tone and presents strategies for developing essay content and methods of organizing information.

- **Section 3. Writing to Describe and to Narrate.** The chapters in this section examine in more depth the two most common writing purposes—to describe and to narrate. Each chapter demonstrates how to accomplish one of those purposes effectively.

- **Section 4. Writing to Inform and to Persuade.** Each chapter in this section explores a strategy that can be used to develop essay content effectively: example, process, cause/effect, comparison/contrast, classification, definition, and argument.

The Appendix to *Improve Your Essays* includes five enrichment chapters that explore special essay applications: essay tests, summaries, reports, résumés and application letters, and research papers. The Appendix also contains additional grammar-related activities as well as a Writer's Guide—an easy-reference handbook of grammar and style.

To make the best use of this text, take charge—participate actively in the writing process. Active writing involves awareness of the elements and steps of the writing process and application of that awareness to everything you write. The activities and assignments in this text make it easy for you to apply what you are learning, not only to your work in this course but to your other courses and in your daily life.

Doug Emory

ACKNOWLEDGMENTS

The author thanks the following educators for reviewing manuscript and offering suggestions for enhancing *Improve Your Essays*.

CONSULTANTS

Hunter R. Boylan
Appalachian State University
Boone, North Carolina

Pura G. Gonzalez
Microcomputer Technology Institute
Houston, Texas

Bertha Murray
Tallahassee Community College
Tallahassee, Florida

Lettie Wong
De Anza College
Cupertino, California

REVIEWERS

Caroline Dennis
University of Florida
Gainesville, Florida

J. R. Dudley
Tacoma Community College
Tacoma, Washington

Barbara Feldman
National-Louis University
McLean, Virginia

Kathleen Jacquette
State University of New
York-Farmingdale
Farmingdale, New York

Diane Janowiak
Prairie State College
Chicago Heights, Illinois

Cecilia Macheski
LaGuardia Community College
Hudson, New York

Emory Maiden
Appalachian State University
Boone, North Carolina

Judith Olson-Fallon
Case Western Reserve University
Cleveland, Ohio

Mark Reynolds
Jefferson Davis Community
College
Brewton, Alabama

Maria Valeri-Gold
Georgia State University
Atlanta, Georgia

The Writing Process

A process is a series of actions, preparations, or procedures made to get something done. You carry out the steps of a process every time you register for your college courses, plan and cook a meal, or apply to school or for a job. Now you'll use a process to take charge of your essay writing.

In Section 1 of *Improve Your Essays*, you will learn skills and techniques that will help you carry out the essay writing process successfully. Chapter 1 draws on what you already know about paragraphs and their structure and helps you relate to the process of writing essays. Chapters 2 and 3 explore the steps of the writing process. Chapter 2 focuses on planning and writing a first draft. Chapter 3 deals with revising and editing and then with proofreading and preparing a final copy of what you have written. These two chapters will provide opportunities for you to follow the steps of the writing process to create essays.

1

FROM PARAGRAPH TO ESSAY

OBJECTIVES:

Composition

- To review the elements of a paragraph.

- To define *essay, central point*, and *thesis statement*.

- To describe the parts of an essay.

- To describe three essential characteristics of effective writing: *unity, support,* and *coherence*.

- To begin a journal and a portfolio of writing assignments.

- To work in collaborative groups.

Grammar

- To distinguish sentence fragments from complete sentences.

How Do I Apply My Skills To Essays?

Your ability to express your ideas in writing enables you to communicate in school, on the job, and in your personal life. Sometimes you need to write only a few sentences or a paragraph or two to convey your meaning. Other times, however, you may need to write several related paragraphs to develop your ideas or communicate information. Writing a multiple-paragraph composition—an essay—calls upon many skills you already have. In fact, just as you use your knowledge of words and sentences to write paragraphs, so you can apply your paragraph-writing skills to create essays.

GETTING STARTED

Answer the following questions about your writing.

- What writing have you done in recent months? List examples from school, from work, and from your personal life. Include only examples that consisted of *more than one paragraph* about a particular subject.

  _____

  _____

  _____

- For the examples that you listed, why wouldn't writing just one paragraph have been adequate?

  _____

  _____

  _____

For *one* of your examples, answer the following questions.

- The **central point** of an essay is the principal idea that the writer presents and develops. In which paragraph did you introduce your central point? Why?

  _____

  _____

  _____

- How well were you able to support or develop your central point? Give reasons for your answer.

  _____

  _____

  _____

- Did all of your paragraphs work together to form a coherent whole? Explain.

  _____

  _____

  _____

WRITING IN YOUR JOURNAL

As you read this book, you'll have opportunities to record your thoughts and ideas in a **journal**. Expressing yourself on paper will help you clarify and focus your thinking.

Your journal is a place to express yourself freely—to try out ideas; jot down impressions of people, places, and things; and experiment with different kinds of writing. In your journal you can explore possible writing topics, note your reactions to political or social issues, or simply comment on everyday events. Often you'll be able to use the thoughts from your journal as a springboard for writing.

Journal entries may take various forms. Sometimes you may want to express yourself by writing sentences or whole paragraphs. Other times a few scribbled words and phrases—or even a drawing—will be sufficient. At times you may want to clip or staple newspaper or magazine articles or photocopied book excerpts in your journal, perhaps with your comments attached. You may also want to record in your journal interesting facts that you encounter, notable quotations, and thought-provoking statistics. Any of these items may later inspire your thinking when you're searching for a writing topic.

The writing you do in your journal is for yourself. What you write is not graded and need not be perfect.

Your journal also provides a place to write specific goals for improving your writing. As you develop and polish your writing skills, you can monitor your progress toward your goals.

IN YOUR JOURNAL

Use your answers to the questions on page 4 to evaluate your ability to write multiple-paragraph compositions. Then set one or more goals in your journal. Here are some examples:

GOALS:
1. I will adequately support or develop my central point.
2. I will organize my paragraphs in a logical order.

YOUR COLLABORATIVE GROUP

Throughout this book you will have many opportunities to work within a collaborative group to discuss ideas and complete activities and assignments. When people **collaborate**, they work together to achieve a common goal. As a member of a group, you have certain responsibilities that will enable the group to function effectively.

- Be an active participant, contributing ideas and examples from your experience and observation.

- Complete your part of the activity or assignment to the best of your ability.

- Be considerate of other group members. Avoid interrupting other members when they are speaking. Try not to dominate the group.

Collaborating with other group members has a number of benefits. Doing a task together with other people will help prepare you to do that same task on your own. If the task is one that you feel uneasy about—writing an essay, for example—sharing your feelings with group members may lessen your anxiety. Also, as you get to know the other members of your class, you'll feel more comfortable discussing your writing with one another and giving and receiving helpful suggestions.

COMPARING PARAGRAPHS AND ESSAYS

GROUP
ACTIVITY

Consider what you know about the features of a paragraph. This knowledge will help you gain an understanding of the features of an essay.

A. The paragraph and the essay on pages 7-9 both deal with the same topic. Read the two selections independently, and consider how they are similar and how they differ.

B. After you've read the selections, discuss with group members similarities and differences between paragraphs and essays. Consider both the content and the structure of the two selections, as well as the manner in which each selection supports and develops ideas. Work together with your group to identify similarities and differences between paragraphs and essays.

- Similarities between paragraphs and essays:

1. A paragraph is a part of an essay.
2. Both give information to the reader

- Differences between paragraphs and essays:

1. A paragraph is short wereas an essay is long
2. A paragraph discusses a topic in brief wereas an essay discusses the topic in detail.
3. A paragraph just consists of a body wereas an essay consists of a heading, Introduction, body and conclusion

Paragraph: Let's Speak for Ourselves

Most of us depend too much on preprinted greeting cards to express our feelings on special occasions. Instead of making an effort to say what we feel, we communicate almost exclusively through words written by professional card writers. We send preprinted cards for birthdays, anniversaries, graduations, major holidays, and numerous other events. We use these cards to express love, longing, regrets, and congratulations. Most of these cards communicate their messages—*our* messages—through corny rhymes or silly jokes or through heavy-handed prose dripping with false sincerity. What an improvement it would be if we purchased cards that were blank inside and took the time to write our own words, or if we telephoned or sent a handwritten note. Our words might not be as slick or funny as store-bought sentiments, but they would certainly be more genuine.

Essay: Write From the Heart

When was the last time you wrote a card to a friend or loved one wishing the person a happy birthday? I don't mean *sent* a card. I mean actually *wrote* one. Unfortunately, most of us rely on professional greeting card writers to express our feelings for us. The preprinted cards that we purchase use corny poetry, silly jokes, and heavy-handed prose to communicate what should be personal and sincere sentiments.

Look around any greeting card shop and you'd think that people were incapable of putting into words their feelings about *any* life situation. The racks are filled with cards for observing birthdays, anniversaries, and holidays; for expressing affection, friendship, and gratitude; for celebrating weddings and graduations. Cards exist that encourage a speedy recovery or wish someone bon voyage or a happy retirement. Cards exist that offer apologies for wrong deeds, congratulations on the birth of a baby or the purchase of a home, or sympathy for a death in the family. Incredibly, cards even exist that fabricate make-believe sentiments: *Happy holidays from our dog to yours!*

Why do we depend so much on words that others write to convey our feelings? Perhaps we're afraid that our writing won't measure up to slick, assembly-line verses. Maybe we're just too lazy to take the time to formulate our thoughts and commit them to paper. Either way, the result is the same. Instead of sending a message from the heart, we send a neatly wrapped word package that a stranger created without knowing either us or the person we're addressing. This same neat little package will be sent by thousands of people to thousands of other people, with all these senders and receivers acting as though their prepackaged, ready-to-consume communication is original and unique.

Perhaps the element of self-revelation is what keeps most of us from buying cards that are blank inside and penning our own messages. Writing to someone does involve risk, especially if we're communicating strong feelings such as love or sadness. When we write our own words, we risk the possibility that the reader may not share or appreciate our feelings.

If we did make the effort to express our true feelings in our own words, then the cards we send would more genuinely reflect *us* as individuals. The sentiments expressed would come from within ourselves, not off the rack. Moreover, instead of just smiling and thinking, "what a clever card" or "what a cute poem," the people to whom we write would focus on the thoughts we're trying to convey.

THE BUILDING BLOCKS OF WRITING

All writing is made up of parts. Words are formed from letters, and these words in turn are joined into sentences. Writers combine sentences into paragraphs, and then use paragraphs to construct essays, articles, books, and other written works.

In this book you'll focus on writing essays. Building on skills and knowledge that you already have, you'll learn to present ideas and information in a carefully planned series of paragraphs that together make up an essay.

REVIEWING PARAGRAPH BASICS

A **paragraph** is a group of related sentences joined together to develop one idea. This idea is usually called the **main idea**. The particular subject that a paragraph (or essay) deals with is its **topic**.

The main idea of a paragraph is usually stated in a **topic sentence**. A topic sentence is often, but not always, the first sentence in a paragraph. The other sentences of the paragraph relate to the topic sentence and provide **supporting information** to support or develop the main idea. Supporting information includes facts, details, examples, reasons, statistics, and anecdotes.

Activity A: Identifying Paragraph Elements

Reread "Let's Speak for Ourselves" on page 7. Then answer the following questions.

- What is the topic of "Let's Speak for Ourselves"?

Excessive dependence on PREPRINTED GREETING CARDS

- What is the main idea of the paragraph?

Most of the people depend too much on pre-printed greeting cards to express their feelings on special occasions. instead we should use our own ideas

CHAPTER 1: FROM PARAGRAPH TO ESSAY **9**

- In which sentence does the writer state the main idea?

  First sentence of first paragraph

- What kinds of supporting information does the writer use to develop the main idea? *use of example to support his point*

Sending pre-printed cards for all purposes, using these cards to express feelings to others

UNITY, SUPPORT, AND COHERENCE

To create effective paragraphs, writers strive to achieve three essential characteristics of effective writing: unity, support, and coherence.

- When a paragraph has a clear main idea and all sentences of the paragraph relate to that idea, the paragraph has **unity**. A unified paragraph remains focused on the main idea and does not include unrelated details or ideas.

- When the main idea of a paragraph is supported or developed by specific information, the paragraph has **support**. Supporting information such as facts, details, and examples gives depth and dimension to the main idea.

- When the supporting information of a paragraph is logically organized and smoothly connected, the paragraph has **coherence**. For example, to explain how to take a picture, you might say: "First, decide how close to come to the subject. Next, consider the amount of available light. Then determine the best angle from which to shoot." By organizing information in sequence and using such words as *first*, *next*, and *then* to connect ideas, the writer creates a smooth and logical paragraph flow. The *final* or *concluding sentence* connects the whole paragraph.

Look again at "Let's Speak for Ourselves" on page 7. In this paragraph the writer achieves unity, support, and coherence. The topic sentence that begins the paragraph clearly states the main idea, and the other sentences all relate to that idea. Specific examples and reasons support the main idea. A smooth progression from the opening sentence to the strong closing point in the last sentence creates coherence.

GROUP ACTIVITY

Activity B: Achieving Paragraph Unity, Support, and Coherence

In the following first-draft paragraph, the writer has encountered some difficulty in achieving unity, support, and coherence. Read the paragraph and then work with your group to answer the questions that follow. Be specific in your answers.

The Benefits of Antioxidants

Recent studies indicate that taking vitamin E, vitamin C, and beta carotene may help protect your health. For example, a five-year study conducted by U.S. researchers in China concluded that consuming beta carotene and vitamin E daily contributed to a 13 percent reduction in cancer deaths. The Chinese study involved almost 30,000 people. In the body, beta carotene becomes vitamin A. A previous study in England drew a connection between cancer and low levels of vitamin E in the blood. The English study involved more than 20,000 people. These substances are known as *antioxidants*. Researchers caution that studies of antioxidants are not conclusive. Nevertheless, many physicians and scientists themselves take them. Of course, you can't live on greasy hamburgers and fatty french fries and expect that swallowing a few vitamin supplements will counteract the damage you're doing to your body. Just think what all that fat does to blood vessels. No wonder there's a link between cholesterol and heart disease. Instead of eating so much high-cholesterol fast food, people should eat healthy foods like fruits and vegetables. Regular exercise is important too. Antioxidants seem to work by offsetting damage to cells. Researchers point out, however, that in most studies the subjects take doses of antioxidants that are ten or more times greater than the currently recommended dietary allowance.

• What suggestions would you make to this writer to improve paragraph unity? Consider, for example, whether the paragraph has a clear main idea and whether all ideas or details in the paragraph relate to the main idea.

_____

_____

_____

_____

- What suggestions would you make to this writer to improve paragraph support? Consider, for example, whether the supporting information is both specific and adequate.

_____

_____

_____

- What suggestions would you make to this writer to improve paragraph coherence? Consider, for example, whether the paragraph has a smooth and logical progression.

_____

_____

_____

_____

WHAT IS AN ESSAY?

An **essay** is a series of related paragraphs that examines a single topic from the writer's viewpoint. Essays appear in newspapers, magazines, professional journals, and collections of nonfiction writing. Editorials, book and movie reviews, daily columns, articles on travel, and even some letters qualify as essays. In fact, any short nonfiction composition that explores a single topic and expresses a personal point of view on that topic can be called an essay.

The French writer Montaigne first used the term *essay* in the sixteenth century to refer to his informal reflections and commentaries about a wide range of subjects. However, people had already been writing essays for centuries. The first essays were written in ancient Rome and Greece by such writers as Seneca and Plutarch. These compositions were intended to educate people about moral and civic issues. They dealt with topics such as envy, hate, and greed. The great essayists of the Renaissance (about 1400 to 1600) similarly wrote essays about moral topics such as truth, conscience, and self-conduct.

Present-day essays typically explore the writer's viewpoint on topics relating to society and people's attitudes and lifestyles. For example, an essay might express a writer's thoughts and feelings about marriage, nuclear power, traffic congestion, or childcare centers. As in the past, most essays today are written for the purpose of presenting information or persuading others to think or act in a certain way.

IN YOUR JOURNAL

Clip or photocopy at least three examples of interesting, amusing, or thought-provoking essays from newspapers, magazines, or books and save them in your journal. Write your reasons for including the particular pieces you select. Also keep a running list of topics you might want to explore in an essay. Refer to this list when you're seeking a topic for an essay assignment.

In your daily life both in and out of school, you'll encounter numerous occasions when writing an essay is essential to communicating your ideas and information effectively. Indeed, your ability to write well is not only important in everyday life but also can be vital to success on the job. Even workers who do not have office jobs must often do a certain amount of job-related writing. How well you express yourself through the written word will therefore play a significant part in determining the impression you make on supervisors, coworkers, and peers. By adding the writing skills you'll learn in this book to those you already have, you'll be able to write the reports, papers, letters, and other documents for which a single paragraph would not be adequate.

In some ways writing an essay is similar to writing a single-paragraph composition. For example, both paragraphs and essays require writers to do careful planning to convey ideas clearly and to support these ideas adequately. Both paragraphs and essays also require writers to decide what information to include and what information to omit and to determine how best to organize this information.

In other ways, however, writing an essay is different from writing a paragraph. An essay is longer than a paragraph and has a more involved structure, so writers must think in terms of an expanded structure. Furthermore, because an essay consists of multiple paragraphs, writers have more space to develop their ideas in greater depth and to provide more detailed supporting information. In creating an essay, writers also have greater flexibility in determining what combination of strategies to use to develop content.

What essays have you read recently that were especially effective? Choose one, and answer the following questions about that essay.

- What was the topic of the essay?

  TV Addiction

- What was the central point of the essay—the principal idea that the writer presents and develops? Where in the essay did the writer state the central point?

  T.V addiction can cause people to lose their families, leave their jobs, and distort their perspective on life
  Last sentence of introductory paragraph.

- How did the writer present the ideas of the essay?

  The author provides examples makes comparisons, etc.

- What features made the essay particularly effective?

  The method of developing the essay by comparing T.V addiction with drug and alcohol addiction.

- Could the writer have handled this topic just as well in a single paragraph? Why or why not?

  No - making it all in one para would make the essay to look detailed.

THE PARTS OF AN ESSAY

In a sense, an essay is an expanded version of a paragraph. A paragraph is built around a main idea, usually expressed in a topic sentence. An essay is built around a central point, which is expressed in a thesis statement. A paragraph develops the main idea with supporting sentences. An essay develops the central point with supporting paragraphs.

The following chart compares the structure and features of a paragraph and an essay.

Paragraph	Essay
Topic sentence (states main idea)	Title Introduction Thesis statement (states central point)
Supporting information (supports main idea)	Body—supporting paragraphs (support central point)
Concluding sentence (connects entire paragraph)	Conclusion (reinforces thesis statement)

The structure of an essay is more elaborate than that of a single paragraph. Most essays contain four parts: an introduction, a body, a conclusion, and a title. Let's examine each of these parts.

THE INTRODUCTION AND THE THESIS STATEMENT

The **introduction** to an essay usually consists of one paragraph. This paragraph serves two important functions. First, the introduction draws readers into the essay, engaging their interest in the topic and making them want to read on. To accomplish this, a writer may begin with a thought-provoking statement, a question, an unusual fact, a quotation, or a brief story or anecdote. Here, for example, is the opening sentence of an essay about the plight of Native Americans:

In *Bury My Heart at Wounded Knee*, Dee Brown's disturbing book about the American West, the author quotes an anonymous Indian: "They made us many promises, more than I can remember, but they never kept but one; they promised to take our land, and they took it."

The second important function of the introduction of an essay is to present the thesis statement. The **thesis statement** is a single sentence that introduces and limits the central point of the essay—the principal idea that the writer will develop. This statement often, but not always, appears at the beginning or the end of an introduction and guides readers into the body of the essay. The rest of the introduction may be general or specific, depending on the topic and the length of the essay and on the writer's purpose. In some essays, the writer begins developing the thesis statement immediately. In other essays, the writer waits until the second paragraph to begin developing the thesis statement. Notice how each of the following thesis statements is specific enough to define and focus the topic yet broad enough to allow for development in the body of the essay.

Topic: Earning extra money for college expenses
Thesis statement: Working a daytime job and a nighttime job is a sure way to earn extra money, but not the only way.

Topic: The hazards of do-it-yourself home repairs
Thesis statement: Do-it-yourselfers who don't know what they're doing pose a danger to themselves and others.

Topic: Why televised sports are popular
Thesis statement: Televised sports can get viewers so involved in the excitement of the competition that the viewers almost feel as though they're in the arena.

In addition to engaging readers' interest and presenting the thesis statement, the introduction may also provide necessary background information that readers will need in order to understand what follows. The introduction may also preview the main points to be covered in the body of the essay.

Read and compare the following introductions. As you read, do the following:

■ Circle the thesis statement in each paragraph—the single sentence that expresses the central point of the essay.

■ In the margin, note how each writer engages your interest.

Introduction 1

The writer uses a question to engage our interest

There's a book out called *Is There Life after High School?* It's a fairly silly book, maybe because the subject matter is the kind that only hurts when you think. Its thesis—that most people never get over the social triumphs or humiliations of high school—is not novel. Still, I read it with the respectful attention a serious hypochondriac[1] accords the lowliest "dear doctor" column. [Thesis I don't know about most people, but for me, forgiving my parents for real and imagined derelictions[2] has been easy compared to forgiving myself for being a teenage reject.]

[1] **hypochondriac:** a person always worried about getting sick
[2] **dereliction:** neglect, abandonment
(Ellen Willis, from "Memoirs of a Non-Prom Queen")

Introduction 2

The writer uses a thought-provoking statement

It's easy to predict what jobs you *shouldn't* prepare for. Thanks to the wonders of fluoride, America, in the future, will need fewer dentists. Nor is there much of a future in farming. The federal government probably won't provide long-term employment unless you aspire to work in the Pentagon or the Veterans Administration (the only two departments accounting for new federal jobs in the last decade). And think twice before plunging into higher education. [Thesis The real wages of university professors have been declining for some time, the hours are bad, and all you get are complaints.]

(Robert B. Reich, from "The Future of Work")

Questions

1. In which introduction does the writer immediately begin developing the thesis statement with supporting information?

2nd Introduction

2. Which introduction provides background information to help readers understand what will follow?

1st Introduction

3. Which introduction was most effective in engaging your interest? Why?

The 2nd introduction was most effective in engaging my interest because the information to be conveyed begins immediately after the thesis statement.

THE BODY OF AN ESSAY

The ideas, facts, details, and examples presented in the **body** of an essay support and develop the central point stated in the introduction. The number of paragraphs in the body of an essay can vary depending on what the writer is trying to accomplish. While the body paragraphs of an essay relate directly to the thesis statement in the introduction, each paragraph has a main idea—often stated in a topic sentence—and information that supports that main idea. Thus you can plan the number of body paragraphs in an essay by determining how many main ideas are needed to support the central point.

In this book you will learn how to develop short essays consisting of several paragraphs. Developing such essays will prepare you to tackle longer writing projects, from a three-paragraph memo to a twenty-paragraph research report. As you work, keep in mind that the length of an essay will vary depending on the subject matter and the purpose for writing.

The following chart shows the relationship of the body of an essay to the introduction and the conclusion. This chart applies to the essay "Learning on the Job," on pages 19-20, which contains three body paragraphs.

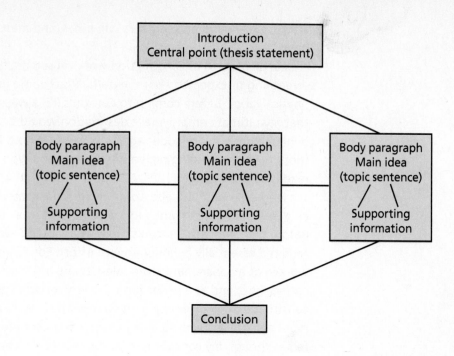

Read the essay "Learning on the Job" that follows. As you read, notice how the body paragraphs relate back to the thesis statement in the introduction.

Learning on the Job

When I went to work part-time for Carlton's Construction Concepts, I expected to learn about home renovation, but the job also taught me a great deal about myself. Carlton's is a six-person construction company that specializes in renovating older houses. During a particularly busy time, Carlton's was looking for an extra pair of hands. This job offered more money than anything else available to me at the time. Even though I had limited experience, I had no trouble getting the job. William Carlton, the company's owner, is my uncle.

At first, I thought my education would be limited to carpentry and related matters. Indeed, my coworkers taught me how to put in insulation, how to attach sheetrock, how to install windows and doors, and how to use tools that I'd never known existed. I also furthered my education by watching electricians run wires, plumbers join pipes, and masons build brick steps.

Several months of construction work caused me to realize something unexpected about myself: I *liked* doing hands-on, physical labor. Before coming to Carlton's, I'd always assumed that my ultimate employment destination would be a chair behind a desk, not a ladder against a beam. Who'd have thought that pounding nails and sawing wood would have made me this happy?

I learned something else about myself too, something probably even more important. I loved being part of a "team." Before working with Carlton's crew, every job I'd ever held required essentially an independent effort. For example, I'd worked as a department store salesperson, as a cashier in a coffee shop, and as a driver for a delivery service. Doing home construction day after day with six other people made me feel more personally involved in my work than ever before. I also felt as though my contribution to the team effort really mattered, a feeling that had been missing from my previous jobs.

It's funny how some of life's most meaningful lessons occur so unexpectedly. I'm truly grateful to my uncle for providing a learning experience that's proved more significant than either of us could have imagined.

In "Learning on the Job," the writer introduces the central point of the essay in the opening sentence, which is the thesis statement: *When I went to work part-time for Carlton's Construction Concepts, I expected to learn about home renovation, but the job also taught me a great deal about myself.* The rest of the introduction provides explanatory background information.

The three body paragraphs support and develop the central point. Notice how the main idea and supporting information of each body paragraph directly or indirectly relate back to the thesis statement:

INTRODUCTION/THESIS STATEMENT: Working part-time for Carlton's Construction Concepts taught me much more about myself than I'd anticipated.

BODY PARAGRAPH 1—MAIN IDEA: The writer describes the excitement of learning new skills.

SUPPORTING INFORMATION: Examples of skills learned

BODY PARAGRAPH 2—MAIN IDEA: The writer explains the surprising pleasure of "doing hands-on, physical labor."

SUPPORTING INFORMATION: Description of change in writer's self-image

BODY PARAGRAPH 3—MAIN IDEA: The writer explains the satisfaction of "being part of a 'team.'"

SUPPORTING INFORMATION: Explanatory reasons, facts, and details

Activity C: Identifying Essay Elements

Reread "Write From the Heart" on pages 7-8. Then answer the following questions.

- What is the central point of the essay?

  The pre-printed cards that we purchase use corny poetry silly jokes, and heavy handed prose to communicate what should be personal and sincere sentiments

- What is the main idea of the second paragraph? How does the writer support or develop this idea?

  People are incapable of putting into words their feelings about any life situation. The writer develops this idea by giving examples of various cards available for various situations.

- What is the main idea of the third paragraph? How does the writer support or develop this idea?

  "Why people depend on the words that others write to convey their feelings" is the main idea of the 3rd para. The writer supports this my provdes facts.

- What is the main idea of the fourth paragraph? How does the writer support or develop this idea?

  "Why some people buy blank cards" is the main idea. The writes supports this by providing explanatory reasons.

THE CONCLUSION

In their closing arguments at a trial, attorneys strive to wrap up their case in a clear and forceful manner. In the **conclusion** to an essay, the writer's goal is much the same. The writer summarizes or reinforces the central point and main ideas to leave readers with a memorable final thought or image.

In some essays, especially short ones, the conclusion may be as brief as a sentence or two. In most essays, the conclusion will generally consist of a full final paragraph. Regardless of length, the conclusion to an essay should be strong and interesting. Strategies for concluding an essay include summarizing key points, calling for action, or asking a pointed question.

Reread the conclusion of "Learning on the Job" on page 20. Notice how the writer summarizes and extends what's been said in previous paragraphs, restating the central point in the final sentence.

Activity D: Evaluating a Conclusion

Review the conclusion of "Write From the Heart" on page 8.

- Describe the strategy the writer uses to conclude the essay.

  _____

  _____

  _____

- Is the conclusion effective? Why?

  _____

  _____

  _____

  _____

THE TITLE

An effective essay title performs two basic functions. The title suggests the topic of the essay and arouses readers' interest. Sometimes a title also communicates the writer's purpose. The title of "Write From the Heart" on page 7, for example, indicates that the writer wants to persuade readers to put more "heart" into their writing.

Titles may be single words, phrases, or complete sentences. Sometimes titles take the form of questions or are divided into two parts. Here are some examples of different kinds of titles:

Word: Equality
Phrase: The True Meaning of Courage
Sentence: *Your* Smoking Is Hazardous to *My* Health
Question: Will There Ever Be Peace in Haiti?
Two Parts: Toni Morrison: Nobel Prize Winner

IN YOUR JOURNAL

Review the examples of essays you've collected from newspapers, magazines, and books. Choose one or two favorites. Does the essay have an interesting title? If so, what makes the title interesting? If not, can you create a better one?

UNITY, SUPPORT, AND COHERENCE IN ESSAYS

On page 10 you read about the importance of unity, support, and coherence in paragraphs. To be effective, essays must have these same characteristics. Compare the following definitions with those that appear on page 10.

- When an essay has a clear central point and all paragraphs of the essay relate to that point, the essay has *unity*. A unified essay remains focused on the central point and does not include unrelated details or ideas.

- When the central point of an essay is supported or developed by specific information, the essay has *support*. Supporting information such as facts, details, and examples, gives depth and dimension to the central point.

- When the supporting information of an essay is logically organized and smoothly connected, the essay has *coherence*. For example, in an essay that discusses the African-American artist Romare

Bearden, the writer might devote each body paragraph to a different period of the artist's life and arrange these paragraphs in chronological order to create a smooth and logical flow.

Look again at "Write From the Heart" on pages 7-8. In this essay the writer achieves unity, support, and coherence. The writer introduces a clear central point in the opening paragraph: how unfortunate it is that *most of us rely on professional greeting card writers to express our feelings for us*. The writer develops this point in subsequent paragraphs, first giving specific examples and then exploring possible reasons why people don't write their own words. The essay concludes by focusing on the benefits of expressing your own thoughts rather than relying on preprinted words.

Activity E: Recognizing Unity, Support, and Coherence in an Essay

How would you rate "Learning on the Job" on pages 19-20 for unity, support, and coherence? Review the definitions of these terms on page 23. On a scale of 1 to 5, with 5 being the best score, rate the essay for each of these characteristics, and give specific reasons to explain each rating you assign.

• Unity: _____

  Reasons:

  _____

  _____

  _____

• Support: _____

  Reasons:

  _____

  _____

  _____

• Coherence: _____

  Reasons:

  _____

  _____

  _____

Activity F: Achieving Unity, Support, and Coherence in an Essay

Has the writer achieved unity, support, and coherence in the following first-draft essay? Read the essay, and then answer the questions that follow.

Winter Woes

This winter's harsh weather has left people physically and mentally exhausted. Subzero temperatures, bitter winds, frequent snowstorms, and accumulated layers of ice have combined to make driving difficult and walking all but impossible.

The first storm of winter deposited six inches of snow. Then the temperature abruptly shot up to fifty degrees. The next day, plunging temperatures froze all the melting snow. That same cycle repeated itself several times over the next few weeks. At first, most people took the severe weather with good humor. After several weeks of below-average temperatures and above-average precipitation, however, people have begun to get testy. The freezing air is filled with loud complaints from homeowners who had to shovel snow one day and chop blocks of ice the next. Since stores have run out of snow shovels, ice choppers, and even salt, many people who are normally polite have become impatient with storekeepers.

Traveling by car has become almost impossible. If drivers manage to dig their cars out of shoulder-high snow, they often find that their car batteries have died. If they can get as far as the street, they find that their wheels do not roll along the icy roads—they slide. The number of accidents has been mounting steadily, most of them the result of ice-slicked roadways. The worst was a seven-car collision on Tremont Boulevard. That accident was nearly as bad as the one that occurred in 1987, when eleven cars collided on Highway 101. Heavy fog was to blame for that memorable chain-reaction disaster. In addition to making roads slippery, the ice has actually damaged the pavement. Alternating freezes and thaws have created innumerable potholes, some large enough to destroy a tire or even break an axle.

Walking isn't any easier than driving. Sidewalk intersections are mounded with snowdrifts, forcing pedestrians to become mountain climbers just to cross a street. Even worse, both sidewalks and streets are glazed with dangerous ice. Many people have given up trying to leave their houses at all until they run out of groceries and get desperate.

Skiers are probably the only people delighted with this winter's weather. Ski conditions at local areas have been excellent, and cross-country skiing trails are busier than ever. Snowboarding, too, seems to have caught on, especially among the younger crowd.

People are so sick of this weather. Some people have found themselves feeling depressed as a result of the daily difficulties in attempting the simplest tasks. Fortunately, this cold spell is one problem that time will definitely cure. In another month, no one will even remember that sinking feeling we all got as the latest weather map, dotted with snowflakes, flashed onto our TV screens. We'll be too busy watching the flowers bloom.

- UNITY: What is the central point of "Winter Woes"? Does the writer stay focused on the central point, or does the writer include unrelated details or ideas? Explain.

  _____

  _____

  _____

  _____

- SUPPORT: Has the writer provided adequate specific information to support or develop the central point of the essay? Explain.

  _____

  _____

  _____

  _____

- COHERENCE: Is the organization of ideas and information logical? Does the essay flow smoothly? Give reasons for your answer. What suggestions would you make for improvement? Be specific.

  _____

  _____

  _____

  _____

Writing on a computer not only saves you time but also helps you get your words flowing. If you've never used a computer before, relax. Writing on a computer requires little or no technical knowledge. Easy-to-use software programs enable you to write, revise, and store your work for later use. These **word processing programs** offer such user-friendly features as built-in Help screens and simple menus of choices that respond to the touch of a key.

Throughout this book you'll see suggestions for using a computer to plan and write essays. Don't be afraid to experiment. You'll discover that by using a computer, you'll spend less time rekeying, and you'll have more time to spend writing and improving your work.

YOUR WRITING ASSIGNMENTS

Each chapter in this book contains two kinds of writing assignments: group assignments and individual assignments. For group assignments you will combine efforts with other students to complete work collaboratively. Individual assignments will give you an opportunity to apply your skills independently.

Set aside a folder or a large envelope as a **portfolio** in which to collect and save your writing assignments. Your instructor will periodically review the work in your portfolio and discuss it with you. Together, you and your instructor will evaluate your progress. You can also refer to the items in your portfolio at any time to reexamine and assess the work you've completed.

GROUP ACTIVITY

Assignment 1:
Evaluating an Essay With Your Group

In this assignment you will work with your group to evaluate and improve an essay. Use the following guidelines:

A. Read "Overcome Your Fears" on page 29.

B. Work with your group to identify the central point of the essay. Is the central point clearly expressed in a thesis statement?

C. Assess whether the introduction effectively engages readers' interest and makes them want to read on.

D. Evaluate the essay for unity, support, and coherence:

- Does the essay have unity? Does the writer stay focused on the central point, or does the writer include irrelevant details or ideas? Do the body paragraphs of the essay relate directly to the thesis statement?

- Does the essay have support? What specific information does the writer provide to support or develop the central point?

- Does the essay have coherence? Is the organization of ideas and information logical? Does the essay flow smoothly?

E. Assess whether the conclusion effectively summarizes or reinforces the central point and main ideas.

F. Evaluate whether the title is effective and appropriate.

G. Discuss how you can improve the essay. Be specific in your comments. As you discuss the essay, consider these questions:

- How can you improve the introduction or the thesis statement?

- Should you eliminate any information in the essay because this information is unnecessary or unrelated to the central point?

- Do you need to rearrange or reword any sentences or paragraphs to give the essay a more logical flow or make the ideas easier to understand?

- How can you make the conclusion stronger?

- How can you improve the title?

H. Agree on the changes your group will make. Then work together to improve the essay. For example, one group member might rewrite the first paragraph, another member might rewrite the second paragraph, and so on, or the group might work together to shape each paragraph.

PORTFOLIO

Record the names of all group members on the essay. Make a photocopy for every group member. Save your copy of the revised essay in your portfolio.

Overcome Your Fears

Are you the kind of person who would like to spend more time hiking or camping but your fears of the outdoors are holding you back? You're not alone. Countless people dream of wilderness outings, canoe trips, and backpacking expeditions but never set foot in the woods. This is such a beautiful country with so many marvelous sights—such as the Grand Canyon, Yosemite National Park, the Florida Everglades—but too few people know that from firsthand experience. They're afraid—afraid of wild animals, bugs, and afraid of getting lost. If you have similar fears, be assured that knowledge and advance planning can help you overcome your apprehension of the outdoors.

Many people are afraid of snakes, poisonous or not. They have good reason to be wary of snakes, of course, but snakes should not keep you out of the woods. Knowing that sharks are in the ocean doesn't keep you from going to the beach, does it? Instead, read about snakes' habits and habitats, stay on marked trails, and learn to be careful where you step and where you place your hands when climbing. Maybe viewing snakes in the zoo would also help.

Bears are another source of fear. This is ironic considering how many kids grow up clutching teddy bears and reading stories about cute bears. Besides, who would be afraid of Smokey the Bear, who tells us, "Only *you* can prevent forest fires." You can minimize the chances of a bear wandering into your campsite by keeping the area clear of food and garbage. Raccoons, too, like to visit in search of leftovers. Raccoons are persistent creatures when it comes to food, though they generally won't bother people. When you leave your campsite, put all your food in a sack, and tie the sack to a high branch some distance away. If you do encounter a bear in the woods, do not bother the animal, and chances are the animal will avoid you. Any animal will be dangerous if it feels threatened or trapped, even a dog, cat, or bird.

Besides snakes and bears, people are afraid of spiders, ticks, fire ants, yellow jackets, tarantulas, scorpions, and numerous other creatures. Mosquitos, though not poisonous, are itch-causing pests that can make a camper's life miserable. In some parts of the country, people now have the so-called killer bees to worry about too. If you take a little care planning your campsite, however, and use bug repellent, you can protect yourself from creepy-crawlies.

For many people, however, far more anxiety-producing than bugs is the thought of getting lost in the woods. People imagine themselves wandering around in the dark, slowly starving to death (if they don't freeze to death first). However, if you travel with a compass and a map and remain calm, you can generally find your way back from wherever you have wandered. Remember that old Boy Scout motto: Be prepared. You should also have with you certain basic supplies and some warm clothing, just in case.

Exploring the outdoors is one of the great pleasures life has to offer. The woods are alive with sights, sounds, and smells you won't find at home. So leave your fears behind, and experience nature.

Assignment 2:
Evaluating an Essay on Your Own

In this assignment you will work independently to evaluate an essay and make suggestions for improvement. Use these guidelines:

A. Read "Smoking Facts" on page 31.

B. Identify the central point of the essay. Is the central point clearly expressed in a thesis statement?

C. Assess whether the introduction effectively engages readers' interest and makes them want to read on.

D. Evaluate the essay for unity, support, and coherence:

- Does the essay have unity? Does the writer focus on the central point, or does the writer include irrelevant details? Do the body paragraphs relate directly to the thesis statement?
- Does the essay have support? What specific information does the writer provide to support or develop the central point?
- Does the essay have coherence? Is the organization of ideas and information logical? Does the essay flow smoothly?

E. Assess whether the conclusion effectively summarizes or reinforces the central point and main ideas.

F. Evaluate whether the title is effective and appropriate.

G. Consider how you might improve the essay. For example:

- How can you improve the introduction or the thesis statement?
- Should you eliminate any information or ideas in the essay because this information is unnecessary or unrelated to the central point?
- Do you need to rearrange or reword any sentences or paragraphs to give the essay a more logical flow or make the ideas easier to understand?

PORTFOLIO

- How can you make the conclusion stronger?
- How can you improve the title?

H. Describe the changes you would make to improve "Smoking Facts." Be sure to consider the introduction, the body, the conclusion, and the title. Include specific suggestions and examples where appropriate. Save your suggestions in your portfolio.

Smoking Facts

Considering how bad smoking is for the body, it's surprising that anyone continues to smoke. Smoking has been linked to cancer, heart disease, emphysema, bronchitis, and other ailments. In pregnant women, smoking increases the likelihood of miscarriage. Even smokers spared serious illness still typically suffer side effects ranging from a chronic cough to bad breath. The dangers of smoking are never hinted at in the image of glamorous smokers in movies and magazine advertisements.

Smoking impairs blood circulation by constricting blood vessels. Tobacco smoke is poison. Among other irritants, it contains carbon monoxide, the same gas found in automobile exhaust. How many people would willingly breathe car exhaust? Taking carbon monoxide into the body can reduce the blood's capacity for carrying oxygen by nearly 10 percent. As a result, the heart must work harder. Cigarettes are also very expensive.

Some cigarette makers promise less tar and nicotine in their product. Tobacco tars—the sticky black or brown substances that smoke deposits on the lungs—are the main cancer-causing agents. Cigarette smokers often think they can protect themselves by smoking filter-tip cigarettes that promise to be low in tar and nicotine. Other smokers trade their cigarettes for a pipe. However, smokers who switch to "safer" cigarettes commonly end up inhaling more deeply or increasing the number of cigarettes they smoke. Pipe smokers may not inhale smoke into their lungs, but they significantly increase their likelihood of getting cancer of the lips, mouth, larynx, and esophagus. Cigar smokers are no better off.

Then there is the issue of secondary smoke. Do smokers have the right to poison those around them? Do smoking parents have the right to poison their children? Smoking injures the body in many ways and can cause various kinds of cancer. People who are concerned about their health and the health of those around them should learn the facts. Smoking can be fatal.

Grammar Gremlins

A **sentence** is a group of words that contains a subject and a verb and expresses a complete idea. A **sentence fragment** is part of a sentence. It does not by itself express a complete idea.

SENTENCE FRAGMENT:
Reads mystery novels.
(*Who* reads mystery novels?)

COMPLETE SENTENCE:
My friend Tanya reads mystery novels.

Complete sentences can vary in length provided they have a subject and a verb and express a complete idea.

COMPLETE SENTENCES:
Joe fell.
Entering the dark room, Joe fell over a chair.

SENTENCE FRAGMENT:
Destroyed the building.
Destroyed the building is incomplete because it does not say who or what destroyed the building. The word group has no subject.

SENTENCE FRAGMENT:
A strong earthquake.
A strong earthquake is incomplete because it has no verb and does not express a complete idea about the earthquake.
You can combine the two fragments to form a complete sentence:
A strong earthquake destroyed the building.
This word group is now a sentence because it has a subject and a verb and expresses a complete idea.

Sometimes word groups resemble sentences because they have a subject and a verb, start with a capital letter, and end with a period. However, such a word group is still a fragment if it does not express a complete idea.

SENTENCE FRAGMENTS:
After you return.
Which he gave to my sister.

To begin painting the house next week.
Speeding around the corner.

All of these word groups are fragments because they leave the reader hanging, unsure of the writer's meaning. You can make these fragments complete sentences by adding information.

COMPLETE SENTENCES:
After you return, I'll make dinner.
Martin found a kitten, which he gave to my sister.
Janet hopes to begin painting the house next week.
A witness to the accident saw a blue sedan speeding around the corner.

Activities

A. Each group of sentences contains at least one sentence fragment. Circle the fragment or fragments in each group.

1. Rena called twice last night. Missed both calls. I finally reached her early this morning. Amazing news. She won the lottery.

2. Rena hadn't won a huge amount. She was able to pay her bills. Put some away in her savings account. Enough left for a trip to a tropical island.

3. Rena invited me along for company on her trip. We flew. I had never been to an island. The weather was terrific. Wonderful scenery too.

B. Read the following paragraph. Circle the sentence fragments.

The basketball game had brought the crowd to its feet. Cheering and applauding. Both teams were determined to win. The Cougars and the Black Hawks. The score was tied. Final seconds of the game. Danson grabbed the ball and passed it to Robinson. Robinson fired it to Greene. Wild shouts. Flash of cameras. Greene faked to his left, then took a long shot. The ball sailed through the air. People screamed. Couldn't believe it. The Cougars had won.

C. In Chapter 2 you will learn how to correct sentence fragments. For additional practice in distinguishing fragments, see page A 67.

WRAPPING IT UP

SUMMARY

- A *paragraph* is a group of related sentences joined together to develop one main idea. The subject of a paragraph is its *topic*, which is stated in the *topic sentence*. Other sentences provide supporting information.

- An *essay* is a series of related paragraphs that examines a single topic from the viewpoint of the writer. The *central point* of an essay is the principal idea that the writer presents and develops. Just as a paragraph is built around a main idea that is often expressed in a topic sentence, an essay is built around a central point that is expressed in a *thesis statement*. Just as a paragraph develops its main idea with supporting sentences, so an essay develops its central point in a series of paragraphs.

- Most essays contain four parts: an introduction, a body, a conclusion, and a title. The introduction presents the thesis statement and engages readers' interest. The body, the longest part of the essay, presents ideas, facts, details, and examples to support and develop the central point expressed in the thesis statement. The number of paragraphs in the body of an essay can vary. The conclusion wraps up the writer's presentation of the central point. The title highlights the topic, draws the readers' attention, and sometimes suggests the purpose of the essay.

- An effective thesis statement is specific enough to limit the central point yet broad enough to allow for development of ideas in the body of the essay.

- Three essential characteristics of effective writing are *unity, support*, and *coherence*. An essay has unity when it has a clear central point and all paragraphs of the essay relate to that point. An essay has support when the central point of the essay is supported or developed by specific information. An essay has coherence when the supporting information of the essay is logically organized and smoothly connected.

- How will your knowledge of writing paragraphs help you write essays?

  _____

  _____

  _____

- What are the main similarities and differences between planning and writing a paragraph and planning and writing an essay? Be specific.

  _____

  _____

  _____

  _____

  _____

- How will an awareness of the characteristics of unity, support, and coherence help you in developing essays?

  _____

  _____

  _____

  _____

IN YOUR JOURNAL

Review the goals that you set at the beginning of this chapter. In your journal, evaluate your progress toward these goals. Add additional goals as you continue through the course.

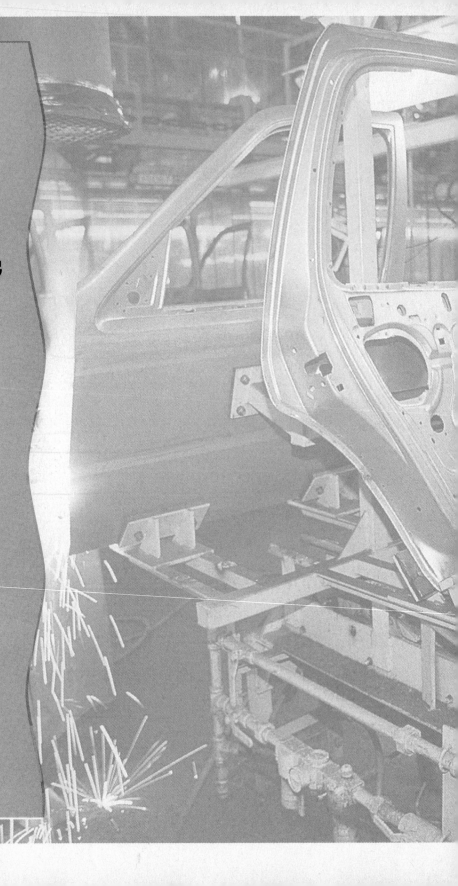

2

BEGINNING THE WRITING PROCESS

OBJECTIVES:

Composition

- To carry out the prewriting and first-draft steps of the writing process.

- To choose and narrow topics.

- To write thesis statements.

- To use the invention techniques of brainstorming, questioning, freewriting, mapping, and outlining.

- To define chronological order, spatial order, and order of importance or interest.

- To create first drafts of essays.

Grammar

- To write complete sentences.

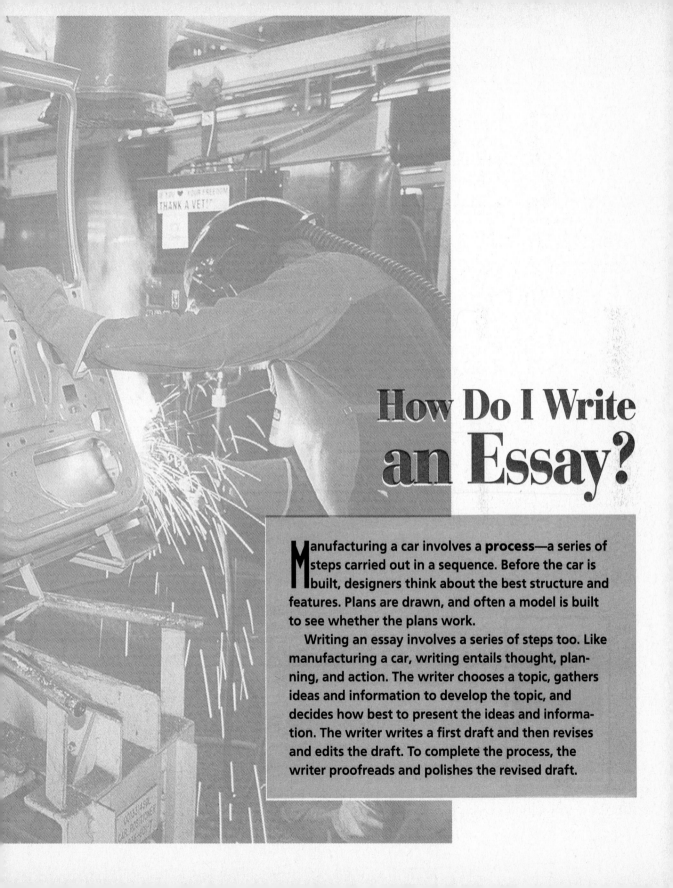

How Do I Write an Essay?

Manufacturing a car involves a **process**—a series of steps carried out in a sequence. Before the car is built, designers think about the best structure and features. Plans are drawn, and often a model is built to see whether the plans work.

Writing an essay involves a series of steps too. Like manufacturing a car, writing entails thought, planning, and action. The writer chooses a topic, gathers ideas and information to develop the topic, and decides how best to present the ideas and information. The writer writes a first draft and then revises and edits the draft. To complete the process, the writer proofreads and polishes the revised draft.

People approach writing in various ways. One person may sit and make notes, then write several paragraphs. Another person may pace the room, write a sentence or two, then go get a snack.

What's *your* approach to writing? Answer the following questions.

• What planning do you generally do before writing?

_____

_____

• How does this planning help you?

_____

_____

• Which task do you find more challenging: deciding what to write about a topic or deciding what *not* to write? Why?

_____

_____

• How is your approach to writing a multiple-paragraph composition different from your approach to writing a paragraph?

_____

_____

• What is the greatest strength of your writing approach? What is the greatest weakness?

_____

_____

IN YOUR
JOURNAL

Evaluate your approach to writing. Then set one or more goals in your journal. Here are some examples:

GOALS:
1. I will spend more time planning before beginning to write.
2. I will look for new ways to generate ideas.

BREAKING A PROCESS INTO STEPS

GROUP ACTIVITY

Every day you complete many tasks without realizing that you've followed specific steps—a process—to accomplish a goal.

A. Each of the following goals involves a series of steps—a process. Working with your group members, select two goals and list the steps you would carry out to accomplish each goal.

- To plan a picnic
- To organize a New Year's Eve party
- To put up bookshelves
- To redecorate a room
- To go fishing or scuba diving

GOAL 1: _____

STEPS:

_____

_____

_____

_____

_____

GOAL 2: _____

STEPS:

_____

_____

_____

_____

_____

B. *Thought*, *planning*, and *action* are key components used in combination to carry out a process. Describe each of the steps you identified above. Discuss whether each step primarily involves thought, planning, or action.

THE STEPS OF THE WRITING PROCESS

Writing is a creative activity. You, the writer, determine what ideas and information to convey. You select words that convey your meaning, and you decide the manner in which these words will be organized.

Because writing is creative, you may think that each writing task you face requires an altogether new approach. On the contrary, all writing involves a process that entails four basic steps, with each step leading to the next:

1. *Prewriting*: thinking and planning on paper or on the computer screen.

2. *Writing the first draft*: putting your plans into action.

3. *Revising and editing the first draft*: improving the content, structure, wording, and sentence structure of your draft until you are satisfied.

4. *Proofreading the revised draft and preparing a final copy*: proofreading to eliminate factual errors and mistakes in spelling, punctuation, and grammar.

These four steps reflect the combination of thought, planning, and action that is essential to clear and effective writing. Whether

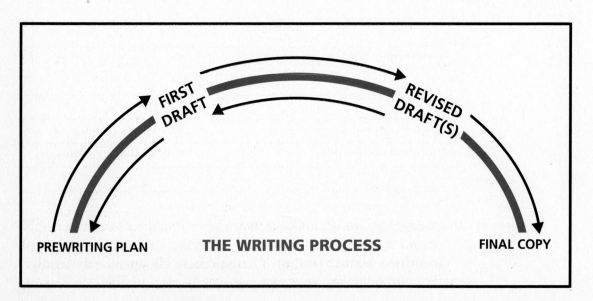

PREWRITING PLAN   THE WRITING PROCESS   FINAL COPY

you realize it or not, you may already carry out most of these steps when you undertake a writing task.

DISCOVERY ACTIVITY

- What was the most recent substantial writing task you did, such as a report for school or a letter to a prospective employer?

  _____

- What thinking or planning did you do before starting to write or while you were writing? For example, how did you decide what content to include and how to organize that content?

  _____

  _____

  _____

- Describe how you went about translating your thoughts and plans into writing.

  _____

  _____

  _____

- Did you make any changes in what you wrote before presenting your writing to the reader? Why?

  _____

  _____

  _____

Depending on what you're writing and why, you may not always carry out all four steps of the writing process. Writing a note to a friend, for instance, requires considerably less planning than preparing an essay. When you do carry out all four steps, you may perform them in a different order from the one described in this chapter. For example, as you're writing the first draft of an essay, you may realize that you need to return to the prewriting step to generate more supporting information for the body paragraphs. Later, as you revise your draft, you may suddenly see a different way of organizing your ideas, one that will enable you to convey your central point more clearly.

The flexible nature of the writing process allows you to develop, change, and improve your writing at any step in the process. In addition, the writing process provides ample opportunities for you to ensure that your essays achieve the three essential characteristics of effective writing discussed in Chapter 1:

Unity: presenting a clear central point and relating all paragraphs of an essay to that point.

Support: providing specific information to support or develop the central point of an essay.

Coherence: organizing and connecting supporting information to give the essay a smooth flow.

As you work through the steps of the writing process to create essays, keep these three characteristics in mind.

PREWRITING: THINKING AND PLANNING

If you've ever sat and stared at an empty computer screen or a blank piece of paper and found yourself unable to write, you've experienced **writer's block**. Getting started on a writing task is sometimes difficult even for professional writers. Fortunately, there are ways to overcome writer's block, several of which you'll learn in this chapter. Just remember that when you tackle a writing assignment, you don't have to produce perfect writing on your first attempt. You'll have ample opportunity to explore and rework your ideas in a series of drafts before you complete the final copy.

The thinking and planning that you do before beginning to write make up the *prewriting* step of the writing process. During the prewriting step, you gather ideas and information about a topic and establish your purpose for writing. You also determine exactly what you want to communicate to readers and decide how best to present your ideas.

The prewriting step is essential to writing because it sets the stage for all that follows. Writing without first doing prewriting would be like setting out on a trip without planning the route you'll take.

The prewriting step includes the following:

- Choosing and narrowing a topic.
- Writing a thesis statement.

- Gathering ideas and information to support your thesis statement.
- Adding and deleting ideas and supporting information.
- Planning how to organize your ideas and information.

In carrying out the prewriting step, you may use various techniques, sometimes called **invention techniques,** to explore topics and ideas. Invention techniques include the following:

- **Brainstorming**: writing a list of all the ideas you can think of about a topic.
- **Questioning**: asking and answering a series of questions about your topic.
- **Freewriting**: writing nonstop about a topic for a short period of time.
- **Mapping**: using a diagram to visualize the relationship between the central point of your essay and the main ideas and supporting information.
- **Outlining**: arranging your central point and main ideas and information according to a logical sequence of numbered and lettered headings and subheadings.

Brainstorming, freewriting, and questioning are especially useful for gathering ideas and information. Mapping and outlining are most helpful for organizing the ideas and information you have gathered.

Let's examine the prewriting step of the writing process.

INTRODUCING THE CENTRAL POINT

You learned in Chapter 1 that an essay is built around a central point—the principal idea that the writer presents and develops—and that this point is expressed in a thesis statement. The writer introduces the central point in the introduction and then develops it in subsequent paragraphs.

Before you can decide on a central point, you must first select a workable topic. Once you've settled on the topic and determined the central point, you can write the thesis statement.

Choosing and Narrowing the Topic

Choosing an appropriate topic for an essay is a task worth spending time on. You should select a topic that interests you. If you are interested in the topic, you're more likely to be able to interest readers in the topic.

After you select a topic, you need to determine if the topic is narrow enough to focus on in an essay of several paragraphs. For example, you might be interested in music videos, but this topic covers too much ground. Instead, you might narrow the topic "music videos" to discuss your favorite music video. Narrowing your topic in this way makes it workable.

Once you've settled on a topic, you need to come up with ideas that you'd like to discuss. For example, in an essay on your favorite music video, you could devote a paragraph each to discussing the setting, costumes, lighting, and sound.

After you've selected and narrowed your topic, your next concern is to write a thesis statement that expresses the point you want to make in your essay.

Consider the following examples of how to narrow a topic that is too broad.

Broad Topic: Great sports stars
Narrowed Topic: Outstanding football players
Specific Topic: The top three NFL quarterbacks of all time

Broad Topic: Optimism
Narrowed Topic: Having an optimistic attitude
Specific Topic: How an optimistic attitude helps you succeed at work

Broad Topic: Impressionism
Narrowed Topic: Impressionist paintings
Specific Topic: The paintings of Claude Monet

Broad Topic: Winter
Narrowed Topic: Harsh winter weather
Specific Topic: The effect of winter weather on people's moods

• How is a narrow or focused topic different from a broad topic?

1: A narrow topic is a part of a broad topic
2. A narrow topic limits our ideas to an essay wereas a broad topic is very vad. and payer can written about it.

- How will narrowing a topic help you plan and write an essay? Give an example.

Narrowing a topic will help us limit our ideas to a certain extent. Narrowing also helps us to make our essay effective and interesting.

Activity A: Narrowing Essay Topics

Narrow each of the following topics for an essay.

Broad Topic: College
Narrowed Topic: *2-year college*
Specific Topic: *Cost of studying in two year college*

Broad Topic: Clothing styles
Narrowed Topic: *Children's clothing styles*
Specific Topic: *Use of cartoon characters in children's clothing*

Broad Topic: The realities of parenthood
Narrowed Topic: *Parents duties towards children.*
Specific Topic: *Educating the child is every parent's duty*

Writing the Thesis Statement

Like a topic sentence in a paragraph, a thesis statement in an essay clarifies what you want to say about your topic. A thesis statement should be specific enough to establish the boundaries of your essay, yet should cover all the main ideas in the body of your essay. To make a thesis statement specific, use language that is precise, not vague, and provide concrete information rather than general ideas. Here is an example:

Too vague: Hawaii is a group of beautiful islands, similar yet different.
Better: The Hawaiian islands of Maui and Kauai share a natural beauty but are very different in regional flavor.

After you choose and narrow your topic, write a rough draft of your thesis statement. Writing your thesis statement first will help you focus on your topic and develop ideas for each of the supporting paragraphs. You may decide to revise your thesis statement at any time if you find you need a more specific statement or if you alter your approach to the topic.

Study the following pairs of thesis statements. Put a check mark next to the thesis statement in each pair that is more specific.

_____ *Mankiller: A Chief and Her People* by Wilma Mankiller is a terrific book about a woman who has led an exciting and important life.

✓_____ *Mankiller: A Chief and Her People* by Wilma Mankiller is the fascinating account of a Cherokee woman who became an activist for Native American civil rights and the first female principal chief of the Cherokee Nation.

_____ Golf is the dullest sport I know, and why anyone would play it I can't understand.

✓_____ What could be more boring that hitting a small white ball into a hole, and then repeating the process seventeen more times?

_____ Newspapers print far too much bad news and not enough good news.

✓_____ Newspaper publishers should balance negative stories with positive, uplifting news.

In the preceding examples, the first thesis statement of each pair is too vague. In the first pair, the first thesis statement contains general comments about *Mankiller: A Chief and Her People* and tells us nothing about the book. In the first thesis statement of the second pair, the writer's statement about golf is too general to be meaningful. In the third pair, the first thesis statement does not clearly state what the writer wants newspaper publishers to do differently.

Activity B: Writing Thesis Statements

Write a thesis statement for each of the three topics you narrowed in Activity A on page 45. Keep in mind what you have just learned about making a thesis statement specific rather than general.

1. The Cost of Tution in 2-year College is Very low compared to 4 year Colleges -

2. Many cartoon Characters are used in Children's clothing styles to make it attractive.

3 It is every parent's duty to Provide basic

Activity C: Narrowing Essay Topics and Writing Thesis Statements

Choose three of the following general topics, or select three topics of your own for an essay. Narrow each topic, and then write a specific thesis statement appropriate for an essay. Your thesis statement should both introduce and limit the topic.

- A worthwhile hobby
- Sharing an apartment
- Taking lessons
- One moment you would love to relive
- A celebrity too much in the news

WRITER'S TIP

Tip: Before writing the thesis statement, be sure your topic is sufficiently focused. To check whether your topic is too general, ask yourself a "What about _____ ?" question. For example, if you narrowed "taking lessons" to "taking driving lessons," ask yourself: What about taking driving lessons? Can I narrow that topic further?

GENERAL TOPIC 1:

A worthwhile hobby

SPECIFIC TOPIC:

Writing books

THESIS STATEMENT:

The process of writing books is time consuming

GENERAL TOPIC 2:

Television

SPECIFIC TOPIC:

Addiction to T.V

THESIS STATEMENT:

T.V. addiction can cause people to lose their families, leave their jobs and distort their perspective on life.

GENERAL TOPIC 3:

Computers Professionals

SPECIFIC TOPIC:

Demand for Computer professionals

THESIS STATEMENT:

The use of computers in every field has these by created new job vacancies for computer professional.

educate to their children for their better future

Engaging Readers' Interest

As you read in Chapter 1, the introduction to an essay serves another important function besides presenting the thesis statement. The introduction also engages readers' interest in the topic.

To decide how best to begin an essay, imagine yourself as a reader. What information would get your attention, making you want to read on? Here are some techniques you might use:

- *Begin with an unusual fact or idea:* By the year 2000 people may be using sunshine, not gasoline, to power their automobiles.

- *Start by asking a question:* What would you do with twenty million dollars?

- *Begin with a quotation:* In his book *How to Live Longer and Feel Better*, Linus Pauling asserts that taking vitamins can help you "extend your life and years of well-being by twenty-five or even thirty-five years."

- *Open with a brief story or anecdote:* When I was nine years old, I brought home a stray dog. My father told me that only one of us could stay.

Sometimes the thesis statement itself works effectively as an attention-getter at the beginning of the introduction. Other times you'll want to begin your essay using one of the techniques described above and place the thesis statement at the end of the introduction. As you write the first draft, experiment with different openings for the introduction and use the one that works best.

Writing your introduction as you begin drafting your essay helps you determine the way in which the essay will focus on your topic. As you continue writing, however, you might find a reason to recast your introduction. For instance, in the course of your research, you might come upon a quotation or fact that would make the perfect introduction. You can always go back and make changes that you feel would improve the introduction and add to its impact on readers.

DISCOVERY ACTIVITY

- Look back at the two introductions you compared in Chapter 1, page 17. In which introduction does the writer begin with a thesis statement that also serves as an attention-getter?

GATHERING SUPPORT

After deciding on a topic and a central point and writing a thesis statement, you're ready to gather ideas and information to support and develop the thesis statement. A well-supported essay is one in which all the main ideas are sufficiently backed up by accurate information. Supporting information may include facts, details, examples, reasons, statistics, or observations.

Just as you develop the main idea of a paragraph with supporting sentences, you develop the central point of an essay with a series of paragraphs, all of which relate directly to the thesis statement. Each paragraph has its own main idea, often stated in a topic sentence, and its own supporting information.

To gather support for an essay, use one of these two basic methods:

1. *Collect-and-sort method*: Begin by collecting a large range of ideas and information. Then sort the items you have collected into groups, with each group representing possible content for one paragraph. Once you sort your ideas and information, you can refine your groups by thinking in terms of the specific main idea, topic sentence, and supporting information for each paragraph of your essay.

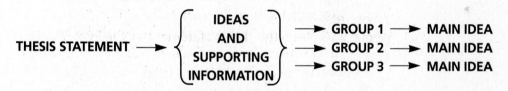

2. *Main-ideas-first method*: Begin by identifying the main ideas that will likely be the focus of your body paragraphs. Your thesis statement should point you toward these ideas. Express each main idea in a topic sentence. Then generate supporting information for each topic sentence.

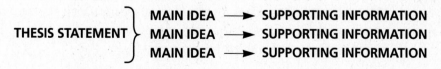

An example of the collect-and-sort method appears on the following page.

THESIS STATEMENT: Many people think of rodeo as just an entertainment attraction, but it is a true sport, with a governing body, an organized system of competition, and set rules for each event.

GROUP 1:

—Professional Rodeo Cowboys Association (PRCA) and the Profesional Women's Rodeo Association (PWRA) govern rodeo sports

—Original purpose: to combat unfair practices by rodeo promoters

—Functions include sponsoring competitions, setting rules, and maintaining records

GROUP 2:

—Organizational structure of rodeos: the circuit system

—12 regional circuits

—Contestants must be members or permit holders of the PRCA or the PWRA

—Winners on the circuits may accumulate enough prize money to qualify for National Finals

GROUP 3:

—Saddle bronc riding, bareback riding, and bull riding: must stay on the animal for at least 8 seconds; rider must use only one hand to hold on during the ride

—Calf roping, steer wrestling, steer roping, team steer roping: these events are timed; winners have shortest time

—Barrel racing: rider must make a full circuit of each barrel without knocking any barrels down

MAIN IDEA FOR GROUP 1: Rodeo has two governing bodies, the Professional Rodeo Cowboys Association (PRCA) and the Professional Women's Rodeo Association (PWRA).

MAIN IDEA FOR GROUP 2: Rodeo events are organized into a system.

MAIN IDEA FOR GROUP 3: Each event has specific rules.

Here is an example of the main-ideas-first method:

THESIS STATEMENT: Even in the age of computerized special effects, some of the most startling effects in science fiction movies or TV shows are often achieved by makeup.

MAIN IDEAS:

—Many makeup effects are created by hand.

—The process of applying makeup might take hours each day.

—Makeup can include false features called appliances, which can create extraordinary changes in a face or body.

—Also included in the makeup process might be mechanical additions such as wiring or flashing lights.

Examples of supporting information for first main idea:
—Even simple effects like beards often made individually so each character looks just right
—During filming each actor must be made up daily
—Applying makeup may include shadowing or blending the makeup, gluing on features such as false noses, putting on wigs and beards, even making up the hands and feet

Examples of supporting information for second main idea:
—Complete facial and hand makeup that aged the main character in *2010*, the sequel to *2001: A Space Odyssey*; 5 1/2 hours to put on
—Complete head and neck makeup, including fixing hair, for evil Cardassians on *Star Trek* TV programs; 2 1/2 hours to apply, with two makeup artists working together

Examples of supporting information for third main idea:
—May include noses, ears, ridged foreheads (the Klingons in *Star Trek*), pointed heads (*Coneheads*) horns, pointed teeth (the Ferengi in *Star Trek*), fangs (most vampires), claws
—May be made of latex, fiberglass, foam, or other materials

Examples of supporting information for fourth main idea:
—May include exposed circuitry to make an actor look like a "wounded" cyborg (as in *The Terminator*), mechanical eyes that flash lights, and so on
—May be made out of leftover model parts, lenses from old binoculars, remote-controlled lights, wires, even lasers

Which method of gathering support should you use? That depends on how clear a concept you have of your main ideas in the body of the essay. For example, if you were writing an essay about the dangers of bungee jumping, you might begin by first listing every idea, fact, example, and statistic you could find about bungee jumping, and then sort your list into possible paragraph groupings—the collect-and-sort method. On the other hand, if you were writing an essay about the three most important people in your life, you'd probably focus on one person in each of your body paragraphs. In this case, you'd use the main-ideas-first method.

Gathering supporting information lays the groundwork for the decisions you must make about the content and structure of your essay. Of course, you will be able to revise any of your decisions later on in the writing process if you find that you need to.

Generating Supporting Information

Because an essay consists of multiple paragraphs, you need to gather a considerable amount of supporting information at this step of the writing process. To help you identify main ideas and supporting information, use these three invention techniques: brainstorming, questioning, and freewriting.

Brainstorming. Brainstorming to solve a problem or come up with an idea is already familiar to you. Whenever you face a problem and think of possible solutions, you're brainstorming.

Brainstorming for ideas and supporting information means listing as many ideas, facts, details, and examples about a topic as you can think of, in any order, without worrying about which ones you will actually use. Your only concern is getting your mind working and putting ideas on paper or on the computer screen.

Consider the following example of how a writer brainstormed ideas and supporting information for an essay. The topic the writer chose was "the benefits of comparison shopping." The thesis statement is "Comparison shopping before buying can save you money and help ensure your satisfaction with your purchases."

—It pays to comparison shop.
—Keeps you from buying first item that looks good.
—Increases likelihood of satisfaction with product.
—Pays off in dollars saved.
—I got a great buy on a TV set last year.
—Don't believe all the advertisements you see.
—You have a better chance of finding exactly what you want.
—Not all stores sell same product at same price.
—Watch out for high-pressure salespeople.
—Happy Harry's Hangout has great prices on VCRs.

—You can learn about new products on the market.
—Comparison shopping requires time and effort.
—Have a basic idea of what you want before shopping.
—Go from store to store to see what's there.
—You can comparison shop by phone.
—It's smart to check newspaper advertisements.
—Talk to knowledgeable salespeople.
—Make a list of questions about products you're considering.
—Ask questions, take notes.
—Some products break down a month after you buy them.
—Gina's a terrific shopper.
—The cheap clock radio I bought is a hunk of junk.
—Some stores may offer discounts or special deals.
—Reading <u>Consumer Reports</u> can be a big help.
—Comparison shopping teaches you about available products.
—Lisa saved 50 dollars on her new desk.
—Price isn't everything; quality and service matter.
—You may find the item you want on sale.

Questions

1. Has the writer listed enough ideas and information to develop an essay? Give reasons for your answer.

_____

_____

_____

_____

2. Which listed items might serve as the main ideas of an essay based on the writer's thesis statement?

_____

_____

_____

_____

3. Should the writer include all of the listed items in the essay? Give reasons for your answer.

_____

_____

_____

Here are some brainstorming tips:

- Use brainstorming either before or after you write a thesis statement. However, you will usually find that writing at least a rough draft of a thesis statement first will help focus your brainstorming efforts.
- Write your brainstormed items on paper or on the computer screen in whatever order or form they occur to you—words or phrases, complete sentences, even drawings. Don't interrupt your flow of thoughts to evaluate the items you list; you will do that later.
- Use brainstorming with both methods for gathering support described on page 49, collect-and-sort and main-ideas-first.
- Use brainstorming at any point in the writing process when you think the technique might help you. For example, you might brainstorm to explore a topic or to determine what supporting information to develop.
- After you've finished brainstorming, take a break and then review the items on your list. Place a check mark beside the ideas or bits of information that stand out as especially interesting or important. Often these items will lead you to think of additional items to add to your list.

Questioning. Asking yourself questions to stimulate your thinking is another invention technique you can use to gather supporting information. This technique is familiar to journalists, who usually try to answer six basic questions when covering a story: who, what, where, when, why, and how. For example, when covering a fire, a news reporter would try to learn *who* was injured, *what* property burned, *where* and *when* the fire occurred, and *why* or *how* the fire happened.

You can use these same questions to focus on an event or issue that you want to write about in an essay. In some cases you might want to create your own questions to ask about a particular topic. For example, if you wanted to write an essay describing a person or place, you might ask yourself questions such as these:

- What makes this person/place unique?

- How long have I known this person/place?

- How does this person/place make me feel? Why?

- Do others share my feelings? Why or why not?

- What would most interest my readers about this person/place?

- Suppose you were writing an essay either for or against lengthening the school year to eleven months. How might you answer the following six questions?

DISCOVERY
ACTIVITY

WHO: _____

WHAT: _____

WHERE: _____

WHEN: _____

WHY: _____

HOW: _____

Activity D: Gathering Main Ideas and Supporting Information

Choose one of the thesis statements you wrote for Activity C on page 47. Gather support using either the collect-and-sort method or the main-ideas-first method, both described on page 49. Use brainstorming and questioning to develop at least three main ideas. For each main idea, list three or more supporting facts, details, reasons, or examples. Include only items that support the central point presented in your thesis statement. If you need more space, use a separate sheet of paper.

THESIS STATEMENT:

_____

_____

MAIN IDEA 1:

_____

_____

SUPPORTING INFORMATION:

_____

_____

_____

_____

MAIN IDEA 2:

_____

_____

SUPPORTING INFORMATION:

_____

_____

_____

_____

MAIN IDEA 3:

_____

_____

SUPPORTING INFORMATION:

_____

_____

_____

_____

PORTFOLIO

If you used a separate sheet of paper, save the work you did in your portfolio. You will continue working on this topic in Activity E on page 61.

Freewriting. A third useful invention technique is freewriting. Freewriting involves writing freely for ten to fifteen minutes, without stopping, about any aspect of your topic. To generate ideas and information, you can use freewriting by itself or in combination with brainstorming or questioning. Freewriting is an especially useful technique for overcoming writer's block.

When you freewrite, you're not concerned about spelling, punctuation, correct English, or even whether what you're writing makes sense. Your goal is to get your thoughts down on paper, letting one idea lead to the next. If you get stuck, write *I can't think of what to write next* until another idea comes to mind.

Here's how one writer used freewriting to come up with ideas and information about the topic "buying a home." The writer's thesis statement was: "Buying a home is so expensive that few young couples can afford to own their own home."

How can young couples buy their own home these days? Average couple doesn't have enough money to afford a home, even with both people working. Can't even come up with enough money for a down payment. Have to borrow from relatives and friends. That's never a terrific idea. My friend Jessica borrowed twenty thousand, and her father-in-law won't let her forget it for a minute. Can't think of what to write next. I should talk about how much more it costs these days to buy a home than it did when my parents were just starting out. Maybe I should mention the effects this has on the lives and hopes of young couples, who remain in cramped apartments they've outgrown. What can young people do? Is there anywhere they can go to borrow low-interest money? Have to find out.

IN YOUR
JOURNAL

Freewrite for ten to fifteen minutes about the topic you narrowed and developed in Activities C and D (pages 47 and 55). Compare your journal entry with the main ideas and supporting information you listed in Activity D on page 55. What new ideas or supporting information did you discover? Did your freewriting experience bring to mind any particular ways of organizing or developing the content?

CREATING UNITY

After you've gathered ideas and information to support and develop the thesis statement, you need to decide which items to keep and which to discard. Choosing supporting information carefully will ensure that you create a unified essay—an essay in which all paragraphs relate to a central point.

Adding and Deleting Ideas and Supporting Information

At this point in the process, your list of possible main ideas and supporting information is probably much longer than you need. Having a long list to choose from is beneficial because it gives you flexibility in developing your essay. That is, you can select the best items for your purpose, rather than feel as though you have to make do with what you've got.

As you evaluate the ideas and information you've generated, remember that your decisions are not final. Because writing is a fluid process, you can add, delete, or change ideas and supporting information as you continue writing.

DO YOU WRITE ON A COMPUTER?

Using a computer with word processing software facilitates both brainstorming and freewriting. You can key in your ideas, facts, details, and examples almost as they occur to you, and you can easily change or add to what you've written. Some writers find it helpful to turn down the brightness of their computer screen so that they can't see what they're keying. Doing so helps keep thoughts flowing by preventing the writer from being distracted or tempted to edit what's on the screen. After brainstorming or freewriting, you can turn up the brightness and use the underline feature to highlight key items. Then save and print your work. You can circle key items, make notes in the margin, or otherwise mark up the paper copy.

Here are some guidelines for evaluating main ideas and supporting information:

- *Choose a manageable number of main ideas.* Normally, you need one main idea for each body paragraph in an essay. Use your central point and supporting information as a guide for determining how many main ideas are needed to cover your topic. In one essay you may feel that you can adequately develop only two main ideas, while in another you can comfortably handle four or more. In general, remember that it's better to include a smaller number of main ideas and develop them well than to include a larger number of ideas and not support them adequately.

- *Include only ideas and information that advance the central point of your essay.* All the paragraphs of an essay should relate directly to the thesis statement in the introduction. Eliminate unrelated, unimportant, and uninteresting ideas or supporting information that would distract your readers from the central point and weaken your essay. Also avoid repeating essentially the same fact or detail in different words. For example, writing "houses are too expensive for young couples to buy" in one paragraph and "young couples cannot afford houses" in the next paragraph would be repetitive.

- *Make facts, details, reasons, examples, and other supporting information specific enough to be meaningful.* The more specific and concrete your supporting information, the better. "A sixteen-year-old Toyota" is more specific than "a very old car," and "64 percent of the students" is clearer than "most of the students." To make your writing come alive for readers, use details that appeal to the senses. For example, describing onion soup as "a thick, bitter-tasting, yellow broth that reeked of onions" is more descriptive than "a bad-tasting broth."

Let's consider an example of how the decision-making process works. After brainstorming the list of ideas and supporting information on pages 52-53, the writer sorted the items into three groups, each group representing possible content for one paragraph. The writer then tentatively decided upon a main idea for each paragraph grouping. Notice that the writer also had several "leftovers" that did not seem to fit with any one main idea.

Next, the writer reviewed the list of main ideas and supporting information and designated which items to use in the first draft by labeling each item *Y* (yes), *N* (no), or *M* (maybe). Note that an alternate method would have been to cross out rejected items and put parentheses around the maybe's. Use whichever method you prefer.

As you look over the list on pages 60-61, remember that the topic chosen by the writer is "the benefits of comparison shopping." The thesis statement is "Comparison shopping before buying can save you money and help ensure your satisfaction with your purchases."

As you read, do the following:

- Consider whether you agree or disagree with the writer's *Y-N-M* decisions.

- Circle the items that should be further developed.

Main idea: It pays to comparison shop.
N—I got a great buy on a TV set last year.
Y—Not all stores sell same product at same price.
Y—Some stores may offer discounts or special deals.
Y—Pays off in dollars saved.
Y—You may find the item you want on sale.
Main idea: Comparison shopping requires time and effort.
Y—Have a basic idea of what you want before shopping.
Y—Go from store to store to see what's there.
Y—You can comparison shop by phone.
Y—It's smart to check newspaper advertisements.
Y—Talk to knowledgeable salespeople.
Y—Make a list of questions about products you're considering.
Y—Ask questions. take notes.
Y—Reading Consumer Reports can be a big help.
Main idea: Comparison shopping increases likelihood of satisfaction with product.
M—Keeps you from buying first item that looks good.
Y—You have a better chance of finding exactly what you want.
M—You can learn about new products on the market.
Y—Comparison shopping teaches you about available products.

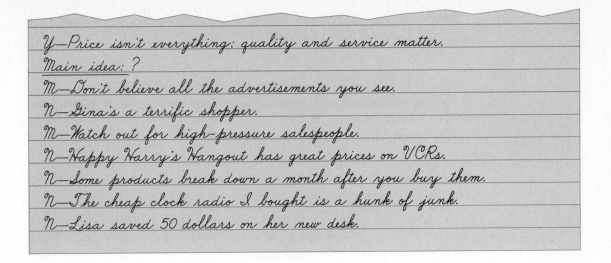

Y—Price isn't everything; quality and service matter.

Main idea: ?

M—Don't believe all the advertisements you see.

N—Gina's a terrific shopper.

M—Watch out for high-pressure salespeople.

N—Happy Harry's Hangout has great prices on VCRs.

N—Some products break down a month after you buy them.

N—The cheap clock radio I bought is a hunk of junk.

N—Lisa saved 50 dollars on her new desk.

The writer may decide not to include in the essay all items designated *Y* or *M*. However, the writer can now compare the most promising possibilities and choose the best ones.

As you review the ideas and information you've collected for an essay, you will often think of new groupings or additional items. Sometimes you may even see a whole new approach to your topic. Use the prewriting step of the writing process to try out different options until you're satisfied with your plan.

Activity E: Evaluating Main Ideas and Supporting Information

Review the ideas and information that you gathered for Activity D on page 55. Label items *Y* (yes), *N* (no), or *M* (maybe), or cross out rejected items and put parentheses around the maybes. Remember to follow the guidelines discussed on pages 58-61.

ESTABLISHING COHERENCE

The way in which you organize or structure your supporting information is important in two ways. First, ideas that have a logical flow will be easier for your readers to follow. Second, the order in which you present your information can influence the effect your writing has on readers. If you structure an essay well, the result will be a coherent essay—an essay in which the supporting information is logically organized and smoothly connected.

Organizing Main Ideas and Supporting Information

When you write an essay, you have several options for organizing ideas and information. Suppose, for example, you are writing an essay about key events in the career of the architect Frank Lloyd Wright. You might begin by discussing Wright's first major building and then move forward in time to focus on other important buildings he created. When you organize information or events according to time, you're using **chronological order**.

By comparison, suppose you are writing an essay not about Wright himself but about a particular building that he designed. In this case you might describe the building floor by floor or perhaps room by room. When you organize details in the order your eye might follow them, you're using **spatial order**.

Now suppose you're writing an essay in which you argue that Wright was the finest architect of the twentieth century. You might organize your reasons and supporting information in order of increasing importance or interest, building up to your conclusion; or, you might organize your essay in order of decreasing importance or interest, starting with your strongest argument. When you organize information in this way, you're using **order of importance or interest**.

You will learn more about these methods of organization in Chapter 5.

Questions

1. If you were writing an essay about the effects of the Los Angeles earthquake in January 1994 on the local economy, in what order would you organize information? Why?

   I will begin by discussing the damages caused to life and property and then move forward to discuss the effects on the local economy.

2. If you were writing an essay proposing the banning of all pesticides, in what order would you organize information? Why?

   I will begin by discussing the harmful affects of pesticides and then proceed to discuss how pesticides can be replaced.

Once you've used invention techniques to gather ideas and information, use the following guidelines to help you plan the organization of an essay:

- *Think about the main ideas in terms of overall essay structure.* How does each main idea relate to the central point? How do the main ideas relate to one another? Is one idea more important than another? Do you need to present one idea first in order for readers to understand other ideas? Should paragraphs be arranged in a certain order to build to a dramatic conclusion?

- *Consider what ideas or information you may want to include in your introduction and conclusion.* For example, in your introduction you may need to provide certain background facts in order for readers to understand what follows in subsequent paragraphs, or you may want to preview the content of the body of the essay.

- *Consider the arrangement of information within paragraphs.* Just as the entire essay should have a smooth and logical flow, each individual paragraph must be similarly well organized. Each paragraph should have a clear main idea developed with supporting facts and details, and each paragraph should lead smoothly to the next.

- *Mark up your list of main ideas and supporting information.* Circle the main ideas you plan to concentrate on in your essay. Cross out those you intend to eliminate. For each main idea, underline the supporting information that is most important, interesting, or relevant. Cross out items you plan to discard. Draw lines linking items you intend to combine (or dotted lines if you're not certain). If necessary, rewrite your amended list to make it easier to read.

- *Plan how to order your paragraphs.* Will you arrange information in chronological order? Spatial order? Order of importance or interest? To plan overall essay structure, first number the main ideas that you've identified in the order you plan to write about them. Then number the supporting items for each main idea in the order you plan to use them in the particular paragraph. Keep in mind that your numbering represents a working plan that you may change later if you decide that a different order would be more effective.

Activity F: Planning Structure

Follow the guidelines on pages 62-63 to help you organize the main ideas and supporting information you listed in Activity D on page 55 and evaluated in Activity E on page 61. Rewrite your list in the order you've planned.

_____

_____

_____

_____

_____

_____

_____

_____

_____

_____

_____

Mapping. To visualize the essay you plan to write, you can use mapping, a technique in which you make a conceptual map or drawing of the essay content. A conceptual map can help you plan both content and structure by enabling you to see relationships between ideas and supporting information.

Study the following example of a conceptual map.

In this conceptual map, the writer has drawn six principal circles, corresponding to the six paragraphs of the planned essay: the introduction, four body paragraphs, and the conclusion. Note that the introduction circle contains the thesis statement, and the four body paragraph circles contain the main ideas. Since this is a planning tool, the writer may decide to change the arrangement of circles, alter the content they include, or add additional circles.

How you draw a conceptual map for a particular essay will vary with the content you're planning to include and the basic structure you have in mind.

INTRODUCTION

Thesis statement: Chinese cuisine is popular in the United States, and for good reason.
Background/other information:
— Restaurants and take-out shops everywhere
— Widely used in homes

BODY PARAGRAPH 1

Main idea: Economical
Cost of ingredients
Usually inexpensive — e.g., rice
Meat used only in small amounts
Cost of meals eaten out
Most restaurants inexpensive
Take-out inexpensive

BODY PARAGRAPH 2

Main idea: Quick to prepare
Before cooking
Ingredients sliced thinly
Thin strips cook quickly
Cooking
Many foods stir-fried
This method very quick

BODY PARAGRAPH 3

Main idea: Generally healthful
Mostly vegetables, grains
Little meat, no cheese or butter

BODY PARAGRAPH 4

Main idea: Delicious
Unusual combination of foods
Can be mild or spicy

CONCLUSION

Chinese cuisine one of the world's most interesting cooking styles
Varied — everyone bound to find something to like

You can make a conceptual map while you're in the process of gathering main ideas and supporting information or after you've completed the process. Sometimes you may find it helpful to rough out a conceptual map *before* you begin to gather support, as an aid to brainstorming.

Assignment 1:
Making a Conceptual Map

In this assignment you will work independently to create a conceptual map for the main ideas and supporting information you organized in Activity F on page 64.

Use a separate sheet of paper. Begin by writing your thesis statement at the top. Think about what other information you might want to include in your introduction. Next, branch off into your main ideas, and then into the supporting information for these ideas. Finally, consider how your conclusion will follow from the preceding paragraphs. Use the map on page 65 as a model, but remember that every conceptual map is unique. Save your completed map in your portfolio.

Outlining. Outlining is another technique that can help you plan both the content and structure of an essay. There are both formal and informal outlines, but they serve essentially the same purpose: to organize ideas and information in a logical sequence according to their level of importance. Use whatever outlining approach you're comfortable with, provided the format gives you a clear picture of essay content and structure.

In a formal outline such as the following one, each paragraph of your essay is assigned a roman numeral. This gives each main idea (the key element of each body paragraph) a roman numeral. The most important supporting facts, details, and examples begin with capital letters. Less important details begin with arabic numerals and lowercase letters. Indent each new level of supporting information to show its relative importance to the main facts and details.

You can make a more informal outline if you prefer, as long as the format gives you a clear feel for both the structure and the sequence of your information. Remember, your outline is useful to you only if it helps you plan a clear, logical essay.

Compare the following sample outline with the conceptual map on page 65, which is based on the same ideas and information.

I. Introduction
  A. Thesis statement: Chinese cuisine is popular in the United States, and for good reason.
  B. Background/other information
    1. Chinese restaurants and take-out shops everywhere
    2. This style widely used in homes
II. Main idea: Economical
  A. Cost of ingredients
    1. Inexpensive ingredients such as rice
    2. Meat used only in small amounts
  B. Cost of meals eaten out
    1. Most restaurants inexpensive
    2. Take-out inexpensive
III. Main idea: Quick to prepare
  A. Before cooking
    1. Ingredients sliced into thin strips
    2. Thin strips cook more quickly
  B. Cooking
    1. Many foods stir-fried
    2. A quick method of cooking
IV. Main idea: Generally healthful
  A. Mostly vegetables, grains (rice, noodles)
  B. Uses little meat, no cheese or butter
V. Main idea: Delicious
  A. Unusual combinations of foods
  B. Can be mild or spicy
VI. Conclusion
  A. Chinese cuisine one of the world's most interesting cooking styles
  B. Varied—everyone bound to find something to like

- How are conceptual maps and outlines alike? How do they differ?

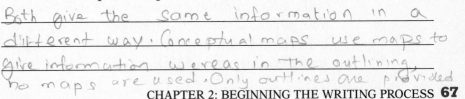

Both give the same information in a different way. Conceptual maps use maps to give information wereas in the outlining, no maps are used. Only outlines are provided.

- If you were the writer planning an essay about the popularity of Chinese food, which technique—mapping or outlining—would you find more useful? Why?

  I will prefer outlining.

Activity G: Using an Outline

Use the outline format of your choice to arrange the main ideas and supporting information you organized in Activity F on page 64. Use a separate sheet of paper to create your outline. Save your outline in your portfolio.

IN YOUR JOURNAL

Writing without first doing prewriting would be like setting out on a trip without planning the route you'll take. Think carefully about the meaning of this statement from page 42. In your journal, write a paragraph or two explaining why this is an important statement for writers to remember.

Shaping the Body of an Essay

The skeleton of any essay is found in the thesis statement and main ideas. To flesh out each paragraph, some writers use their thesis statement as a springboard for brainstorming or freewriting about their topic. Then they create a conceptual map or an outline to help them organize ideas and information into separate paragraphs. Other writers begin by creating a detailed outline or conceptual map for each individual paragraph in the essay. Then they write a first draft according to their plan.

Try various methods of shaping your essays, and use the ones you feel most comfortable with. Be sure that any supporting information you generate through invention techniques develops your thesis statement. Delete any facts, details, or examples that are unrelated to the central point of your essay.

CONCLUDING AND TITLING THE ESSAY

Once you've written the introduction and the body paragraphs, you're ready to conclude the essay and create a title. During the writing process you may have come up with new ideas or a new direction for your essay, and these may have an influence on your conclusion and your title.

Writing the Conclusion

Concluding an essay effectively is essential to achieving both unity and coherence. The conclusion sums up what has been said in the body paragraphs and ties in with the central point stated in the introduction. Here are several common techniques for writing effective conclusions. You can use these techniques, alone or in combination, to bring your essays to a smooth and logical conclusion.

- *Sum up key points:* "Whether you're buying a car or investing in a mutual fund, learn the facts before you spend your money. Never rely solely on the word of a salesperson, a friend or acquaintance, or even a relative without doing your own research. You work hard to earn your money. Work equally hard to spend it wisely."

- *Call for action:* "If you want to feel better and work more productively, get up off the couch and exercise!"

- *Make a final point:* "The ultimate irony is that some actors become so closely identified with the characters they play that audiences have difficulty accepting them in any other roles."

- *Ask a question:* "If we continue to squander our natural resources, what will remain for our children?"

As you write the conclusion to an essay, avoid using dull or overused phrases such as "in conclusion," "to sum up," "as I said," or "let me repeat." Just make your point.

Tired conclusion: I want to end by saying again that people who don't vote have no right to complain about our elected officials.

Effective conclusion: Voting is more than a privilege. It is your responsibility as a citizen. If you fail to live up to that responsibility, you forfeit the right to complain about elected officials.

Activity H: Improving Conclusions

Rewrite the following conclusions to make them stronger.

1. To sum up what I've been saying, friendship means knowing how to listen.

_____

_____

2. Employers must address the child care needs of their employees. They really must.

_____

_____

Writing the Title

As you read in Chapter 1, an effective title suggests the topic of the essay and arouses readers' interest. Review the examples of titles on page 23 of Chapter 1. The examples will help you create an interesting and appropriate title.

Even though the title appears before an essay, writers usually wait until they have completed at least a first draft before composing an essay title. To come up with an effective title, reread your essay, giving special attention to your thesis statement and your conclusion. Then write several possible titles that concisely convey the central point of the essay. Select the title that you as a _reader_ would find most intriguing.

GROUP ACTIVITY

Assignment 2:
Using Prewriting Steps and Invention Techniques With Your Group

In this assignment you will work with your group to use the prewriting steps of the writing process to plan an essay.

A. _Choose and narrow a topic._ Choose one of the following topics, or work together to select another topic. Narrow the topic to make it specific enough to cover adequately in an essay. Ask "What about _____?" questions (see page 47) to help narrow the topic.

- Pests
- The power of music
- Cheating on exams
- The importance of safe sex

TOPIC:

_____

_____

B. *Write a thesis statement.* Work together to write a clear and specific thesis statement expressing your central point.

THESIS STATEMENT:

_____

_____

C. *Gather ideas and information to support your thesis statement.* Work as a group to gather ideas and information to support and develop the thesis statement. Use either the collect-and-sort method or the main-ideas-first method (see pages 49-51). Also use the invention techniques you've learned—brainstorming, questioning, and freewriting. Write your ideas and information on a separate sheet of paper.

D. *Add and delete ideas and supporting information.* Working together, review the ideas and information you've gathered. Mark the items you intend to keep and develop, eliminate those that are irrelevant or unimportant, and add any new items. Be sure you have a manageable number of main ideas and enough supporting information to develop your central point.

E. *Plan how to organize your ideas and information.* Work together to organize the main ideas and supporting information for your essay. Discuss which organizational approach would be most effective—chronological order, spatial order, or order of importance or interest. Number the main ideas and supporting items in the order you plan to use them. Use the techniques for organizing ideas and information—mapping and outlining (see pages 64-68)—to help you plan.

Record the names of all group members on your list of main ideas and supporting information. Make a photocopy for every group member. Also make copies of any conceptual maps or outlines your group develops. Save your copies in your portfolio. You will use your prewriting work in Assignment 3 on page 75.

PORTFOLIO

THE FIRST DRAFT: PUTTING YOUR PLANS INTO ACTION

The more time and effort you devote to the prewriting step of the writing process, the easier it will be to write your first draft. This is true because the content and structure of your first draft follows directly from the planning and thinking you've already done.

Once you start writing, you may think of changes or additions you want to make to your plan. You may even find that you have to rethink some aspect of your approach or set aside your writing and do additional brainstorming or mapping. Such adjustments are a natural part of the writing process. Just remember that your goal is to support your thesis statement and develop your main ideas.

Let's see how the writer who brainstormed the list of ideas and supporting information on pages 52-53 advanced from the prewriting step to the first draft. Remember that at this point the writer has not corrected any errors in grammar, spelling, punctuation, and capitalization. As you read, do the following:

- Circle the thesis statement—the sentence in which the writer expresses the central point of the essay.

- Underline the main ideas in the body paragraphs that the writer uses to support or develop the central point.

- Note the supporting information that the writer uses to support or develop each main idea.

- Note the order in which ideas and information are arranged.

- Cross out any information that is unnecessary.

First Draft: **Comparison Shopping Is Worth Your While**

Think about this. Would you spend $250 for a product if

you could buy the same product for just $200? Would you

by a product that has only some of the things you want if

you could get everything you like for the same price? If

your answer to both of these questions is no. Then you

can appreciate the benefits of comparison shopping.

Comparison shopping before buying can save you money and help ensure your satisfaction with your purchases. That's a smart thing to do.

uses examples

Comparison shopping pays off in dollars saved. As you shop around, you'll see that some stores sell exactly the same things as other stores for less. A discount apliance store, for example, may sell something more cheaply than a department store, even when the department store supposedly has the same something on sale. Some stores also offer special promotional deals.

Comparison shopping does require some work. You know what they say: There's no such thing as a free lunch. You should have a basic idea of what your looking for in an item before you get out there. In other words, do your homework! Learn as much as you can from friends. Read consumer information publications such as *Consumer Reports*. There are other good magazines too. Check newspaper advertisements to see what's going on. Once you've checked things out, make your product comparisons either in person by visiting stores or over the telephone. Prepare a list of questions you want answer, and talk to knowledgeable salespeople. Ask questions and take notes. Get as much information as you can before committing yourself.

Comparison shopping also increases the likelihood that you'll be satisfy with your purchase. Rather than buying the first thing that looks good to you, take your time and compare, looking for exactly the things you want. This gets your feet wet before you dive into the pool. Learn about the range of products out there and their various good points and not-so-good points. as you do, you'll develop an understanding of differences in quality and will learn about available warrenties and service.

Comparison shopping is well worth your time and effort. It really is. Not only will you save money, but you will also maximize your chances of being satisfied with what you buy. In addition, comparison shopping will make you a Wiser and better informed consumer.

- Compare the essay with the main ideas and supporting information the writer listed on pages 52-53. How did the prewriting work help the writer develop the first draft? Be specific in your answer.

  _____

  _____

- Has the writer adequately supported or developed the central point? Explain your answer.

  _____

- Has the writer effectively organized ideas and information? Give reasons for your answer.

  _____

  _____

  _____

- Would you suggest that the writer make any changes in the essay? If so, what would those changes be?

  _____

  _____

  _____

As noted previously, the first draft of "Comparison Shopping Is Worth Your While" contains a number of errors. That's because first drafts are not perfect—and do not have to be. You will have ample opportunity later in the writing process to revise and edit your writing. At the first-draft step your main concerns are to get your ideas and information down on paper and to develop your central point adequately. You will focus on making revisions and corrections later in the writing process.

Assignment 3:
Writing a First Draft With Your Group

In this assignment you will work with your group to write the first draft of an essay using the prewriting notes your group developed in Assignment 2.

A. Carefully review the planning work you did for Assignment 2 on pages 70-71. Make any necessary changes.

B. Work together to write the first draft of your essay. Divide the workload in any way acceptable to both your group members and your instructor. For example, one group member might write the first paragraph, another might write the second paragraph, and so on, or the group might work together to shape each paragraph. Your first draft should consist of an introduction, body paragraphs that each contain a main idea, and a conclusion. After you review the draft, work together to develop a title that suits the topic.

Record the names of all group members on the draft. Make a photocopy for every group member. Save your copy in your portfolio. You will have an opportunity to revise and edit this draft in Chapter 3.

Assignment 4:
Prewriting and Writing a First Draft

In this assignment you will work independently to plan and write the first draft of an essay.

A. *Choose and narrow your topic.* Choose one of the following topics, or select your own topic. Narrow the topic to make it specific enough for you to cover adequately in an essay. Ask yourself "What about _____ ?" questions (see page 47) to help you bring the topic into focus.

- Secret wishes
- Doing the right thing
- Fears
- Privacy

TOPIC:

_____

B. *Write a thesis statement.* Write a clear and specific thesis statement expressing your central point.

THESIS STATEMENT:

_____

_____

C. *Gather ideas and information to support your thesis statement.* Use either the collect-and-sort method or the main-ideas-first method (see pages 49-51). Also use the invention techniques you've learned—brainstorming, questioning, and freewriting. Write your ideas and information on a separate sheet of paper.

D. *Add and delete ideas and supporting information.* Review the ideas and information you've gathered. Mark the items you intend to keep and develop, eliminate those that are irrelevant or unimportant, and add new items that occur to you. Be sure you have a manageable number of main ideas and enough supporting information to develop your central point.

E. *Plan how to organize your ideas and information.* Organize the main ideas and supporting information for your essay. Think about which organizational approach would be most effective—chronological order, spatial order, or order of importance or interest. Number the main ideas and supporting items in the order you plan to use them. Use the techniques for organizing ideas and information—mapping and outlining—to help you plan.

F. *Share your plan.* At this point, you have spent some time exploring the prewriting step of the writing process. You have chosen and narrowed a topic, written a thesis statement, and gathered ideas and supporting information. Talk to your group members about the topic you are considering. Ask for constructive advice about the topic. Also discuss any problem areas that you foresee.

As you work with your group, be ready to evaluate the plans of other group members. As with all group activities, listen and comment respectfully. Offer specific and constructive suggestions. Your goal is to provide encouragement and to help group members make their first drafts as effective as possible.

PORTFOLIO

G. *Write the first draft of your essay.* Your first draft should consist of an introduction, body paragraphs that each contain a main idea, and a conclusion. After you review your essay, develop a title that suits the topic. Save your first draft in your portfolio. You will have an opportunity to revise and edit this draft in Chapter 3.

Assignment 5:
Reading as a Stimulus for Writing

In this assignment you will read a selection and then work independently to plan and write the first draft of an essay.

A. Read "Don't Expect Me to Be Perfect" by Sun Park, on page A 119. As you read, think about how the writer has been affected by other people's expectations of her.

B. Use the selection as a stimulus for planning and writing the first draft of an essay. Use your answers to the following questions to help you decide on a specific topic and generate a thesis statement. Freewrite for approximately ten or fifteen minutes on the topic you select.

- How did the expectations of her classmates make Sun Park feel? How does her parents' attitude make her feel?

- In what ways has the pressure on Sun Park helped her? How has it hurt her?

- What pressure do you feel now or have you felt in the past in terms of someone expecting you to act in a certain way or accomplish certain tasks? How have you responded to this pressure? Has the pressure helped or hurt you?

- Who are the people who expect something of you? Your mother or father, perhaps, or your spouse? Your instructors, friends, or work colleagues?

- Are the expectations that people have of you reasonable or unfair? How do they make you feel?

PORTFOLIO

C. Work through the prewriting step and write the first draft. Your draft should have an introduction, body paragraphs that each contain a main idea, and a conclusion. After you review the draft, develop a title that suits the topic. Save your draft in your portfolio. You will have an opportunity to revise and edit this draft in Chapter 3.

ELIMINATING SENTENCE FRAGMENTS

In Chapter 1 you learned that a sentence is a group of words that contains a subject and a verb and expresses a complete idea. You also learned that a fragment is only part of a sentence. To eliminate fragments from your writing, you can take one of two approaches:

- Combine the fragment with another word group nearby.
- Rewrite the fragment to form a complete sentence.

Combining:

Look for a nearby word group that you can combine with a fragment to form a complete sentence. You may or may not need to add or rearrange words to make a smooth sentence.

SENTENCE FRAGMENTS:

Hispaniola is an island in the West Indies. *Divided between Haiti and the Dominican Republic.*

Sushi consists of thin strips of raw fish wrapped around rice. *A Japanese dish.*

COMPLETE SENTENCES:

Hispaniola is an island in the West Indies that is divided between Haiti and the Dominican Republic.

Sushi, a Japanese dish, consists of thin strips of raw fish wrapped around rice.

The writer uses the words *that is* to join the sentence fragment about Haiti and the Dominican Republic with a nearby complete sentence. The writer moved the sentence fragment about sushi to a position within the nearby complete sentence.

Rewriting or Recasting:

You can rewrite a sentence by adding a missing element, or you can recast the sentence by moving the words around.

SENTENCE FRAGMENT:

Janice to the library on Wednesday to borrow a book about architecture.

COMPLETE SENTENCES:

Janice went to the library on Wednesday to borrow a book about architecture.

On Wednesday Janice borrowed a book about architecture from the library.

This sentence fragment can be corrected either by adding a verb (*went*) or by recasting the word *borrowed* as a verb.

You may need to add new information to correct a fragment.

SENTENCE FRAGMENTS:
Learned to carve a Halloween pumpkin.
Since Mike met Kathy.

COMPLETE SENTENCES:
I learned to carve a Halloween pumpkin by watching my Dad.
Since Mike met Kathy, he talks only about her.
The fragments about carving a pumpkin and Mike and Kathy need information that only the writer can supply. These details cannot be determined by reading the fragment.

Activities

A. Each group of sentences contains a sentence fragment. Correct the fragment using one of the methods you have learned.

1. When she began working at Prescott, Lisa was given a list of tasks to be done. ~~Ten~~ that had items on the list. Lisa wondered how she'd ever get them all done.

2. Lisa listened carefully and learned quickly. She became more confident of her abilities. After three weeks on the job., she became more confident of her abilities.

B. Eliminate any fragments in the following paragraph by combining, rewriting, or recasting fragments to form sentences.

My younger brother has a bizarre concept of interior design. The walls of his room are painted green and his room's ~~Painted the walls of his room green. Bright~~ carpet is bright orange ~~orange carpet.~~ and the in color. The window curtains are yellow. Bed-
The
spread is red. his room gives me a headache. He said that
His once the ceiling is painted blue
it would look better, ~~Once he painted the ceiling blue.~~

C. For additional practice in correcting sentence fragments, see page A 68.

WRAPPING IT UP

SUMMARY

- Writing is a process that involves thought, planning, and action. This process includes prewriting, writing a first draft, revising and editing drafts, and proofreading and preparing a final copy.
- The prewriting step involves choosing and narrowing a topic, writing a thesis statement, gathering ideas and information to support a thesis statement, evaluating ideas and supporting information, and organizing ideas and supporting information.
- Brainstorming, freewriting, and questioning are useful invention techniques for gathering ideas and information. Mapping and outlining are helpful invention techniques for organizing ideas and information.
- To gather support for an essay, you can use the collect-and-sort method or the main-ideas-first method.
- Organize ideas and information in chronological order, spatial order, or order of importance or interest.

THINKING IT OVER

- What have you learned from this chapter about the writing process that you did not know before?

  _____

  _____

  _____

  _____

  _____

  _____

- How can using invention techniques help you plan and write effective essays?

  _____

  _____

  _____

  _____

  _____

- Why is planning essential to writing a unified and coherent essay?

  _____

  _____

  _____

  _____

  _____

IN YOUR JOURNAL

Review the goals that you set at the beginning of the chapter. In your journal, evaluate your progress toward these goals.

CHAPTER

3

COMPLETING THE WRITING PROCESS

OBJECTIVES:

Composition

- To revise and edit, and to proofread and prepare a final copy as two steps of the writing process.

- To evaluate the content, structure, and wording of first drafts.

- To revise and edit essays to improve content, structure, and wording.

- To proofread essays to correct errors.

Grammar

- To eliminate run-on sentences.

How Do I Revise an Essay?

An architect who designs a building can make it fit exact specifications. The architect draws a plan that shows the building's size and style. The architect can work on the plan until it is exactly what is wanted. The building made from this plan will be a product of imagination and technical skill.

You can make your writing fit your specifications in much the same way. As you revise and edit the first draft of an essay, you adjust the content, structure, and wording to express your ideas more clearly. You trim irrelevant facts or details and incorporate new supporting information. When you proofread, you correct errors in grammar, spelling, and punctuation. Your end product will be a custom-made piece of writing that effectively communicates your ideas.

Review the following list of revision tasks. If you currently do the task, explain how doing the task is helpful. If you don't currently do the task, explain how doing the task might be helpful.

- Determine whether the introduction engages readers' interest.

  _____

  _____

- Evaluate the paragraphs of an essay to see whether they all support or develop the central point.

  _____

  _____

- Verify that information is logically organized and connected.

  _____

  _____

- Evaluate whether the essay has an effective conclusion.

  _____

  _____

- Check for errors and correct them.

  _____

  _____

IN YOUR JOURNAL

Evaluate your approach to making revisions. Then set one or more goals in your journal. Here are some examples:

GOALS:
1. I will give more thought to my introduction.
2. I will make sure each paragraph supports the central point.

MAKING REVISIONS

GROUP ACTIVITY

The word *revise* means literally "to look again." **Revising** means making changes or corrections for the purpose of improving or updating material. For example, authors revise books, speech writers revise speeches, and government officials revise tax tables.

A. What kinds of revision have you done? Share your experiences with group members. Here are some examples:

- Rethinking a plan
- Adjusting a budget
- Revising a list
- Rethinking an idea or opinion

_____

_____

_____

B. In general, how do you go about making revisions? Is there a particular thought process you follow? Do you approach all kinds of revisions in the same way? Discuss and compare with group members the general steps you follow in carrying out your revisions.

_____

_____

_____

C. What aspects of your approach to making revisions would also apply to the revision of written work? With your group, brainstorm a list of steps that you might follow to revise the first draft of an essay.

_____

_____

_____

In Chapter 2 you explored the prewriting and first-draft steps of the writing process. In this chapter you will focus on the remaining two steps: revising and editing the first draft, and proofreading the revised draft and preparing a final copy.

As you work through these steps, keep in mind that at any time you can use the invention techniques you've already learned: brainstorming, questioning, freewriting, mapping, and outlining. For example, you can brainstorm to come up with additional main ideas or supporting information to develop your central point, or you can devise a new conceptual map to help you visualize a different organizational approach to your topic.

HOW MUCH REVISION IS ENOUGH?

DISCOVERY ACTIVITY

Do you agree or disagree with each of the following statements? Give reasons for your answers.

- Good writers don't have to revise their work.

_____

_____

_____

- Every first-draft essay requires the same amount of revision.

_____

_____

_____

- A writer can never do too much revision.

_____

_____

_____

For the most part, revision is a personal matter. Certainly, if an essay lacks support for the main ideas or the organization isn't clear, some revision is required. However, exactly how much revision and what specific kinds of revision are up to the writer.

Some writers are so concerned with the amount of revision that they lose sight of the purpose and value of the revision process itself. These writers dwell on questions like *How many drafts do I have to write?* or *How much time should I spend on revision?* Such questions miss the point. Revision is not an activity with time limits or rules dictating a specific number of drafts. In fact, some essays may require just a light revision after one draft, while other essays will require multiple drafts before they're ready for presentation.

To determine how much revision is enough, ask yourself this: *Am I satisfied with what I've done? Does my essay represent my best effort?* Your answers to these questions will tell you whether your essay is finished or whether you need to work on it further.

There are limits, of course. Doing your best doesn't mean becoming such a perfectionist that you can never let go of a paper you've written. What it does mean is that you invest the amount of effort needed for you to feel satisfied with what you've written.

REVISING A FIRST DRAFT

As you read at the beginning of this chapter, revising your writing requires you to be a critic. Like any critic, you need to have certain standards by which you make your evaluations. Three of the basic standards by which to evaluate an essay are unity, support, and coherence:

- Does the essay have a clear central point? Do all paragraphs relate to that point?

- Is the central point supported by specific information?

- Is the supporting information logically organized and smoothly connected?

If you can answer yes to these three questions, your essay has unity, support, and coherence. If you can't, take the time to further revise to make your essay as effective as possible.

In addition to unity, support, and coherence, you also want to evaluate your writing for clear and precise wording. Remember: the sharper you can make your language, the more effective your communication will be. Here are some guidelines to help you revise:

- *Distance yourself from what you've written.* Let some time pass—a day or two—before reviewing your first draft. You'll have a clearer, more objective view of your work if you can approach it with fresh eyes. You'll also be more likely to catch errors.

- *Read aloud what you've written, and listen to your words as though they were written by someone else.* Listen for sentence flow and logic, for variety in structure, for connections between paragraphs. Does the introduction "hook" the reader? Do the body paragraphs support the central point with effective examples and facts? Does the conclusion effectively wrap up the essay? Does the essay seem complete?

- *Ask someone whose opinion you value to give you written or oral feedback.* Did your reader understand your central point and main ideas? Did any parts of the essay seem confusing or incomplete to your reader? Ask for specific suggestions for improvement.

LEVELS OF REVISION

Although the revising and editing step and the proofreading and final-copy step of the writing process are closely related, they are separate and distinct levels of revision. Your goal during the revising and editing step is to evaluate and improve overall content, structure, wording, and sentence structure. You view the essay as a whole and also examine its components: the introduction, body paragraphs, and conclusion. You want to ensure that you've presented your central point clearly and developed it effectively.

As you prepare to fine-tune and polish your work, you move into the proofreading and final-copy step. In this step of the writing process, you carefully reread your draft, proofreading every word and sentence and correcting factual mistakes and errors in grammar, spelling, and punctuation.

Let's look first at the revising and editing step of the writing process.

REVISING AND EDITING DRAFTS

To evaluate the draft of an essay, you'll need to consider such aspects as content, overall structure, wording, and sentence structure. You'll usually find it easiest to concentrate on one aspect at a time as you revise your work. Remember, however, that the content and structure of your writing are closely linked, and making changes in one usually requires some adjustment of the other.

- *Content:* Did you include a manageable number of main ideas—that is, a number that you were able to develop adequately? Do all main ideas and supporting information advance the central point? Is the supporting information specific and concrete? What material should be eliminated? What material should be added?

- *Structure:* Have you structured your essay effectively?
  Do ideas flow smoothly from paragraph to paragraph?

- *Wording and Sentence Structure:* Have you chosen your words carefully? Is the sentence structure interesting and varied? Did you use **transitions**—connecting words and phrases such as *however*, *next*, and *in addition*—to link sentences and paragraphs?

The Checklist for Revising and Editing on page 90 can guide you in evaluating and revising a first draft. You will learn more about the various elements of the checklist later in this chapter.

Evaluating Content

Read the content of a draft carefully to make sure that you have clearly communicated and adequately supported your central point and main ideas. Use the *Content* section of the Checklist for Revising and Editing on page 90 as a guide. If you find that you need to expand or alter what you've written, use the invention techniques of brainstorming, questioning, or freewriting to gather additional ideas and information.

Checklist for Revising and Editing

CONTENT

- Is your topic too narrow or too broad?
- Does the introduction engage readers' interest?
- Have you presented the central point and main ideas clearly?
- Does your essay have unity—do all paragraphs relate to the central point?
- Does your essay have support—is there enough specific information to support or develop the central point?
- Did you make the facts and details specific enough to be meaningful?
- Did you select concrete details and examples?
- Have you included unimportant information that should be deleted?
- Does the conclusion effectively wrap up the essay?

STRUCTURE

- Is your thesis statement focused and interesting?
- Are your ideas and information organized and presented effectively?
- Does your essay have coherence—is supporting information logically organized?
- Do you move smoothly from one thought to the next?
- Does the conclusion follow logically from the preceding paragraphs?

WORDING AND SENTENCE STRUCTURE

- Have you used specific language and concrete details?
- Can you make any words or phrases more specific?
- Have you used any words that you should explain?
- Are your sentences varied in terms of length, wording, and structure?
- Do you need transitions within or between paragraphs to lead readers from one thought to the next?

Activity A: Evaluating the Content of a Draft

Read and evaluate the following first draft of an essay. Use the *Content* section of the Checklist for Revising and Editing above as a guide. As you read, underline the sentence that states the central point. In the margin, note how well the ideas are explained or developed.

First Draft: **Missing Out**

     Ever since George Ramirez took over his father's store last year, he's done nothing but work. He arrives at the store by seven in the morning and doesn't leave until eight at night. He does paperwork at home every evening and spends most Saturdays and Sundays at the store as well. George is a man who has made work his sole priority and has lost sight of everything else of value.

     George rarely allows himself a free moment to do anything other than work. He used to do many things. Now the only things he does are work related, and the only activities he participates in take place at the store.

     George has forgotten the meaning of *family*. His working hours leave him little time to spend with his wife, and even less to spend with his two children. In fact, in some respects his wife and children feel and act as though theirs is a one-parent family.

     George has abandoned his friends. For example, he used to play basketball in a local gym once or twice a week. He was a terrific player who knew how to handle the ball and had a deadly jump shot. Even though he isn't tall, George used to outscore most of the other players.

     George is a sad case. He neglects himself, his family, and his friends. Whatever internal demons have been driving him to work so fanatically are also pushing him away from the simple joys of life and, more importantly, from the people who love him. George always used to say, "Call me, and I'll be there." Now, he's never "there" anymore. I miss my husband.

Questions

1. Who is the writer of "Missing Out"? How is the revelation of the writer's identity made especially effective?

   Another Person : His wife

2. The central point of this essay is stated in the last sentence of the introduction. How does the writer use details to lead up to and support the thesis statement?

The writer says that George has forgotten about his family, and even doesn't spend time with his friends which he used to do before.

3. The second paragraph is too vague. How might the writer improve it?

By making it specific about something like the 2nd, 3rd para.

4. The third paragraph of "Missing Out" is a key paragraph, yet the writer does not adequately develop the main idea about what things George used to do with his family. How might the writer improve this paragraph? List specific suggestions.

Give more details about what George used to do within his family. Provide some examples.

5. How might the writer improve the fourth paragraph?

Be specific about his "friends".

6. Does the essay have adequate support? Explain your answer.

No,

7. To be effective, a conclusion should summarize or reinforce the central point and leave readers with a memorable final thought or image. Is the conclusion of "Missing Out" effective? Explain.

Not effective. No summarization of central point nor does it leave readers with a memorable final thought.

Evaluating Structure

Structure, or organization, is the backbone of an essay. How you organize and present ideas and information determines not only how well readers will understand your meaning but also how strongly they will be affected by your words. As you read in Chapter

2, page 62, there are various organizational approaches to use in essays, including chronological order, spatial order, and order of importance or interest. You'll learn more about these methods in Chapter 5.

Use the *Structure* section of the Checklist for Revising and Editing on page 90 to guide you in evaluating the organization of your essay. If you need to rethink your organizational approach, use mapping or outlining. Often these techniques can help you identify and correct structural flaws. Keep in mind how closely content and structure are linked. As you analyze one, you'll often need to make changes in the other.

Activity B: Evaluating the Structure of a Draft

A. Reread the first draft of "Missing Out" on page 91. Evaluate the structure of the essay using the *Structure* section of the Checklist for Revising and Editing on page 90.

- If you were the writer, how would you improve the organization of the essay? Be specific.

  _____

  _____

B. Study the following outline of "Missing Out" that the writer prepared *after* writing the first draft on page 91. Notice how the outline helped the writer find weaknesses in both structure *and* content. Answer the questions that follow the outline.

Missing Out
  I. Introduction
    A. Thesis statement: George is a man whose work has become his priority. —Is this focus correct for my central point?
    B. Background information
      1. Took over his father's store last year
      2. Works all the time now, weekdays and weekends

II. Main idea: George no longer participates in leisure activities.
   A.   Used to do what?
   B.   Now does what?
III. Main idea: George is neglecting his family.
   A. No time for wife
      1. ?
   B. No time for kids
      1. ? — This paragraph is more important than the one
   C. Like a one-parent family before and the one after.
      1. ?
IV. Main idea: George has no time for friends.
   A. Used to play basketball
      1. Terrific player ——————→ This doesn't fit!
      2. Outscored other players
   B. ?   Wouldn't this conclusion work better
V. Conclusion   with a different paragraph right
   A. George losing out on simple joys of life   before it?
   B. George distancing himself from people who love him
   C. I miss him Can I strengthen the conclusion?

- What content weaknesses has the writer found?

   _____

   _____

   _____

- What structural weaknesses has the writer found?

   _____

   _____

   _____

- How might making content revisions in "Missing Out" affect the structure of the essay?

   _____

   _____

Activity C: Evaluating the Content and Structure of a Draft

Read the following revised draft of "Missing Out." As you read, compare the revised draft with the first draft on page 91 and with the outline of the essay on pages 93-94.

Revised Draft:

Missing Out

Why does a person turn into a workaholic? Ever since George Ramirez took over his father's store last year, he's done nothing but work. He arrives at the store by seven in the morning and doesn't leave until eight at night. He does paperwork at home every evening and spends most Saturdays and Sundays at the store as well. George is a man who has made work his sole priority and has lost sight of everything else of value.

George rarely allows himself a free moment to do anything other than work. He used to read books, play cards, and go biking. Now the only reading he does is work related, and the only activities he participates in involve invoices, purchase orders, and store inventory.

George has abandoned his friends. For example, he used to play basketball in a local gym once or twice a week with two old buddies. He hasn't seen or even spoken to either one for months. Even Daniel, his closest friend, rarely talks with George anymore. When Daniel phones him at the store, George's assistant intercepts the call. "Tell him I'll call back later," George tells his assistant, but he seldom does.

Most disturbing of all, George has forgotten the meaning of *family*. His working hours leave him little time to spend with his wife, and even less to spend with his two children. In fact, in some respects his wife and children feel and act as though theirs is a one-parent family. Family activities such as going to the playground, checking homework, and visiting the library or a museum have all become exclusively his wife's domain. George's children no longer expect his presence or participation and seem surprised on those rare occasions when their father is around.

George is neglecting himself, his friends, and his family. Whatever internal demons have been driving him to work so fanatically are also pushing him away from the simple joys of life and, more important, from the people who love him. George always used to say, "Call me, and I'll be there." Now he's never "there" anymore. It's not just his friends and children who are hurt by his absence. I miss George too. I miss my husband.

Questions

1. What revisions did the writer make to the introduction? How do these changes improve the paragraph?

make use of a question to
attract reader's attention
The paragraph will attract reader's attention.

2. What revisions did the writer make to the second paragraph? How do these changes improve the paragraph?

Provides specific examples of what other things
George used to do. The improvement
provides support to the main topic.

3. Why did the writer change the order of paragraphs? What effect has this revision had?

To provide co-herence

4. On the outline, the writer noted "This doesn't fit!" next to the paragraph about George's friends. How did the writer revise this paragraph?

It provides details about his friends

5. On the outline, why did the writer note that the paragraph about family was "more important than the one before and the one after"? How did the writer revise the paragraph?

6. Review the writer's comments on the outline regarding the conclusion. How did the writer deal with these comments?

Makes the conclusion to summarize
the central point.

Evaluating Wording and Sentence Structure

After you've incorporated revisions in content and structure, turn your attention to wording and sentence structure. Follow these guidelines to help you evaluate the wording and sentence structure of your essay:

- Choose your words with care.
- Vary your sentences.
- Explain the unfamiliar.
- Use transitional words and phrases.

Choose Your Words With Care. Use language that brings your writing to life. Make details specific and concrete, and use words that appeal to the senses.

Read the following paragraph. As you read, underline words and phrases that appeal to the five senses and help you picture the scene.

Crackling yellow flames shot up the side of the old tenement, licking at the dirt-smudged windows. Black smoke rose in curls and billows that blended into the night. Fleeing tenants lined the streets, most of them wearing little more than robes or T-shirts. Light from the flickering flames reflected off their grim, sweat-streaked faces. Helplessly they stood there, coughing, crying, and hugging one another. They heard the wail of distant sirens, but knew the fire engines would arrive too late.

- How does the writer's choice of words help you "experience" the scene? Give examples to support your answer.

_____

_____

_____

_____

Vary Your Sentences. Writing is more interesting to read when sentences are varied in length, wording, and structure. To vary sentence length, mix short and long sentences. To vary wording, start sentences in different ways. If too many sentences in a row begin with the same word (such as *the* or *I*), begin some sentences with a word such as *Next* or a phrase such as *In one room*. To vary sentence structure, look for the subject and verb in each sentence. If too many sentences in a row begin with a subject and then state the verb, vary this pattern. Beginning some sentences with a word or phrase will help. Another solution is to use descriptive words or phrases between the subject and the verb.

For additional information on achieving sentence variety, see pages A 115–A 118 of the Writer's Guide.

Compare the following paragraphs. How do they differ? Which is more interesting to read? Why?

The river was calm when we began our rafting trip. The river soon got rough, though. The river tossed us around. We held on to the raft. The river put a lot of obstacles in our path. Our guides got us around them. The ride on the river was exciting.

Though the river was calm when we began our rafting trip, it soon turned into a raging torrent. We gripped our paddles as the inflatable raft bucked, rolled, and swirled. Our guides expertly maneuvered around boulders, log jams, and small waterfalls. We felt like rodeo riders on bucking broncos.

Questions

1. What makes the second paragraph more interesting than the first? Give specific examples.

   In 1st para, too many sentences in a row begin with the same word whereas it is not so in the 2nd para. The sentences are combined

2. Compare the verbs used in the two paragraphs. Which paragraph has more vivid verbs? Give examples.

   2nd para has more vivid verbs. turned, bucked, rolled, swirled.

3. Which paragraph contains more descriptive details? Give examples to support your answer.

   2nd para.

Explain the Unfamiliar. If you need to use words or expressions that your readers may not know, be sure to explain or define them. For example, read the following sentence:

> My father's cataract makes everything look cloudy to him.

If you didn't know the meaning of the word *cataract*, you wouldn't understand the sentence. Compare this revised version:

> My father suffers from a cataract. This is an eye condition that causes the lens of the eye, which is supposed to be clear, gradually to become cloudy. As a result, less light passes into the eye, and everything looks dim to him.

Use Transitional Words and Phrases. Transitions provide connections between sentences and paragraphs to guide readers from one thought to the next. *Transitions* are words or phrases that signal a relationship between one sentence and another or between one idea and another.

The italicized words and phrases in the following paragraph are transitions. Note how these transitions make the sentences flow in a logical order.

> I promised Amy that I would serve her a terrific meal on Saturday night. *First*, I went to the supermarket and bought all the ingredients I needed. *As soon as* I got home, I set to work. I gathered together all my pots and utensils. *Then* I carefully followed the recipe. *After* two hours, I opened the oven. I screamed. *Inside*, I found not the delicious meal of lasagna I had envisioned, but a lumpy mass of blackened pasta. Amy was due to arrive in half an hour. In a panic, I raced out to the Captain's Galley and ordered two meals to go. *When* Amy sat down to dinner, I was true to my word. I did *indeed* serve her a terrific meal.

In essays, transitions are needed within paragraphs to link sentences and between paragraphs to show connections between ideas. You can use transitional words and phrases to compare or contrast two people or places, to indicate time or sequence, to signal a conclusion, or to add emphasis. In the preceding paragraph, for instance, the transitions *first* and *after* show sequence while *indeed* signals emphasis. You will learn more about using transitions in Chapter 5.

Use the *Wording and Sentence Structure* section of the Checklist for Revising and Editing on page 90 to help you evaluate the wording and sentence structure of a draft.

Activity D: Evaluating a Revision

Let's examine the revised draft of the essay you read in Chapter 2 on pages 72-74, "Comparison Shopping Is Worth Your While." Keep in mind that the writer has focused on revising content and structure and hasn't yet corrected errors in grammar, spelling, punctuation, and capitalization.

Revised Draft:

Comparison Shopping Is Worth Your While

~~Think about this.~~ Would you spend $250 for a product if you could buy the same product for just $200? Would you by a product that has only some of the ~~things~~ *features* you want if you could get everything you like for the same price? If your answer to both of these questions is no. Then you can appreciate the benefits of comparison shopping. Comparison shopping before buying can save you money and help ensure your satisfaction with your purchases. ~~That's a smart thing to do~~

Comparison shopping pays off in dollars saved. As you shop around, you'll ~~see~~ *discover* that some stores sell exactly the same ~~things~~ *products* as other stores ~~for less~~ *but at a lower price.* A discount apliance store, for example, may sell ~~something~~ *a television set* more cheaply than a department store, even when the department store supposedly ~~has the same something~~ *is offering the same set* on sale. Some stores also offer special promotional deals *such as "buy this printer and get a two-year service contract."*

Comparison shopping does require some work. ~~You know what they say: There's no such thing as a free lunch.~~ You should have a basic idea of what your looking for in an item before you ~~get out there.~~ *begin shopping.* In other words,

do your homework! Learn as much as you can from

friends. Read consumer information publications such as

Consumer Reports. ~~There are other good magazines too.~~

Check newspaper advertisements to see ~~what's going on.~~ *what items are available.*

Once you've ~~checked things out,~~ *done the background research,* make your product com-

parisons either in person ~~by visiting stores~~ or over the

telephone. Prepare a list of questions you want answer,

and talk to knowledgeable salespeople. Ask questions

and take notes. Get as much information as you can

before ~~committing yourself.~~ *making a final decision.*

Comparison shopping also increases the likelihood that

you'll be satisfy with your purchase. Rather than buying

the first ~~thing~~ *item* that looks good to you, take your time and

compare, looking for exactly the ~~things~~ *features* you want. ~~This~~

~~gets your feet wet before you dive in the pool.~~ Learn

about the range of products out there *offered* and their various

~~good points~~ *advantages* and ~~not-so-good points.~~ *disadvantages* as you do, you'll

develop an understanding of differences in quality and

will learn about available warrenties and service.

make this paragraph 3.

Comparison shopping is well worth your time and

effort. ~~It really is.~~ Not only will you save money, but you

will also maximize your chances of being satisfied with

what you buy. In addition, comparison shopping will

make you a Wiser and better informed consumer.

Questions

1. In what way did deleting two sentences in the third paragraph improve unity in the essay? Be specific.

Removes the unnecessary sentences. and provides unity

2. How did adding the words to the last sentence in the second paragraph increase support for the main idea of that paragraph?

Provides an example.

3. How did moving two paragraphs around increase coherence?

Presents the details in a chronological order.

4. What other revisions would you make if you were the writer of this essay? (Consider only changes in content, structure, and wording and sentence structure.)

Assignment 1:
Revising and Editing a First Draft With Your Group

In this assignment you will work with your group to revise and edit the first draft of the essay the group worked on in Chapter 2, Assignments 2 and 3.

A. Carefully reread and evaluate the content, structure, and wording of your first draft from Assignment 3 in Chapter 2. Discuss any changes, additions, deletions, and corrections needed to improve the draft. If necessary, do additional brainstorming or research. Use the Checklist for Revising and Editing on page 90 as a guide.

B. Work together to revise the first draft. Make as many revisions as needed for the group to agree that the essay represents your best combined effort. Record the names of all group members on the revised draft. Make a photocopy for every group member. Save your copy in your portfolio. You will have an opportunity to proofread this essay in Assignment 3.

GROUP
ACTIVITY

PORTFOLIO

Assignment 2:

Revising and Editing a First Draft

In this assignment you will work independently to revise and edit one of the two first drafts you wrote independently in Chapter 2, Assignments 4 and 5, and saved in your portfolio.

A. Reread the first drafts you wrote on your own for Assignments 4 and 5 of Chapter 2. Select the one you want to revise.

B. Share with your group or a peer editor the essay that you have chosen. Use the comments and suggestions from your partner or group in conjunction with the Checklist for Revising and Editing on page 90 to help you make revisions.

If you are working with your group, be ready to evaluate the essays of other group members. If you are working with a peer editor, evaluate and discuss each other's essays using the following guidelines. After sharing essays, you will work independently to revise your draft until you are satisfied with it.

Guidelines for Sharing

Writer

- Tell your evaluator(s) what concerns you about your draft.
- Maintain a positive attitude.
- Don't be defensive.

Group Member or Peer Editor

- Be sensitive to the writer's feelings.
- Point out techniques the writer has used that are particularly effective.
- Offer specific and constructive suggestions for improvement.
- Focus on essay content and organization, not errors in grammar, spelling, punctuation, or capitalization.
- Help the writer understand a weakness by asking questions.
- Give the writer your undivided attention.

C. Evaluate the content, structure, and wording of the draft you've chosen. Make any changes, additions, deletions, and corrections needed to improve your draft. If necessary, do additional brainstorming or research. Use the Checklist for Revising and Editing on page 90 as a guide.

D. Make as many revisions as needed for you to feel that you've done your best work. Save your revised essay in your portfolio. You will have an opportunity to proofread this essay in Assignment 4.

PROOFREADING AND PREPARING A FINAL COPY

After revising and editing your draft, you're ready to move on to the last step in the writing process, proofreading the revised draft and preparing a final copy. **Proofreading** is the step in the writing process where you eliminate any factual errors you may have missed; correct mistakes in grammar, spelling, and punctuation; and do whatever other final polishing may be necessary.

Allow some time to pass between the revision and proofreading steps. You'll find it easier to detect errors and make final changes if you can read your draft as though it were a fresh piece of writing.

To proofread your revised draft, you'll read it several times. Here are some tips to help you proofread:

- First, read your draft aloud for sense. You may want to begin by reading the entire essay and then carefully rereading each individual paragraph, or you may prefer focusing on one paragraph at a time and then reading the entire essay from start to finish.

- Next, read your draft backwards, one word at a time. This is an effective trick that professional proofreaders use to detect errors and omissions.

- Finally, ask a classmate, friend, or coworker to read your draft. Another reader may catch errors that you've overlooked.

To prepare your final copy, use the Checklist for Proofreading on page 105. Use proofreaders' marks from the box on page 105 to mark changes and corrections.

After proofreading your draft, key the final copy. Follow the "Guidelines for Preparing a Final Copy" that appear on page 106.

Checklist for Proofreading

- **Factual accuracy.** Have you double-checked all your facts? If you're not sure whether a fact is correct, recheck your sources.

- **Correct numbers.** If your essay contains any dates, addresses, or other numbers, examine *each digit* to be sure of accuracy.

- **Correct spelling.** Are you certain you've spelled the names of persons and places correctly? If a word can be spelled two ways, have you spelled the word consistently throughout the essay? If you are unsure of the spelling of a word, check a dictionary.

- **Grammatical accuracy.** Do all subjects and verbs agree? Are all sentences complete?

- **Correct punctuation.** Have you used punctuation marks, such as commas, quotation marks, apostrophes, and end punctuation, correctly?

- **Correct capitalization.** Have you capitalized the first letter of every sentence and proper noun? Have you capitalized words in the title as needed?

Consult the Writer's Guide that begins on page A 80 to review key points of grammar, punctuation, and capitalization.

Proofreaders' Marks

Mark	Meaning	Example
∧	insert a word or letter	typwriter (e)
—℮	delete a word or letter	do ~~not~~ ℮
/	lowercase a letter	He said /Hello
≡	capitalize	My friend ịnez
∩	transpose a word or letter	recieve
⊙	insert a period	Mr⊙ Sam Burns
∧	insert a comma	he, she∧and it
∨	insert an apostrophe	we∨ll
¶	start a new paragraph	¶As a result,
#	insert space	no#one

When you're done, look over your final copy and make any additional corrections that may be necessary. Rekey the final copy if you have to make many corrections.

For most school assignments and work-related writing tasks, you'll be required to key your final copy. If you plan to submit a handwritten final copy, check with your instructor in advance to make sure that a handwritten copy is acceptable.

GUIDELINES FOR PREPARING A FINAL COPY

- Use full-size typewriter or theme paper, 8½ by 11 inches.
- Use only one side of the paper.
- Double-space the lines.
- Leave one-inch margins at the top, sides, and bottom.
- Number all pages except the first page. Place the page number in the upper right-hand corner.

- Skip a line between the title and the first line of text.
- Indent the first line of each paragraph.
- Correct any keyboarding errors and produce a clean copy.
- Use the style your instructor requests for your name, the date, and the course number.

Activity E: Proofreading a Revised Draft

After making revisions, the writer of "Comparison Shopping Is Worth Your While" keyed a revised draft of the essay.

A. Proofread the following revised draft and correct any factual, keyboarding, grammatical, spelling, and punctuation errors. Use the proofreaders' marks on page 105 to mark corrections.

Revised and
Rekeyed Draft: **Comparison Shopping Is Worth Your While**

Would you spend $250 for a product if you could buy the same product for just $200? Would you by a product that has only some of the features you want if you could get everything you like for the same price? If your answer to both of these questions is no, Then you can appreciate the benefits of comparison shopping. Comparison shopping before buying can save you money and help ensure your satisfaction with your purchases.

Comparison shopping pays off in dollars saved. As you shop around, you'll discover that some stores sell exactly the same products as other stores but at a lower price. A discount apliance store, for example, may sell a television set more cheaply than a department store, even when the department store is offering the same set on sale. Some stores also offer special promotional deals such as "buy this printer and get a two-year service contract."

Comparison shopping also increases the likelihood that you'll be satisfy with your purchases. Rather than buying the first item that looks good to you, take your time and compare products, looking for exactly the features you want. Learn about the range of products offered and their various advantages and disadvantages. as you do, you'll develop an understanding of differences in quality and will learn about available warrenties and service.

Comparison shopping does require some work. You should have a basic idea of what your looking for in an item before you begin shopping. In other words, do your homework! Learn as much as you can from friends. Read consumer information publications such as *Consumer Reports*. Check newspaper advertisements to see what items are available. Once you've done the background research, make your product comparisons either in person or over the telephone. Prepare a list of questions you want answer, and talk to knowledgeable salespeople. Ask questions and take notes. Get as much information as you can before making a final decision.

Comparison shopping is well worth your time and effort. Not only will you save money, but you will also

maximize your chances of being satisfied with what you
buy. In addition, comparison shopping will make you a
wiser and better informed consumer.

B. Compare your corrections with those your classmates made to
help develop a sense of your skill as a proofreader.

Here's a time-saving tip for handling hard-to-spell words. If you find
yourself repeatedly misspelling a particular word—say, *receive*—as
you work on an essay, simply abbreviate the word—*rec*, for example—instead of spelling it out. Write down the abbreviation you
decide on so you'll remember what it is. After you've completed your
draft, use the search-and-replace feature of the word-processing program to replace every instance of *rec* with *receive*.

GROUP ACTIVITY

Assignment 3:
Proofreading a Revised Draft and Preparing a Final Copy With Your Group

In this assignment you will work with your group to proofread and
prepare the final copy of the essay you revised and edited as a group
in Assignment 1.

A. Carefully reread your revised draft. Using the Checklist for
Proofreading on page 105, work together to prepare the final
copy. Consult the Writer's Guide that begins on page A 80 to
review key points of grammar, punctuation, and capitalization.
First, have each group member proofread the revised draft independently. Use proofreaders' marks from the box on page 105 to
mark corrections. Then compare your corrections. Incorporate
all the changes on one draft.

PORTFOLIO

B. Have one group member key the final copy. Proofread the final
copy as a group. Correct any errors in keying. Record the names
of all group members on the final copy. Make a photocopy for
every group member. Save your copy in your portfolio.

Assignment 4:
Proofreading a Revised Draft and Preparing a Final Copy

In this assignment you will work independently to proofread and prepare the final copy of the essay you revised and edited independently in Assignment 2.

A. Carefully reread your revised draft. Use the Checklist for Proofreading on page 105. Consult the Writer's Guide that begins on page A 80 to review key points of grammar, punctuation, and capitalization. Use proofreaders' marks from the box on page 105 to mark your corrections.

B. Key the final copy. Look over the final copy and correct any errors in keying. Save your final copy in your portfolio.

PORTFOLIO

Assignment 5:
Working Through the Steps of the Writing Process

In this assignment you will work independently to carry out all the steps in the writing process.

A. Choose a topic from this list, or select your own topic.
- The worst teacher I ever had
- Campus life
- Honesty in relationships
- Why I'm in college

B. Narrow your topic for an essay that has an introduction, a body, and a conclusion. Use the invention techniques you learned in Chapter 2 to help gather and organize ideas.

C. Use mapping or outlining to organize main ideas and supporting information.

D. Use your planning notes to write a first draft.

E. Revise the essay as many times as needed to improve the content, structure, and wording. Use the Checklist for Revising and Editing on page 90 as a guide.

F. Proofread the revised draft. Use the Checklist for Proofreading on page 105 to help you.

G. Key the final copy. Proofread the final copy to correct any errors. Save your final copy in your portfolio.

PORTFOLIO

RUN-ON SENTENCES

Grammar Gremlins

A **run-on sentence** appears to be one sentence but is actually two (or more) separate sentences run together. Run-on sentences are grammatically incorrect and difficult to understand. The reader can't see where one thought ends and the other begins.

There are four common ways to correct run-on sentences. You will learn two ways in this chapter and two more ways in Chapter 4.

INCORRECT:
Elana draws beautifully, she should be an artist.
My brother sold his house, he moved to Michigan.

The sentences above each state two complete thoughts. Using a comma alone to divide the two thoughts is not enough to separate them. This error is called a **comma splice** and creates a run-on sentence. A break stronger than a comma is needed between two complete thoughts. One way to correct a run-on sentence is to break it into two separate sentences.

CORRECT:
Elana draws beautifully. She should be an artist.

Another way to correct a comma splice is to use a comma plus a conjunction such as *and* or *but*. **Conjunctions** are words used to connect two or more words, phrases, or sentences.

CORRECT:
My brother sold his house, and he moved to Michigan.

Now consider a slightly different example. Some writers string together a series of thoughts with conjunctions. The result is a long, awkwardly written run-on sentence.

INCORRECT:
Sperry biked to the market and bought bread and milk and then biked over to the music store but the store was closed and she decided to return on Thursday.

Let's correct this run-on sentence by taking out the *ands* and adding a comma and a few periods.

CORRECT:
Sperry biked to the market. She bought bread and milk. Then she biked over to the music store, but the store was closed. She decided to return on Thursday.

and
but
or
nor
for
yet
so

Activities

A. Correct the following run-on sentences. Use the proofreaders' marks on page 105 of this chapter to mark your corrections.

1. As the temperature fell, ice formed on the roadway, *and* many cars skidded.

2. Snow began to fall heavily, *and* drivers could scarcely see.

3. I started to drive across town, *but* I changed my mind.

4. By noon, the roads were nearly impassable, and cars were stranded all along the highway, and even the snowplows had difficulty moving, and the snow kept falling.

5. The weather forecaster predicted six more inches of snow by evening, people didn't want to believe what they were hearing.

6. The next morning the city was buried under two feet of snow, and schools closed and all the kids went sledding, and I went outside and built a snowwoman.

B. Read the following paragraph. Correct any run-on sentences.

Mr. and Mrs. Kobray, the couple next door, are celebrating their *fiftieth* wedding anniversary. I asked Mrs. Kobray what their secret was, she told me that her spouse is also her best friend. Mrs. Kobray made a very wise observation. As important as love and passion are, the person with whom you're living must also be your close friend, if that's not the case, the relationship can't last. Later on I met Mr. Kobray in the park and I asked him the same question I had asked his wife earlier, and he smiled and said that the secret to their long marriage was that they both liked Italian food. I laughed and wished the Kobrays fifty more happy years together.

C. For additional practice in identifying and correcting run-on sentences, see page A 69.

WRAPPING IT UP

SUMMARY

- In revising and editing a draft, you evaluate and improve the content, structure, wording, and sentence structure of your essay.
- In proofreading a draft, you correct factual and keyboarding errors and incorrect numbers, spelling, grammar, capitalization, and punctuation.

THINKING IT OVER

- How can revision help you create a unified and coherent essay?

  _____

  _____

- Why is proofreading an important part of the writing process?

  _____

  _____

IN YOUR JOURNAL

Review the goals that you set at the beginning of this chapter. In your journal, evaluate your progress toward these goals.

The Elements of Essays

In your lifetime you have handled projects that required you to juggle a number of considerations at one time. Think of parties you have planned, alone or with friends. Perhaps you had to decide on a theme for a party. You had to decide the type of food you would serve: a birthday cake, chips and dip, or sandwiches. You planned the guest list, the date and time of the party, and whether the party would be formal or casual. When you write an essay, you also do a lot of planning beforehand. You must coordinate many elements when you write an essay. Section 2 of *Improve Your Essays* will help you take charge of all the aspects of essay writing. Chapter 4 introduces the five key elements of writing: writing purpose, content development, structure, audience, and tone. Chapter 5 presents strategies for developing and organizing content to create a coherent essay.

4

THE ELEMENTS OF WRITING

OBJECTIVES:

Composition

- To analyze essays written for four purposes: to describe, to narrate, to persuade, and to inform.

- To establish a writing purpose.

- To apply the five key elements of writing: purpose, content, structure, audience, and tone.

- To develop content that supports the thesis statement.

- To define and address the intended audience.

- To determine the tone of an essay.

Grammar

- To eliminate run-on sentences.

How Can I Plan an Essay?

Think about the planning and preparation that musicians must do before a concert. Each musician has to learn and practice the music individually. In addition, all the musicians must practice the piece together to blend the different musical instruments. The orchestra members must also work to blend together the different elements of the music—melody, beat, and the volume and speed at which each section is played.

Writing an essay, like giving a concert, requires thoughtful planning. To convey your meaning effectively, you need to begin with a clear concept of what you want to communicate. Then you have to determine how best to organize your presentation and tailor it for your particular audience.

A composer blends and balances elements of sound to create a harmonious musical composition. A writer creates harmony on paper by blending and balancing the elements of writing. To address these elements, writers devote considerable time to thinking and planning before they begin to write. They think carefully about their topic. They mull over their purpose for writing and the ideas they plan to include. They consider how to appeal to their particular audience, and they think about how their words will "sound" to this audience. Answer the following self-survey questions to help you gauge how well you already understand and balance the elements of writing.

- Name something you've written for which you have done the following: established a specific writing purpose and topic before you began to write, planned how to organize ideas and information, and tailored the approach for a specific audience.

  _____

  _____

- Did the piece you wrote accomplish your writing purpose? Give reasons for your answer.

  _____

  _____

- Did you stick to your topic? How well did your ideas and information blend together to develop the topic? Explain.

  _____

  _____

- How closely did you follow your organizational plan? Was your structure clear and logical? Explain.

  _____

  _____

- Did the piece of writing affect your audience as you'd intended? Explain your answer.

  _____

  _____

Read the following list of writing-related tasks. Circle *E* if you generally find the task "easy," *C* if you find it "challenging," or *I* for "in between."

1. Establishing a clear reason for writing. (Purpose)   E   C   I

2. Deciding what ideas and information to include. (Content)   E   C   I

3. Organizing ideas and information logically. (Structure)   E   C   I

4. Maintaining a clear sense of who the readers will be. (Audience)   E   C   I

5. Using language that is appropriate for the intended audience. (Tone)   E   C   I

IN YOUR JOURNAL

Review your answers to the self-survey questions. What do they reveal about your ability to address the elements of writing? In your journal, write one or more goals. Here are some examples:

GOALS:
1. I will establish a clear writing purpose before I begin to write.
2. I will use language that is suitable for my audience.

ELEMENTS OF SPEAKING AND WRITING

GROUP ACTIVITY

Speaking and writing have much in common. Whether you are communicating orally or in writing, you consider several interrelated elements.

- *Why* you're communicating—your purpose for speaking or writing.
- *What* you're communicating—the ideas and information you want to convey.
- *How* you're communicating—the way in which you organize and express your ideas and information.
- *Whom* you're addressing—the people who will hear or read your words.

Work with your group to compare the following two situations. As you discuss the questions, think about how purpose shapes all the other elements. Try to arrive at a group consensus in answering each question.

SITUATION A: You have been asked to make an oral presentation to a sixth-grade class warning the children about the dangers of drug abuse.

SITUATION B: You have been asked to prepare a written report for the mayor about drug abuse in your community. Your report is to describe the extent of drug abuse and recommend ways of addressing the problem.

- What is the purpose of the presentation? Be specific.

PRESENTATION TO SIXTH GRADE:

_____

_____

REPORT TO MAYOR:

_____

_____

- What will be the content of the presentation? What ideas and information will you include? How will you develop your ideas?

PRESENTATION TO SIXTH GRADE:

_____

_____

REPORT TO MAYOR:

_____

_____

- How will you introduce your topic? How will you organize your ideas and information? How will you conclude your presentation?

PRESENTATION TO SIXTH GRADE:

_____

_____

REPORT TO MAYOR:

_____

_____

- How will your audience affect your choice of content and your method of organization?

PRESENTATION TO SIXTH GRADE:

_____

_____

REPORT TO MAYOR:

_____

_____

- What tone will you use for each presentation? How will your audience affect your choice of tone?

PRESENTATION TO SIXTH GRADE:

_____

_____

REPORT TO MAYOR:

_____

_____

ESTABLISHING A WRITING PURPOSE

WHY ARE YOU WRITING?

All writing has a purpose. Newspaper reporters present information. Novelists tell stories. Advertising copywriters try to persuade you to purchase products. For what purposes do *you* write?

DISCOVERY ACTIVITY

- Think back over the past few weeks. What have you written? List six examples of your writing. Include items of any length or form—school reports, greeting cards, letters to friends, whatever comes to mind.
- Next to each item, briefly describe your purpose for writing.

_____

_____

_____

_____

_____

_____

Your specific purpose for writing, whether you're doing a report or sending a postcard, determines what information you will include and how you will present that information. For this reason, having a clear purpose in mind is essential. Unless you clearly establish *why* you're writing, you can't plan your writing effectively.

Each writer has a distinct writing style, but all writers write for the same four basic purposes:

1. To *describe* something or someone.
2. To *narrate*, or give an account of, an event or experience.
3. To *persuade* others to think or act in a certain way.
4. To *inform*, explain, or present information.

Let's examine each of these writing purposes.

DESCRIPTIVE WRITING: PAINTING A VERBAL PICTURE

Descriptive writing paints a verbal picture. That is, the writer uses words to help readers "see" a person, place, or thing. You might, for example, write an essay describing the appearance of the African plains or the thrill of snowboarding down a mountain. Descriptive writing uses **sensory language**—words or phrases that appeal to one or more of the five senses: sight, hearing, touch, smell, and taste. Examples of sensory language include *shimmering*, *rumbling*, *smooth*, *icy*, *bitter*, *as hot as a flame*, and words that describe color, size, or shape.

You'll encounter descriptive writing in all sorts of contexts, from magazine articles to novels, from travel brochures to product advertisements.

Read the excerpt from "The Little Store" below. As you read this descriptive selection by Eudora Welty, underline words and phrases that the writer uses to paint a verbal picture.

Excerpt from   **"The Little Store"**

Our Little Store rose right up from the sidewalk; standing in a street of family houses, it alone hadn't any yard in front, any tree or flowerbed. It was a plain frame building covered over with brick. Above the door, a little railed porch ran across on an upstairs level and four windows with shades were looking out. But I didn't catch on to those.

Running in out of the sun, you met what seemed total obscurity inside. There were almost tangible[1] smells—licorice recently sucked in a child's cheek, dill-pickle brine that had leaked through a paper sack in a fresh trail across the wooden floor, ammonia-loaded ice that had been hoisted from wet croker sacks and slammed into the icebox with its sweet butter at the door, and perhaps the smell of still-untrapped mice.

Then through the motes of cracker dust, cornmeal dust, the Gold Dust of the Gold Dust Twins that the floor had been swept out with, the realities emerged. Shelves climbed to high reach all the way around, set out with not too much of any one thing but a lot of things—lard, molasses, vinegar, starch, matches, kerosene, Octagon soap (about a year's worth of octagon-shaped coupons cut out and

[1]**tangible:** able to be touched

saved brought a signet ring addressed to you in the mail. Furthermore, when the postman arrived at your door, he blew a whistle). It was up to you to remember what you came for, while your eye traveled from cans of sardines to ice cream salt to harmonicas to flypaper (over your head, batting around on a thread beneath the blades of the ceiling fan, stuck with its testimonial catch).

Its confusion may have been in the eye of its beholder. Enchantment is cast upon you by all those things you weren't supposed to have need for, it lures you close to wooden tops you'd outgrown, boy's marbles and agates in little net pouches, small rubber balls that wouldn't bounce straight, frazzly kitestring, clay bubble-pipes that would snap off in your teeth, the stiffest scissors. You could contemplate those long narrow boxes of sparklers gathering dust while you waited for it to be the Fourth of July or Christmas, and noisemakers in the shape of tin frogs for somebody's birthday party you hadn't been invited to yet, and see that they were all marvelous.

You might not have even looked for Mr. Sessions when he came around his store cheese (as big as a dolls' house) and in front of the counter looking for you. When you'd finally asked him for, and received from him in its paper bag, whatever single thing it was that you had been sent for, the nickel that was left over was yours to spend.

(Eudora Welty, from "The Little Store," in *The Eye of the Story*)

Questions

1. Like many other pieces of descriptive writing, this selection does not have an explicit thesis statement. Rather, the piece of writing as a whole conveys the central point. What is the central point of "The Little Store"?

Description of the store.

Memories make the shop appear more magical than the shop was in actuality

2. How does the writer develop the description of the store? Be specific and give examples.

Location of the store, Items sold in the store

3. To which senses does the writer appeal in the selection? Support your answer with specific examples.

rose right up — sight

plain frame building — sight

sweet butter — taste

smell of stuff wrapped unwrapped milk — smell

4. How might the writer have written about the same basic topic but for a *different* purpose? Explain your answer.

By narrating

NARRATIVE WRITING: TELLING WHAT HAPPENED

Narrative writing gives readers an account of events that have happened or are happening. When writers narrate, they tell either a true story or a fictional one. A magazine article such as "How One Family Survived the Los Angeles Earthquake," a newspaper account such as "Repairing the Hubble Telescope," and a short story such as "I Saw Elvis at the Post Office" are all examples of narrative writing.

Narrative writing is usually structured chronologically, presenting events in the order they occur. Often the writer of a narrative piece includes dates or times, or time words such as *first*, *next*, or *afterward*, to help indicate sequence.

Read the following narrative excerpt from *Blue Highways* by William Least Heat Moon. In *Blue Highways*, William Least Heat Moon tells about a journey he took along the back roads of the United States. As you read, underline any words or phrases that indicate time or that otherwise help you understand the sequence of events.

Excerpt from **Blue Highways**

New Pass Station, under cliffs of the Desatoya Mountains and half an hour west of Austin, used to be a stagecoach stop. The cold morning I pulled in to make breakfast, it was a tumble of stone walls and the willow-thatch roof had long since gone to compost. These stations were crude shelters even when the Overland ran the route; a traveler in 1861 described Cold Spring, the next stop west, as a "wretched place, half-built and wholly unroofed." He spent the night in a haystack. What I took for a ruin was, perhaps, a reconstruction.

I found my cooler empty except for some sardines and the can of chopped liver so I went on along the stage road, also once the Pony Express trail and the route of the first transcontinental telegraph. Add to those the journeys of Indians and Forty-niners, and highway 50 is one archaeological layer of communication upon another.

Regardless of the utter fierceness of desert winters and summers, the Pony Express riders, they say, always rode in shirtsleeves; considering the real hazards of the job, that may be true. The Central Overland California and Pike's Peak Express (the actual name of the Pony Express) used to run notices that are models for truth in advertising. An 1860 San Francisco newspaper printed this one:

WANTED
Young, skinny, wiry fellows not
over eighteen. Must be expert
riders willing to risk death
daily. Orphans preferred.

Despite or because of such ads, never was there a shortage of riders.

The only baggage the boys carried—in addition to the mail mochila[1]—was a kit of flour, cornmeal, and bacon, and a medical pack of turpentine, borax, and cream of tartar.[2] Not much in either one to keep a rider alive. A letter cost $2.50 an ounce, and, if the weather and horses held out and the Indians held off, it might go the two thousand miles from Missouri to California in ten days, as did Lincoln's Inaugural Address. But the primary purpose of the service was neither the speedy delivery of news or correspondence; rather, the Express comprised part of the Northern defense strategy during the Civil War by providing a fast, central link with California that Southern raiders couldn't cut. For the seventeen months the Pony Express existed, it helped to hold California in the Union; what's more, this last of the old-world means of communication before mechanical contraptions took over left a deep mark on the American imagination. The riders, going far on little, became touchstones of courage and strength.

[1]**mochila:** a pack or knapsack
[2]**borax** and **cream of tartar:** chemical powders that were used as medicines

(William Least Heat Moon, from *Blue Highways*)

Questions

1. What is the topic of the selection from *Blue Highways*?

   Pony express riders

2. The writer presents two narrative situations in the selection. What are they?

   smy of his own journey and story of pony express
   riders

3. In narrative essays a writer will often use descriptive details to present a clear image of a certain time or event. What descriptive details make the time of the Pony Express riders stand out most clearly to you?

4. Why does the writer decide to present the narrative about the riders instead of just narrating his own experiences at New Pass Station? Which clues from the story helped you decide on your answer?

PERSUASIVE WRITING: USING WORDS TO INFLUENCE OR CONVINCE

Persuasive writing tries to influence how readers think or feel or convince them to act in a certain way. You encounter persuasive writing in many different forms, including editorials, advertisements, movie reviews, political pamphlets, and letters to the editor.

To be persuasive, a writer emphasizes or supports an opinion with facts, reasons, or other information. The writer may also use words or phrases that carry an emotional charge—positive or negative—to help sway readers, such as *devious, vital,* or *insidious.*

To make a persuasive piece effective, a writer gives careful consideration to the intended readers. Keeping the particular audience in mind enables the writer to tailor information and arguments appropriately. For example, if you were writing a persuasive essay about the value of sex education in school, you would take a different approach for preteen readers than you would for parents.

Read "Passports to Understanding" below. As you read this persuasive essay, mark places where the writer makes clear that her purpose is to persuade readers to think or act in a certain way.

Passports to Understanding

Human beings are more alike than unalike, and what is true anywhere is true everywhere, yet I encourage travel to as many destinations as possible for the sake of education as well as pleasure.

It is necessary, especially for Americans, to see other lands and experience other cultures. The American, living in this vast country and able to traverse three thousand miles east to west using the same language, needs to hear languages as they collide in Europe, Africa, and Asia.

A tourist, browsing in a Paris shop, eating in an Italian *ristorante*,[1] or idling along a Hong Kong street, will encounter three or four languages as she negotiates the buying of a blouse, the paying of a check, or the choosing of a trinket. I do not mean to suggest that simply overhearing a foreign tongue adds to one's understanding of that language. I do know, however, that being exposed to the existence of other languages increases the perception that the world is populated by people who not only speak differently from oneself but whose cultures and philosophies are other than one's own.

Perhaps travel cannot prevent bigotry, but by demonstrating that all peoples cry, laugh, eat, worry, and die, it can introduce the idea that if we try to understand each other, we may even become friends.

[1]**ristorante:** *restaurant* in Italian

(Maya Angelou, from *Wouldn't Take Nothing for My Journey Now*)

✓ **Questions**

1. What is the topic of "Passports to Understanding"?

The importance of Travelling for promoting understanding

2. What is the central point of the essay?

For the sake of education as well as pleasure travel to as many destinations as possible

3. How does the writer support or develop the central point? Be specific.

Persuade Americans to see other lands

4. Is the conclusion effective? Give reasons for your answer.

Yes,

5. Overall, has the writer been persuasive? Explain your answer.

Yes,

INFORMATIVE WRITING: EXPLAINING SOMETHING

Informative writing presents information to readers or explains how to do something. Informative writing differs from persuasive writing in that the writer is not trying to convince readers to believe or act on the information presented. Instead, the writer is presenting information to increase readers' understanding and knowledge of a topic. You encounter informative writing in textbooks, news articles, encyclopedias, instruction manuals, and many other contexts.

Read "Working Together for Multicultural Education" on pages 128-129. Note that this informative essay is somewhat similar in subject matter to "Passports to Understanding." The writer's purpose, however, is not to persuade but to inform. As you read "Working Together for Multicultural Education," note in the margin the kinds of supporting information the writer includes to support the main idea of each paragraph.

Working Together for Multicultural Education

A growing number of schools across the country are actively promoting understanding and acceptance of cultural and racial differences. From grade school through high school, administrators and teachers are working together to implement a wide range of multicultural programs and activities. These undertakings may involve entire schools or districts, individual classes, or individual students.

Several factors are at the root of this trend. One factor is that the United States is an increasingly multicultural country. This development is due largely to changing sources of new citizens in recent decades. Where once the bulk of immigrants to the United States came from Western European countries such as England and Germany, now an increasing proportion of immigrants come from Latin America and the Caribbean, Africa, and Asia. The result is that in some states such as California, more than 25 percent of the population is some combination of ethnic groups such as Hispanic, African American, Asian, and Native American. Some city school systems, such as those in Los Angeles and New York City, serve as many as 100 different ethnic groups. Another factor in the rise of multiculturalism is that, largely as a result of the civil rights movement in the 1960s, many minority groups have been inspired to explore, assert, and share the uniqueness of their cultures.

On a school-wide or district-wide basis, schools are incorporating multicultural themes into their daily curriculum. Special assemblies and festivals introduce students to music and dance from all over the globe. Guest speakers from different countries and different ethnic backgrounds talk to students about cultural similarities and differences. School-wide celebrations of other cultures include poster-design contests built around multicultural themes or performances of plays from around the world, with the student actors often wearing authentic costumes. Some schools even have "special food days" on which students sample foods from other cultures.

On an individual class basis, teachers are linking classroom activities with a particular country, culture, or part of the world. For example, one class may "adopt" Spain for the year. Students in this class study the history of Spain and read library books written by Spanish writers. They learn basic Spanish vocabulary, write reports about notable Spaniards, and carry out assignments relating to Spanish art or music.

Some multicultural activities take a more personal track. Students are encouraged to share with the class their own multicultural knowledge and experiences and to invite to school friends and relatives of different cultures and backgrounds.

Educators and parents agree that understanding how people from various backgrounds are both alike and different is an important life lesson. By teaching children this lesson at an early age, schools are encouraging young people to become open-minded adults. Multicultural programs alone cannot eliminate all the difficulties people have accepting one another's differences, but such programs are a promising beginning.

Questions

1. What is the topic of "Working Together for Multicultural Education"?

   Importance of Schools Multicultural Programs.

2. What is the central point of the essay?

   From grade school to high school, administrators and teachers are working together to implement a wide range of multicultural programs and activities.

3. How does the writer support or develop the central point? Be specific.

By providing facts / to prove US is increasingly multicultural country

4. How might the writer have written about the same basic topic but for a _different_ purpose? Explain your answer.

_____

_____

_____

CAN YOU HAVE MORE THAN ONE WRITING PURPOSE?

As you may already have concluded, writers often set out to accomplish one purpose and in so doing accomplish a second purpose as well. For example, the purpose of "Working Together for Multicultural Education" on pages 128-129 is to inform. However, because the essay is obviously positive in tone—especially the conclusion—the writer also shows an intention to persuade readers that multicultural programs should be part of every school curriculum. Similarly, a descriptive essay such as the selection from "The Little Store" on pages 121-122 or a narrative essay such as the selection from _Blue Highways_ on pages 123-124 also serves to inform readers.

Don't let this overlap of purposes confuse you. When you plan an essay, clearly establish your writing purpose. Then set about accomplishing this purpose. If you accomplish a secondary purpose as well, that's simply an extra achievement.

IN YOUR
JOURNAL

Find examples of newspaper editorials and feature columns. Select one and examine this piece of writing to determine its purpose. Assess whether there is a secondary purpose. Was the writer successful in accomplishing both purposes? Tell why you answered as you did.

FIRST DRAFT: ADDRESSING FIVE KEY ELEMENTS

If you are a musician, whether you perform with a rock group or a symphony orchestra, you have to play well on your own *and* in combination with the other musicians. The collective sound of the various instruments would have to blend and flow together to create the overall melody.

When you develop an essay, you address five key elements that must similarly "play well" both individually and in combination in order to create an effective written piece. These five elements are purpose, content, structure, audience, and tone. To understand how these five basic elements interrelate, study the Writing Focus Chart on page 132.

USING THE WRITING FOCUS CHART

Note that *Writing Purpose* appears at the center of the Writing Focus Chart. As you learned in Chapter 2, your first task in planning an essay, after selecting and narrowing your topic, is to establish your writing purpose. Your writing purpose determines the ideas you will present and how you will express them.

As you study the Writing Focus Chart, you will see that *Writing Purpose* is directly linked with each of the other four elements, and all of these elements are themselves connected with one another.

The other elements in the chart are:

- *Content Development:* the information and ideas you communicate through your writing and how you develop them.

- *Structure:* the way in which you organize and connect these ideas and information.

- *Audience:* the intended readers for your writing.

- *Tone:* the way in which you express your feelings and your attitude toward a topic to your audience.

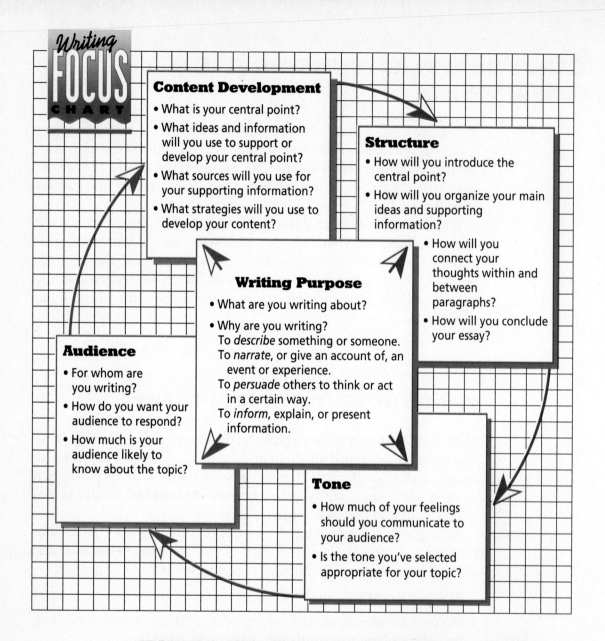

Writing Focus Chart

Content Development
- What is your central point?
- What ideas and information will you use to support or develop your central point?
- What sources will you use for your supporting information?
- What strategies will you use to develop your content?

Structure
- How will you introduce the central point?
- How will you organize your main ideas and supporting information?
- How will you connect your thoughts within and between paragraphs?
- How will you conclude your essay?

Writing Purpose
- What are you writing about?
- Why are you writing?
  To *describe* something or someone.
  To *narrate*, or give an account of, an event or experience.
  To *persuade* others to think or act in a certain way.
  To *inform*, explain, or present information.

Audience
- For whom are you writing?
- How do you want your audience to respond?
- How much is your audience likely to know about the topic?

Tone
- How much of your feelings should you communicate to your audience?
- Is the tone you've selected appropriate for your topic?

HOW DO THE FIVE KEY ELEMENTS WORK TOGETHER?

The five key elements of writing are interdependent, just as the melody, harmony, and beat in a piece of music are. To develop an effective essay, you need to consider all five elements singly as well as collectively. Using the Writing Focus Chart as a planning tool can help you do just that.

Let's see how a writer used the Writing Focus Chart to develop an essay.

Read the following essay, and then reread it. On your second reading, do the following:

■ Circle the thesis statement.

■ Underline the main ideas the writer uses to support or develop the central point.

■ Mark places in the essay where the writer expresses feelings about the topic.

The Truth About Cats

Even though cats now outnumber dogs as house pets, many people persist in believing—and repeating—certain myths about felines. These untruths are offered as reasons for not owning a cat. Cats are unfriendly, they say. Cats are sneaky, they say. Cats can't be trained, they say. The time has come to dispel these false and unfairly negative ideas. If someone doesn't want to own a cat, that's a matter of personal choice. However, people should not damage the reputation of our feline companions with opinions masquerading as facts.

The notion that cats are unfriendly is due largely to the inevitable comparisons made between cats and dogs. True, cats do not go into a tail-wagging, slobbering frenzy over every visitor who enters the house. Cats are by nature shyer, quieter creatures than dogs. However, most cats are affectionate, companionable, even occasionally clingy animals who greet their owners at the door (with raised, not wagging, tails) and then settle down wherever the owner is, often in the owner's lap.

The idea that cats are sneaky comes from the fact that they can move about noiselessly. Unlike an eighty-pound golden retriever, cats do not bound through living rooms like bulls across an arena, nor do they smash fragile objects to the floor with relentless back-and-forth swipes of their tail. Cats walk, run, and jump with grace and in silence. Such agile movement is properly characterized as "elegant," not "sneaky."

As for the assertion that cats can't be trained, this idea is at most a half-truth. Cats do not take to training the way dogs do because cats are more independent by nature. The typical cat has no interest in learning to fetch the morning paper or roll over on command. However, cats can be taught certain behaviors, such as to come when called or not to jump on the kitchen table. In addition, while their canine cousins are scratching and howling at the front door, cats are using the litter box, a behavior they learned as kittens.

Dog lovers sometimes talk as though dogs have a monopoly on all desirable pet traits. They don't. Dogs make *different* pets than cats, not *better* pets. As happy as a dog owner may feel strolling down the block with a loyal canine, a cat owner feels equally gratified stroking a purring bundle of fluff curled up close by. People who don't want to own a cat are free to offer whatever reasons they choose for their preference. However, their reasons should not include unfair and unkind characterizations about cats that simply aren't true.

Questions

1. What is the topic of "The Truth About Cats"?

Mistaken Beliefs some people have about Cats

2. What is the writer's purpose for writing? Does the writer accomplish any secondary writing purpose as well? Explain.

To inform readers that certain beliefs about cats are not based on fact. Also to persuade readers not to spread such belief.

3. What is the central point of the essay?

People should not damage the reputation of cats by making false negative statements.

4. What main ideas does the writer use to support the central point?

Main idea of second paragraph:

Cats are by nature shyer, quieter creature than dogs. [Cats are friendly]

Main idea of third paragraph:

Cats walk, run and jump with grace and in silence.

Main idea of fourth paragraph:

Cats can be taught certain behaviours

5. What audience does the writer have in mind?

People who don't know much about cats.

6. Is the organization of the essay effective? Why?

Yes, it has unity and support since

7. Describe the tone of the essay.

Humorous

In planning and writing "The Truth About Cats," the writer addressed the five key elements of writing. To see how this was done, let's examine the writer's responses to the questions on the Writing Focus Chart. As you read the writer's planning notes, compare them with the essay on pages 133-134.

ESTABLISHING THE WRITING PURPOSE

Two questions appear at the center of the Writing Focus Chart: *What are you writing about?* and *Why are you writing? What are you writing about?* refers to your topic. Choosing and narrowing a topic is the first step in planning an essay. *Why are you writing?* refers to establishing your writing purpose. Your purpose guides you in determining what ideas you will present and how you will express them. When planning an essay, you should begin by addressing both questions.

Here is how the writer of "The Truth About Cats" answered the *Writing Purpose* questions.

Writing Purpose

- *What are you writing about?*

  the mistaken beliefs some people have about cats

- *Why are you writing?*

  to inform readers that certain beliefs about cats are not based on fact; also to persuade readers not to spread such beliefs

Activity A: Establishing Your Writing Purpose

In this activity you will choose a topic and establish a writing purpose for an essay. You will use the questions on the Writing Focus Chart on page 132 to guide you.

A. Choose a topic and narrow a topic to make it specific enough for you to cover adequately in an essay with an introduction, a body, and a conclusion.

Use the questions on the Writing Focus Chart to assess whether your topic is suitable for an essay. If some of the questions do not apply to your topic, consider exploring another topic. You will have less of a problem modifying or changing your topic in this planning step than you would later on.

Answer the first of the two *Writing Purpose* questions:

• *What are you writing about?*

_____

B. Establish your writing purpose. Review the four basic writing purposes discussed earlier in this chapter, and choose one of the four purposes. Once you have established your writing purpose, answer the second of the two *Writing Purpose* questions:

• *Why are you writing?*

_____

_____

C. Write a thesis statement that communicates your writing purpose and the central point of your essay.

_____

_____

You will develop support for your thesis statement in Activity B on pages 140-141.

DEVELOPING THE CONTENT

In developing the content of an essay, you gather ideas and information to support your central point. You also decide on appropriate strategies for presenting your ideas. The *Content Development* questions on the Writing Focus Chart will help you plan.

Here's how the writer of "The Truth About Cats" answered the *Content Development* questions. Compare the writer's planning notes against the actual essay on pages 133-134.

Content Development

- *What is your central point?*

  People should not make false negative statements about cats.

- *What ideas and information will you use to support or develop your central point?*

  refute three common untruths: cats are unfriendly, sneaky, and untrainable; cats may be shyer than dogs, but they are affectionate; cats move with noiseless grace, not "sneakiness"; although cats are less trainable than dogs, they can learn various behaviors.

- *What sources will you use for your supporting information?*

  my personal experience with cats as well as stories friends and acquaintances have shared with me

- *What strategies will you use to develop your content?*

  provide facts, examples, and descriptive details about cats to refute misconceptions; compare and contrast cats and dogs

Choosing a Suitable Source

Once you've determined the central point of your essay, you'll need to consider what information you'll use to support and develop that point and what sources you'll use to gather information. Sources may include personal observations and experience, reference books, newspapers, magazines, and interviews that you conduct.

Both your writing purpose and your intended audience affect your choice of sources. For example, when writing a narrative essay, you'd most likely draw on your personal observations and experience unless you're writing about a historical event or a situation experienced by someone else. In such cases, you would need to do library research or conduct one or more interviews. A descriptive essay might draw on your personal observations or on material from reference books. For a persuasive essay, you might research facts, statistics, and other information to support an opinion. To write an informative essay about a person or a political issue, you might conduct one or more interviews.

When using published materials such as books, magazines, and newspapers as research sources, be careful not to copy information word-for-word or in almost the same form as it appears in the original source. This practice is known as **plagiarism**, and it is both unethical and illegal.

To avoid plagiarizing material, read the information in the source and then put the source away, think the information over, and rephrase the main points in different words. Next, decide which facts, statistics, examples, or other information you want to use to develop your central point. Then express this information in your own words. For some essays you will be required to supply **footnotes**, notes that document the sources of research information.

Through the use of invention techniques such as brainstorming, questioning, and freewriting (see Chapter 2), you gather the information you'll need to write about your topic. In deciding what information to include in your essay and what information to discard, you need to consider your writing purpose as well as your intended audience.

Choosing a Strategy

A **strategy** is a plan for reaching a goal. The strategy or strategies you use to develop the content of an essay will largely be determined by your writing purpose. For example, if you were writing a persuasive essay about the value of regular exercise, you might compare and contrast statistical information about the health of people who exercise regularly with that of people who don't. Strategies for developing content include the following: giving examples, explaining causes and effects, making comparisons and contrasts, giving descriptions, and providing definitions. You'll learn about these and other strategies for developing content in Chapter 5.

Activity B: Planning and Developing Content

In this activity you will develop content to support the thesis statement you wrote in Activity A, pages 136-137. You will use the questions on the Writing Focus Chart on page 132 and the invention techniques you learned in Chapter 2 to plan your essay.

A. Review the thesis statement you wrote in Activity A. Answer the following *Content Development* questions from the Writing Focus Chart. Note that the last question is not included here because the strategies for developing content are discussed in detail in Chapter 5.

- *What is your central point?*

  _____

  _____

  _____

- *What ideas and information will you use to support or develop your central point?*

  _____

  _____

  _____

  _____

- *What sources will you use for your supporting information?*

  _____

  _____

  _____

  _____

B. Gather ideas, facts, details, examples, and other information to support your thesis statement. Use either the collect-and-sort method or the main-ideas-first method (see Chapter 2, pages 49-51). Use brainstorming, questioning, and freewriting to generate as many items as possible. Use a separate sheet of paper for your work.

C. Review the ideas and information you've listed. Add, delete, or combine items as needed. Be sure you have a manageable number of main ideas and enough specific supporting information to develop your central point.

D. On a separate sheet of paper, create a conceptual map or outline for your essay. When you finish, use your map or outline to evaluate whether you have enough main ideas and supporting information. To review how to construct a conceptual map or an outline, refer to Chapter 2.

PORTFOLIO

Save your conceptual map or outline in your portfolio. You will use the map or outline and your planning notes for Activity C on pages 142-143.

PLANNING STRUCTURE

Writing FOCUS CHART

To plan the structure of an essay, you need to consider several related aspects: how to begin the essay, how to organize and connect ideas and information, and how to bring the essay to a conclusion. The *Structure* questions on the Writing Focus Chart will help you zero in on each of these aspects.

As you read in Chapters 1 and 2, organizing ideas and information effectively is essential to achieving coherence. Whether you use chronological order, spatial order, or order of importance or interest, a sound essay structure will help ensure that you get your central point across to readers and accomplish your writing purpose. In Chapter 5 you will explore in detail ways of organizing and connecting ideas and information in an essay.

Here's how the writer of "The Truth About Cats" answered the *Structure* questions. Compare the writer's answers to the actual essay on pages 133-134.

Structure

- *How will you introduce the central point?*

  state that many people have mistaken ideas about cats; preview three misconceptions that the essay will focus on; stress that people should not spread unfounded ideas about cats

- *How will you organize your main ideas and supporting information?*

  focus on one misconception in each body paragraph—stating and then refuting each belief; compare cat and dog behavior as needed

- *How will you connect your thoughts within and between paragraphs?*

  The opening paragraph introduces the three "myths" to be considered, followed by body paragraphs about each of the myths mentioned. Each paragraph will include cat-dog comparisons to link ideas.

- *How will you conclude your essay?*

  point out that dog lovers and cat lovers both love their pets; reiterate that people shouldn't make untrue statements about cats

Activity C: Planning Structure

In this activity you will continue planning the essay you began in Activity A (pages 136-137) and continued in Activity B (pages 140-141). You will use the questions from the Writing Focus Chart on page 132 to plan the structure.

A. Answer the *Structure* questions on the Writing Focus Chart. For the second question, consider which organizational approach would work best—chronological order, spatial order, or order of importance or interest. Number the main ideas and supporting information that you listed in Activity B in the order you plan to use them. Use the organizational techniques you learned in Chapter 2—mapping and outlining—to help you plan the structure and flow of your essay.

- *How will you introduce the central point?*

  _____

  _____

  _____

- *How will you organize your main ideas and supporting information?*

  _____

  _____

  _____

- *How will you connect your thoughts within and between paragraphs?*

  _____

  _____

  _____

- *How will you conclude your essay?*

  _____

  _____

  _____

PORTFOLIO

B. Review the conceptual map or outline you created in Activity B. Are you satisfied with your planned content and structure? Make any changes that you feel will improve your plan.

Save your planning work in your portfolio. You will have an opportunity to define the audience for your essay in Activity D, page 148.

TARGETING A SPECIFIC AUDIENCE

Stage performers use acting technique, facial expressions, gestures, and tone of voice to affect their audience. In a similar fashion, writers use ideas, language, style, and tone to affect their audience.

When you plan an essay, consider who your intended readers are and how you can most effectively reach them. By tailoring your writing to your particular audience, you help to ensure that readers will listen to, identify with, and understand what you're trying to communicate.

You've been developing a sense of audience all your life. You know, for example, that telling jokes is appropriate at parties, but inappropriate at funerals. You also know that you must use simpler words to communicate with a child than with an adult. Indeed, every day you instinctively adjust the language you use to make it suitable for different audiences.

Television commercials are carefully targeted for specific audiences. Compare several commercials shown during children's morning shows with commercials shown after 9 P.M. What specific differences do you notice? What clues tell you for whom each commercial is targeted? Write a paragraph or more summarizing your observations and conclusions about the commercials.

The Audience questions on the Writing Focus Chart can help you tailor your writing for your intended audience. Answering these questions will help you picture the readers for whom you're writing and enable you to tailor your content, structure, and language accordingly. For example, if you were discussing the spread of AIDS, you would take a different approach in writing for children than you would for adults. Similarly, you would use different sources for information, depending on your audience.

To see how answering the *Audience* questions can aid you in targeting an audience, read "So You're Getting a Cat" on pages 145-146. This essay deals with a topic that is similar to the topic of "The Truth About Cats" on pages 133-134. However, "So You're Getting a Cat" is clearly intended for a different audience.

After you read "So You're Getting a Cat," compare it with "The Truth About Cats" on pages 133-134. Then compare the two sets of planning notes on pages 147-148 that answer the *Audience* questions, to see how different audiences led to different writing approaches.

So You're Getting a Cat

Once you decide to get a cat, you need to make a few preparations before you welcome your new pet home. Like any other pet, cats have certain basic needs. Understanding your cat's needs will help you make a better home for your new companion.

Have a water dish and a food dish ready for your cat. A cat always needs a supply of clean, fresh water. As for food, most people find that the best and most convenient way to feed a cat is to use commercially prepared cat foods. Since cats have a much higher protein need than dogs, never feed your cat commercial food designed for dogs.

An advantage that cats have over dogs as pets is that cats are litter-trained. You'll never have to drag yourself outside on a rainy night to walk your pet. Be ready for your cat with a litter box made of enamel or plastic. The litter box should be large enough for the cat to sit in comfortably. Fill the box about one-third full with cat litter. Have a long-handled "pooper scooper" ready. Since cats are very clean animals, they won't use the litter box if it gets too dirty or damp. You'll use the "pooper scooper" to scoop out waste every day, and about once a week you'll need to empty the pan, clean it with mild soap, and put in fresh litter.

Except in emergency situations such as accidentally sticking a paw into your honey jar, your cat won't need to be bathed. Cats groom themselves by washing with their tongues, which are pleasingly rough—almost like fine sandpaper. A cat's tongue delivers an effective bath-and-brushing that keeps its fur shining clean. However, you'll have a job in this process too. Have on hand a special cat brush or a regular comb. You'll use one or both to groom your cat's fur every day or two. Brushing or combing gets rid of loose fur that the cat would otherwise swallow during its grooming. When a cat swallows too much fur, the fur forms hairballs in the cat's digestive system. The cat will "cure" hairballs in a way that you probably won't approve of—by throwing up to get rid of the hairball.

The most important supply for you to have on hand for your cat is affection. Cats are not as standoffish as most people think. Although many outdoor cats have learned to do without human companionship, nearly all indoor cats yearn for attention. While your cat will get used to spending time alone when you are at work, it will expect you to make up for lost time once you get home. Cats love to be stroked. In addition, although cats are not usually as fond of roughhousing as dogs, they do enjoy playing. A popular cat pastime is chasing a toy or even a piece of crinkled cellophane across the floor. Whatever attention your cat enjoys will prove enjoyable for you too.

If you prepare for your cat, you'll find that the transition to pet ownership is easy. Your cat will quickly get used to its new home, and soon you'll wonder how you ever got along without this friendly, graceful creature in your life.

···

Questions

1. How does "So You're Getting a Cat" differ from "The Truth About Cats" in content, language, and structure? Include specific examples to support your answers.

CONTENT:

_____

_____

_____

_____

_____

LANGUAGE:

_____

_____

_____

_____

_____

STRUCTURE:

_____

_____

_____

_____

_____

2. Compare the introductions of "So You're Getting a Cat" and "The Truth About Cats." How are they alike? How are they different? Be specific.

_____

_____

_____

_____

_____

Now look at the *Audience* planning notes on pages 147-148. Compare the two sets of notes with each other and with the finished essays.

Here is how the writer of "The Truth About Cats" answered the *Audience* questions.

Audience

- *For whom are you writing?*

  an audience of people who don't know much about cats, have heard many false statements about cats, and spread these false ideas

- *How do you want your audience to respond?*

  to understand that cats are often inaccurately characterized; to stop contributing to cats' bad reputation

- *How much is your audience likely to know about the topic?*

  My readers don't know much about cats, or they wouldn't hold the opinions they do.

The following example shows how the writer of "So You're Getting a Cat" answered the *Audience* questions.

Audience

- *For whom are you writing?*

  <u>people who are about to get a pet cat for the first time</u>

- *How do you want your audience to respond?*

  <u>to prepare for the arrival of the new pet by having certain supplies on hand and being aware of the cat's needs</u>

- *How much is your audience likely to know about the topic?*

  <u>My readers will be fond of cats but will have limited experience caring for a cat</u>

Activity D: Focusing on a Specific Audience

In this activity you will focus on the audience for the essay you worked on in Activity C on pages 142-143. Answer the *Audience* questions on the Writing Focus Chart as you focus on your intended readers.

- *For whom are you writing?*

  _____

- *How do you want your audience to respond?*

  _____

  _____

- *How much is your audience likely to know about the topic?*

  _____

  _____

  _____

You will continue planning this essay in Activity E on page 151.

SETTING THE TONE

When you speak to someone, your tone of voice conveys your feelings and helps get your point across. You may, for example, want to sound affectionate, angry, concerned, or sarcastic. Your tone is a combination of the sound of your voice and the actual words you speak. For instance, if a friend is always late for appointments, you might express your thoughts by using any of various tones:

- "If you know that you won't be able to meet me at the designated time, just call and let me know."

- "You know I enjoy getting together with you, but could you please try to show up on time?"

- "Do you think maybe you ought to buy a watch so that you can keep track of the time?"

- "How inconsiderate can you be? I have better things to do than wait around for you all the time."

When you write, you also use a certain tone. Even though no one spoke the preceding three examples aloud, you "heard" the tone of each one as you read. In your writing, you convey tone through your choice of language. The words you use and the way that you use them let readers know how you feel about your topic. The *Tone* questions on the Writing Focus Chart will help you set the tone for an essay.

In answering the first *Tone* question, you determine the extent to which you will communicate or reveal your feelings about the topic. If you were offering your opinion of a movie, for example, you would communicate more of your feelings than if you were explaining a bank's customer relations policy. In answering the second question, you determine the appropriateness of the tone you plan to use. For example, a lighthearted tone might be suitable for an essay about a surprise bridal shower, but inappropriate for an essay about cancer research.

To see how answering the *Tone* questions can serve as a planning aid, reread "The Truth About Cats" on pages 133-134 and "So You're Getting a Cat" on pages 145-146. The two essays have similar topics, but the writers have used different tones.

Questions

1. Describe how the tone of "The Truth About Cats" differs from the tone of "So You're Getting a Cat."

_____

_____

_____

_____

2. What differences in content and language create the difference in tone in each essay? Include specific examples in your answer.

_____

_____

_____

_____

_____

Now look at the *Tone* planning notes for both essays on pages 150-151. Compare the notes with each other and with the finished essays.

Here is how the writer of "The Truth About Cats" answered the *Tone* questions.

Tone

- *How much of your feelings should you communicate to your audience?*

  Since I'm a cat lover and am defending the reputation of all cats, I'm going to include my feelings with the information I present.

- *Is the tone you've selected appropriate for your topic?*

  My tone is earnest but humorous, which is suitable to a lighthearted piece on pets.

Here is how the writer of "So You're Getting a Cat" answered the *Tone* questions.

Tone

- *How much of your feelings should you communicate to your audience?*

  I can make readers aware of my own fondness for cats, but showing my feelings too much will get in the way of the important information I want to communicate.

- *Is the tone you've selected appropriate for your topic?*

  Using a straightforward tone with touches of humor will show that I am knowledgeable and interested.

Suppose you were the writer planning "The Truth About Cats" on pages 133-134. If you were writing for an audience made up mainly of dog lovers, would you use the same tone as for an audience composed mainly of cat lovers? Explain your reasoning.

_____

_____

_____

_____

Activity E: Choosing the Right Tone

In this activity you will continue to plan the essay you worked on in Activity D on page 148. Answer the *Tone* questions on the Writing Focus Chart as they apply to your essay.

- *How much of your feelings should you communicate to your audience?*

  _____

  _____

  _____

- *Is the tone you've selected appropriate for your topic?*

  _____

  _____

  _____

In Assignment 2 on pages 155-156, you will work independently to create the first draft of an essay from the planning work you've done.

DO YOU WRITE ON A COMPUTER?

To keep the Writing Focus Chart questions handy when you plan an essay, key the questions on the computer and save the file on a disk for future use. To try out a particular approach, make a copy of your Writing Focus Chart and key in your answers to the questions. Save your answers as part of your planning work. You can also print out your questions and answers and discuss them with a classmate or your instructor. If you want to try an alternative approach for an essay, remember to save each working file under a different name, such as "NARRATE.1," "NARRATE.2," and so on. If you save two files with the same name, the one you save later will erase the one saved earlier.

BLENDING THE ELEMENTS

Now that you are familiar with the five key elements of writing, you can put your knowledge to work. Whether you write out all your answers to the Writing Focus Chart questions or simply think through most of the answers, the chart will help you blend the elements of purpose, content, structure, audience, and tone. Use the Writing Focus Chart on page 132 to guide you in planning not just essays for this course but other kinds of writing as well, from history papers to letters to prospective employers.

REVISING AND EDITING YOUR FIRST DRAFT

As you revise drafts of essays, use the following Checklist for Revising and Editing to help you evaluate the content, structure, and wording of each draft.

Checklist for Revising and Editing

WRITING PURPOSE

- Does the essay have a clear writing purpose?
- Have you accomplished this purpose?

CONTENT

- Is your topic too narrow or too broad?
- Does the introduction engage readers' interest?
- Have you presented the central point and main ideas clearly?
- Does your essay have unity—do all paragraphs relate to the central point?
- Does your essay have support—is there enough specific information to support or develop the central point?
- Did you make the facts and details specific enough to be meaningful?
- Did you select concrete details and examples?
- Have you included unimportant information that should be deleted?
- Does the conclusion effectively wrap up the essay?

STRUCTURE

- Is your thesis statement focused and interesting?
- Are your ideas and information organized and presented effectively?
- Does your essay have coherence—is supporting information logically organized?
- Do you move smoothly from one thought to the next?
- Does the conclusion follow logically from the preceding paragraphs?

WORDING AND SENTENCE STRUCTURE

- Have you used specific language and concrete details?
- Can you make any words or phrases more specific?
- Have you used any words that you should explain?
- Are your sentences varied in terms of length, wording, and structure?
- Do you need any transitions within or between paragraphs to lead readers from one thought to the next?

AUDIENCE

- Is the essay appropriate for its audience in content and language?

TONE

- Is the tone appropriate for the subject matter?
- Is the language appropriate for the topic?

GROUP
ACTIVITY

Assignment 1:
Creating an Essay With Your Group

In this assignment you will work with your group to plan, write, edit, and proofread an essay about the challenges students face in adjusting to college.

A. Freewrite for ten to fifteen minutes about your early experiences in college. What did you find easy about getting started in, or returning to, college? What did you find difficult? Why? Are there things that you wish you had known before you started college? How would such knowledge have helped you? Were your expectations about college realistic?

B. Share and compare with group members the most important ideas from your freewriting. Discuss common challenges students face when they enter or return to college. Agree on two or three difficulties the group would like to explore in an essay.

Writing
FOCUS
CHART

C. Working as a group, use the questions on the Writing Focus Chart on page 132 to guide you as you plan the first draft. Use any of the invention techniques you learned in Chapter 2 to develop content. If necessary, review the material in this chapter that discusses each of the key elements of writing.

D. Use your group's planning notes to write the first draft. Your first draft should consist of an introduction, a body, and a conclusion and should clearly accomplish your writing purpose. Review the draft and work together to develop an appropriate title.

E. Carefully reread and evaluate the content, structure, and wording of your first draft. Pay special attention to how the five elements of writing are blended. Discuss any necessary changes, additions, deletions, and corrections. Using the Checklist for Revising and Editing on page 153 as a guide, work together to revise the first draft. Complete as many revisions as needed.

F. When you are satisfied that your draft is the best work that your group can produce, choose someone to key a revised draft. Make a photocopy for every group member.

G. Carefully reread your revised draft. Using the Checklist for Proofreading on page 105, work together to prepare the final copy. Consult the Writer's Guide that begins on page A 80 to review key points of grammar, punctuation, and capitalization. Have each group member proofread the revised draft independently and use proofreaders' marks from the box on page 105 to mark corrections. Then compare corrections. Incorporate all the changes on one draft.

PORTFOLIO

H. Have one group member key the final copy. Proofread the final copy as a group and correct any keyboarding errors. Record the names of all group members on the final copy. Make a final copy for every group member. Save your final copy in your portfolio.

Assignment 2:
Creating an Essay

In this assignment you will work independently to plan, write, edit, and proofread the essay you worked on in Activities A, B, C, D, and E.

A. Retrieve your planning notes from your portfolio. Review your thesis statement and your answers to the Writing Focus Chart questions.

B. Share your ideas with members of your group or with a peer editor. Discuss the topic you are considering for your essay. Ask for constructive advice about the topic. Also discuss any problem areas you foresee.

C. Use your planning notes and the questions on the Writing Focus Chart on page 132 to write the first draft. Your first draft should consist of an introduction, a body, and a conclusion and should clearly accomplish your writing purpose. Review your draft and develop an appropriate title.

D. Share your draft with members of your group or with a peer editor. Use the comments and suggestions from your group or partner, in conjunction with the Checklist for Revising and Editing on page 153, to help you make revisions. After sharing essays, work independently to revise your draft.

E. Evaluate the content, structure, and wording of your essay. Using the Checklist for Revising and Editing as a guide, make any necessary changes, additions, deletions, and corrections. When you are satisfied, key your revised draft.

PORTFOLIO

F. Carefully reread your revised draft. Using the Checklist for Proofreading on page 105, prepare a final copy. Consult the Writer's Guide that begins on page A 80 to review key points of grammar, punctuation, and capitalization. Use proofreader's marks from the box on page 105 to mark your corrections.

G. Key the final copy. Look over the final copy and correct any keyboarding errors. Save your final copy in your portfolio.

Assignment 3: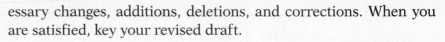
Reading as a Stimulus for Writing

In this assignment you will read a selection and then work indepen-dently to plan, write, edit, and proofread an essay.

A. Read "Easy Job, Good Wages" by Jesus Colon on pages A 120-A 12 The writer recalls his youth and tells about a job he got that d not turn out as expected. As you read, think about how writer has blended the five key elements of writing in his essay

B. Use the selection as a stimulus for planning and writing a draft of your own. Here are a few questions to start you th ing.

- What memories of your early jobs or other attempts to tak adult responsibilities come to mind? What makes these pa ular experiences memorable?

- What details in "Easy Job, Good Wages" help you ider strongly with the writer's situation?

- What do you learn about the writer from this recollection short-lived job? What would you like your readers to le about you in an essay you write about a similar topic?

  Use your answers to help you select a topic, generate a thesi statement, and establish a writing purpose. Freewrite for approx imately ten or fifteen minutes on the topic you select.

C. Share your ideas with members of your group or with a peer edi-tor. Discuss the topic you are considering for your essay. Ask for constructive advice about the topic. Also discuss any problem areas that you foresee.

D. Use your planning notes and the questions on the Writing Focus Chart on page 132 to write the first draft. Develop your content using invention techniques you learned in Chapter 2. If you would find it useful, make a conceptual map to help you visualize the content and structure of your essay. Your first draft should have an introduction, a body, and a conclusion and should clearly accomplish your writing purpose. Review your draft and develop an appropriate title.

E. Share your draft with members of your group or with a peer editor. Use the comments and suggestions from your group or your partner, in conjunction with the Checklist for Revising and Editing on page 153, to help you make revisions. After sharing essays, work independently to revise your draft.

F. Using the Checklist for Revising and Editing as a ᵗ le, evaluate the content, structure, and wording of your draft. any necessary changes, additions, deletions, and correction

G. Carefully reread your revised draft. Using the (for Proofreading on page 105, prepare the final copy. 'he Writer's Guide that begins on page A 80 to review kᵉ ᵒf grammar, punctuation, and capitalization. Use prᵢ marks from the box on page 105 to mark your correctiᵢ

H. Key the final copy. Look over the final copy and correcᵗ boarding errors. Save your final copy in your portfolio.

Grammar **G**remlins

In Chapter 3 you learned that run-on sentences are actually two or more separate sentences run together, and you learned two ways to correct them. In this chapter you will learn two more ways to correct run-on sentences.

INCORRECT:
Nicole can repair anything, she even fixes computers.

The sentence above consists of two independent clauses that state two complete thoughts. Dividing the two thoughts with just a comma is not enough to separate them. As you have learned, this error is called a comma splice. You can, however, correct a comma splice by separating the thoughts with a semicolon.

A **semicolon** signals a pause stronger than a comma but not quite as strong as a period. You can use a semicolon to join two independent clauses that contain ideas that are closely related.

CORRECT:
Nicole can repair anything; she even fixes computers.

Another way to correct a run-on sentence is by subordinating one of the clauses—that is, giving one idea lesser importance than the other. The subordinate idea starts with a **subordinating conjunction** such as *after, as, because, before, if, since, though, unless, until, when, where,* or *while.* If the subordinate clause comes before the main clause, it is set off by a comma. Otherwise, there is no comma.

INCORRECT:
The telephone rang, I was taking a shower.

CORRECT:
When the telephone rang, I was taking a shower.
I was taking a shower when the telephone rang.

In the above examples, the subordinate clause is *when the telephone rang.* In the first example, the subordinate clause comes first and is set off by a comma. In the second example, there is no comma since the subordinate clause follows the main clause.

Activities

A. Correct the following run-on sentences. Refer to the following examples for help in subordinating a clause.

INCORRECT:

The elevator was broken we walked up the stairs.

CORRECT:

The elevator was broken; we walked up the stairs.

Because the elevator was broken, we walked up the stairs.

We walked up the stairs because the elevator was broken.

[margin note: Run on]

1. The job advertisement first appeared in the Sunday newspaper it ran again on Monday and Tuesday.

[margin note: Comma Splice]

2. Response to the advertisement was overwhelming more than 400 people answered in three days.

[margin note: Run on / Since]

3. So many qualified applicants were competing I didn't think I stood a chance.

[margin note: Comma Splice / After]

4. Ms. Edwards called to tell me the job was mine, I nearly dropped the telephone.

B. Read the paragraph below. Correct any run-on sentences. Make at least one correction using a semicolon and restructure at least one sentence to include a subordinate clause.

I dislike standing in line waiting is such a waste of time. Still, sometimes you have no choice. When that's the case, I try to make the best use of my time. I plan out the rest of the week while waiting in line. Often I play games in my head, such as trying to name all fifty states I may think of song titles containing the word *blue.* These games soon get boring I find another way to pass the time. Sometimes I close my eyes and imagine myself on vacation in Hawaii or another tropical paradise. I envision myself dozing on a sunny beach the crash of ocean waves is the only sound I hear. The one problem with my fantasy is that eventually the line moves, and my vacation is abruptly cut short.

C. For additional practice in identifying and correcting run-on sentences, see page A 70.

WRAPPING IT UP

SUMMARY

- Writing purpose is the central element of writing. All other elements work together to effectively express the writer's purpose. There are four basic writing purposes: to *describe* something or someone; to *narrate,* or give an account of, an event or experience; to *persuade* others to think or act in a certain way; and to *inform,* explain, or present information.

- The five key elements of writing are *Writing Purpose* (why you are writing), *Content Development* (central point supported by ideas and information), *Structure* (organization of information), *Audience* (intended readers), and *Tone* (communicated feelings). These elements are interconnected and influence one another.

- Use the questions on the Writing Focus Chart to guide you in planning, researching, and writing an essay.

THINKING IT OVER

- How can establishing your writing purpose before starting to write help you write effective essays?

  _____

  _____

  _____

  _____

  _____

  _____

- In what ways will using the Writing Focus Chart as a tool help you plan and write essays? Be specific.

_____

_____

_____

_____

_____

_____

Review the goals that you set at the beginning of this chapter. In your journal, evaluate your progress toward these goals.

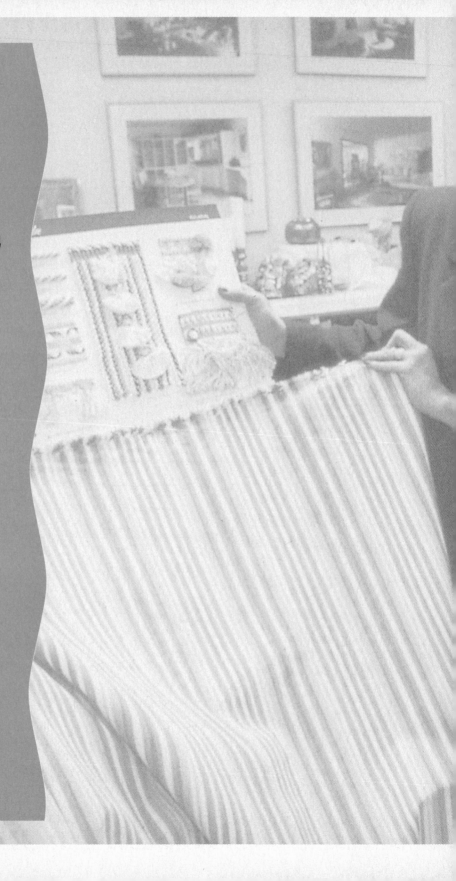

5

DEVELOPING AND ORGANIZING CONTENT

OBJECTIVES:

Composition

- To analyze ten strategies for developing content and to select and use appropriate strategies.

- To organize ideas and information by using chronological order, spatial order, and order of importance or interest.

- To connect ideas and information by using transitions, repeated words, pronouns, and synonyms.

- To create essays that have coherence.

Grammar

- To create sentences in which subjects and verbs agree.

How Can I
Develop and
Structure an Essay?

Someone who is choosing fabrics to decorate a home has many decisions to make, such as which fabrics to choose, how they should coordinate with the color scheme, what the price range should be, and the amount of fabric to purchase.

Like decorating a home, writing is a process of choices and decisions. What will you write about? How will you approach your topic? What tone will you take? In previous chapters you learned how to answer such questions. In this chapter you'll focus on two other writing-related choices: determining what strategies to use to develop your content and deciding how to organize and connect ideas and information. In choosing the strategies and structure for an essay, you create a coherent design for your readers to follow in your writing.

Whenever you communicate—orally or in writing—you make decisions about how to present ideas and information. Sometimes you make these decisions only after careful thought and planning. Other times you make them automatically. As you answer the following questions, consider what factors influence your communication decisions.

- Imagine that you are telling a friend about a camping trip that you took. Place a check mark next to the strategies you would use to relate your experience.

    _____ Present specific facts about the trip.

    _____ Give examples of what you did.

    _____ Describe in detail places or people you saw.

    _____ Compare this trip with others you've taken.

    _____ Relate memorable experiences you had during the trip.

    _____ Define important words or phrases.

    _____ Explain how camping is like some other activity.

- Of the strategies you checked, which ones would you use most? Why?

    _____

    _____

    _____

    _____

- How would you organize your account? Would you describe events in the order that they occurred? Would you instead describe the most important event first, followed by other events? Explain why.

    _____

    _____

    _____

    _____

- Now suppose you were writing an essay about your camping trip. Would you choose the same strategies and method of organization? Explain your answer.

_____

_____

_____

_____

_____

_____

_____

_____

_____

IN YOUR
JOURNAL

Review your answers to the Getting Started questions. Then set one or more goals in your journal. Here is one example:

GOAL:
I will carefully consider the way I organize the content of my essays.

Often you can ask specific questions to clarify information. The questions you decide to ask will depend on the type of information that you want clarified.

A. With your group, decide on a topic that you could explain or describe orally. Choose a topic from one of the following categories, or agree on another topic.

- A particular skill or hobby
- An event that group members are familiar with
- A monument, landmark, or public building
- Caring for a particular pet

B. The following questions are ones a listener might ask about your topic. Discuss with group members how you would address these questions in your oral presentation.

- What facts do I have to know to understand this topic?

  _____

- What examples can you give me to make the topic more understandable?

  _____

- What does that place/item/part look like?

  _____

- What does that word mean?

  _____

- How do you do that?

  _____

- Is what you're describing similar to anything I might be familiar with?

  _____

C. With group members, work up a brief oral presentation. Which questions were most helpful to you as you worked?

Shaping Content and Structure

As you learned in Chapter 4, a strategy is a plan for reaching a goal. When you write, that goal is your writing purpose. The strategy or strategies you use to develop the content of an essay help determine how successful you are in conveying your central point and accomplishing your writing purpose.

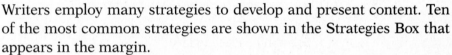

Using Strategies to Develop Content

Writers employ many strategies to develop and present content. Ten of the most common strategies are shown in the Strategies Box that appears in the margin.

STRATEGIES:

Facts

Examples

Description

Compare/Contrast

Narration

Definition

Process

Classification

Cause/Effect

Analogy

In Chapter 4 you'll recall that the last *Content Development* question of the Writing Focus Chart (page 132) is *What strategies will you use to develop your content?* In planning and writing an essay, you can use the strategies in the Strategies Box—alone or in combination—to answer this question. Which strategy or strategies you choose will depend on several factors: your writing purpose, the central point of your essay, your intended audience, and your preferences as a writer.

The same strategies writers use to develop the content of individual paragraphs can also serve to develop the content of an essay. However, because an essay consists of multiple paragraphs instead of just one, you have greater flexibility in deciding how to apply and blend strategies when you write an essay.

For example, suppose you wanted to compare life in a large city with life in a small town. If you were writing only a single paragraph, you'd have to focus on a few key similarities and differences and cover these briefly. However, if you were writing an essay, you might devote an entire body paragraph to similarities and another body paragraph to differences. You might even devote a third paragraph to another strategy—drawing an analogy, for instance, or relating an anecdote.

Sometimes an entire essay is built around one strategy. For example, an essay entitled "How to Find a Job" may describe a process for getting a job. Such an essay can be referred to as a *process essay*. Similarly, you may encounter a *compare/contrast essay*, a *definition essay*, a *classification essay*, and so on, depending on whatever the dominant strategy happens to be. You'll learn more about such essays in Sections 3 and 4 of this book.

STRATEGY: FACTS

Presenting facts is the most basic strategy for developing content. A **fact** is something known to be true or real. Facts are *objectively* true: they are true regardless of anyone's feelings or beliefs. By contrast, **opinions** are statements based on feelings or beliefs. When someone expresses an opinion, the statement may or may not be true.

Read "Selecting a Place to Live," which follows. Note how the writer uses facts to develop the content.

Selecting a Place to Live

North American Indian communities chose with great care the sites of their villages and encampments. They would seek, first of all, a place offering maximum shelter from the elements. In addition, they would look for a site located near water—a stream, a river, or a natural water hole. In this way the community would have a ready source of water (and perhaps fish as well). Moreover, deer and other animals coming to drink could be hunted for food. Another crucial factor the community considered when selecting a site was how effectively that place could be defended against enemy attack.

Questions

1. What is the main idea of the paragraph?

How North American Indian Communities choose their sites.

2. What facts does the writer use to support the main idea?

STRATEGY: EXAMPLES

An **example** is a detail or illustration that supports an idea. Writers provide examples to help explain or clarify their meaning or to make a point. Examples make writing more concrete and interesting by adding specific information.

Read the paragraph that follows. Note how the writer uses examples to develop the content.

Food for Thought

Many food-related words have interesting and unexpected origins. *Onion*, for example, comes from the Latin word *unio*, meaning "oneness or unity," because the layers of an onion together form a whole. *Spaghetti* is derived from the Italian word *spago*, meaning "small cord." *Ketchup* comes from the Malay *kĕchap*, meaning "fish sauce." Originally this sauce was made of fish broth and mushrooms. The English, however, added tomatoes to the recipe and altered the taste.

Questions

1. What is the main idea of "Food for Thought"?

   Many food-related words have interesting
   and unexpected origins

2. What examples does the writer use to develop the main idea?

   Provide examples of how Onion, ketchup, Spaghetti
   derive their name

Writers frequently use a combination of facts and examples to support or develop an idea. Indeed, facts often serve as examples, and examples are typically based on facts. For instance, in "Selecting a Place to Live" on page 168, the writer gives examples of water sources that a North American Indian community might look for in choosing a site for a village or encampment.

Reread "Food for Thought" and answer the following questions.

- What examples of food-related words does the writer give?

  Onion, Ketchup Spaghetti

- What factual material is included in these examples?

  _____

• How do these examples help you understand the writer's point?

Helps understand what writer wants
to convey interestingly

STRATEGY: DESCRIPTION

A **description** is a word picture of a person, place, or thing. Writers use language to create word pictures much as artists use lines and colors to create paintings. The more specific and vivid your descriptions are, the more alive your writing will be. Sensory details—those that appeal to the five senses of sight, hearing, touch, smell, and taste—are particularly effective in bringing your descriptions to life. For example, you might describe an old car as "rusty brown with an engine that coughed and wheezed like an aging smoker."

Read "The Climb," which follows. What descriptive details does the writer use in this paragraph to develop the content?

The Climb

As I gazed into the misty distance, I felt small and insignificant. The momentary silence of my companions told me they shared my feelings. As far as we could see to the west ran an unbroken line of gray-brown peaks patched with snow. Smoky clouds raced low and fast above them. Nearer and below us was the stark wilderness of Glacier Gorge, a deep, V-shaped chasm filled with alpine lakes that glistened like aqua jewels. A strong wind blew upslope, and I pried my fingers from the cold granite and hugged myself against the chill. Peering in the direction of the wind, I suddenly felt afraid. Below and around us were a series of sheer gray cliffs. The trail, a thin dusty ribbon, led precariously across the top of them. That treacherous path would be where this hike would take us.

Questions

1. How does the description help you share the writer's experience?

misty - sight

gray brown - sight

2. To what senses do the descriptive details appeal?

Momentary silence - hearing

Look outside through a nearby window. If you were writing a description of what you see, what specific details would you include? Use your imagination. In your journal, list specific visual details that you could use to bring your description to life. Then write a paragraph or more describing the scene.

STRATEGY: COMPARE/CONTRAST

When you **compare** one person, place, or thing with another, you identify similarities or common features—how your two sisters are alike, for example, or how jazz is similar to blues. When you **contrast** one person, place, or thing with another, you identify differences: how Rome differs from Athens, for instance, or how today's movies are so much more graphic than movies were 20 years ago.

To develop content using a compare/contrast strategy, you can present ideas and information in one of three ways:

1. Compare *and* contrast, discussing similarities as well as differences between two or more persons, places, or things.

2. Compare only, discussing just similarities.

3. Contrast only, discussing just differences.

Which of these options you choose will depend on your writing purpose and on the central point of your essay.

When you use a compare/contrast strategy, you can structure your approach in various ways. For example, you can move back and forth between items, comparing and contrasting information in a parallel, point-by-point manner, either sentence by sentence or paragraph by paragraph. Alternatively, you might first present all your information about one item and then all your information about the other item. Whatever structural approach you take, plan ahead by listing parallel information in side-by-side columns. In this way you'll have a clear view of the ideas and information to be compared and contrasted.

Suppose you were writing an informative essay discussing birds commonly seen in a local park. Two kinds of birds you plan to mention in your essay are crows and ravens. Because many people can't tell these two birds apart, you decide to devote one paragraph to a comparison of the two.

Read the following two paragraphs. The writer uses the same facts and descriptive details in both paragraphs. However, the organizational approaches differ.

Approach A: **Crows and Ravens**

People often confuse crows and ravens, but the two birds are really not so difficult to distinguish. Crows are intelligent, mischievous birds whose bodies are covered with glossy black feathers. They are large, about 18 to 20 inches long, with a wingspan up to 39 inches. They have high, shrill voices. Crows build their nests in trees. Ravens are clever and mischievous birds, too, and they are also glossy black. However, ravens are larger than crows, sometimes exceeding 26 inches in length, with a wingspan up to 56 inches. Their voices are deep, harsh, and croaky. Ravens sometimes nest in trees but more often build their nests on rocky cliffs.

Approach B: **Crows and Ravens**

People often confuse crows and ravens, but the two birds are really not so difficult to distinguish. Both crows and ravens are large, intelligent, mischievous birds whose bodies are covered with glossy black feathers. However, while crows are about 18 to 20 inches long, with a wingspan up to 39 inches, ravens sometimes exceed 26 inches in length and have a wingspan up to 56 inches. Crows have high, shrill voices while ravens' voices are deep, harsh, and croaky. Crows build their nests in trees. Ravens sometimes nest in trees but more often build their nests on rocky cliffs.

Questions

1. What information is presented to show how crows and ravens are alike?

_____

_____

2. What information is presented to show how crows and ravens are different?

_____

_____

3. Which organizational approach compares crows and ravens point by point? Which approach first presents all the information about crows and then all the information about ravens?

Approach B - point by point

Approach A

4. Which approach provides a more effective comparison? Why?

Approach B - It compares side by side.
The reader does not have to look back
and forth.

STRATEGY: NARRATION

Narrating a story or anecdote can be an effective way to support or illustrate a point that you want to make. **A story** relates an event or series of events in a certain sequence. An **anecdote** is a short account of an interesting or humorous incident.

Here's an example of how a writer used narration in an essay about unpleasant chores. The following body paragraph from the essay focuses on the chore the writer most dislikes:

The Most Unpleasant Chore of All

My least favorite chore is moving furniture. Shifting around sofas, cabinets, tables, beds, and desks is sweaty, backbreaking labor. Worst of all is moving bookcases. Last summer I helped my aunt move furniture from the first floor of her house to the second floor. She had a six-foot oak bookcase that nearly killed me. First, I had to remove dozens of hardcover books from the shelves of the bookcase and lug them up a flight of stairs. Then, already exhausted, I had to carry the bookcase itself. This monster weighed as much as a rhinoceros and was nearly as wide as the staircase. Even with my uncle's help, I think I must have pulled every muscle in my back. Someone should invent disposable furniture.

Questions

1. What is the main idea of the paragraph?

Moving furniture is the author's
least favorite chore.

2. How does the writer's narration help to support this idea?

_____

_____

_____

STRATEGY: DEFINITION

Supplying a definition or meaning for a word, phrase, or concept is one way to ensure that your audience understands the ideas and information you are conveying. Providing definitions is particularly important when you write about a specialized topic or about subject matter that may be unfamiliar to your audience.

You can provide a definition in several ways. You can supply a **synonym**—a word or words that have the same or similar meaning as the word being defined. A synonym for _microbe_, for example, is _germ_. If you want to find synonyms for words you are using, look in a **thesaurus**—a reference book containing words and their synonyms—or a dictionary.

Another way to provide a definition is to use an **explanatory phrase** for definition when one word does not make the meaning clear. For example, you can define the term _impermeable_ as "not allowing fluids to pass through." Sometimes you may want to write a full definition consisting of one or more sentences. How much definition you need to provide will depend on the difficulty of your subject matter, the knowledge level of your audience, and the particular context. Sometimes the meaning of a term or concept becomes clear to the reader simply from reading the surrounding text.

Read the following excerpt from an essay about emergency care. As you read, circle five terms that the writer defines or explains.

Covering a Wound

Dressing refers to the sterile, or germ-free, material applied directly to a wound, while _bandage_ refers to the material that covers the dressing. Several types of bandages are commonly used, depending on the injury to be treated. A roller bandage is a rolled strip of gauze or other cloth. A triangular bandage is a three-cornered bandage about

54 or 60 inches long across the base. An adhesive bandage is a combination of dressing and bandage, such as a Band-Aid. Whatever kind of bandage is applied, it must be secured firmly enough to control bleeding but not so tightly as to cut off circulation.

Questions

1. What explanatory phrase does the writer use to define *bandage*? What other explanatory phrases does the writer use?

_____

_____

_____

_____

2. Suppose you did not know the meaning of *gauze*. What meaning could you infer from the context, or surrounding text?

_____a type of cloth_____

_____

3. What is the writer's purpose in this paragraph: to describe, to narrate, to persuade, or to inform? Is providing definitions appropriate for this purpose? Why or why not?

_____Inform, Yes, people can know what_____

_____the items and_____

_____

Defining a word, phrase, or concept is an effective strategy for communicating or clarifying information. Remember, however, that it is often better to avoid using complex terms rather than break your writing flow to insert a definition. If you feel a particular term is essential, first decide whether or not a definition is required for your audience. If so, determine whether to provide a synonym, an explanatory phrase, or a full-sentence definition.

Also remember that you can use other strategies you've learned—especially giving examples—in combination with the definition strategy. For instance, if you are explaining the term *textile*, you might give cotton and wool as examples. What example does the writer give in the paragraph on page 174 for an adhesive bandage?

Activity A: Recognizing Strategies

Reread "The Truth About Cats" on pages 133-134. What synonym does the writer give for *myths* in the first paragraph?

_____*untruths*_____

- Cite a specific example that the writer uses in the second paragraph.

_____*notion*_____

- Cite two facts that the writer uses in the essay.

___*They (cats) can move about noiselessly*___
___*Cats are by nature quieter, shyer*___
___*creature than dogs.*___

STRATEGY: PROCESS

A **process** is a series of steps or actions leading to a specific end. Baking cookies, following instructions to install a smoke alarm, and refinishing a table are all processes.

In an essay you may want to explain a process to help readers understand how something operates or how something happens—how a caterpillar changes into a butterfly, for instance. Other times you may want to explain a process to help readers carry out that process—how to run a computer program, for example.

Read "Building the Egyptian Pyramids," which follows. Notice how the writer describes the steps of the process in the order that they occur. Presenting the steps of a process in chronological order aids readers in understanding the process.

Building the Egyptian Pyramids

The ancient pyramids of Egypt continue to fascinate and amaze people nearly five thousand years after the Egyptians built them. Constructing each massive pyramid was difficult and dangerous labor, requiring thousands of workers and years of toil. First, heavy limestone blocks were taken from quarries located near the Nile River. Then the blocks were transported by wooden boats to a point as close as possible to the intended building site of the pyramid. Next, the blocks were unloaded and slowly hauled to the actual site by means of sledges positioned atop wooden rollers. As construction proceeded, the Egyptians moved each successive block into position using ramps made of bricks of dried mud. Incredibly, the huge pyramids were completed] ' without the aid of bulldozers, cranes, trucks, or other modern-day construction equipment. Even so, the tallest pyramid rose higher than a forty-story building! Equally remarkable, numerous pyramids still stand today, almost fifty centuries since their construction.

Questions

1. List briefly the steps involved in constructing a pyramid, in the order in which these steps would be performed.

_____

_____

_____

2. How do words like *first*, *then*, and *next* help you understand the process?

They help us understand the process
in chronological order

_____

STRATEGY: CLASSIFICATION

To **classify** information means to sort similar or related facts and details and arrange them into groups or categories according to common features. For example, insurance companies may classify drivers by age, gender, and geographic area. Biologists classify each animal and plant into a group and subgroup called *genus* and *species*. Athletes are categorized as amateurs or professionals, depending on whether or not they earn their living at their sport.

Classification is useful because it helps people find and grasp information quickly and easily. Instead of searching through a random collection of data, you can focus on a particular grouping that contains the information for which you're looking. Think how difficult it would be to find your way through the classified advertisements in a newspaper if those ads *weren't* classified!

When you write an essay, you can use classification to help your readers understand the ideas and information you're presenting, as in the following paragraph.

The ABO System

When people ask, "what's your blood type?" they are referring to the ABO system for classifying human blood. According to this system, there are four specific blood types: A, B, AB, and O. People with blood type A carry what's known as antigen A in their red blood cells and antibody b in their plasma. (*Antigens* are substances that cause the body to produce *antibodies*; antibodies are proteins that act against disease-producing bacteria.) People with blood type B carry antigen B and antibody a. People with blood type AB carry both antigen A and antigen B, but neither of the antibodies. Those with blood type O have both antibodies, but neither antigen. All this may sound confusing, but categorizing blood by the ABO system has saved numerous lives. The reason is that certain antigens and antibodies are incompatible. If they are mixed together during a blood transfusion, the result can be a blocked blood vessel that proves fatal to the transfusion recipient.

Questions

1. What information is classified by the ABO system?

Human Blood Types

2. In what way might the strategies of facts or definition be used effectively in combination with classification in an essay? Use examples from "The ABO System" in your answer.

Definition must be written at the
end of the essay

STRATEGY: CAUSE/EFFECT

What caused the crash of an airplane? How do fatty foods affect the body? What impact does inflation have on the economy? Such questions examine **cause/effect relationships** that ask either what event or series of events (the cause) led to a particular outcome (the effect) or what will happen (the effect) as a result of a particular occurrence (the cause).

To develop content using the cause/effect strategy, you can organize ideas and information in various ways. You can start by discussing a cause and then explore its actual or projected effects. For example, you might discuss the problem of unchecked population growth and then describe how shortages of food and housing will result. Another organizational approach is to focus first on effects and then analyze the cause or causes. For example, you might describe how civil war has devastated a nation and then discuss the factors that led to the outbreak of war.

In using the cause/effect strategy, keep in mind that a single cause may lead to multiple effects, or several interrelated causes may together produce only one effect.

Read the following excerpt from an essay about the Industrial Revolution. What causes and effects can you identify?

How the Industrial Revolution Changed England

Before the Industrial Revolution, British workers made most products by hand or with the aid of simple tools and machines. However, in the eighteenth and nineteenth centuries, numerous new inventions—from spinning and weaving machines to James Watt's steam engine—changed the way products were made and significantly increased both productivity and profitability. Machine and power tools replaced hand tools, and large-scale factory production took the place of in-home employment. Workers and their families moved closer to their factory jobs, causing towns and cities near the factories to grow. Farmers turned to new methods of production to meet the cities' increasing demand for food, thereby further encouraging technological development. Before long, Britain had been transformed from an agricultural country into an economically powerful industrial nation.

Questions

1. What cause/effect relationships does the writer include in this paragraph?

_____

_____

2. What other strategy or strategies does the writer use in combination with cause/effect?

Facts examples

_____

STRATEGY: ANALOGY

When writers draw a comparison between two items for the purpose of explanation or illustration, they create an **analogy**. Two forms of analogy are the simile and the metaphor.

A **simile** is a comparison of two items using the word *like* or *as*. What two items is the writer comparing in the following simile? What specific features are being compared?

> The cave was as cold and dark as a tomb.

A **metaphor** is an implied comparison made without the use of *like* or *as*. What two items is the writer comparing in the following metaphor? What specific features are being compared?

> On the soccer field, Kerri was a bull on the rampage, charging through anyone who blocked her path.

Brief comparisons such as these make writing lively and interesting. In some cases writers develop a more sustained analogy to convey their point. For example, a writer may compare the parts of the human eye with the parts of a camera or discuss how the functioning of the human heart is similar to the operation of a pump.

Read the following paragraph. As you read, be alert to the writer's use of analogy.

A Star Comes to Town

As soon as word got out that the rock star was vacationing in Maywood, an ocean of teenage fans materialized, engulfing the entire town. Wave after wave of people swept through the quiet streets, damaging property, drowning lawns in sandwich wrappers and soda cans, and eroding the carefully planted flower beds. Within days, Maywood began to resemble a coastal town struck by a tropical storm.

Questions

1. What comparison does the writer make?

Compares Maywood to resemble a
coastal town struck by a tropical
storm
Compares teenage fans to ocean

2. How does the writer develop the analogy? Be specific.

_____

_____

_____

Activity B: Identifying Strategies

Using books, magazines, and newspapers, work with group members to identify at least one example of each of the ten strategies for content development that you've read about in this chapter. If possible, clip or photocopy the examples you find to share with your group.

After you've found your examples, work independently to answer the following questions. Then compare your responses and examples with those of the other group members.

- For which strategies was it easiest to find examples?

_____

_____

_____

_____

- For which strategies was it most difficult to find examples?

_____

_____

_____

- Which strategy was used most frequently in combination with other strategies?

_____

_____

_____

_____

Have one member save the examples your group collected. You will use them again in Activity G on page 196.

DECIDING WHICH STRATEGIES TO USE

When you write an essay, you can combine strategies to suit your purpose, content, and audience. Use the following guidelines to choose a strategy or combination of strategies wisely.

- *Consider your writing purpose.* Certain strategies are especially appropriate for accomplishing particular purposes. For example, for an informative or persuasive essay, facts and examples can support your ideas and a compare/contrast or cause/effect strategy can help to explain them. For a descriptive essay, you'll want to use description, perhaps in combination with analogy.

- *Consider the complexity of your ideas and information and the knowledge level of your audience.* Using examples and definitions helps to clarify difficult content. Classification, too, can make complicated content easier to understand. An analogy can be helpful as long as the analogy is clear and sound.

- *Stay focused on your central point.* Strategies should help to convey the central point of an essay without distracting readers. For example, narration can effectively reveal aspects of someone's personality, if you choose a relevant story or anecdote. However, if the central point of your essay is how kindhearted your cousin is, any stories or anecdotes should reflect this trait. An anecdote that deals with, say, your cousin's love of music will blur the focus of your essay.

- *Put yourself in the reader's place.* If you're not sure whether the strategy or strategies you've chosen are the "best" to use, try to view your content as a reader rather than as the writer. Suppose, for example, you're planning an essay to persuade readers that college courses be graded on a pass/fail basis. What approach would be most likely to convince a reader? Facts and examples? An analogy? Some other strategy? Viewing matters from the reader's vantage point may help you choose your approach.

- *Be flexible.* Make your writing richer and more expressive by experimenting with different strategies and different combinations of strategies. For example, in an informative essay about how exercise improves muscle tone even in elderly people, you might use narration to tell about a specific elderly person's improved strength after beginning an exercise program.

PLANNING ESSAY STRUCTURE

You learned in Chapter 1 that when the main ideas and supporting information of an essay are logically organized and smoothly connected, an essay has *coherence*. The word *cohere* is derived from a Latin word meaning "to stick together." In a coherently written essay, the paragraphs "stick" together to form a logically connected whole.

In planning and writing an essay, you can achieve coherence in two ways:

- By carefully organizing main ideas and supporting information.
- By connecting main ideas and supporting information to create a smooth flow.

Organizing and connecting content are the twin aspects of coherence. Both of these aspects are essential to effective writing. The following diagram illustrates methods of achieving coherence.

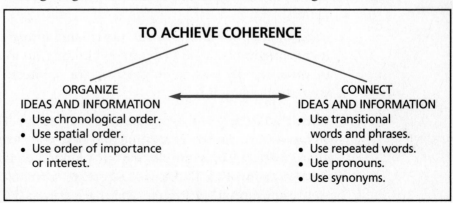

TO ACHIEVE COHERENCE

ORGANIZE
IDEAS AND INFORMATION
- Use chronological order.
- Use spatial order.
- Use order of importance or interest.

CONNECT
IDEAS AND INFORMATION
- Use transitional words and phrases.
- Use repeated words.
- Use pronouns.
- Use synonyms.

The paragraphs that make up an essay, and the sentences that make up each individual paragraph, must be both organized *and* connected for your thoughts to flow smoothly from the beginning of the essay to the end. As you saw in Chapter 4, the Writing Focus Chart includes two *Structure* questions that deal specifically with organizing and connecting information: *How will you organize your main ideas and supporting information?* and *How will you connect your thoughts within and between paragraphs?* What you'll learn in the remainder of this chapter will help you address these two questions as you plan and write essays. We'll first examine methods of organizing content and then discuss methods of connecting content.

Reread "Learning on the Job" on pages 19-20 and "The Truth About Cats" on pages 133-134.

DISCOVERY ACTIVITY

- Which essay is organized so that you learn what happened first, what happened next, and so on?

  Learning on the job

- Why is this organization a logical way to present the material in this essay?

  _____

  _____

ORGANIZING CONTENT

In Chapter 2 you learned about three basic methods of organization:

- *Chronological order*: organizing information or events according to time
- *Spatial order*: organizing details in the order your eye might follow them
- *Order of importance or interest*: organizing information in order of increasing importance or interest, building up to a conclusion; or in order of decreasing importance or interest, beginning with your strongest point.

Which approach will work best for an essay? That depends on such factors as why you're writing and how your ideas and information are related. For example, if your planned content for an informative essay involves a sequence of events, chronological order may be most appropriate. If you're writing a persuasive essay in which you present increasingly strong arguments, order of importance will probably create maximum impact.

Keep in mind that most content can be organized in more than one way. As you plan an essay, try to find the organizational approach that will most effectively accomplish your writing purpose and communicate your central point.

Using Chronological Order

Writers use *chronological order* to show a sequence of events. For example, you might use chronological order to explain a step-by-step process (how to change a flat tire), to describe a chain of events (how a bill becomes a law), or to relate a humorous anecdote ("On my way to school this morning . . ."). Because the progress of events over time naturally follows chronological order, news reports and historical accounts tend to organize information chronologically, proceeding either from past to present or sometimes from present to past.

Read "Anne Frank's Unforgettable Diary," which follows. As you read, circle words or phrases that signal the progress of time.

Anne Frank's Unforgettable Diary

On June 14, 1942, Anne Frank received a diary covered in red-checked cloth for her thirteenth birthday. Although she doubted that she had anything of value to say, her diary would become a remarkable record of the life of a Jewish family in hiding in Nazi-occupied Holland during World War II.

The early diary entries don't suggest that drastic changes were about to befall Anne Frank and her family. At first she writes about ordinary subjects—her school friends, a boy she has a crush on. Then, matter-of-factly, she mentions the anti-Jewish laws her family suffers under. All Jews must wear a yellow star. They cannot ride bikes or trams, attend movies, sit outside (even in their own gardens) after 8 P.M. Anne must attend Jewish-only schools. Her family can buy groceries only from Jewish storekeepers. On July 8, 1942, Anne reports that the Franks have received a deportation notice from the Gestapo, the Nazi secret police, and the family must now go into hiding or else be sent to a concentration camp.

The very next day Anne and her family left their house and most of their belongings behind to live in hiding in the Secret Annexe. The Annexe was located on the upper back floors of an office building on Prinsengracht Street, in Amsterdam. The door to the Annexe was concealed by a bookcase. Some of the workers in the office knew the Franks were hiding upstairs; others did not.

For two years Anne described what life was like in hiding. The Franks and four others—Mr. and Mrs. Van Daan and their son Peter and Mr. Dussel, a dentist—lived in constant fear of discovery. They were dependent on loyal Dutch friends for food, books, and news of the war. Anne tells of long, boring afternoons when all the hidden occupants had to remain silent so that no one in the office below would discover their whereabouts. She describes what she reads, what she dreams about, her hopes for the future, her feelings of loneliness and despair. We learn about Anne's conflicts with her mother and her deep attachment to her father. After one and a half years of confinement, she tells us that she has fallen in love with Peter Van Daan. By the time the diary is interrupted, Anne has grown in wisdom and courage far beyond her fifteen years.

On August 4, 1944, German Security Police and Dutch Nazis raided the office and broke into the small rooms of the Secret Annexe. The Franks, the Van Daans, and Mr. Dussel were arrested and sent to concentration camps. Only Anne's father, Otto Frank, survived. During the police raid nobody stopped to confiscate Anne's diary. It was left amidst the rubble, later to be found by an office worker and held in safekeeping by friends until the end of the war. Anne's father published her diary in 1947. Since that time *Anne Frank: The Diary of a Young Girl* has been translated into many languages and read by millions of people worldwide. The diary has been adapted for stage, screen, and television. Long after Anne Frank's tragic death, her diary continues to impart a young girl's enduring faith in the goodness of life.

Questions

1. What is the writer's main purpose in "Anne Frank's Unforgettable Diary": to describe, to narrate, to persuade, or to inform?

Narrate Describe and
some Narration

2. How does using chronological order help the writer accomplish this purpose?

_____

_____

Activity C: Organizing Information in Chronological Order

Think back to an especially enjoyable week you recently spent.

• Write five sentences telling about five different events that occurred during the week.

• Number the sentences in chronological order.

_____

_____

_____

_____

_____

Using Spatial Order

Organizing information by *spatial order* means arranging details in the order someone might view them. Spatial order is especially effective for describing a place, an object, or a person because it helps the reader picture one item as it relates to other items.

Read the following example of a paragraph organized by spatial order. The paragraph describes a museum that was made from the home of Sarah Orne Jewett, a writer who was known for her books set in Maine.

Excerpt from "Sarah Orne Jewett"

Although the house is officially known as the Sarah Orne Jewett House, the interior reflects the interests and tastes of both sisters. Sarah's bedroom, a cozy room in the back of the house, contains several items that she preserved from her childhood, including her riding crops, her skater's lantern, and two slates she had used when she was learning how to write. The furnishings consist of a simple sleigh bed, a writing desk, and several chairs. Mary's bedroom, which is located in the front part of the upstairs, is a large and elegant room with French flock wallpaper and carved woodwork. An impressive four-poster bed with a canopy dominates the room. Because the presence of the two sisters is so strongly felt in the house, visitors who are familiar with *Betty Leicester* can easily imagine that Betty's eccentric aunts are upstairs awaiting the arrival of their niece.

(Mark I. West, from *Wellsprings of Imagination.*)

Questions

1. What are the two main locations that the writer describes?

_____

_____

2. Why is spatial organization a good method of organization for the material in this paragraph?

_____

_____

When you organize information using spatial order, the position of your "viewing eye" is your **vantage point**. A vantage point may be *fixed* or *moving*. Gazing through a window, for example, your vantage point is fixed. You're viewing everything from one place, and what you see does not change. If you were hiking up a mountain trail, however, you would have a moving vantage point. Your surroundings would be continuously changing, and you would see different places and objects as you continued along the trail.

Whether to use a fixed or moving vantage point will depend on your topic and on your personal preference. With a fixed vantage point, you have to decide in what direction your "viewing eye" will look. With a moving vantage point, you have to determine how and where your "viewing eye" will move. Once you've chosen a vantage point, use that same vantage point throughout the essay.

Reread the excerpt from "Sarah Orne Jewett" on pages 187-188.

• Does the writer use a fixed or a moving vantage point? Explain.

_____

_____

Activity D: Organizing Information in Spatial Order

Picture in your mind either a place you've visited or a person you know well. Imagine that you are writing a description of this place or person.

- List five or six specific descriptive details that you would include.

_____

_____

_____

_____

_____

- Number the details in the order that you would present them.

- Would you use a fixed or moving vantage point for your description? Why?

_____

_____

_____

Using Order of Importance or Interest

To organize the main ideas and supporting information of an essay in *order of importance or interest*, you can use either an ascending or a descending approach. An **ascending approach** is one in which you present ideas and information in order of *increasing* importance or interest, often leading up to a specific climax or conclusion. An ascending approach is effective in a persuasive essay, where you want to convince readers to agree with your point of view. A **descending approach** is one in which you start with your strongest point and then present additional information in *decreasing* order of importance or interest. A descending approach works well when you plan to "hook" readers from the start with an important fact or a surprising idea.

Read "Recognizing Our Differences" on pages 189-191. As you read, note how the writer has organized the information.

Recognizing Our Differences

American visitors to East Asia are often surprised and puzzled by how Asian cultures and customs differ from life in the United States. What's considered typical or proper social conduct in one country may be regarded as odd, improper, or even rude in the other.

For example, people from some East Asian countries (Taiwan, for example) may begin a conversation with a stranger by asking personal questions about family, home, or work. Such questions are thought to be friendly, whereas they might be considered intrusive in the United States. On the other hand, people in most Asian cultures are far more guarded about expressing their feelings publicly than most Americans are. Openly displaying annoyance or anger—yelling, arguing loudly, and so forth—is considered ill-mannered in countries such as Japan. Many East Asians prefer to hold their emotions in check and instead express themselves with great politeness. They try not to be blunt, and they avoid making direct criticisms. In fact, they often keep their differences of opinion to themselves and merely smile and remain silent rather than engage in a confrontation. By comparison, Americans are often frank about displaying both positive and negative emotions on the street and in other public places. Americans visiting Asia should keep in mind that such behavior may cause offense.

A major difference between the American culture and most East Asian cultures is that in East Asia the community is more important than the individual. Most Americans are considered a success when they "make a name for themselves"—a very revealing figure of speech. In parts of East Asia such as Hong Kong, people instead strive to do honor to such community units as their family, their school, or their company. This position is reflected in many aspects of behavior. For instance, a member of a Korean sports team is more likely to play for the glory of the team rather than for recognition as an individual star. Complimenting a good player might therefore be a source of embarrassment for that player.

The East Asian concept of "face" is perhaps the most important difference for American visitors to keep in mind, because ignorance of this concept can cause distress. Americans are of course familiar with the common notion of "saving face"—that is, preserving one's dignity. In East Asian cultures, saving face is a much more serious matter. Face encompasses prestige, self-respect, personal worth, and—most important—respect of others. In countries throughout East Asia, Americans must be especially careful to avoid causing someone to lose face. This means, for instance, that American tourists should avoid criticizing a hotel worker or restaurant waiter where others can overhear, and that Americans at a business meeting should be very careful about criticizing East Asian businesspeople in the presence of colleagues.

American travelers to Asia, like all travelers to other countries, encounter many differences in culture and customs. Although these differences may at first cause confusion, frustration, or embarrassment, they can be smoothed over with a little understanding and effort. Ultimately such differences help people understand that each of the world's innumerable communities is unique.

Questions

1. What is the writer's purpose in "Recognizing Our Differences": to describe, to narrate, to persuade, or to inform? What pattern of organization does the writer use to structure the essay to accomplish this purpose? Explain your answer.

To inform

Order of Importance or Interest

2. Could the writer have organized the information differently? Explain.

3. What strategy or strategies does the writer use in "Recognizing Our Differences"? Explain.

Facts, Example, Contrast, Analogy

Activity E: Organizing Information in Order of Importance or Interest

As you develop an essay, you'll usually find that ideas and information can be organized in more than one way. Review the five sentences that you wrote for Activity C on page 187. Suppose you are planning an essay based on these sentences. Organize the sentences in ascending or descending order of importance or interest.

_____

_____

_____

_____

_____

_____

_____

_____

CONNECTING IDEAS AND INFORMATION

As you learned earlier in this chapter, the paragraphs that make up an essay and the sentences that form these paragraphs must be smoothly connected to create a coherent whole. There are several ways to connect ideas and information. You can use transitional words, phrases, and sentences; repeat key words; use pronouns; and substitute synonyms.

All such "connectors" serve to link your thoughts and lead readers to see the connections between your ideas.

Using Transitional Words, Phrases, and Sentences

As you read in Chapter 3, **transitional words and phrases** signal a relationship between one sentence and another or between one idea and another. Transitional words and phrases may appear at the beginning of a sentence or within a sentence. In addition, you will often want to include a transitional sentence at the end of one paragraph or at the start of the next paragraph to indicate that you're shifting your focus to a new idea.

Transitional words and phrases may be grouped by the function they perform. The chart on page 193 presents some common transitions and their functions.

TRANSITIONAL WORDS AND PHRASES	
Function	**Examples**
Show time or sequence	after, at present, at the same time, before, during, eventually, finally, first (second, third, and so on), immediately, later on, meanwhile, next, soon, then
Add information	also, and, another, as well, besides, first (second, third, and so on), furthermore, in addition, next, too
Indicate position	above, across, before, behind, beside, below, beyond, close by, farther, in front of, inside, in the distance, nearby, next to, opposite, outside, over, there, under
Provide an illustration	for example, for instance, in particular, namely, one such, specifically, such as, that is
Indicate a result or conclusion	as a result, because of, consequently, finally, for this reason, therefore, thus
Add emphasis	above all, especially, indeed, in fact
Compare or contrast	also, although, both, but, by contrast, even though, however, instead, likewise, neither, nevertheless, on one hand, on the contrary, on the other hand, rather, similarly, still, yet

You'll recognize the following paragraph from earlier in this chapter. Notice the words in italics. These are examples of transitional words and phrases.

> North American Indian communities chose with great care the sites of their villages and encampments. They would seek, *first of all*, a place offering maximum shelter from the elements. *In addition*, they would look for a site located near water—a stream, a river, or a natural water hole. In this way the community would have a ready source of water (*and* perhaps fish *as well*). *Moreover*, deer and other animals coming to drink could be hunted for food. *Another* crucial factor the community considered when selecting a site was how effectively that place could be defended against enemy attack.

Activity F: Identifying Transitional Words and Phrases

Reread "Building the Egyptian Pyramids" on pages 176-177. Underline at least three transitional words or phrases. In the margin beside the selection, list what function each one serves.

Because each new paragraph in an essay signals to readers that the writer is moving on to a new idea, a transitional sentence, rather than just a transitional word or phrase, is used to link one paragraph with the next. Full-sentence transitions, like transitional words and phrases, help readers follow the writer's train of thought and understand the organization of the essay.

Reread "Working Together for Multicultural Education" on pages 128-129.

- What full-sentence transitions does the writer use in the body paragraphs of the essay to link ideas and guide readers?

    _____

    _____

    _____

- How do these transitional sentences relate back to the introduction of the essay?

    _____

    _____

    _____

IN YOUR JOURNAL

Write a paragraph about one of your dreams or fantasies. Use at least three transitions from the chart of transitional words and phrases on page 193 to connect your thoughts.

Reread your paragraph. Could you substitute different transitions from the chart for the ones you used? How would your substitutions affect paragraph flow?

Repeating Key Words

Another way to connect ideas and information in an essay is by repeating key words. Using the same word or phrase in several sentences or paragraphs helps readers see how the thoughts in those sentences or paragraphs are related. Repeating words is also a means of emphasizing ideas, as when a candidate repeatedly promises no new taxes during a campaign speech.

- Reread "Building the Egyptian Pyramids" on pages 176-177. Which key word is repeated to help link the third, fourth, fifth, and sixth sentences?

_____

Using Pronouns

A **pronoun** is a word that replaces or stands for a noun. Pronouns include the words *I, you, he, she, it,* and *they.* Using pronouns is a third method of connecting ideas and information. Pronouns not only help you link sentences but also help you avoid needless repetition of names and other nouns.

Reread the opening paragraph of "Anne Frank's Unforgettable Diary" on pages 185-186.

- What pronouns does the writer use to connect the sentences?

  she, her, they

- What noun do these pronouns replace?

  Anne Frank   Jews

Substituting Synonyms

A *synonym* is a word that means the same or almost the same as another word. For example, *automobile* and *vehicle* are two synonyms for *car.* You can connect ideas and information by substituting synonyms for key words. In the following paragraph, the writer uses five different synonyms for *song.* Circle them.

Singing in the Shower

There's something about taking a shower that makes me want to sing a song. I like to start with a sentimental (ballad) or two. Then I move on to a show (tune) or perhaps a somber (hymn.) I usually end with some silly (ditty) or advertising (jingle) that pops into my head. If I can't remember the words to a song, I'm content to hum the melody.

Instead of a synonym, you may at times want to substitute a descriptive phrase. For example, in "The Climb" on page 170, notice how the writer uses the phrases *thin dusty ribbon* and *treacherous path* in the last two sentences to mean *trail*. These colorful phrases function much as synonyms would, but they make for livelier reading.

GROUP
ACTIVITY

Activity G: Identifying Connectors

Look back at the examples of strategies your group collected from books, magazines, and newspapers for Activity B on page 181. Identify two examples of each of the following kinds of connectors. If necessary, clip or photocopy additional materials for reference.

- Transitional words and phrases

  _____

  _____

- Transitional sentences

  _____

  _____

- Repeated words

  _____

- Pronouns

  _____

- Synonyms

  _____

BLENDING THE ELEMENTS

The Writing Focus Chart on page 132 can guide you in blending the key elements of writing to create an interesting and effective essay. Use the questions on the chart as you consider the purpose, content, structure, audience, and tone for an essay.

GROUP
ACTIVITY

Assignment 1:
Creating an Essay With Your Group

In this assignment you will work with your group to plan, write, edit, and proofread an essay using one or more of the strategies you've learned in this chapter.

A. Brainstorm a list of people that group members agree qualify as heroes or heroines. Decide on a topic and a writing purpose related to the person you selected. For example, you may choose to write an essay telling about the person's accomplishments, or you may want to write an essay that expresses an opinion about the person. Narrow your topic as necessary to make it specific.

B. Working as a group, use the questions on the Writing Focus Chart on page 132 to guide you as you plan the first draft. Use any of the invention techniques you learned in Chapter 2 as well as the strategies from the Strategies Box on page 182 to develop content. Carefully organize and connect the information in your essay to create a coherent whole.

C. Use your group's planning notes to write the first draft. Your first draft should consist of an introduction, a body, and a conclusion and should clearly accomplish your writing purpose. Review the draft and work together to develop an appropriate title.

D. Carefully reread and evaluate the content, structure, and wording of your first draft. Discuss any necessary changes, additions, deletions, and corrections. Using the Checklist for Revising and Editing on page 153 as a guide, work together to revise the first draft. Complete as many revisions as needed.

E. When you are satisfied that your draft is the best work that your group can produce, choose someone to key the revised draft. Make a photocopy for every group member.

F. Carefully reread your revised draft. Using the Checklist for Proofreading on page 105, work together to prepare the final copy. Consult the Writer's Guide that begins on page A 80 to review key points of grammar, punctuation, and capitalization. Have each group member proofread the revised draft indepen-

PORTFOLIO

dently and use proofreaders' marks from the box on page 105 to mark corrections. Then compare corrections. Incorporate all the changes on one draft.

G. Have one group member key the final copy. Proofread the final copy as a group. Correct any keyboarding errors. Record the names of all group members on the final copy. Make a final copy for every group member. Save your final copy in your portfolio.

Assignment 2:
Creating an Essay

In this assignment you will work independently to plan, write, edit, and proofread an essay about an event or experience from your life.

A. Recall a memorable event or experience from your recent past. Once you decide on the event or experience, try to remember as many specific details as possible.

B. Share your ideas with members of your group or with a peer editor. Discuss the topic you are considering for your essay. Ask for constructive advice about the topic. Also discuss any problem areas you foresee.

C. Use the questions on the Writing Focus Chart on page 132 to guide you as you write the first draft. Use the invention techniques you learned in Chapter 2 as well as strategies from the Strategies Box on page 182 to develop content. Carefully organize and connect the information in your essay to create a coherent whole. Your first draft should consist of an introduction, a body, and a conclusion and should clearly accomplish your writing purpose. Review your draft and develop an appropriate title.

D. Share your draft with your group or a peer editor. Use the comments and suggestions from your group or partner, in conjunction with the Checklist for Revising and Editing on page 153, to help you make revisions. After sharing essays, work independently to revise your draft.

E. Evaluate the content, structure, and wording of your essay. Using the Checklist for Revising and Editing as a guide, make any necessary changes, additions, deletions, and corrections. When you are satisfied, key your revised draft.

PORTFOLIO

F. Carefully reread your revised draft. Using the Checklist for Proofreading on page 105, prepare the final copy. Consult the Writer's Guide that begins on page A 80 to review key points of grammar, punctuation, and capitalization. Use proofreaders' marks from the box on page 105 to mark your corrections.

G. Key the final copy. Look over the final copy and correct any keyboarding errors. Save your final copy in your portfolio.

Assignment 3:
Reading as a Stimulus for Writing

In this assignment you will read a selection and then work independently to plan, write, edit, and proofread an essay.

A. Read "Enough Bookshelves" by Anna Quindlen on pages A 121-A 123. As you read this essay, think about what the writer is saying about how we change as we grow up and how children can help us reclaim some of what we've lost.

B. Use the selection as a stimulus for planning and writing a first draft of your own. Use your answers to the following questions to help you decide on a specific topic and establish a writing purpose. Freewrite for approximately ten or fifteen minutes on the topic you select.

- What qualities or abilities have you lost as you've grown up? What have you gained?

- The writer explains that "Reading has always been life unwrapped to me, a way of understanding the world and understanding myself. . . ." How was reading important to you as a child? How is it important to you as an adult?

Use the questions on the Writing Focus Chart on page 132 to guide you as you plan your first draft. Use the freewriting you did as a stimulus for your essay. Develop your content using invention techniques you learned in Chapter 2 and one or more of the strategies you've learned in this chapter.

C. Share your ideas with members of your group or a peer editor. Discuss the topic you are considering for your essay. Ask for constructive advice about the topic. Also discuss any problem areas that you foresee.

D. Write your first draft. Your first draft should have an introduction, a body, and a conclusion and should clearly accomplish your writing purpose. Review your draft and develop an appropriate title.

E. Share your draft with your group or with a peer editor. Use the comments and suggestions from the group or your partner, in conjunction with the Checklist for Revising and Editing on page 153, to help you make revisions. After sharing essays, work independently to revise your draft.

F. Using the Checklist for Revising and Editing as a guide, evaluate the content, structure, and wording of your draft. Make any necessary changes, additions, deletions, and corrections.

PORTFOLIO

G. Carefully reread your revised draft. Using the Checklist for Proofreading on page 105, prepare a final copy. Consult the Writer's Guide that begins on page A 80 to review key points of grammar, punctuation, and capitalization. Use proofreaders' marks from the box on page 105 to mark your corrections.

H. Key the final copy. Look over the final copy and correct any keyboarding errors. Save your final copy in your portfolio.

SUBJECT-VERB AGREEMENT

Grammar Gremlins

A verb must agree in number with its subject. A singular subject requires a singular verb, and a plural subject requires a plural verb. There are four common sentence patterns that may cause difficulties in subject-verb agreement. You will learn about two patterns in this chapter and two other patterns in Chapter 6.

INCORRECT:
Katherine drive to work.   Most employees arrives on time.

CORRECT:
Katherine drives to work.   Most employees arrive on time.

When the verb directly follows the subject, as in the preceding examples, it's easy to see when a subject and verb do not agree.

When words come between the subject and verb, mistakes in subject-verb agreement may be less apparent.

INCORRECT:
A box of tissues cost very little.
Club members who do not pay dues loses voting privileges.

In the first sentence, the subject is *box* and the verb is *cost*. The verb should be singular to agree with its subject. In the second sentence, the subject is *members* and the verb is *loses*. The verb should be plural to agree with its subject.

CORRECT:
A box of tissues costs very little.
Club members who do not pay dues lose voting privileges.

INCORRECT:
There is countless stars in the sky.
Just west of the city was two small towns.

The subject of the first sentence is *stars*, not *There*. *Stars* requires a plural verb. The subject of the second sentence is *towns*, which also requires a plural verb.

CORRECT:
There are countless stars in the sky.
Just west of the city were two small towns.

Activities

A. Underline the subject in each sentence. Circle the form of the verb in parentheses that correctly agrees with the subject.

1. To find employment, a <u>job seeker</u> (need, ~~needs~~) a résumé.

2. An effective <u>résumé</u> (describe, ~~describes~~) the job seeker's relevant experience and qualifications.

3. Unless they are work related, <u>personal details</u> (~~do~~, does) not belong on a résumé.

4. <u>Résumés</u> frequently (~~include~~, includes) details of the job seeker's educational background.

5. <u>People</u> who prepare their résumés with care usually (~~find~~, finds) a job more quickly than those who don't.

B. Read the following paragraph. Correct any mistakes in subject-verb agreement using proofreaders' marks from page 105.

As I ~~boards~~[ed] the bus to my first job interview, I ~~am~~[was] a nervous wreck. Two people ~~is~~[were] already waiting in the outer office when I ~~arrive~~[d]. Both of them ~~seems~~[ed] utterly calm, which ~~makes~~[made] me feel worse. They both ~~appears~~[ed] better dressed too, which ~~does~~[did] not help my self-confidence. Finally, I ~~am~~[was] called into the manager's office. On top of a huge desk ~~is~~[were] four towering stacks of files and records. Next to these ~~are~~[was] a tall metal basket filled with even more papers. The manager ~~stands~~[stood] up and ~~extend~~[ed] her hand. I ~~shake~~[d] it, hoping that when I speak, my voice won't show how terrified I ~~am~~[was].

were – wrong

wanting in present tense

C. For additional practice in identifying and correcting mistakes in subject-verb agreement, see page A 71.

SUMMARY

- Strategies for developing content include the following:

Facts	Definition
Examples	Process
Description	Classification
Compare/Contrast	Cause/Effect
Narration	Analogy

- To determine which strategy or strategies to use, consider your writing purpose, the complexity of your content, and your audience. Choose an approach that will effectively convey your central point. Be flexible; don't be afraid to try new strategies.

- You can create coherence in an essay by carefully organizing main ideas and supporting information. Methods of organization include chronological order, spatial order, and order of importance or interest. You can also create coherence in an essay by connecting ideas and information to create a smooth flow.

THINKING IT OVER

- How will selecting and using strategies from the Strategies Box help you write effective essays?

_____

_____

_____

_____

- On page 183 you read: "Organizing and connecting content are the twin aspects of coherence." Why is this an important statement to keep in mind when developing an essay?

_____

_____

_____

_____

- In Chapter 1 you learned that essays should have unity, support, and coherence. How are these three characteristics different? How are they related?

_____

_____

_____

_____

IN YOUR
JOURNAL

Review the goals that you set at the beginning of this chapter. In your journal, evaluate your progress toward these goals.

Writing to Describe and to Narrate

As you know from your experience, having a purpose for any task you do helps you perform that task effectively. Your purpose also helps you decide your approach to accomplishing the task. Suppose you ride a bike for exercise. You probably pay more attention to things like distance, speed, heart rate, and stamina. If instead, your purpose for bike riding is to see the scenery, you probably pay more attention to choosing your route or stopping occasionally to take photographs. Behind every piece of writing you do there also is a purpose. Section 3 of *Improve Your Essays* provides an in-depth examination of how to take charge of your writing to accomplish each of two main purposes: to describe and to narrate. Chapter 6 explores descriptive essays and will guide you in the methods of creating vivid descriptions. Chapter 7 investigates narrative essays and explains how to write essays that have a well-organized story line.

6

DESCRIPTIVE ESSAYS

OBJECTIVES:

Composition

- ○ To explore similarities between oral and written description.

- ○ To use description to develop essay content.

- ○ To write essays that describe in vivid detail a person, place, or thing.

- ○ To create and revise descriptive essays.

Grammar

- ○ To create sentences in which subjects and verbs agree.

How Do I Describe
People, Places, and Things?

Suppose you were visiting an amusement park. How would you share this experience with your friends back home? You would probably use description to re-create what the park looked like. In addition, you might describe things you heard, smelled, touched, and tasted while you were there.

Every day you use description to convey both ordinary and unusual feelings and experiences. You describe your child's flu symptoms to a doctor. You describe the taste of homemade pastry to a friend. You describe your college campus to your relatives. Through description, you help others imagine and understand your experiences. In this chapter you will learn how to develop essays that use description to convey meaning.

When Melvyn describes the costume he made for a Halloween party, the guests laugh. When Lydia describes her fear during a recent earthquake, her mother shudders on the phone miles away. As Claudie tells her grandchildren about the house she lived in as a child in Cuba, they ask her for more details.

Melvyn, Lydia, and Claudie are all using description to share an experience and to re-create that experience for their listeners.

Recall situations in which you have used description to share an experience. List specific instances in which you used the senses of sight, hearing, touch, smell, or taste to describe what something was like.

- With friends or relatives:

  _____
  _____
  _____

- At work:

  _____
  _____
  _____

- At school:

  _____
  _____
  _____

For *one* example you listed, consider these questions:

- What dominant impression were you trying to convey in your description?

  _____
  _____
  _____

- Did all of your details work together to convey this dominant impression, or were some details unrelated?

  _____

  _____

  _____

- How thorough was your description? Did you use all or most of your senses to describe this person, place, or thing?

  _____

  _____

  _____

- How did your audience respond to your description? Was this the response you had hoped to create?

  _____

  _____

  _____

IN YOUR
JOURNAL

Evaluate your ability to use description orally and in writing. Then set one or more goals in your journal. Here are some examples:

GOALS:
1. When I describe an experience, I will use vivid sensory details.
2. To present a clear impression, I will eliminate unnecessary facts.

DESCRIBING SOMETHING ORALLY

GROUP
ACTIVITY

When you describe something, how would you decide what words and details to use?

A. Each member of your group will choose a person, a place, or an object to describe. You might select one of the following: a person you know well or once noticed, a place you pass by often, or an object such as a rubber band or a feather. Use as many senses as possible (sight, touch, and, if applicable, hearing, smell, and taste) to describe the object. After describing what the person, place, or object is like in terms of appearance and so forth, think about what the person, place, or object means to you or reminds you of in your own life. For example, a rubber band might remind you of a time when you were so tense you felt close to snapping. Include at least one such imaginative detail in your description.

B. Each member of the group should take turns presenting a description orally to the group.

C. Work together to assess every description for effectiveness. Identify features that make a description vivid, logical, and useful.

D. Work with your group to create a list of five or more specific guidelines to evaluate the effectiveness of a description.

E. Evaluate the guidelines your group developed. Work together to improve them. Then write the revised guidelines in the following space.

_____

_____

_____

_____

_____

_____

_____

USING DESCRIPTION

FEATURES OF DESCRIPTIVE ESSAYS

A **descriptive essay** uses word pictures to re-create a person, place, thing, event, or feeling in the mind of the reader. To paint vivid word pictures, writers use **sensory language** to appeal to the senses of sight, hearing, touch, smell, and taste. Descriptive essays occur in newspapers, magazines, travel books, textbooks, and other sources.

Descriptive essays can be extremely subjective, or personal. In a personal essay, for example, you might describe how you felt about returning to Puerto Rico to visit a childhood friend. In such a description the writer describes feelings, memories, and personal experiences to convey an impression to readers. Descriptive essays can also be primarily factual and objective. In an objective description the writer records precise observations and physical characteristics, with little or no mention of personal opinions or feelings. For instance, in an objective essay you might describe the parts of a flowering plant or the bone structure of a chicken.

For each of the following writing tasks, would you use subjective description, objective description, or both? Write *S* for "subjective," *O* for "objective," or *B* for "both."

DISCOVERY
ACTIVITY

_____ A memo to a coworker describing the organization of your files.

_____ An essay about the death of a friend or family member.

_____ A written statement to a lawyer about a crime you witnessed.

When you write descriptive essays, you may use one of the following approaches to develop your content:

- Focus on subjective (personal) experiences.
- Focus on objective facts and characteristics.
- Include both subjective and objective facts, details, and examples.

Most of the descriptive essays you write will contain a blend of objective and subjective information. The approach you choose will depend on your topic, your purpose for writing, and the dominant impression or central point you want to convey.

USING SENSORY LANGUAGE

Sensory language contains details that convey strong images to a reader. Sensory details include such factors as size, shape, color, sound, texture, aroma, and flavor. To create effective sensory details, use precise, vivid words. In the following descriptions, notice how precise and particular the language is and how the words appeal to the five senses.

> As the storm approached, the sky took on the color of newspaper that had been yellowed by age.
> Her heels clicked along the pavement as she walked.
> The stone's pitted surface felt rough against his palm.
> After the rainstorm, the scent of moist earth and grass wafted up from the ground.
> Pickles taste salty and sour at the same time.

USING ANALOGIES, SIMILES, AND METAPHORS

As you learned in Chapter 5, writers often use *analogy*, or a comparison between two items for the purpose of explanation or illustration. There are two basic forms of analogy, similes and metaphors. A *simile* is a stated comparison that uses *like* or *as*. A *metaphor* is an implied comparison that does not use *like* or *as*. Look at the following examples:

> Simile: Their conversation is like a gently wicked dance. . . .
> —Toni Morrison
> Metaphor: Stories are antibodies against illness and pain.
> —Anatole Broyard

You can use figurative analogies to create vivid associations and images in a reader's mind. A **figurative analogy** uses comparison to make an imaginative connection between two seemingly dissimilar things. To understand the difference between a literal and a figurative comparison, read the following sentences.

Agent Smith is as talented as Agent Jones.
Agent Smith is a time bomb waiting to go off.

The first sentence makes an implied comparison between Agents Smith and Jones. The second sentence makes an unrealistic comparison between Agent Smith and a bomb. We know that Agent Smith isn't actually like a bomb. Comparing Agent Smith to a bomb suggests that he has a volatile, or explosive, personality. Like the second sentence about Agent Smith, the simile and metaphor examples on page 212 are figurative comparisons.

A writer can extend an analogy over several sentences or a full paragraph. The following paragraph is an example of an extended analogy. As you read, note in the margins specific comparisons the writer is making.

Excerpt from

The Years with Ross

Having a manuscript under Ross's scrutiny was like putting your car in the hands of a skilled mechanic...a guy who knows what makes a motor go, and sputter, and wheeze, and sometimes come to a dead stop; a man with an ear for the faintest body squeak as well as the loudest engine rattle. When you first gazed, appalled, upon an uncorrected proof of one of your stories and articles, each margin had a thicket of queries and complaints—one writer got a hundred and forty-four on one profile. It was as though you beheld the works of your car spread all over the garage floor, and the job of getting the thing together again and making it work seemed impossible. Then you realized that Ross was trying to make your Model T or old Stutz Bearcat into a Cadillac or Rolls-Royce. He was at work with the tools of his unflagging perfectionism, and after an exchange of growls or snarls, you set to work to join him in his enterprise.

(James Thurber, from *The Years with Ross*)

In the preceding example, notice how James Thurber compares a manuscript to a car and compares Ross's editing to the work that a mechanic does. Use similes and metaphors such as these to make your essays more lively and enjoyable to read. Avoid overused similes and metaphors such as *strong as an ox*, *sweet as sugar*, or *he's a busy little bee*. Make fresh comparisons that come from your own unique perceptions and experiences.

USING TRANSITIONS IN DESCRIPTIVE ESSAYS

WRITER'S TIP

In a descriptive essay, transitional words and phrases guide the reader from one detail to another in space, time, or some other logical order. Use transitional words and phrases such as *above*, *beside*, *farther*, *inside*, *next to*, *outside*, and *under* to clarify relationships between physical details such as the placement of people and objects. Consult the chart on page 193 for additional transitional words and phrases that can be used.

UNDERSTANDING DESCRIPTIVE ESSAY TASKS

You will use description in many school and job-related tasks. Often description will be part of a larger task. For example, in a how-to essay about first aid techniques, you may describe cardiopulmonary resuscitation (CPR). Other times, description will be the focus of an entire essay. How do you know that you are required to describe a person, place, or thing? Some instructions, such as the following examples, tell you outright to use description.

- *Describe* a friend or family member who has had a great influence on your life.
- *Describe* the vacation policy to new employees.
- *Describe* the parts of a flower.
- *Describe* the setting in William Faulkner's story "The Bear."

Other descriptive tasks will not be worded as directly. If you are asked for personal reactions and feelings about a person, place, or thing, you should include some description in your writing. If you are asked to explain what a person, place, or thing is like, respond with description. In addition, clue words such as *characteristics*, *traits*, *qualities*, *size*, *shape*, *speed*, or *mood* often mean that you are being asked to describe.

Activity A: Finding Descriptive Clue Words

Underline the clue words for description in the following questions.

- What qualities in Jacob Lawrence's paintings do you find most striking?

- What characteristics make you ideally suited for this nursing job?

- What will colleges be like in the year 2000?

- What traits do you look for in a friend?

FIRST DRAFT: PLANNING AND WRITING DESCRIPTIVE ESSAYS

The Writing Focus Chart on page 132 can guide you in blending the key elements of writing to create interesting and effective descriptive essays. Use the questions on the chart as you consider the purpose, content, structure, audience, and tone for a descriptive essay.

CHOOSING A TOPIC

For the topic of a descriptive essay, choose a person, place, or thing that you know well and can describe accurately and in detail. If you are writing a subjective descriptive essay, choose a topic that you feel strongly about or one that made a strong impression on you. The force of your feeling will help you brainstorm or freewrite memories, associations, and physical details that will help you choose a topic. If you are writing an objective descriptive essay, choose a topic that you know well or can observe closely so that you can include concrete observations and precise details in your description.

ESTABLISHING THE WRITING PURPOSE

Once you have chosen a topic, establish your writing purpose. The purpose of descriptive essays is usually either to describe or to inform. Some descriptive essays are also used to persuade. If your purpose is simply to describe, use description to re-create an impression of your topic. For example, you might use description to create a word picture of the home you lived in as a child. If your purpose is to inform, use description to explain some point about your topic. For instance, you might describe the parts of an airplane and show how an airplane is similar to a car. If your purpose is to persuade, use description to present an opinion or argument. For example, you might describe the effects of radiation sickness in order to persuade readers that nuclear energy is dangerous.

WRITING A THESIS STATEMENT

After narrowing your topic and establishing your writing purpose, decide what dominant impression or central point you want to convey about this person, place, or thing. Expressing a dominant impression or central point in a thesis statement will help you develop and structure your essay.

A thesis statement for a descriptive essay should do one or both of the following:

- Mention the person, place, or thing you plan to describe.
- Present a dominant impression or central point about the person, place, or thing you will describe.

Even though a thesis statement helps to unify the content of a descriptive essay, some writers don't include one. Instead they rely on the essay as a whole to imply a central point or to create a dominant impression. Usually, however, you should try to state your topic and dominant impression in one or two sentences in your introduction to help readers follow the details and central point of your description.

DEVELOPING THE CONTENT

After selecting a topic and writing a thesis statement, you are ready to gather sensory facts, details, and examples about your topic. Use the invention techniques you learned in Chapter 2 to brainstorm a list of details or to freewrite an impression about your topic.

PLANNING THE STRUCTURE

The structure of a descriptive essay will depend on your topic. If you are describing a walk through city streets, you may decide to use chronological order to follow the actual progress of your walk—the stores, people, and streets you passed in the order in which you passed them. If you are describing a fixed object, you may decide to structure your essay in spatial order (near to far; left to right; top to bottom). You may use order of importance or interest in many descriptive essays, either presenting the strongest point first or building up to the strongest point. Finally, you may organize a descriptive essay around a single mood that the essay keeps returning to. For example, in an essay describing an unbearably gloomy restaurant, each paragraph could describe an aspect that makes the restaurant gloomy. Whatever method you use to structure a descriptive essay, your organization should work to create a unified, dominant impression in the reader's mind.

IN YOUR
JOURNAL

Clip or photocopy for your journal examples of interesting descriptive writing you encounter in newspapers, magazines, or books. Describe the topic and purpose of each example, and explain how the writer has made the description come to life.

Select one description you particularly like. Then note how the writer has structured the description. Does the writer use chronological order, spatial order, order of importance or interest, or a combination of methods to organize the description? How does the structure of the piece clarify the content?

Read the following essay, "My Grandfather's Place." As you read, underline specific sensory details the writer uses to support or develop the central point or dominant impression of the essay.

My Grandfather's Place

Whenever I breathe the salty odor of sea air, I recall my grandfather and his house by Penobscot Bay in Maine. I was only seven the summer I spent there, but I clearly remember his small white house. My parents' Boston apartment was not that far away—only several hundred miles—but in Maine I felt as if I were in another world.

My memory of my grandfather is inseparable from that of his surroundings. Like the shaggy pine trees by his house, my grandfather looked large and windblown. Because he spent the bulk of the day outdoors, my grandfather seemed to be part of the landscape. In the front of the house, facing the road, my grandfather had planted many flowers, shrubs, and trees. On a typical day he would spend the morning tending his roses. He moved so smoothly and made so little noise that chickadees and blue jays would come to drink from a birdbath right next to the roses as if my grandfather wasn't even there. He spoke very little as he gardened. When he did speak, I could hear the pleasing tunefulness of his Italian accent.

As soon as my grandfather had completed his gardening chores, he would take me down to the beach. The grass along the way felt stubbly and hard under my feet. A set of wooden steps led to the beach which was peppered with pebbles, rocks, and boulders. At first, the pebbles hurt my feet, but my feet soon toughened, and I could walk barefoot with ease like my grandfather.

We usually spent most of the day by the water, with my grandfather showing me many wonders. He pointed out starfish clinging to the undersides of large rocks. He showed me mussels whose shells were rainbow-colored inside and a huge purple jellyfish that had washed up on the beach. As we walked along the shore, we would look for our marker—a large rock fifty feet from our sea wall. At low tide, the rock looked like a buffalo rising out of the water. Its craggy hump was covered with thousands of rough barnacles and with strips of curly black seaweed.

My grandfather's daily rituals were not complete until we had watched the sun set. We would walk to the end of the jetty and sit gazing out at the water until the sun rested on the surface of the water, then disappeared.

After my grandfather died, I learned that he had come to the United States when he was thirteen years old. Before that he had lived in a town in southern Italy that overlooked the Mediterranean Sea. I went there years later. Staring out over the shimmering blue expanse of water, I realized that my grandfather had re-created in America some of the beauty he had left behind in Italy.

Questions

1. What central point or dominant impression does the writer convey in this descriptive essay? his landscape

   Grandfather and House in Maine

2. What concrete sensory details does the writer use to create a dominant impression of the topic? Be specific.

Shaggy pine trees

3. How does the writer achieve unity in the essay? Be specific.

Each paragraph is dependent on the topic sentence

4. How does the writer use chronological order and spatial order to structure the essay? Be specific.

DO YOU WRITE ON A COMPUTER?

Use a word processor to determine the best structure for a descriptive essay. First, key your brainstormed lists and freewriting right on the screen. When you have gathered enough details and examples, save the material. Then make a copy and work with the information. Delete unnecessary details and place information in a logical sequence. If additional facts, details, and examples occur to you, insert them where they belong. Add, delete, and move information until you have created a satisfactory informal outline of your topic.

TARGETING A SPECIFIC AUDIENCE

When writing a descriptive essay, consider how you want your readers to respond to the person, place, or thing you are describing. In personal descriptive essays you will want your audience to respond to the topic in the same way that you did. Provide enough sensory details and background information so that readers can picture the dominant impression you want to convey. If the audience has some knowledge of the topic, try to present familiar details in your own unique way to provide a fresh view of the topic. In "My Grandfather's Place," the writer conveys a unique impression of a rock by saying that it looked "like a buffalo rising out of the water."

The writer of "My Grandfather's Place" had a clear audience in mind for the essay. This writer was writing for fellow students in a writing workshop. Because the audience had no way of knowing what the grandfather and his place were like, the writer included many concrete, specific details to convey a clear sensory image. If the writer of "My Grandfather's Place" was describing the grandfather in a letter to relatives, how might the content and wording of the description change?

SETTING THE TONE

The tone you set for a descriptive essay should reflect the purpose of your essay, your attitude toward the person, place, or thing you are describing, and the feelings you wish to convey. Tone is conveyed by your choice of words and by the details you include. In a subjective, descriptive essay, you may want readers to come away with a certain mood or feeling. If you are writing about a person who is sloppy, you can lead readers to feel the same way by choosing words and details to reflect your attitude. On the other hand, if you are writing an impersonal, objective essay about orchids, a phrase such as "orchids are more beautiful than any other flowers" would distract readers because your feelings and opinions are not appropriate for your topic and purpose.

In "My Grandfather's Place," the writer used tone to convey his feelings about his grandfather and about the landscape associated with his grandfather. The writer didn't state these feelings directly but allowed the choice of details to convey this attitude.

Questions

1. How would you describe the tone of "My Grandfather's Place" on page 217? Be specific.

   _____ Positive _____

   _____

2. How does the writer feel about the grandfather and his place? Locate and describe specific instances where tone reveals the writer's feelings.

   _____

   _____

Activity B: Planning a Descriptive Essay

In this activity you will plan the purpose, content, structure, audience, and tone for a descriptive essay. Refer to the Writing Focus Chart on page 132 for help in addressing these five key elements. Use separate sheets of paper for your work.

A. Narrow one of the following general topics for a descriptive essay:

- A person who has greatly influenced me
- A place I'd love to return to
- An object that I have a sentimental attachment to

   For example, if you select the general topic "A place I'd love to return to," your narrowed topic could be Taos, New Mexico.

B. Once you have selected and narrowed your topic, establish your writing purpose. Freewrite for ten to fifteen minutes about the person, place, or thing you have chosen to describe. Close your eyes and imagine your topic in detail. Use as many of your senses as possible to describe what this person, place, or thing is like. If possible, observe the person, place, or thing firsthand and write down physical details. Use brainstorming to gather as many sensory details, facts, and examples as you can.

C. Based on your prewriting, write a thesis statement.

D. Based on your prewriting, decide how you want to structure your descriptive essay. Determine whether you will use chronological order, spatial order, order of importance or interest, or a combination of methods to structure your essay. Prepare a conceptual map or an outline of your essay. Delete any unrelated facts, details, and examples from your map or outline.

E. Target an audience for your essay. After considering your intended audience, decide what tone is most appropriate for your topic and writing purpose.

   Save your work in your portfolio. You will use your prewriting work to develop a descriptive essay in Assignment 2 on pages 227-228.

REVISING, EDITING, AND PROOFREADING DESCRIPTIVE ESSAYS

The Checklist for Revising and Editing on page 153 can guide you in evaluating and revising the first draft of a descriptive essay. The Checklist for Proofreading on page 105 can help you turn a revised draft into a final copy.

Read the following first draft of a descriptive essay, which includes the writer's handwritten revisions. Remember that the writer has not yet corrected errors in grammar, spelling, punctuation, and capitalization. What changes did the writer make to improve the essay?

....

Revised Draft: **A Trip to the Great Outdoors**

Before I visited Glacier National Park, I had never been anywhere that made me feel that the earth was a grand, magnificent place. I lived in a city full of skyscrapers but its crowds made everything seem cramped. *The park made me understand the concept of largeness for the first time.*

I became aware of the sheer immensity of everything the night i arrive. There was so much sky! The stars were uncountable. The most brightest ones seemed so close that they appeared to dangle from the sky. ~~Light from the smaller stars seemed to flutter.~~ Tired from drinking in all this space, I looked down and saw the Big Dipper, *perfectly mirrored* in the nearby lake.

Early Everything around us seemed of an immense scale. *the next morning we drove to the hiking trail.* The mountains that towered over us were so high that we couldn't see their peeks. Waterfalls ~~flowed~~ *tumbled* from a great hieght to the valley floor.

Once we started hiking on the trail, Our view of the mountains was largely obscured by the Woods we were passing through. Some of the pine and fir trees have ~~thick~~ trunks, *so thick that two of us couldn't join hands around them.* Soon we started to see orange signs warning us that this was a "grizzly freqenting

area." Even the animals here were super-size!

Near the summit We came out of the trees. *Sweaty and breaching hard,* We stopped to rest. Now we

had a view again. We stood in the center of a vast,

breathtaking panorama. *On all sides* Mountain after mountain stood *my eyes seemed to fill with sky,*

fiercely in the sun. When I looked up, ~~I could see sky on all~~

~~sides.~~ My thought's would never again be as small as they

once had been. At that moment I knew that this aware-

ness of magnificent size would remain with me forever.

On pages 224-225 of this chapter you'll see a rekeyed version of "A Trip to the Great Outdoors" that incorporates the writer's handwritten revisions. You'll use that version to proofread the essay for errors in spelling, punctuation, and so on.

Questions

1. How has the writer improved the effectiveness of this descriptive essay? Be specific.

By improving the content. By providing a good central topic.

2. Why did the writer add a sentence to the introduction?

To help the readers understand the central point.

3. Why did the writer take a sentence out of the second paragraph?

It did not support the central point

4. What transitions did the writer add to create a smooth flow from one detail to the next?

next,

5. Why did the writer change the order of sentences in the conclusion of the essay?

To make the essay in chronological order.

6. If you were the writer of this essay, what additional changes would you make in content, structure, and wording?

Read the revised and rekeyed draft of "A Trip to the Great Outdoors" that follows. Proofread the revision, and correct any mistakes in spelling, capitalization, and punctuation as well as any factual, keyboarding, and grammatical errors.

Revised and Rekeyed Draft:

A Trip to the Great Outdoors

Before I visited Glacier National Park, I had never been anywhere that made me feel that the earth was a grand, magnificent place. I lived in a city full of skyscrapers but its crowds made everything seem cramped. The park made me understand the concept of largeness for the first time.

I became aware of the sheer immensity of everything the night i arrive. There was so much sky! The stars were uncountable. The most brightest ones seemed so close that they appeared to dangle from the sky. Tired from drinking in all this space, I looked down and saw the Big Dipper perfectly mirrored in the nearby lake.

Early the next morning we drove to the hiking trail. Everything around us seemed of an immense scale. The mountains that towered over us were so high that we couldn't see their peeks. Waterfalls tumbled from a great hieght to the valley floor.

Once we started hiking on the trail, our view of the mountains was largely obscured by the Woods we were passing through. Some of the pine and fir trees have trunks so thick that two of us couldn't join hands around them. Soon we started to see orange signs warning us that this was a "grizzly freqenting area." Even the animals here were super-size!

Near the summit we came out of the trees. Sweaty and breathing hard, we stopped to rest. Now we had a view again. We stood in the center of a vast, breathtaking panorama. On all sides mountain after mountain stood fiercely in the sun. When I looked up, my eyes seemed to fill with sky. At that moment I knew that this awareness of magnificent size would remain with me forever. My thought's would never again be as small as they once had been.

GROUP
ACTIVITY

Writing
FOCUS
CHART

Assignment 1: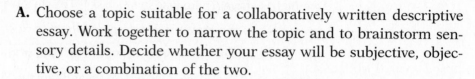
Creating a Descriptive Essay With Your Group

In this assignment you will work with your group to plan, write, edit, and proofread a descriptive essay.

A. Choose a topic suitable for a collaboratively written descriptive essay. Work together to narrow the topic and to brainstorm sensory details. Decide whether your essay will be subjective, objective, or a combination of the two.

B. Working as a group, use the questions on the Writing Focus Chart on page 132 to guide you as you plan the first draft. Use any of the invention techniques you learned in Chapter 2 to develop the thesis statement, introduction, main ideas, supporting details, and conclusion. Also use any of the strategies from Chapter 5 to develop content.

C. Use your group's prewriting to write the first draft. Your first draft should consist of an introduction, a body, and a conclusion and should clearly accomplish your writing purpose. Review your draft and work together to develop an appropriate title.

D. Carefully reread and evaluate the content, structure, and wording of your first draft. Discuss any necessary changes, additions, deletions, and corrections. Using the Checklist for Revising and Editing on page 153 as a guide, work together to revise the first draft. Complete as many revisions as needed.

E. When you are satisfied that your draft is the best work that your group can produce, choose someone to key the revised draft. Make a photocopy for every group member.

F. Carefully reread your revised draft. Using the Checklist for Proofreading on page 105, work together to prepare the final copy. Consult the Writer's Guide that begins on page A 80 to review key points of grammar, punctuation, and capitalization. Have each group member proofread the revised draft independently and use proofreaders' marks from the box on page 105 to mark corrections. Then compare corrections and incorporate all the changes on one draft.

G. Have one group member key the final copy. Proofread the final copy as a group and correct any keyboarding errors. Record the names of all group members on the final copy. Make a photocopy for every group member. Save your final copy in your portfolio.

Assignment 2:
Creating a Descriptive Essay

In this assignment you will work independently to plan, write, edit, and proofread the descriptive essay you began developing earlier in this chapter.

A. Review the planning you did in Activity B on page 221, including your prewriting, thesis statement, and outline. Reread the freewriting you did on your topic.

B. Use your prewriting and the questions on the Writing Focus Chart on page 132 to guide you as you plan the first draft of the essay. Use any of the invention techniques you learned in Chapter 2 to develop the introduction, main ideas, supporting details, and conclusion. Also use any of the strategies from Chapter 5 to develop content.

C. Write the first draft of your essay. Your first draft should consist of an introduction, a body and a conclusion and should clearly accomplish your writing purpose. Review your draft and develop an appropriate title.

D. Share your draft with members of your group or with a peer editor. Use the comments and suggestions from the group or peer editor, in conjunction with the Checklist for Revising and Editing on page 153, to help you make revisions. After sharing essays, work independently to revise your draft.

E. Evaluate the content, structure, and wording of your essay. Using the Checklist for Revising and Editing as a guide, make any necessary changes, additions, deletions, and corrections. Make as many revisions as needed. When you are satisfied, key your revised draft.

PORTFOLIO

F. Carefully reread your revised draft. Using the Checklist for Proofreading on page 105, prepare the final copy. Consult the Writer's Guide that begins on page A 80 to review key points of grammar, punctuation, and capitalization. Use proofreaders' marks from the box on page 105 to mark your corrections.

G. Key the final copy. Look over the final copy and correct any keyboarding errors. Save your final copy in your portfolio.

Assignment 3:
Reading as a Stimulus for Writing

In this assignment you will read a selection and then work independently to plan, write, edit and proofread a descriptive essay about a person, place, or thing in your neighborhood.

A. Read "A Pothole From Hell" by Mark Goldblatt on pages A 123-A 124. In this essay Goldblatt describes a gigantic pothole in his neighborhood that has assumed an exaggerated significance for him.

B. Use the selection as a stimulus for a descriptive essay. For example, you might write a description of an unusual building or public sculpture in your neighborhood. Here are a few questions to start you thinking.

- What sensory details does Goldblatt use to describe the pothole in his neighborhood? How do these details create a funny impression?

- Is there a person, place, or thing in your neighborhood that you find humorous?

- Why has the pothole come "to represent a source of justice" for Goldblatt?

- Has a person, place, or thing in your neighborhood assumed an exaggerated significance for you? What does this person, place, or thing represent? Why?

  Use your responses to the preceding questions to help you select a specific topic, generate a thesis statement, and brainstorm sensory details. Decide whether your essay will be subjective, objective, or a combination of the two. Freewrite for approximately ten or fifteen minutes on the topic you select.

C. Share your ideas with members of your group or with a peer editor. Discuss the topic you are considering for your essay. Ask for constructive advice about the topic. Also discuss any problem areas that you foresee.

D. Use your prewriting and the questions on the Writing Focus Chart on page 132 to guide you as you write your first draft. Use any of the invention techniques from Chapter 2 and any of the strategies from Chapter 5 as needed. Your first draft should consist of an introduction, a body, and a conclusion and should clearly accomplish your writing purpose. Review your draft and develop an appropriate title.

E. Share your draft with members of your group or with a peer editor. Use the comments and suggestions from the group or peer editor, in conjunction with the Checklist for Revising and Editing on page 153, to help you make revisions. After sharing essays, work independently to revise your draft.

F. Evaluate the content, structure, and wording of your draft. Using the Checklist for Revising and Editing as a guide, make any necessary changes, additions, deletions, and corrections. Make as many revisions as needed. When you are satisfied, key your revised draft.

G. Carefully reread your revised draft. Using the Checklist for Proofreading on page 105, prepare the final copy. Consult the Writer's Guide that begins on page A 80 to review key points of grammar, punctuation, and capitalization. Use proofreaders' marks from the box on page 105 to mark your corrections.

H. Key the final copy. Look over the final copy and correct any keyboarding errors. Save your final copy in your portfolio.

MORE ABOUT SUBJECT-VERB AGREEMENT

Grammar Gremlins

In Chapter 5 you learned that subjects and verbs must agree in number. When a subject is singular, the verb must be singular. When a subject is plural, the verb must be plural. In Chapter 5 you learned about two types of sentences that may be confusing when you are trying to determine whether the subject and verb agree. This chapter will present practice for working with three other sentence types that may cause problems with subject-verb agreement.

When subjects are joined by the conjunction *and*, the subjects usually take a plural verb.

INCORRECT:
The wolf and the fox is members of the dog family.

CORRECT:
The wolf and the fox are members of the dog family.

When subjects are joined by the correlative conjunctions *either...or* or *neither...nor*, the verb agrees with the subject *closer* to the verb.

INCORRECT:
Neither the stars nor *the moon give* enough light to read by.

CORRECT:
Neither *the stars* nor *the moon gives* enough light to read by.
Neither *the moon* nor *the stars give* enough light to read by.

If the subject is an indefinite pronoun, it always takes a singular verb. Common indefinite pronouns include *one, anyone, everyone, someone, nobody, anybody, everybody, somebody, nothing, anything, everything, something, each, either, neither.*

INCORRECT:
Everybody seem to enjoy watching elephants.
Nothing in this room *match* the wallpaper.

CORRECT:
Everybody seems to enjoy watching elephants.
Nothing in this room *matches* the wallpaper.

[handwritten top margin: tries-singular, plural / try] *[handwritten: verb]* *[handwritten: if s is There it is singular]*

Activities

A. Underline the subject in each of the following sentences. Circle the verb in parentheses that correctly agrees with the subject.

1. Neither Blake nor Willie (like, likes) doing crossword puzzles.

2. Everyone else in the family (excel, excels) at puzzles.

3. Blake and Willie (try, tries) to solve crossword puzzles.

4. Either the boys or their mother (begin, begins) a puzzle.

5. The only way that everything in a crossword puzzle (get, gets) completed is if one of their parents fills in the last squares.

B. Read the following paragraph. Correct any mistakes in subject-verb agreement.

Everyone use *[s]* stamps to mail letters. To many people, stamps are also a fascinating collector's item. Some collectors concentrate on old stamps, which can be expensive. Everyone are *[is]* able to afford current stamps, though. Current stamps cost just the price printed on the stamp, and they are easy to obtain. Each are *[is]* available at the local post office. No one enjoy *[s]* standing in a long line at the post office, but a stamp collector might get in line with a smile. The new flower stamps or the latest air mail stamp *[s]* wait at the postage window for the patient collector *[s]* Neither children filling their first stamp album nor experienced collectors expresses disappointment at the sight of a new stamp.

C. For additional practice in identifying and correcting mistakes in subject-verb agreement, see page A 71.

WRAPPING IT UP

SUMMARY

- Use a descriptive essay to re-create in vivid detail what a person, place, or thing is like.

- A descriptive essay can be subjective (personal) or objective. Most descriptive essays contain a mixture of subjective and objective information.

- Select key sensory details, use vivid figurative comparisons, and supply appropriate transitions to add unity, coherence, and support to a descriptive essay.

- The purpose of a descriptive essay can be to describe, to inform, or to persuade. If your purpose is simply to describe, use description to paint a unified picture of a topic. If your purpose is to inform, use description to explain or make a central point. If your purpose is to persuade, use description to make a convincing argument.

- Convey a central point or dominant impression in a descriptive essay through supporting information that appeals to the senses of sight, hearing, touch, smell, and taste.

- Structure the information in a descriptive essay in one or more of the following ways: chronological order (presenting details in the order in which the writer encountered them), spatial order (following the writer's eye across a scene), or order of importance (presenting key details first or last).

- Use tone in a descriptive essay, to impart your attitude toward the person, place, or thing you are describing.

- How is description important in daily life? Discuss two or three of the most useful aspects of description that you learned in this chapter.

_____

_____

_____

_____

- How can description help you share your experiences in conversations and in writing?

_____

_____

_____

_____

- How will what you have learned in this chapter help you write descriptive essays at work and at school?

_____

_____

_____

_____

IN YOUR
JOURNAL

Review the goals that you set at the beginning of this chapter. In your journal, evaluate your progress toward these goals. Revise or add to your goals as appropriate.

OBJECTIVES:

Composition

- To explore similarities between oral and written narration.

- To use narration to develop essay content.

- To write essays that narrate a story or event.

- To create and revise narrative essays.

Grammar

- To construct sentences in which pronouns agree with their antecedents.

How Do I Use
Stories to Make a
Point?

People love to hear and tell a good story. Not only are stories entertaining, they are also an effective way to make a point. Whenever you tell the story of what happened, you are using narration. In a narrative you give an account of an experience in a logical sequence. You include dialogue, description, and details to give the audience the feeling of *being there*.

Stories can be fictional, but many of the stories you hear and tell are about real-life situations. You listen to a news story about a conflict overseas. To ease your child's fears about entering first grade, you tell the story of your first day in school. In this chapter you will learn how to develop essays that use narration to make a point.

In a letter to her mother, Beverly recounts her first day of substitute teaching. In the hospital, Francesca tells her friends what happened when her car skidded on ice and hit a tree. Frank tells about the long train trip his family took from Mississippi to Chicago during the 1930s. Beverly, Francesca, and Frank are all using their ability to tell a story. They are narrating, or giving an account of, an event or experience. Think of situations in which you have narrated an event orally or in writing. List specific instances in which you told stories about real-life events.

- With friends or relatives:

  _____

- At work:

  _____

- At school:

  _____

For *one* example you listed, consider these questions:

- What was the central point of your story?
- Did your facts/details work together to convey a central point?
- What ideas, facts, details, and quotations did you include?
- How did your audience respond to your story? Was this the response you had hoped to create?

IN YOUR JOURNAL

Evaluate your ability to use narration orally and in writing. Then set one or more goals in your journal. Here are some examples:

GOALS:

1. When I narrate an event or experience, I will include only those facts, details, and quotes that relate to my central point.
2. I will structure my narrative in time order so that readers will understand how the event unfolded.

NARRATING AN EVENT ORALLY

GROUP
ACTIVITY

What would you say if you were recounting an unforgettable personal experience?

A. Each member of your group will choose an event or experience from his or her life or the life of a close friend or relative to tell about. Select an event that would make a good story—something scary (the night your building was on fire), or embarrassing (the day you unwittingly wore two different shoes to work), or weird (the morning you ran into a long-lost friend you had dreamed about the night before).

B. Each member of the group should take turns telling a story to the group.

C. Work together to assess every story for effectiveness. Identify features that make a narrative lively, absorbing, and something with which you could easily identify.

D. Work with your group to create a list of five or more specific guidelines to evaluate the effectiveness of a narrative.

E. Evaluate the guidelines your group developed. Work together to improve them. Then write the revised guidelines in the following space.

_____

_____

_____

_____

_____

_____

_____

_____

_____

_____

USING NARRATION

FEATURES OF NARRATIVE ESSAYS

A **narrative essay** gives an account of an experience or event. In a narration, a writer blends **internal responses**—what people *think* and *feel* with **external actions**—what people *do*—to make the account come alive for readers. Narrative essays occur in newspapers, magazines, travel books, history books, letters, diaries, and other sources. In narrative essays writers often give an account of a real-life event in order to make a point.

Narrative essays use facts, details, and dialogue (quotes of what people said) to re-create an actual event or experience in the mind of the reader. Usually a narrative is presented in time order with transitions to mark the passage of time. In an effective narrative essay, the writer maintains a consistent point of view and uses strong, precise verbs and rich descriptive details so that readers can see and identify with what's happening.

Many of the narrative essays you write will be about events in your personal life. Other times you will write about what happened to a character in a book or about an important historical person or event. How you approach a particular narrative essay will depend on your topic, your purpose for writing, and the central point you want to make.

USING STORY TIME INSTEAD OF REAL TIME

In real time, every minute you live through is the same length. The purpose of a narrative, however, is not to give an exact record of passing time. Rather, a narrative should present events that move toward a **climax**, or final conclusion. In order to keep the narrative moving toward the climax, a writer narrates what happens in **story time** instead of in **real time**. In story time, each event of a narrative is weighted according to its importance to the narrative. The writer might spend a large part of the narrative on a small but very important event, giving details about the action and descriptions of the surroundings. Less important events might be presented in only a sentence or even a few words. Still less important events might be eliminated entirely. For instance, you might take the same amount of real time to brush your hair as you take to look out the window and see a suspicious person entering your apartment building. In a narrative about a mysterious event in your building, however, you would devote more story time to the important event of noticing the stranger enter the building.

DISCOVERY ACTIVITY

If you were writing an essay about the time your apartment building caught on fire, which of the following items would take more story time to narrate? Put a check mark next to those items.

_____ ate pizza, apple juice, and a mixed green salad for supper
_____ on television, watched a movie that lasted almost two hours
__✓__ woke up to loud noises from somewhere in the building
_____ heard a nearby church tower clock chime twelve times
__✓__ ran to the door and saw dense, white smoke in the hallway
__✓__ opened the window and went out on the fire escape
__✓__ firefighters helped me down the ladder to the street
_____ heard a radio playing in a neighboring building

USING FLASHBACKS

When writers move backward in time from the present to the past, they are using **flashbacks**. In this variation on strict chronological order, a writer might begin a narrative in the present and then narrate an event in the past. For instance, from the safety of your kitchen, you might recall the terrifying incidents that occurred when you found yourself on the street in the midst of a hurricane.

Using flashbacks can be an unusually effective technique. It can allow you to present a person who behaves oddly and then reveal an incident that caused that person to behave in such a manner. It can allow you to describe a deserted building and then take readers into the past to learn how a single disastrous event caused the building to be abandoned.

Flashbacks should be used carefully, however. Like any technique, overuse of flashbacks can take away from their impact. Also, when using a flashback, follow standard time order when you narrate the incident that occurred in the past. Otherwise you will confuse your readers.

MAINTAINING A CONSISTENT POINT OF VIEW

To maintain a consistent relationship to the event or experience you are recounting in a narrative, use consistent pronouns and verb tenses throughout the essay. If you are narrating a personal experience in which you take an active part, use the first-person pronouns *I* or *we*. If you are reporting an event or experience that happened to someone else, use the third-person pronouns *he, she, it,* or *they*. Choose the verb tense (either past or present) that shows readers your relationship to the order of events in the narrative. Using the present tense (*is, yell, laugh*) creates a sense of immediacy as if the event were happening right now. Using the past tense (*was, yelled, laughed*) creates some distance between you and the event. For example, compare the different effects of the following sentences:

I hear strange footsteps in the room above. (*first person; present*)
He heard strange footsteps in the room above. (*third person; past*)

Be consistent in your use of verb tenses. Don't shift unnecessarily from the past to the present or the present to the past in a narrative. If you do shift between tenses, do so for a reason, such as indicating an actual shift in time.

USING TRANSITIONS IN NARRATIVE ESSAYS

Like most stories, narrative essays unfold in time. In your narratives, use transitions such as the following that signal a change in time or sequence: *before, after, soon, next, meanwhile,* and *finally*. Consult the chart on page 193, for additional transitional words and phrases that guide readers from one moment to the next.

UNDERSTANDING NARRATIVE ESSAY TASKS

Narration is an important part of many school- and job-related tasks. Sometimes narration will be part of a larger task. For example, in an essay about the causes and effects of the civil rights movement, you might need to recount Rosa Parks's experiences in the bus boycott in Montgomery, Alabama, in 1955. Other times, narration will be the focus of an entire essay. For instance, on a college application you might be asked to recount a key experience that influenced your desire to go to college. How do you know that you are being asked to tell the story of an event or experience? Narrative essay tasks often contain clue words such as *narrate, tell what happened, describe what took place,* and *recount key events.* Here are several examples.

- *Narrate* an incident in your life that influenced your stand on the legalization of narcotics.
- *Tell exactly what happened* the day the computers were stolen from the office.
- *Describe what took place* when Hitler invaded Poland.
- *Recount* one of your favorite childhood memories.

Often the instructions for a writing task will contain the word *describe.* If you are not sure whether you are being asked primarily for description or narration, analyze the wording of the instructions carefully. If you are asked to focus on physical characteristics and qualities of a person, place, or thing, respond with description. If you are asked to focus on actions and conversations that tell the story of an event, respond with narration.

Activity A: Distinguishing Between Descriptive and Narrative Essay Tasks

Write *N* if the instruction is asking for a narrative essay and *D* if the instruction is asking for a descriptive essay. Underline the clue words that help you decide.

_____N_____ Recount a key event in the early life of Vincent Van Gogh.

_____D_____ Describe Van Gogh's painting "The Potato Eaters."

_____N_____ What happened when you interviewed Jesse Jackson?

_____D_____ Describe what takes place at the end of the novel *One Hundred Years of Solitude.*

FIRST DRAFT: PLANNING AND WRITING NARRATIVE ESSAYS

The Writing Focus Chart on page 132 can guide you in blending the key elements of writing to create interesting and effective narrative essays. Use the questions on the chart as you consider the purpose, content, structure, audience, and tone for a narrative essay.

CHOOSING A TOPIC

For the topic of a narrative essay, choose an event or experience that had an effect on you—one that will make a good story. When an event makes a strong impact on you, the incident is likely to have an equal effect on your readers. Choose an event that is still fresh in your mind so that you can use brainstorming and questioning to gather facts, details, and bits of conversation to re-create what happened. If you are telling the story of a historical event, research your topic thoroughly so that you can tell what happened accurately and in detail.

ESTABLISHING THE WRITING PURPOSE

Once you have chosen a topic, establish your writing purpose. The purpose of narrative essays is usually either to narrate or to inform. Some narrative essays are also used to persuade. If your purpose is to narrate, give a clear account of what happened during a particular event or experience. For example, you might use narration to tell about your frightening experience in a storm in your community. If your purpose is to inform, use your account of an event or experience to explain some point about your topic. For instance, you might narrate an incident between a hiker and a grizzly bear in order to explain how to respond to grizzlies in the wild. If your purpose is to persuade, use narration to present an opinion or an argument. For example, you might present a narrative about a woman who contracted AIDS in order to convince readers to protect themselves from the spread of AIDS.

WRITING A THESIS STATEMENT

After narrowing your topic and establishing your writing purpose, decide what central point you want to convey about this event or experience. Expressing the central point of your story in your thesis statement will help you develop and structure your essay.

A thesis statement for a narrative essay should do one or more of the following:

- Introduce the event or experience that you will narrate.

- Present a dominant impression or central point about the story.

The following sentences are examples of thesis statements for narrative essays:

> I never knew how scary floods could be until this summer.
> The year my father spent in China was the happiest year of his life.

To create suspense in narrative essays, writers often don't include a thesis statement in the introduction. Instead, they use the entire narrative to build up to a central point. Sometimes a writer will not state the central point even at the conclusion but will only imply it. If you do decide to present a thesis statement, use it to suggest but not give away the point of your story. Composing a thesis statement early in the writing process will help you unify your narrative and gather appropriate supporting information.

Here is an introduction from a narrative essay. As you read, circle the sentence or sentences that state or imply what the essay will be about.

On Not Being a Victim

In the early 1970s, I had an experience that could be described as acquaintance rape. Actually, I have had two or three such experiences, but this one most dramatically fits the profile. I was sixteen and staying in the apartment of a slightly older girl I'd just met in a seedy community center in Detroit. I'd been in her apartment for a few days when an older guy she knew came over and asked us if we wanted to drop some acid. In those years, doing acid with complete strangers was consistent with my idea of a possible good time, so I said yes. When I started peaking, my hostess decided she had to go see her boyfriend, and there I was, alone with this guy, who, suddenly, was in my face.

(Mary Gaitskill, from *Harpers*, March 1994)

Questions

1. Based on the introduction, what will this narrative essay be about? *Personal experience*

   ___The rape of the victim___

   _____

2. How does the writer spark your interest in the topic?

_____

_____

DEVELOPING THE CONTENT

After selecting a topic and writing a thesis statement, gather facts, details, and bits of dialogue about the event or experience you have chosen to narrate. Use the invention techniques you learned in Chapter 2 to brainstorm a list of facts and details or to freewrite possible dialogue for your narrative.

PLANNING THE STRUCTURE

The structure of a narrative essay will depend on the story you are telling. Most narrative essays are structured using chronological order. The easiest way to structure a narrative is to follow time order—begin with what happened first, move on to what happened next, and so on. For example, if you were writing about an airplane flight you took, you might begin with your arrival at the airport, continue with events leading up to the flight, and conclude with the plane taking off. Narrative essays may also be structured in the following ways:

- Begin the narrative in the present and then present a flashback that takes place in the past.

- Present the entire story briefly in the introduction, followed by an examination of specific points in detail.

- Divide the story into a series of incidents, presenting each one from least to most important.

When planning the structure of a narrative essay, you can create suspense and drama by building to a climax. If you do so, save the best moments for last so that readers will want to stay with you until the end. You can end a narrative essay in a variety of ways: conclude with the most dramatic aspect of your story; conclude with a return to your central point; or conclude by describing the aftermath of what happened.

To select an appropriate structure for your content, look at the facts, details, and dialogue you gathered. Divide the event or experience into what happened first, what happened next, and so on. Arrange your supporting information in a logical sequence. (For additional information on methods of organization, see Chapter 5.)

IN YOUR JOURNAL

Clip or photocopy for your journal examples of interesting narrative writing you encounter in newspapers, magazines, or books. Describe the topic and purpose of each example, and explain how the writer has made the story come to life.

Select one narrative that you particularly like. Describe how the writer has structured the essay. Does the writer use chronological order, spatial order, order of importance or interest, or a combination of methods to organize the narrative? How does the structure of the story clarify the content?

Read the following essay, "Lost and Found." As you read, underline specific facts, details, and dialogue the writer uses to convey what happened.

Lost and Found

That cold January night, I was growing sick of my life in San Francisco. There I was, trudging home at one in the morning after a disheartening rehearsal at the theater. With opening night only a week away, I was still botching my lines. I was having trouble juggling my temp job at the bank and my acting at night. As I walked, I thought seriously about quitting both acting and San Francisco. City life had become too much for me.

The bus I usually took home sat at the bus stop a block away. I made a run for it, but just as I was crossing the street, the driver pulled away. I yelled "STOP!" at the top of my theater-trained voice, but the bus continued moving. At that hour the next bus wouldn't come soon. I began the long walk home.

As I walked down empty streets under tall buildings, I felt very small and vulnerable. My face stiffened against the sharp wind. I began jogging, both to keep warm and to elude any potential muggers. Very few people were still out, only a few sad-looking homeless people bundled up under blankets or huddled in cardboard boxes.

About a block from my apartment, I heard a sound behind me. I turned quickly, half expecting to see someone with a knife or a gun. The street was empty. All I saw was the glow of a streetlight. Still, the noise had made me nervous, so I started to jog faster. Not until I reached my apartment building, climbed up the six flights, unlocked the door, and plopped down on the couch did I realize what the noise had been. The noise I'd heard hadn't been a stalker. It had been my wallet—with my credit cards, my driver's license, and my ID cards—falling to the sidewalk.

Suddenly I wasn't cold or tired anymore. I was just desperate. I ran out the door and back to where I'd heard the noise. Although I retraced my steps exactly and searched the pavement frantically for fifteen minutes, my wallet was nowhere to be found. As my search slowed to a halt, I heard a garbage truck yawning and moaning nearby. The mournful sound echoed my mood.

Just as I was about to give up the search and go home, I heard the garbage truck pull up to the curb next to me. When a voice called from the inside the cab, "Alisa Camacho?" I thought I was dreaming. How could this guy know my name? The door to the truck swung open, and out popped a small red-haired man with an amused look in his eyes. "Is this what you're looking for?" he asked, holding up a small oblong shape.

I hardly remember walking home; I think I must have floated an inch from the ground. In my memory, I kept hearing my voice thanking the sanitation workers and their laughter as they told me how I had added a little excitement to their evening. After I returned home, I opened my wallet. By this time I was not surprised to see that everything was still there—cash, credit cards, everything.

It was nearly 3 A.M. by the time I collapsed into bed. I wouldn't get much sleep that night, but I had gotten my wallet back. I also had gotten back some enjoyment of city life. I realized that the city couldn't be a bad place as long as people were willing to help each other.

Questions

1. What central point or dominant impression does the writer convey in this narrative essay?

The incidents that took place

life in a big city is not as many time

bud as many time

2. What facts, details, and dialogue does the writer use to tell the story? Be specific.

_____

_____

_____

3. How does the writer achieve unity in the essay? Be specific.

_____

_____

4. How does the writer use chronological order to structure the essay? Be specific.

_____

_____

DO YOU WRITE ON A COMPUTER?

Use a word processor to create a time line for a narrative essay. Try dividing the event or experience you are narrating into stages. Using the columns feature on your program, key in three headings: What Happened First; What Happened Next; What Happened Last. Place the facts, details, and bits of dialogue you have gathered in time order under the appropriate headings. Within each column, check that your supporting information is in a logical sequence. If new information occurs to you, add the item in the appropriate column in the appropriate place. Use this time line to prepare an outline of your essay. When you write your first draft, try devoting a paragraph to each stage of the event or experience you are narrating.

TARGETING A SPECIFIC AUDIENCE

When writing a narrative essay, consider whether or not your readers might have gone through a similar experience. If you are narrating an everyday event, such as a funny thing that happened at the supermarket checkout counter, don't include unnecessary details such as how you pushed the shopping cart around. Focus instead on those aspects of your topic that are truly essential to the point of the story. If you are writing about an unusual topic, such as the time your Volkswagen broke down in the desert, provide enough concrete sensory details, dialogue, and action so that readers can identify with your experience. To set the scene for your story, you might provide some background in the introduction. For instance, you might explain briefly who you are and why you were in a particular place at a particular time.

Questions

1. How does the writer of "Lost and Found" on pages 245–246 help you identify with the experience?

_____

_____

_____

2. Suppose the writer of "Lost and Found" intended to reach an audience of people who had never visited a city of any kind. How might the content and wording of the narrative change?

_____

_____

_____

_____

SETTING THE TONE

The wording and imagery you use in a narrative essay will color the reader's impression of the event or experience you are narrating. Using strong, precise verbs will help you convey feelings and actions accurately in a narrative. If your narrative essay is about a terrifying experience, your wording should convey your terror to the reader. If your narrative essay is about a funny experience, your tone should reflect the humor of the experience.

When you write a personal narrative in which you are an active participant in the story, your tone will also affect how the audience responds to you, the writer. When the writer of "Lost and Found" describes the homeless people in the street, the description implies sympathy for them. If the writer had adopted a contemptuous tone and said "What were these people doing on the streets? Didn't they have anywhere to go?" most readers' sympathy would have been lost immediately.

Questions

1. Is the tone of "Lost and Found" formal or informal? Why has the writer adopted this tone?

_____

_____

2. How does the writer feel about life in the big city? Cite specific instances in the narrative where the tone reveals the writer's true feelings.

_____

_____

Activity B: Planning a Narrative Essay

In this activity you will plan the purpose, content, structure, audience, and tone for a narrative essay. Refer to the Writing Focus Chart on page 132 for help in addressing these five key elements. Use separate sheets of paper for your work.

A. Narrow one of the following general topics for a narrative essay:

- The most thrilling moment in your life
- A scary adventure you shared with a friend
- A story about a family member

For example, if you select the general topic "A scary adventure you shared with a friend," your narrowed topic could be "encountering a shark while snorkeling."

B. Once you have selected and narrowed a topic, establish your writing purpose. Then recall the event you have chosen to narrate. Think about what happened in the order that it happened. Freewrite for ten to fifteen minutes about this event. One way to generate material about the event is to write about it as though you were telling a friend about the event in a letter.

C. Based on your prewriting, write a thesis statement for your narrative essay.

D. With your topic fresh in your mind, answer a series of *who, what, when, where, why, how* questions about the event or experience. Questions might include the following: What happened?

When did the incident occur? Who was there? What did people say? How did things turn out? Why was the experience important? Write your questions and answers. Include as much detail as possible in your answers. Consider brainstorming to gather additional information about your topic.

E. Based on your prewriting, decide how to structure your narrative essay. Determine whether you will use chronological order, order of importance or interest, or some other method or combination of methods. Prepare a conceptual map or an outline of the event or experience you intend to narrate. Delete any unrelated facts, details, and dialogue from your map or outline.

F. Target an audience for your essay. After considering your intended audience, decide what tone is most appropriate for your topic and writing purpose.

PORTFOLIO

G. Save your work in your portfolio. You will use your prewriting work to develop a narrative essay in Assignment 2 on pages 255-256.

REVISING, EDITING, AND PROOFREADING NARRATIVE ESSAYS

The Checklist for Revising and Editing on page 153 can guide you in evaluating and revising the first draft of a narrative essay. The Checklist for Proofreading on page 105 can help you turn a revised draft into a final copy.

Read the following first draft of a narrative essay, which includes the writer's handwritten revisions. Remember that at this point the writer has not yet corrected errors in grammar, spelling, punctuation, and capitalization. What changes did the writer make to improve the essay?

Revised Draft: **The Race**

On the day of our cross country team's last meet, the
air was clear and fresh. We couldn't have asked for better
runing weather. We were standing on a green hill near
Southwestern High School as the Southwestern team pre-

pared to walk the course with us. *Before the beginning of a race,* The tradition is for the home team to walk the course with the visiting team, pointing out the significant landmarks. ("At the top of the hill, you have to run to the right of the oak tree, then follow the path to the left....") This lets the visiting team know which way to run when the race starts. *and gives both teams an equal advantage.*

I was especially nervous as I walked. *with my teammates.* Our team was having a successful season, but I wasn't doing *brilliantly* too well. The previous week our coach, Mr. Wysocki, had told me, "Rivera you're fast and you're tough, but you're not running up to your potential." *I was beginning to think, however, that I just wasn't a very good runner.* Next year, my senior year, I might not go out for the team.

When the starting gun goes off, the runners pounded across the open field. After the first mile, the Southwestern team could no longer keep up with our best runners. *Going into the last half mile,* My team had the first seven places locked up. At the last turn, five member of my team began *sprinting* running across the baseball diamond toward the finish line. "Wait up!" I *called* said breathlessly. "We're supposed to go *around* the field!" One of my teammates looked back and yelled that I was wrong.

I didnt know what to do. Then I decided to run in the direction I thought was the right one. Even if I was wrong, we would still win the meet, because my teammates would have captured the first five positions. I distinctly remembered being told to run around the field, not through it—didnt I? At the risk of seeming like a total fool, I took off by myself, running around the outside of the baseball field.

A few moments later One of my teammates turned around to see the Southwestern team following after me. He raced back. *and was able to pass a couple of Southwestern runners.* When the final score was tallied, my team had four of the first seven spots and barely ~~won~~ *squeaked by* with a one-point victory.

~~Next month basketball practice would begin.~~

I went out for cross country again, *the following year,* and I started to do

really well. *though* the race I remember with the most satisfac-

tion is the last race of my junior year. That's the race in

which I learned to trust my instincts. Speed and tough-

ness are important qualitys in a runner, but confidence is

even more important.

On pages 253-254 of this chapter you'll see a rekeyed version of "The Race" that incorporates the writer's handwritten revisions. You'll use that version to proofread the essay for errors in spelling, punctuation, and so on.

Questions

1. How has the writer improved the effectiveness of this narrative essay? Be specific.

_____

_____

2. Why did the writer add the final phrase to the introduction?

_____

_____

3. Why did the writer change two verbs in the third paragraph?

_____

_____

4. Why did the writer change the order of sentences in the fourth paragraph?

_____

_____

5. Why did the writer cross out the last sentence of the fifth paragraph?

_____

_____

6. What transitions did the writer add to create a smooth flow from one moment to the next?

_____

_____

7. If you were the writer of this essay, what additional changes would you make in content, structure, and wording?

_____

_____

Read the revised and rekeyed draft of "The Race" that follows. Proofread the revision, and correct any mistakes in spelling, capitalization, and punctuation as well as any factual, keyboarding, and grammatical errors.

Revised and Rekeyed Draft:

The Race

On the day of our cross country team's last meet, the air was clear and fresh. We couldn't have asked for better runing weather. We were standing on a green hill near Southwestern High School as the Southwestern team prepared to walk the course with us. Before the beginning of a race, the tradition is for the home team to walk the course with the visiting team, pointing out the significant landmarks. ("At the top of the hill, you have to run to the right of the oak tree, then follow the path to the left....") This lets the visiting team know which way to run when the race starts and gives both teams an equal advantage.

I was especially nervous as I walked with my teammates. Our team was having a successful season, but I wasn't doing brilliantly. The previous week our coach, Mr. Wysocki, had told me, "Rivera you're fast and you're tough, but you're not running up to your potential." I was beginning to think, however, that I just wasn't a very good runner. Next year, my senior year, I might not go out for the team.

When the starting gun ~~goes~~ went off, the runners pounded across the open field. After the first mile, the Southwestern team could no longer keep up with our best runners. Going into the last half mile, my team had the first seven places locked up. At the last turn, five members of my team began sprinting across the baseball diamond toward the finish line. "Wait up!" I called breathlessly. "We're supposed to go *around* the field!" One of my teammates looked back and yelled that I was wrong.

I didnt know what to do. I distinctly remembered being told to run around the field, not through it—didnt I? Then I decided to run in the direction I thought was the right one. Even if I was wrong, we would still win the meet, because my teammates would have captured the first five positions. At the risk of seeming like a total fool, I took off by myself, running around the outside of the baseball field.

A few moments later one of my teammates turned around to see the Southwestern team following after me. He raced back and was able to pass a couple of Southwestern runners. When the final score was tallied, my team had four of the first seven spots and barely squeaked by with a one-point victory.

I went out for cross country again the following year, and I started to do really well. The race I remember with the most satisfaction, though, is the last race of my junior year. That's the race in which I learned to trust my instincts. Speed and toughness are important qualitys in a runner, but confidence is even more important.

GROUP
ACTIVITY

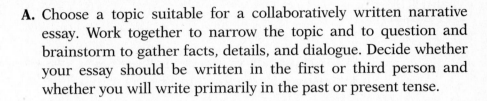

Assignment 1:
Creating a Narrative Essay With Your Group

In this assignment you will work with your group to plan, write, edit, and proofread a narrative essay.

A. Choose a topic suitable for a collaboratively written narrative essay. Work together to narrow the topic and to question and brainstorm to gather facts, details, and dialogue. Decide whether your essay should be written in the first or third person and whether you will write primarily in the past or present tense.

B. Working as a group, use the questions on the Writing Focus Chart on page 132 to guide you as you plan the first draft. Use any of the invention techniques you learned in Chapter 2 to develop the thesis statement, introduction, main ideas, supporting details, and conclusion. Also use any of the strategies from Chapter 5 to develop content.

C. Use your group's prewriting to write the first draft. Your first draft should consist of an introduction, a body, and a conclusion and should clearly accomplish your writing purpose. Review your draft and work together to develop an appropriate title.

D. Carefully reread and evaluate the content, structure, and wording of your first draft. Discuss any necessary changes, additions, deletions, and corrections. Using the Checklist for Revising and Editing on page 153 as a guide, work together to revise the first draft. Complete as many revisions as needed.

E. When you are satisfied that your draft is the best work that your group can produce, choose someone to key the revised draft. Make a photocopy for every group member.

F. Carefully reread your revised draft. Using the Checklist for Proofreading on page 105, work together to prepare the final copy. Consult the Writer's Guide that begins on page A 80 to review key points of grammar, punctuation, and capitalization. Have each group member proofread the revised draft independently and use proofreaders' marks from the box on page 105 to mark corrections. Then compare corrections and incorporate all the changes on one draft.

PORTFOLIO

G. Have one group member key the final copy. Proofread the final copy as a group correct any keyboarding errors. Record the names of all group members on the final copy. Make a photocopy for every group member. Save your final copy in your portfolio.

Assignment 2:
Creating a Narrative Essay

In this assignment you will work independently to plan, write, edit, and proofread the narrative essay you began developing earlier in this chapter.

A. Review the planning you did in Activity B on pages 249-250, including your prewriting, thesis statement, and map or outline. Reread the freewriting you did on your topic.

Writing **FOCUS CHART**

B. Use your prewriting and the questions on the Writing Focus Chart on page 132 to guide you as you plan the first draft of the essay. Use any of the invention techniques you learned in Chapter 2 to develop the introduction, main ideas, supporting details, and conclusion. Also use any of the strategies from Chapter 5 to develop the content.

C. Write the first draft of your essay. Your first draft should consist of an introduction, a body, and a conclusion and should clearly accomplish your writing purpose. Review your draft and develop an appropriate title.

D. Share your draft with members of your group or with a peer editor. Use the comments and suggestions from your group or peer editor, in conjunction with the Checklist for Revising and Editing on page 153, to help you make revisions. After sharing essays, work independently to revise your draft.

E. Evaluate the content, structure, and wording of your essay. Using the Checklist for Revising and Editing as a guide, make any necessary changes, additions, deletions, and corrections. Make as many revisions as needed. When you are satisfied, key your revised draft.

F. Carefully reread your revised draft. Using the Checklist for Proofreading on page 105, prepare the final copy. Consult the Writer's Guide that begins on page A 80 to review key points of grammar, punctuation, and capitalization. Use proofreaders' marks from the box on page 105 to mark your corrections.

G. Key the final copy. Look over the final copy and correct any keyboarding errors. Save your final copy in your portfolio.

Assignment 3:
Reading as a Stimulus for Writing

In this assignment you will read a selection and then work independently to plan, write, edit, and proofread a narrative essay about a personal struggle to gain recognition from a family member or an authority figure.

A. Read "Only Daughter" by Sandra Cisneros on pages A 124–A 127. In this essay Cisneros recounts her efforts to gain her father's attention and approval.

B. Use the selection as a stimulus for writing a narrative essay. For example, you might recount an incident in which you had to compete with a brother or sister for a parent's attention. You might narrate a childhood experience in which you felt isolated or ignored by a teacher, family member, or friend. You might relate an experience in which you felt "invisible" because of your sex or race. Here are a few questions to start you thinking.

- How does Cisneros tell what happened between her and her father? What incidents, details, and dialogue does she include? How does this information help convey her experience?

- Is there a person whose attention and approval you have longed for? Who is this person and what is he or she like? Why is this person's approval important to you?

- When Cisneros's father reads her story and asks for copies, she says the moment was "the most wonderful" thing that happened to her that year. Why is she so happy? Have you ever had a similar experience?

Use your responses to the preceding questions to help you select a specific topic and generate a thesis statement. Freewrite for approximately ten or fifteen minutes on the topic you select.

C. Share your ideas with members of your group or with a peer editor. Discuss the topic you are considering for your essay. Ask for constructive advice about the topic. Also discuss any problem areas that you foresee.

D. Use your prewriting and the questions on the Writing Focus Chart on page 132 to guide you as you write your first draft. Decide on an appropriate pronoun and tense. Use any of the invention techniques from Chapter 2 and any of the strategies from Chapter 5 as needed to generate ideas and develop content. Your first draft should consist of an introduction, a body, and a conclusion and should should clearly accomplish your writing purpose. Review your draft and develop an appropriate title.

E. Share your draft with members of your group or with a peer editor. Use the comments and suggestions from your group or peer editor, in conjunction with the Checklist for Revising and Editing on page 153, to help you make revisions. After sharing essays, work independently to revise your draft.

F. Evaluate the content, structure, and wording of your draft. Using the Checklist for Revising and Editing as a guide, make any necessary changes, additions, deletions, and corrections. Make as many revisions as needed. When you are satisfied, key your revised draft.

G. Carefully reread your revised draft. Using the Checklist for Proofreading on page 105, prepare the final copy. Consult the Writer's Guide that begins on page A 80 to review key points of grammar, punctuation, and capitalization. Use proofreaders' marks from the box on page 105 to mark your corrections.

H. Key the final copy. Look over the final copy and correct any keyboarding errors. Save your final copy in your portfolio.

Grammar Gremlins

A **pronoun** is a word such as *I, me, my, he, she,* it, *her, him, his, they, them,* or *their* that stands for a noun. The word for which the pronoun stands is called its **antecedent**. Remember: A pronoun must agree with its antecedent in number, gender, and person.

CORRECT:

Even though the *kayak* was developed thousands of years ago, *it* is still a popular boat today.

In the sentence above, the pronoun *it* stands for the noun *kayak*. Therefore, *kayak* is the pronoun's antecedent.

INCORRECT:

Rhys, who was late, and *Charlie* got *his* coats off the rack.

The two nouns in this sentence are singular, but they are joined by *and* to create the equivalent of a plural. A plural pronoun is needed.

CORRECT:

Rhys, who was late, and *Charlie* got *their* coats off the rack.

INCORRECT:

Mimi or *Marcia* will play *their* composition for the judges.
The twins or *Pat* will take *her* mother to dinner.

The words *or* and *nor* indicate that one subject or the other, but not both, will do something. In the first example above, either girl, not both, will play a composition. If *or* or *nor* comes between two singular nouns, the pronoun should be singular. If *or* or *nor* comes between a singular and a plural noun, as in the second example, the pronoun agrees with the nearest noun. Since a singular pronoun can sound awkward in such a case, however, it is best to change the order of the nouns in the sentence so that the plural noun is the one nearest the verb.

CORRECT:

Mimi or *Marcia* will play *her* composition for the judges.
Pat or *the twins* will take *their* mother to dinner.

INCORRECT:

Those *jumping beans* surprise the customers. We must move *them.*

Be very sure your pronouns refer to the correct antecedents. In this example, *them* should refer to *jumping beans*, but the word order makes *customers* the antecedent. Changing or reordering words will help here.

CORRECT:

The customers are surprised by those *jumping beans.* We must move *them.*

Those *jumping beans* surprise the customers. We must move the *beans.*

INCORRECT:

Nils runs a coffee shop. He often works twelve-hour days. "*It* is my lifeline—*it's* filling me with purpose," he says.

Avoid using pronouns that float without antecedents. In this sentence group, the pronoun *it* and the contraction *it's* don't refer to anything nearby. Reword to provide a clear antecedent.

CORRECT:

"The *coffee shop* is my lifeline—*it's* filling me with purpose," he says.

INCORRECT:

Everybody will find *their* special place in the workforce.

Indefinite pronouns like *everyone, somebody,* and *no one* are treated as singular words and require a singular pronoun. If the result sounds awkward, you can reword the sentence.

CORRECT:

Everybody will find *his or her* special place in the workforce.

Activities

A. In each group of sentences, one pronoun does not agree with its antecedent. Circle the pronoun. Then rewrite the sentence to be correct. You may reword the sentence as shown in the example.

Example: No one remarked that their stomachs hurt after the meal.
Rewrite: None of the diners remarked that their stomachs hurt after the meal.

1. Knitting dates back before the second century A.D. No one knows when it was invented, but ~~they~~ *Everyone* suspect~~s~~ it may have begun as a way to make fishing nets and sleeping mats.

   No one knows when knitting was invented, but they suspect that it may have begun as a way to make fishing nets and sleeping mats.

2. Whatever, its origin, knitting became very important in the textile industry. Knitters and weavers competed for ~~his or her~~ *their* customers in Europe during the Middle Ages.

   _____

   _____

3. In some parts of the world today, boys and girls learn to knit in school. It is still considered by many to be a necessary life skill.

   Knitting

   _____

   _____

   B. Read the following paragraph. Eliminate any incorrect antecedents. Either change the pronoun or reword the sentence to make it correct.

   As a child, when I opened the newspaper, I read the comics first. The news pages depressed me because ~~it~~ *they* had many articles about war, crime, and famine. ~~The comic strips supplied humor and happy endings.~~ Often at breakfast my brother or my father would read ~~their~~ *his* favorite comic strips aloud. Mom and I laughed when they did funny voices for the characters. ~~It~~ *The voices* gave all of us a lift before we faced the day. Everybody has ~~their~~ *his or her* favorite newspaper section; mine will always be the comics.

   C. For additional practice in working with pronouns and antecedents, see page A 72.

WRAPPING IT UP

SUMMARY

- Use a narrative essay to give a vivid account of an event or experience. Select key facts, sensory details, and dialogue to re-create what took place.

- The purpose of a narrative essay can be to narrate, to inform, or to persuade. The central point may be stated or implied.

- Most narrative essays are structured in chronological order, with events presented in the order that they happen.

- Use consistent pronouns and verb tenses throughout the narrative to maintain a consistent relationship to the event or experience.

THINKING IT OVER

- How is narration important in daily life?

  _____

  _____

- How can narration help you share your life experiences in conversations and in writing?

  _____

  _____

IN YOUR JOURNAL

Review the goals that you set at the beginning of this chapter. In your journal, evaluate your progress toward these goals. Revise or add to your goals as appropriate.

Writing to Inform and to Persuade

In your life, you have probably needed to inform or to persuade people of many things. You might have explained to a friend how to care for your pet while you were away. You might have needed to persuade someone to accept you as a roommate in an off-campus apartment. Knowing how to inform or to persuade effectively can help you take charge of your essay writing too. Once you have those basic skills, you can apply them in your essays.

Section 4 explains seven strategies by which to develop essays that inform or persuade. Chapter 8 explores how to use examples to illustrate or explain a point. Chapter 9 deals with how to describe a process effectively. In Chapter 10 you will learn how to use cause and effect analysis. Chapter 11 handles how to use the compare/contrast strategy. Chapter 12 deals with how to use classification. Chapter 13 explains how to define a word or term. Chapter 14 offers guidelines for arguing for or against an issue or convincing readers to take a specific action.

8

USING
EXAMPLES

OBJECTIVES:

Composition

- To explore similarities between examples used in speech and in writing.

- To use examples to develop essay content.

- To develop examples with facts, incidents, and specific details.

- To create and revise essays that use examples.

Grammar

- To identify regular verbs and use the correct forms.

How Do I Show You Through Examples?

The man in the picture is being interviewed for a job. When asked about his qualifications and skills, he will give several examples to show that his education and work experience qualify him for the position.

Every day, we use examples to show what we mean, and we ask others to give us examples so we can understand what they mean. Examples can clarify a point or supply proof for a general statement.

Examples are also a common way of developing essay content. In this chapter you will learn how to develop essays that use one or more examples to illustrate a central point.

People give examples to clarify what they're saying or to illustrate a point. Cassandra uses an example to illustrate a math formula to a classmate. Leonard cites incidents of vandalism of synagogues and attacks on members of racial minorities to convince his neighbors that Nazism is on the rise again in some parts of Europe. In each case examples are the primary source of information.

List specific instances when you used examples to illustrate a general point. Also tell what examples you used.

- With friends or relatives:

  _____

  _____

- At work:

  _____

  _____

- At school:

  _____

  _____

For *one* of the examples you listed, consider these questions:

- Why did you give examples?
- How thoroughly did you develop your examples?
- How did your audience respond to your examples?

IN YOUR JOURNAL

Evaluate your ability to use examples orally and in writing. Then set one or more goals in your journal. Here are some examples:

GOALS:

1. When I use examples to explain a central point, I will develop each example fully.
2. I will select only examples that relate to the point I'm making.

GROUP ACTIVITY

If you wanted to supply specific details to make a general statement clearer, what details would you use?

A. Each member of your group should choose a topic for which examples can be given to illustrate a point. Consider illustrating a point about child-rearing, marriage, sports and recreation activities, your work, your neighborhood, or your college classes.

B. Each member of the group should take turns presenting examples to make a point orally to the group.

C. Work together to assess how effective each group member's examples were in making the point. Identify features that make examples clear, logical, and useful.

D. Work with your group to create a list of five or more specific guidelines to evaluate the effectiveness of examples used to support a point.

E. Evaluate the guidelines your group developed. Work together to improve them. Then write the revised guidelines in the following space.

_____

_____

_____

_____

_____

_____

_____

_____

_____

_____

_____

Giving Examples

Features of Examples

Good writers often illustrate a central point by means of one or more **examples**. Examples can be brief, extended, or a combination of both, depending on the writer's purpose and audience.

Writers often use examples to hook a reader's attention. A concrete example almost always has more impact than a simple statement. An example can bring an idea to life and convince readers of the believability of the idea.

Sometimes one extended example can be used to illustrate a thesis statement. Suppose you state in an essay that white-water rafting is an exciting sport that brings people close to nature. Since readers may not know what white-water rafting is like, a single, extended example narrating a rafting trip will give substance to your point and clarify readers' understanding.

In some situations, one example may not be sufficient to support a thesis statement. Suppose you state in an essay that hairstyles and clothing styles from the past often come back into fashion. Citing just one example of an old fashion that has become all the rage again will not support such a general point. You will need to provide several examples to illustrate your central point.

The approach you choose in developing examples in an essay will depend on your topic, your purpose for writing, your thesis statement, and your audience.

Giving Examples from Personal Observations or Experience

Examples can include narrative incidents and descriptive facts or details that come from your own observations and experience. For example, suppose you plan an essay stating that getting a job with just a high school diploma is difficult. You may know this because you spent a year after high school applying for jobs that paid a decent wage before landing a job. You may also have observed friends who had the same problem. This information will provide useful details to support your central point.

Use specific details to develop examples based on experience or observation. Vague, blanket statements such as "I know that getting a job without a college degree is hard because that's what happened to me" make ineffective examples. To reach readers, examples must be detailed, vivid, and well developed.

GIVING EXAMPLES FROM OUTSIDE SOURCES

Examples can include specific information such as quotations, facts, statistics, or accounts gathered from sources such as books, newspapers, and magazines. You may recall something you read or heard about that would make an appropriate example to illustrate the central point of your essay. In such a case, track down the example to make sure you use it accurately. This may mean finding a book of quotations, looking through magazines, or even conducting an interview. Information that can be verified provides convincing examples. For instance, if you decide to include examples from outside sources to illustrate an essay about the difficulties of getting a good job with only a high school diploma, you could use any of the following approaches:

- Present a quotation that you read in a newspaper or magazine.
- Give facts about qualifications for various jobs with local businesses; get these facts from classified ads or by questioning people at local businesses.
- Cite statistics showing unemployment rates among college graduates in contrast to unemployment rates among people with just a high school diploma.
- Interview people you know about their job-hunting experiences; cite material from these interviews.

Whenever you use information from outside sources, be sure to present this information accurately and to cite the source of the information. You will learn more about researching and presenting information from outside sources in Enrichment Chapter E.

GIVING HYPOTHETICAL EXAMPLES

A **hypothetical example** is a situation or idea that may not actually exist but that could logically exist. Writers often give examples based on hypothetical situations to test or confirm the truth of an idea. Many hypothetical examples begin with the word *suppose*. For instance, a writer might say, "Suppose everyone in this country was required to spend a year in another country." The writer might then develop this hypothetical example to show how living in another culture could affect the way people would look at their own culture. Consider how using hypothetical examples would work in an essay about high school graduates and jobs. You could describe an imaginary situation in which a job hunter goes out on many interviews and finds that, while jobs are available, the ones open to those with only a high school diploma pay relatively lower wages.

DISCOVERY ACTIVITY

- Think of a recent situation in which you used an example to illustrate a point. Was this example from your own observations or experience, a fact from an outside source, or a hypothetical example? What made this example effective?

  _____

  _____

USING THE INTRODUCTION EFFECTIVELY

Because you may use several examples when developing an essay, you must ensure that all your examples work together to support and develop the central point. Use the introduction of the essay to show the relationship of all the examples to the central point and to preview the range of examples that you will use. You might accomplish this in one of the following ways:

- Make a statement that previews the examples covered in later paragraphs. You might make the statement "People who take the time to relax are often healthier and more energetic than people who give in to stress. Relaxation can be as simple as spending a few minutes sitting quietly in a darkened room or listening to music, or as elaborate as taking up a hobby." The body paragraphs might then give examples of each form of relaxation.

- Start with an anecdote that itself serves as an example of your central point. You might then make the statement: "This incident is one of many that proves how pets improve the quality of life for senior citizens." Such a statement alerts readers that further examples will support the same point as the opening example.
- Begin with a fact or statistic that is related to facts or statistics that you present as examples later in the essay.
- Open by asking a question that will be answered by examples you supply in the body paragraphs.

USING TRANSITIONS TO LINK EXAMPLES

WRITER'S TIP

When giving examples in an essay, use transitional words and phrases to emphasize the connection between examples in a paragraph. Transitions can also connect an example more closely to the central point. Use transitions such as *for example*, *another*, *by contrast*, and *in conclusion* to signal that a new example is beginning, to point out examples that may contradict each other, or to signal that a conclusion will be presented. Consult the chart in Chapter 5, page 193, for additional transitional words and phrases that can be used to link examples in an essay.

UNDERSTANDING WRITING TASKS THAT REQUIRE EXAMPLES

Probably the most common writing tasks are ones that involve giving examples. Among your class assignments may be ones such as these that direct you to give examples:

- *Demonstrat*e your understanding of "dramatic irony" by giving an *example* from everyday life.
- *By means of a clear, well-developed example,* clarify what Freud means when he talks about "the unconscious influence on conscious life."

Many job-related writing tasks also require responses based on examples, including the following:

- On a job application, *illustrate examples* of your previous work experience.

- In a memo, *list three examples* of how production on the assembly line can be improved.

Sometimes it is difficult to detect when you are being asked to provide examples. Clue words such as *show, show specific instances, illustrate, give concrete reasons, support your claim, cite,* or *clarify* let you know that your response should contain examples.

Activity A: Finding Example Clue Words

Underline the clue words that ask for examples in the following directions.

- Cite the consequences of the changed schedule for city garbage collection.
- Give concrete reasons that show why the penalties for driving under the influence should be strengthened.
- Illustrate how Vietnam veterans were largely ignored by American society when they returned home.
- Show how communication styles can influence job performance.

FIRST DRAFT: PLANNING AND WRITING ESSAYS THAT USE EXAMPLES

The Writing Focus Chart on page 132 can guide you in blending the key elements of writing to create interesting and effective essays that make use of examples. Use the questions on the chart as you consider your purpose, content, structure, audience, and tone.

CHOOSING A TOPIC

Select a topic that you already know about through personal experience and observations or a topic you can get information about through reading and research in the library. For instance, you could write about "Quirky Personalities in My Family" without leaving your own living room. On the other hand, to write authoritatively about a topic such as "The New Hi-Tech Household," you would need to read books or articles to inform yourself on the topic.

Once you select a topic, find a focus that will narrow your topic to manageable proportions. A topic that is too broad will be difficult to illustrate even with powerful and vivid examples.

ESTABLISHING THE WRITING PURPOSE

Once you have chosen a topic, establish your writing purpose. The purpose of essays that use examples is usually either to inform or to persuade. If your purpose is to inform, you might supply examples to clarify your point or increase readers' understanding of a difficult or unfamiliar concept. If your purpose is to persuade, you might use examples to prove a statement you make or to convince people of the urgency of your argument.

WRITING A THESIS STATEMENT

After you have generated some ideas, become familiar with your topic, and established your writing purpose, write a thesis statement. The thesis statement will help you develop and structure your essay.

In essays that use examples, the thesis statement should do one or more of the following:

- State the central point you will discuss.
- Clarify the purpose of your essay.
- Present your perspective on the topic.

The following sentences are examples of thesis statements for essays that use examples:

> San Francisco offers terrific vacation possibilities for people of all ages with activities that appeal to every taste.
> Keeping your sense of humor can help you deal with almost any challenge or obstacle you'll face during an ordinary day.

The thesis statement should clearly indicate *why* the examples are being introduced. Writing a thesis statement will also help you generate appropriate examples.

DEVELOPING THE CONTENT

Once you determine a topic and a central point for your essay, begin developing your examples. Use examples that are *representative*—typical rather than highly unusual or uncommon—and *relevant* to your thesis statement—supportive of the central point you make.

For instance, if your thesis statement says "Underage drinkers create a serious problem in our community," your examples wouldn't be representative if they were based on the behavior of just one or two drinkers. Likewise, discussing the behavior of adult drinkers at home would not be relevant.

As you learned earlier in the chapter, you can use several sources for your examples, including the following:

- Personal observations and experience
- Outside sources including newspapers, magazines, books, and encyclopedias
- Hypothetical situations or ideas

You can combine several of these types of examples. You might begin with an example from your personal experience and back up your experience with facts or statistics from a newspaper article. You might instead present a hypothetical example and then show how, from your observations, this situation occurs often in real life.

IN YOUR JOURNAL

Think of a situation in which you could explain something by means of a hypothetical example. How would you present this hypothetical example? How would you connect it to what you are explaining? Write a brief paragraph that presents your hypothetical example. Include one or more sentences that connect the hypothetical example to the topic it is meant to illustrate.

PLANNING THE STRUCTURE

Examples are usually presented in the body paragraphs of an essay, though you can also use an example to create an effective introduction. Any of the three basic methods of organization—chronological order, spatial order, or order of importance or interest—can be used, as shown in the following examples.

- *Chronological order:* In a job application, you might illustrate your trustworthiness by giving three examples of your behavior in time order, starting with the earliest example.

- *Spatial order:* To make a point about the style of the painter Vincent Van Gogh, you might use as your example one of his paintings, describing the details in the painting as they appear from left to right.

- *Order of importance or interest:* You can use ascending order or descending order of importance or interest to present examples. To present instances of great upset victories in sports, you might begin with an upset victory by a local team and build to an example such as the United States victory in ice hockey at the 1980 Winter Olympics. A variation of order of importance or interest is to arrange your examples from least to most difficult or from least to most controversial.

Read the following essay, "The Doubt That Haunts." As you read, underline the first sentence of each example.

The Doubt That Haunts

When most people are asked to produce something creative, they freeze. They panic. They choke. They seize up with self-doubt. "Creativity?" they say. "Not me!" If you disbelieve this statement, consider how often you try new things in your life. How readily do you try something creative, such as writing, drawing, or singing? Most of us believe we can't create and have believed it for so long that the belief has become reality. People possess a large capacity for self-doubt about their creative ability in terms of writing, drawing, and music.

Writing offers a classic example. About 90 percent of adults believe they cannot write, although nearly all young children believe they can write. Self-doubt seems to creep in as we grow older. I witnessed this last year in a college writing class when the instructor asked students if they ever wrote outside of school. One student raised his hand. When the instructor asked how many students thought of themselves as writers, no students—zero out of twenty—raised a hand. By contrast, my daughter's first grade teacher had asked her students the same questions and received quite different responses. Did any first graders write outside of school? Twenty out of twenty-two hands shot up. Did any first graders think of themselves as writers? Twenty-two out of twenty-two hands went up. Plainly, adults are more self-conscious about their creativity than children are.

Drawing is another creative ability that many adults doubt they have. For instance, at a recent family party I suggested we play "Pictionary," which involves drawing clues for secret words. "Absolutely not!" my family said. "We can't draw." The interesting part, however, is that we played "Pictionary" and had a wonderful time with some very creative drawings. This experience showed me that people often doubt they can be creative because they haven't tried.

Self-doubt about musical ability is also common. For example, at sporting events where "The Star-Spangled Banner" is sung, many people just mouth or whisper the words, even though in such a crowd their individual voices would not be heard. Recently, however, I was at a football game when the electricity failed and the tape-recorded national anthem could not be played. The crowd sang without accompaniment and sounded pretty good. Everyone I talked to afterwards admitted to enjoying singing very much, but nearly all of them were convinced that they couldn't "carry a tune in a bucket." I concluded that many people doubt they can be creative because they fear the results will not be perfect.

Self-doubt about creativity in areas such as writing, drawing, or music seems nearly universal among adults. It seems probable, however, that almost all adults have the capacity for creativity in those areas. What keeps people from being creative? I have observed that people are afraid of looking inept, so they hesitate to try creative things. If people would learn to do things to please themselves rather than to please others, maybe their doubts would disappear.

Questions

1. What is the central point of this essay?

_____

_____

2. According to the writer, what are some obvious examples of creative self-doubt?

Writing, drawing and music

3. How does the writer achieve unity in the essay? Be specific.

Every paragraph is Support the central point. Removing unnecessary details and joining necessary details

4. The writer presents several brief examples of creative self-doubt. How is this structure effective?

TARGETING A SPECIFIC AUDIENCE

When writing an essay that uses examples, consider two things about your audience's viewpoint: (1) what kinds of examples will likely "hook" their interest, and (2) what knowledge are they likely to have about the subject. For instance, an essay addressing how college students relieve stress during final exams will have a better chance of hooking readers if it shows *unusual* examples of how students relieve stress (midnight swims in the campus pool, or sitting on ice) rather than more common forms of stress reduction (going to bed early, consuming less caffeine). By analyzing what interests and appeals to your audience, you will have a better chance of reaching that audience.

The writer of "The Doubt That Haunts" had a general audience in mind: people who are reluctant to be creative. The writer wanted those readers to think about what they are missing. In order to do that, the writer gave clear and detailed examples that show how people are plagued with unnecessary and unreasonable doubts about their creativity. If "The Doubt That Haunts" was written for young readers aged ten to twelve, how might the writer have changed the content and wording of the essay?

SETTING THE TONE

The tone of an essay that uses examples should be consistent with the topic. If you are writing about a topic such as child abuse, a serious tone would be appropriate. On the other hand, if you were writing about a lighter subject, such as how the postage stamps you use reflect your mood on the day you are mailing a particular letter, a humorous tone would be more appropriate.

As you consider the tone and language of your examples, eliminate vague words and phrases and replace them with precise, concrete, and authoritative language.

Questions

1. How do the opening sentences of "The Doubt That Haunts" on pages 275-276 establish the tone of the essay? Be specific.

_____

_____

2. In "The Doubt That Haunts," what is the writer's attitude toward people's self-doubt about their creativity? Describe specific instances where the writer reveals this attitude.

_____

_____

_____

_____

**DO YOU WRITE
ON A COMPUTER?**

The advantage of "clean erasing" that a word processor's delete function offers can cause problems. When you delete words, those words are often gone. For this reason, many people create an outtakes file in which they dump copy that they delete from their screen. Create an outtakes file for saving copy you delete but may want to use again. Then, instead of using the delete function, block the material and move it into this outtakes file. If you change your mind and want to use that copy, move it back into your essay.

Activity B: Planning an Essay That Uses Examples

In this activity you will plan the purpose, content, structure, audience, and tone for an essay that uses examples. Refer to the Writing Focus Chart on page 132 for help in addressing these five key elements. Use separate sheets of paper for your work.

A. Narrow one of the following general topics for an essay:

- Problems on your college campus
- Issues in professional sports
- Annoying salespeople
- Telephone manners

For instance, if you select the general topic "Issues in professional sports," you could narrow the topic to focus on whether professional athletes should be allowed to compete in the Olympic Games, and develop the essay with clear examples.

B. Once you have selected and narrowed a topic, establish your writing purpose. Freewrite for ten to fifteen minutes about your topic. Explore as many ideas, facts, descriptive details, and narrative incidents as you can. Your goal is to generate an *abundance* of examples and details.

C. Based on your prewriting, write a thesis statement.

D. Use questioning to help you generate examples. Write at least three questions relating to your topic. Your questions should point you toward examples from your experience or from other sources. Create a list of examples to support your thesis statement. Eliminate examples that don't seem relevant.

E. Based on your prewriting, decide how you want to structure your essay. Determine whether you will use chronological order, spatial order, or order of importance or interest. Prepare a conceptual map or an outline that includes the examples you will use to support your thesis statement. Include any additional details that further support your examples.

F. Target a specific audience for your essay. Consider which of the examples you have generated will most appeal to this audience and hook their interest. After considering your intended audi-

PORTFOLIO

ence, decide what tone is most appropriate for your topic and writing purpose.

Save your work in your portfolio. You will use your prewriting to develop an essay in Assignment 2 on pages 285-286.

REVISING, EDITING, AND PROOFREADING ESSAYS THAT USE EXAMPLES

The Checklist for Revising and Editing on page 153 can guide you in evaluating and revising the first draft of essays that use examples. The Checklist for Proofreading on page 105 can help you turn a revised draft into a final copy.

Read the following revised draft of an essay that uses examples, which includes the writer's handwritten revisions. Remember that at this point the writer has not yet corrected errors in grammar, spelling, punctuation, and capitalization. What changes did the writer make to improve the essay?

Revised Draft: **The Sound of Where I Live**

The place where I live is like the middle of a never-end-

ing concert. Morning, afternoon, and evening, the noise ~rock and roll~

never stops. If I shout loudly enough, maybe you can here

me: IT IS NOISY WHERE I LIVE.

The noise begins early. There's an opra singer who ~On the apartment next to mine,~

practices from 9 A.M. to 12 noon every day. I've listened to ~He sings vocal exercises and bellows out songs in a~ ~huge voice.~

him hit the high notes (hes a tenor) and almost thought I

saw the window glass rattle. MY NEIGHBOR THE OPRA

SINGER SINGS LOUDLY. ~Need I say more?~

~When the singer finishes at noon,~

Then the guy above me starts. He's a boxer who skips ~for an hour and a half.~

rope every day. It builds his quickness and his stamina, he

says. All I know is the sound of thump-thump, thump-

thump as it thump-thumps across my ceiling. ~~If there's a~~ ~~rhythm I could live without, it's the rhythm of thump-~~ ~~thump~~ then he ~~hits~~ punches his speed bag, also loudly. This bracka-bracka-bracka-brack, bracka-bracka-bracka-brack sound could make anyone think that a tap dancer is rehearsing, overhead.

When the boxer quits. The fireworks really start. Usually it is 5 P.M. when the girl who lives in the apartment on the other side of me gets up. That's right. My jazz drummer neighbor *starts* her day at 5 P.M., practicing for a couple of hours to get herself limber for the evening gig ("loosen the chops," she calls it). Jazz people work until the sun comes up six nights a week and sleep all day. Then they try to breathe some life into their bones for another all-night jam.

While the drummer is ~~drumming~~ thundering away, the two kids across the hall are coming home from after-school activitys. They sound like a herd of stampeding buffalo. If the kids have had a bad day, they're usually arguing with each other at full voice. If they've had a good day, they're shrieking with laughter.

A lot of people would hate living in such a building, but not me. You see, Im a college student. Hearing all the bustle and noise in my building gives me a taste of the outside world. For a large part of every day I sit at my desk, studying and writing. The noise provided by my neighbors makes me realize that Im not the only person in the universe.

On pages 282-284 of this chapter you'll see a rekeyed version of "The Sound of Where I Live" that incorporates the writer's handwritten revisions. You'll use that version to proofread the essay for errors in spelling, punctuation, and so on.

Questions

1. How has the writer improved the effectiveness of this essay? Be specific.

_____

_____

2. Why did the writer delete the last sentence in the second paragraph of the essay?

_____ *unnecessary sentence* _____

_____

3. Why did the writer move the sentence in the last paragraph?

_____ *To make the order correct* _____

_____

4. What transitions did the writer add to create a smooth flow from one detail to the next?

_____ *after, while, then, when* _____

_____

5. If you were the writer of this essay, what additional revisions would you make in content, structure, and wording?

_____

_____

Read the revised and rekeyed draft of "The Sound of Where I Live" that follows. Proofread the revision, and correct any mistakes in spelling, capitalization, and punctuation as well as any factual, keyboarding, and grammatical errors.

Revised and Rekeyed Draft:

The Sound of Where I Live

The place where I live is like the middle of a never-ending rock and roll concert. Morning, afternoon, and evening, the noise never stops. If I shout loudly enough, maybe you can here me: IT IS NOISY WHERE I LIVE.

The noise begins early. In the apartment next to mine, there's an opra singer who practices from 9 A.M. to 12 noon every day. He sings vocal exercises and bellows out songs in a huge voice. I've listened to him hit the high notes (hes a tenor) and almost thought I saw the window glass rattle. MY NEIGHBOR THE OPRA SINGER SINGS LOUDLY.

When the singer finishes at noon, the guy above me starts. He's a boxer who skips rope every day for an hour and a half. It builds his quickness and his stamina, he says. All I know is the sound of thump-thump, thump-thump as it thump-thumps across my ceiling. then he punches his speed bag, also loudly. This bracka-bracka-bracka-brack, bracka-bracka-bracka-brack sound could make anyone think that a tap dancer is rehearsing overhead.

When the boxer quits. The fireworks really start. Usually it is 5 P.M. when the girl who lives in the apartment on the other side of me gets up. That's right. My jazz drummer neighbor *starts* her day at 5 P.M., practicing for a couple of hours to get herself limber for the evening gig ("loosen the chops," she calls it). Jazz people work until the sun comes up six nights a week and sleep all day. Then they try to breathe some life into their bones for another all-night jam.

While the drummer is thundering away, the two kids across the hall are coming home from after-school activitys. They sound like a herd of stampeding buffalo. If the kids have had a bad day, they're usually arguing with each other at full voice. If they've had a good day, they're shrieking with laughter.

A lot of people would hate living in such a building, but not me. You see, Im a college student. For a large part of every day I sit at my desk, studying and writing.

Hearing all the bustle and noise in my building gives me a taste of the outside world. The noise provided by my neighbors makes me realize that Im not the only person in the universe.

Assignment 1:
Creating an Essay That Uses Examples With Your Group

In this assignment you will work with your group to plan, write, edit, and proofread an essay that uses examples.

A. Choose a topic suitable for a collaboratively written essay. Work together to narrow the topic and brainstorm examples and illustrations. Decide whether you will use examples from your own observations and experience, examples from outside sources, hypothetical examples, or a combination of examples.

B. Working as a group, use the questions on the Writing Focus Chart on page 132 to guide you as you plan the first draft. Use any of the invention techniques you learned in Chapter 2 to develop the thesis statement, introduction, main ideas, supporting examples, and conclusion. Also use any of the strategies from Chapter 5 to develop content.

C. Use your group's prewriting to write the first draft. Your first draft should consist of an introduction, a body, and a conclusion and should clearly accomplish your writing purpose. Review the draft and work together to develop an appropriate title.

D. Carefully reread and evaluate the content, structure, and wording of your first draft. Discuss any necessary changes, additions, deletions, and corrections. Using the Checklist for Revising and Editing on page 153 as a guide, work together to revise the first draft. Complete as many revisions as needed.

E. When you are satisfied that your draft is the best work that your group can produce, choose someone to key the revised draft. Make a photocopy for every group member.

F. Carefully reread your revised draft. Using the Checklist for Proofreading on page 105, work together to prepare the final copy. Consult the Writer's Guide that begins on page A 80 to review key points of grammar, punctuation, and capitalization. Have each group member proofread the revised draft independently and use proofreaders' marks from the box on page 105 to mark corrections. Then compare corrections and incorporate all the changes on one draft.

PORTFOLIO

G. Have one group member key the final copy. Proofread the final copy as a group and correct any keyboarding errors. Record the names of all group members on the final copy. Make a photocopy for every group member. Save your final copy in your portfolio.

Assignment 2:
Creating an Essay That Uses Examples

In this assignment you will work independently to plan, write, edit, and proofread the essay you began developing earlier in this chapter.

A. Review the planning you did in Activity B on pages 279-280, including your prewriting, thesis statement, and outline. Reread the freewriting you did on your topic.

Writing FOCUS CHART

B. Use your prewriting and the questions on the Writing Focus Chart on page 132 to guide you as you plan the first draft of the essay. Use any of the invention techniques you learned in Chapter 2 to develop the introduction, main ideas, supporting details, and conclusion. Also use any of the strategies from Chapter 5 to develop the content.

C. Write the first draft of your essay. Your first draft should consist of an introduction, a body, and a conclusion and should clearly accomplish your writing purpose. Review your draft and develop an appropriate title.

D. Share your draft with members of your group or with a peer editor. Use the comments and suggestions from the group or peer editor, in conjunction with the Checklist for Revising and Editing on page 153, to help you make revisions. After sharing essays, work independently to revise your draft.

E. Evaluate the content, structure, and wording of your essay. Using the Checklist for Revising and Editing as a guide, make any necessary changes, additions, deletions, and corrections. Make as many revisions as needed. When you are satisfied, key your revised draft.

PORTFOLIO

F. Carefully reread your revised draft. Using the Checklist for Proofreading on page 105, prepare the final copy. Consult the Writer's Guide that begins on page A 80 to review key points of grammar, punctuation, and capitalization. Use proofreaders' marks from the box on page 105 to mark your corrections.

G. Key the final copy. Look over the final copy and correct any keyboarding errors. Save your final copy in your portfolio.

Assignment 3:
Reading as a Stimulus for Writing

In this assignment you will read a selection and then work independently to plan, write, edit, and proofread an essay that uses examples to support a central point.

A. Read "Introductions to New York" by Bob Blaisdell on pages A 127-A 128. In this news article, Blaisdell uses examples to make two very strong points about his subject, life in New York City.

B. Use the selection as a stimulus for an essay about the community where you live. For instance, consider the most dominant impressions that you and many others in your community have experienced. Consider people's attitudes or the specific behaviors they exhibit that strike you as characteristic. Focus on concrete examples—things that people typically say or value. Here are several questions to start you thinking.

- What is the dominant impression of New York City conveyed by Blaisdell's selection?
- What details from the selection best explain that dominant impression?
- Have you had experiences in your community that left a strong impression on you? What were they?
- Can you link your experiences to those that other people in your community might also have had? How?

Use your responses to the preceding questions to help you decide on a specific topic and generate a thesis statement. Freewrite for approximately ten or fifteen minutes on the topic you select.

C. Share your ideas with members of your group or with a peer editor. Discuss the topic you are considering for your essay. Ask for constructive advice about the topic. Also discuss any problem areas that you foresee.

D. Use your prewriting and the questions on the Writing Focus Chart on page 132 to guide you as you write your first draft. Decide what examples you will use to support your central point. Use any of the invention techniques from Chapter 2 and any of the strategies from Chapter 5 as needed. Your first draft should consist of an introduction, a body, and a conclusion and should clearly accomplish your writing purpose. Review your draft and develop an appropriate title.

E. Share your draft with your group or with a peer editor. Use the comments and suggestions from the group or peer editor, in conjunction with the Checklist for Revising and Editing on page 153, to help you make revisions. After sharing essays, work independently to revise your draft.

F. Evaluate the content, structure, and wording of your draft. Using the Checklist for Revising and Editing as a guide, make any necessary changes, additions, deletions, and corrections. Make as many revisions as needed. When you are satisfied, key your revised draft.

G. Carefully reread your revised draft. Using the Checklist for Proofreading on page 105, prepare the final copy. Consult the Writer's Guide that begins on page A 80 to review key points of grammar, punctuation, and capitalization. Use proofreaders' marks from the box on page 105 to mark your corrections.

H. Key the final copy. Look over the final copy and correct any keyboarding errors. Save your final copy in your portfolio.

USING REGULAR VERBS

Grammar Gremlins

The **tense** of a verb indicates the time in which the action takes place. Verbs have four principal forms on which all tenses are based: the present, the past, the past participle, and the present participle.

Form the past tense and the past participle of regular verbs by adding -*ed* or -*d* to the present form. Watch for spelling changes, such as *y* changing to *i*. When in doubt, check a dictionary.

Present Tense:
Manuel loves horses.
Teri washes her car once a month.
In order to grow, plants need nutrients.

Past Tense:
Manuel loved horses until one bit him.
After the class Teri washed her car.
Tyler needed to buy some new shirts.

Past Participle:
Manuel has loved many horses, but only one bit him.
We have carried the groceries to the car.
Teri had washed her car before dinner.

Notice that the past participle is used with a **helping verb** such as *has*, *have*, or *had*.

Form the present participle of regular verbs by adding -*ing* and using the helping verb *am*, *is*, or *are*.

Present Participle:
I am becoming more skeptical of advertising claims.
We are stacking the plates in the sink.

Activities

A. Complete each sentence by filling in the blanks with the appropriate form of the verb in parentheses.

1. This morning I _____ (phone) my office and told them that I was _____ (stay) home with a cold.

2. After I hung up the phone, I _____ crawled (crawl) into bed and _____ (pull) the covers up to my chin.

3. I was _____ (shiver) with chills and _____ (cough) every few seconds.

4. When I get a cold, my throat _____ (burn), and anything I try to eat _____ (taste) like cardboard.

5. When I woke up from a nap, I _____ (look) out the window and _____ (noticed) that the sky was very blue and clear.

6. A bird was _____ (hop) on my windowsill, and the woman next door was _____ (walk) her dog.

7. As I blew my nose for the hundredth time, I _____ (moan) to myself about the bad luck that had _____ (cause) me to get sick on such a lovely day.

8. My friends who were _____ (work) were _____ (enjoy) more of this day than I was at home.

B. The paragraph below contains ten errors in verb forms. Identify the errors and correct them.

When I was born, my parents decide on a name for me right away. They were ready when the nurse walk into Mom's hospital room with the birth certificate. Mom and Dad announce they were call me Charlotte. The nurse praise Mom and Dad for choosing such a lovely name. Mom smile and said that she had pick the name from her favorite book, *Charlotte's Web*. Mom had always enjoy this book. In fact she was read the story to my older sister shortly before I was born. Mom love to tell that story. I wish she wouldn't tell anyone but family members, though. How would you like all your friends to know that you were named after a talking spider?

C. For additional practice in using regular verbs, see page A 74.

WRAPPING IT UP

SUMMARY

- Use examples in an essay to illustrate and support a point in an essay. Examples can be brief, extended, or a combination of the two.

- Examples may be based on personal observations or experience, drawn from outside sources such as newspapers or magazines, or based on hypothetical situations or ideas.

- Use appropriate transitional words and phrases to link examples in an essay.

- The purpose of an essay that uses examples is usually to inform or persuade.

- Structure the examples in an essay in one of three ways. Present the information in chronological order, spatial order, or order of importance or interest.

THINKING IT OVER

- Why is it important to use examples to support a point in daily life? Describe one or two of the most useful aspects of using examples that you learned in this chapter.

  _____

  _____

  _____

  _____

  _____

- How can the strategy of using examples to develop content help you in conversations and in writing?

_____

_____

_____

_____

- How will what you have learned in this chapter help you write essays that use examples at work and at school?

_____

_____

_____

_____

IN YOUR
JOURNAL

Review the goals that you set at the beginning of this chapter. In your journal, evaluate your progress toward these goals.

9

DESCRIBING A PROCESS

OBJECTIVES:

Composition

- To explore similarities between explanations of a process used in speech and in writing.

- To explain a process to develop essay content.

- To write essays that clearly explain how to do something or show how something happens.

- To create and revise essays that describe a process.

Grammar

- To use irregular verbs correctly.

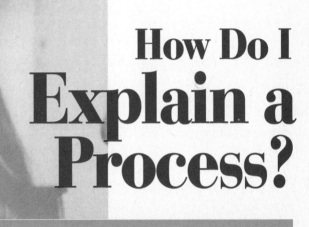

How Do I
Explain a
Process?

Suppose you wanted to learn how to use a camera. How would you do this? You would probably have a knowledgeable person show you how. For you to learn how to make or do something, you have to have a clear explanation of the process. A **process** presents a series of steps in a certain order that need to be followed for something to be done or a skill to be developed.

Situations that involve explanations based on a process are common in your life. You learn how to use a new computer software program, or you show someone how to drive with a stick shift. Describing or explaining a process is just one of the strategies you can use to develop essays. In this chapter you will learn how to develop writing that describes a process.

GETTING STARTED

Sara gives Richard directions on how to drive to the local stadium. Robert presents a report explaining how the human brain works. Sam teaches his son how to swim. These situations all involve explaining a process—how to do or make something, or how something works.

Recall times when you have used a process strategy. List specific instances in which you have presented the steps in a process.

- With friends or relatives:

  _____

  _____

- At work:

  _____

  _____

- At school:

  _____

  _____

For *one* example you listed, consider these questions:

- Why did you describe this process?
- How thoroughly did you develop your explanation?
- What were the strengths and weaknesses of your approach?
- What kinds of details, examples, or illustrations did you use?
- How did your audience respond to your explanation?

IN YOUR JOURNAL

Evaluate your ability to explain a process orally and in writing. Then set one or more goals in your journal. Here are some examples:

GOALS:
1. When I explain a process, I will present the steps in sequence.
2. When describing a process, I will be as exact as possible so that the reader can easily perform each step.

EXPLAINING A PROCESS ORALLY

GROUP ACTIVITY

If you were explaining how to do or make something, how would you go about it?

A. Each member of your group should select a process to describe. You might explain how to do or make something, give directions to a place, or describe how something works. Think about the process you are describing. What ideas, facts, or materials are needed to explain the process?

B. Each member of the group should take turns presenting a process orally to the group.

C. Work together to assess every explanation for effectiveness. Identify features that make the explanation of a process clear, logical, and useful.

D. Work with your group to create a list of five or more specific guidelines to evaluate the effectiveness of an explanation of a process.

E. Evaluate the guidelines your group developed. Work together to improve them. Then write the revised guidelines in the following space.

_____

_____

_____

_____

_____

_____

_____

_____

_____

_____

_____

_____

PRESENTING A PROCESS

FEATURES OF PROCESSES

Writing that describes a **process** explains how to do something or tells how something works. Examples of writing that describes a process include directions on how to assemble something, procedure manuals for a business, self-help articles, and textbooks.

Writing that presents a process usually is one of two basic types:

- A set of instructions that describes how to do something; examples include instructions for completing an income tax return or preparing an agenda for a meeting.

- An explanation of how something works; examples include an explanation of how whales sing or how orchids reproduce.

EXPLAINING HOW TO DO SOMETHING

If you are explaining a process that readers will complete themselves, the explanation must be clear enough for readers to complete the process successfully. To write clear and useful directions, you must understand the process well enough to complete it yourself. Because you need such detailed knowledge of the process, the best processes to write about are ones you are thoroughly familiar with from your experience. You may use outside sources to confirm details, but your best source of material is first-hand knowledge. An alternative is to interview an expert and have the expert demonstrate the process. For best results, however, you should try the process yourself under the expert's direction. Otherwise you might leave out important details in your essay.

EXPLAINING HOW SOMETHING WORKS

Although writing that describes how something works must be clear, a writer does not need to be an expert on the process from direct experience. For example, you may describe how whales sing without personally studying whales in the wild. Instead, you could depend on outside sources such as encyclopedias, books, or magazines. If you use outside sources, make sure these sources are clear and detailed. Also, you should use more than one source, in order to verify that you have identified all the steps in the process and that you have the clearest, most understandable explanation.

INCLUDING CLEAR EXPLANATIONS

Like a set of instructions, the explanation of a process must give readers a clear understanding of the steps involved, whether or not readers are to complete the process themselves. To write a clear explanation of a process, keep these tips in mind:

- Use precise language instead of vague phrases. The phrase "Take the back stairs near the water fountain and walk up two flights" is more precise than "Go up the stairs."
- Include all important details. For instance, if you're explaining how to wallpaper a room, be sure to include instructions on how to estimate how much wallpaper to buy. If you're explaining how electricity works, you may need to define terms such as *circuit* and *electron*.
- Use concise wording. Include only the information the reader needs to know to complete the process.
- Present all the steps in the process in the correct order.
- Give brief reasons for elements or steps of the process where necessary. Giving such reasons can often clarify the process.

To ensure that your explanation is clear, mentally go through the process yourself as you plan and write to make sure you recalled all the steps. When you are finished, read the essay as though you are someone who is unfamiliar with the process, or have a friend or classmate read the essay.

FOLLOWING CHRONOLOGICAL ORDER

Most processes are performed step by step in chronological order: step 1 is usually completed before step 2 is undertaken. An essay that describes a process should reflect the sequence in which the process is undertaken in order to make the procedure logical and easy for readers to understand.

USING TRANSITIONS TO LINK THE STEPS IN A PROCESS

WRITER'S TIP

When presenting a process, use transitional words and phrases such as *before you begin*, *first*, *next*, and *last* to link the steps in the process. Transitions can also point the reader to conclusions that can be drawn once a process has been completed. Consult the chart in Chapter 5, page 193, for additional transitional words and phrases that can be used when explaining a process.

• What writing have you read lately that explained steps you needed to follow to complete a process?

_____

_____

_____

_____

_____

_____

• What writing have you read lately that explained how something worked?

DISCOVERY ACTIVITY

_____

_____

_____

_____

_____

_____

UNDERSTANDING WRITING TASKS THAT REQUIRE A DESCRIPTION OF A PROCESS

How do you know when you need to use the process strategy to complete a writing task? Sometimes you will be asked specifically to explain how something is done, as in the following examples:

• A friend asks you to explain *how to* change the oil in a car.

• Your employer asks you to write instructions for new employees on *how to* fill an order.

Other process-related requests will not be worded as directly, as in the following examples:

- A friend needs written *directions* for traveling to a party.
- On a test you are asked to *explain how* the respiratory system *works*.

Activity A: Identifying Clue Words That Ask for a Description of a Process

Underline the clue words in any of the following directions that ask you to use the process strategy.

- Discuss whether professional athletes should/should not be allowed in the Olympics.
- Explain how to dry flowers.
- Describe the best way to get from here to the mall.
- The person who inspired me the most in high school

FIRST DRAFT: PLANNING AND WRITING ESSAYS THAT DESCRIBE A PROCESS

The Writing Focus Chart on page 132 can guide you in blending the key elements of writing to create interesting and effective essays that describe a process. Use the questions on the chart as you consider your purpose, content, structure, audience, and tone.

CHOOSING A TOPIC

How do you select a topic for a description of a process? Everyone has talents or skills. Maybe you know how to give a great party or arrange a garage sale, or maybe you are good at household repairs or training new employees at work. Processes like these, as well as processes you would enjoy researching, are ones you could explain in an essay.

Essays that describe a process can be either "how to" or explanatory. "How to" topics include how to quit smoking, how to buy or sell a used car, and how to record on a VCR. Examples of explanatory topics include how lions stalk their prey, how perfume is made, and how teddy bears are manufactured.

ESTABLISHING THE WRITING PURPOSE

Once you have chosen a topic, establish your writing purpose. One of the most common purposes of an essay that describes a process is to inform: to explain how to do or make something or to explain how something works.

Some essays that describe a process persuade as well as inform. For example, a writer might say, "There are three ways to change the oil in your car, but here is the best way." As another example, a writer might explain how to set up a home fitness center with the intention of persuading readers that exercising is both easy and important for good health.

WRITING A THESIS STATEMENT

After familiarizing yourself with your topic and establishing your writing purpose, write a thesis statement. The thesis statement will help you develop and structure your explanation of a process.

A thesis statement for an essay that describes a process should do one or more of the following:

- State the process you are describing.
- Preview the steps of the process you will present.
- Clarify the purpose of the process.

You can preview the steps you will present by listing them. Listing the steps is one way to signal what readers will learn about the process. Clarifying the purpose of your process in your thesis statement indicates how readers can apply the information they will learn.

The following sentences are examples of thesis statements for essays that describe a process:

> In order to create a tile mosaic, you must begin with a plan for arranging the tiles.

> Evaluating the development of first grade pupils requires an analysis of the physical, social, and mental aspects of children's behavior.

DEVELOPING THE CONTENT

Once you have selected a topic and written a thesis statement that introduces the process you will describe, identify the steps of the process. Use the invention techniques of questioning and brainstorming to identify the steps in a process and to generate details about the process. For example, if you are explaining how to make something, you might ask the following questions:

- What materials and tools are needed?
- What kind of work space is needed?
- What planning or designing should be done ahead of time?
- Which step comes first? Which step comes next?

PLANNING THE STRUCTURE

In an essay that describes a process, the introduction should provide an overview of the process and tell why the topic is important. The body paragraphs will consist of all the steps or stages involved in the process. These steps must be presented in order. The topic sentence of each body paragraph should signal which step of the process will be explained in that paragraph. The conclusion of the essay should tie together all the steps in the process. In addition, the conclusion can identify the end result of the process or state ways in which the process can be applied.

Using Methods of Organization

As you learned earlier in this chapter, the steps of a process are usually presented in chronological order. This method is particularly useful if readers are expected to use your explanation to complete the process themselves. You should analyze the process carefully, break it down into steps, and present the steps in a logical sequence. If several steps are performed at the same time, or if a step requires advance preparation, allow for that in your planned sequence.

- The following list shows the steps in the process of taking a photograph. Number the steps in chronological order.

_____ taking the photograph

_____ buying the correct film for your camera

_____ posing and/or checking the lighting of your subject

_____ loading the film

_____ aiming the camera correctly

_____ deciding on a suitable subject to photograph

Clip or photocopy for your journal examples of essays that describe a process that you encounter in newspapers, magazines, or books. Describe the topic and purpose of each example, and explain how the process presented is useful to you as a reader.

Select one essay that is particularly effective. Describe how the writer has structured the process. How does the structure clarify the process?

Read the following essay, "How to Prepare for an Interview." As you read, underline important steps in the process.

How to Prepare for an Interview

Being interviewed is a situation that nearly everyone faces at some time in life, whether for college or for a job. Most people face this ordeal with anxiety and even fear. However, people who prepare for an interview avoid much of this anxiety. Preparing for an interview involves doing advance research, choosing the right outfit, and planning appropriate communication with the interviewer.

Doing research before the actual interview will increase the chances for a successful interview. Find out the location of the interview site and decide how to travel there to arrive on time. Nothing makes as poor an impression on an interviewer as arriving late. In addition, learn about the company or institution where you are being interviewed. This will help you ask intelligent questions. If your interview is for admission to a school, find out what courses the school offers in your field of interest. For a job interview, find out about the kind of work the company does. If you already work at the company and are being interviewed for a promotion, research the duties of the job for which you are applying. Such research will show the interviewer that you are interested in obtaining the job or being admitted to the school.

Dressing appropriately for the interview is important because your appearance will be the first thing the interviewer notices about you. This means wearing clean, neatly pressed clothing and subdued color combinations such as brown or navy with white. You want to make a good impression, but at the same time you do not want to attract attention to your clothing. Also, you want to show that you can use good judgment. If you wear loud colors or overly noticeable clothes, the interviewer might question your judgment about what's acceptable behavior for a school or office setting.

Preparing what you might say to the interviewer will help you feel more in control of the situation. From your research, prepare a list of questions that you would like to ask the interviewer. As you prepare what you might say, remind yourself of what *not* to say. For instance, you won't want to ask questions that are too personal. Also, remind yourself not to talk too much. Make a mental note to let the interviewer guide and control the course of the meeting. Also plan to answer the interviewer's questions fully, explaining your answers rather than replying by saying only yes or no. Remember, the interviewer is trying to form an impression of you and how you would fit in at the school or company.

By following these steps, you will be prepared for your interview and feel more confident about the results. You will also increase your chances of making the good impression that is important for getting accepted into the school of your choice or landing the job you want.

Questions

1. What is the central point of this essay?

   How to prepare for an interview.

2. What steps does the writer identify as being involved in preparing for an interview?

3. Are the steps presented in a logical order? Explain your answer.

   Yes

4. How does the writer achieve unity in the essay? Be specific.

   Every para is related to thesis

To chart the sequence of steps in a process, you can use your word processor to list the steps on the computer. Evaluate your list, and then block and move items around to see whether they work better in another order. Add details for each step as needed and revise or combine steps to eliminate repetition. Use this list as the basis for your description of a process.

TARGETING A SPECIFIC AUDIENCE

In considering the audience for an essay that describes a process, put yourself in the readers' place. If you are explaining a process that you do routinely, step back and view the process as if you were completing the process for the first time. What seems difficult or confusing? How can you overcome problems? If readers will not actually be completing the process, will the process have some special interest for them? If the audience is not likely to be familiar with the process, provide enough details to enable readers to follow the steps you are explaining. Explain or define any terms that may be unfamiliar to readers.

Questions

1. If the writer of "How to Prepare for an Interview" on pages 302-304 was writing for an audience of high school students preparing for their first job interviews, how might the content or wording of the essay be changed?

_____

_____

_____

2. If the writer of "How to Prepare for an Interview" was writing for an audience of office workers seeking promotions, how might the content or wording be changed?

_____

_____

_____

SETTING THE TONE

A description of a process can benefit from a tone that is factual, objective, and positive. When giving instructions, avoid making those instructions sound like orders. Using phrases such as *The next step is to . . .* or *It may be helpful for you to . . .* can soften the tone of your instructions.

Essays that describe how to do something are usually written using the present tense of verbs and are usually written in the second person (*you*). Essays that explain how something works can be written in the first person (*I, we*) or the third person (*he, she, it, they*). The important thing to remember is to use verb tenses and pronouns consistently. If you begin your essay using the present tense, don't switch to the past tense (unless, of course, you are explaining something that took place earlier). If you begin using *you*, don't switch to *they* partway through.

In "How to Prepare for an Interview" on pages 302-304, the writer used a factual tone to emphasize the practical nature of the material. By being brisk but not overly aggressive, the writer was able to persuade readers that following the steps for preparing for an interview can make a difference in the success of the interview.

Questions

1. Is the tone of "How to Prepare for an Interview" on pages 302-304 in keeping with an audience of people preparing for college interviews or for their first jobs? Be specific.

_____

_____

_____

2. Locate and describe specific instances in the essay where the tone reveals the writer's purpose.

_____

_____

_____

_____

Activity B: Planning an Essay That Describes a Process

In this activity you will plan the purpose, content, structure, audience, and tone for an essay that describes a process. Refer to the Writing Focus Chart on page 132 for help in addressing these five key elements. Use separate sheets of paper for your work.

A. Narrow one of the following general topics for an essay:
- How to play a musical instrument
- How to procrastinate
- How to study
- How a government system works
- How something is manufactured

For example, if you select the general topic "How to play a musical instrument," your narrowed topic could be an explanation of how to play chords on a guitar.

B. Once you have selected and narrowed a topic, establish your writing purpose. Freewrite for ten to fifteen minutes about the topic of your essay. Explore as many ideas, facts, and examples as you can about the process you plan to present.

C. Based on your prewriting, write a thesis statement.

D. Write a list of questions to help you decide what information you need to present in your essay. Then brainstorm by breaking the process into steps or parts.

E. Based on your prewriting, decide how you want to structure your essay. Prepare an outline that lists the steps in the process in the order you plan to present them. Also include any supporting facts, details, and examples.

F. Target a specific audience for your essay. Consider what your audience is likely to know about the process you are describing and what information you will need to supply. Also consider what your audience will find important or relevant about the process. You may target that angle of the process in your introduction and your conclusion. After considering your intended audience, decide what tone is most appropriate for your topic and writing purpose.

PORTFOLIO

Save your work in your portfolio. You will use your prewriting to create an essay that describes a process in Assignment 2 on page 313.

Revising, Editing, and Proofreading Essays That Describe a Process

The Checklist for Revising and Editing on page 153 can guide you in evaluating and revising the first draft of an essay that describes a process. The Checklist for Proofreading on page 105 can help you turn a revised draft into a final copy.

Read the following revised draft of an essay that describes a process, which includes the writer's handwritten revisions. Remember that at this point the writer has not yet corrected errors in grammar, spelling, punctuation, and capitalization. What changes did the writer make to improve the essay?

Revised Draft:

The Music Makers

When you listen to a tape or CD of your favorite singer, you are actualy listening to the work of many people. Recording a collection of songs takes the efforts of the performer, one or more musician, a producer, various types of engineers, and assorted other workers. *Each of these people has a specific job to do.*

Before the recording session begins, someone has to compose the music and write the lyrics for the songs. Some performers compose their own music. *Others choose to record songs written by someone else.* Once music is chosen, an arranger will style the music for recording. The arranger plans what musical instruments will be used, *and exactly how the singer will perform the song.* Some singers arrange their own musical material, *or work closely with the arranger.*

Many people asist the singer during the *recording stage of the* actual process. The record producer is in charge of everything nontechnical during a recording session. *The record producer obtains studio space.* If musicians are needed to perform the arrangement, the record producer will hire these musicians. The session engineer is responsible for everything technical, such as the microphones and the recording ekwipment. ~~The record producer obtains studio~~

~~space~~. Another of the session engineer's jobs is to decide where all ekwipment should be placed in the studio to achieve the proper effect on the recording. Each musician ^and singer records at a different microphone. ~~Each singer records at a separate microphone also.~~ This method of recording produces separate tracks, or recordings, for each performer. With this method, the engineer has more controle over how each performance will be combined in the finished recording. ^*If there is a mistake in one person's performance,* A mistake is easier to retape than a combined performance would be. ^*When all the tracks are made,* The session engineer mixes the tracks to create the recording.

^*After the recording is completed,* Mastering engineers makes a master tape from the recording. This master tape will be used to ~~make~~ *manufacture* millions of copies ^*of tapes and CDs* for the singer's eager fans.

When you play a recording, you may hear only the ^*voices of the* singers ~~and the musicians~~ but many other people have also worked to create the final product. Some of these people's names may be known only from the fine print on the ~~CD's~~ *recording's* list of credits. These behind-the-scenes workers, however, are just as important to the success of a recording ^*as the performer in the spotlight.*

On pages 310-312 of this chapter you'll see a rekeyed version of "The Music Makers" that incorporates the writer's handwritten revisions. You'll use that version to proofread the essay for errors in spelling, punctuation, and so on.

Questions

1. How has the writer improved the effectiveness of this essay? Be specific.

Removed unnecessary details, Used transitions

Used precise language instead of vague

2. Why did the writer add the sentence in the introduction?

_____

_____

3. Why did the writer insert the sentence *Others choose to record songs written by someone else* in the second paragraph?

To make it specific then
being vague

4. Why did the writer move the sentence *The record producer obtains studio space* in the third paragraph?

_____

_____

5. What transitions did the writer add to create a smooth flow from one detail to the next?

_____

_____

6. If you were the writer of this essay, what additional revisions would you make in content, structure, and wording?

_____

_____

_____

Read the revised and rekeyed draft of "The Music Makers" that follows. Proofread the revision, and correct any mistakes in spelling, capitalization, and punctuation as well as any factual, keyboarding, and grammatical errors.

Revised and
Rekeyed Draft:

The Music Makers

When you listen to a tape or CD of your favorite singer, you are actualy listening to the work of many peo-ple. Recording a collection of songs takes the efforts of the performer, one or more musician, a producer, various types of engineers, and assorted other workers. Each of these people has a specific job to do.

Before the recording session begins, someone has to compose the music and write the lyrics for the songs. Some performers compose their own music. Others choose to record songs written by someone else. Once music is chosen, an arranger will style the music for recording. The arranger plans what musical instruments will be used and exactly how the singer will perform the song. Some singers arrange their own musical material or work closely with the arranger.

Many people assist the singer during the recording stage of the process. The record producer is in charge of everything nontechnical during a recording session. The record producer obtains studio space. If musicians are needed to perform the arrangement, the record producer will hire these musicians. The session engineer is responsible for everything technical, such as the microphones and the recording ekwipment. Another of the session engineer's jobs is to decide where all ekwipment should be placed in the studio to achieve the proper effect on the recording. Each musician and singer records at a different microphone. This method of recording produces separate tracks, or recordings, for each performer. With this method, the engineer has more controle over how each performance will be combined in the finished recording. If there is a mistake in one person's performance, this mistake is easier to retape than a combined performance would be. When all the tracks are made, the session engineer mixes the tracks to create the recording.

After the recording is completed, mastering engineers makes a master tape from the recording. This master tape will be used to manufacture millions of copies of tapes and CDs for the singer's eager fans.

When you play a recording, you may hear only the voices of the singers, but many other people have also worked to create the final product. Some of these people's names may be known only from the fine print on the recording's list of credits. These behind-the-scenes workers, however, are just as important to the success of a recording as the performer in the spotlight.

Assignment 1:
Creating an Essay That Describes a Process With Your Group

In this assignment you will work with your group to plan, write, edit, and proofread an essay that describes a process.

A. Choose a topic suitable for a collaboratively written essay that describes a process. Work together to narrow the topic and to brainstorm steps and details of the process. Decide whether you will describe a process that explains how to do or make something or a process that explains how something works.

B. Working as a group, use the questions on the Writing Focus Chart on page 132 to guide you as you plan the first draft. Use any of the invention techniques you learned in Chapter 2 to develop the thesis statement, introduction, main ideas, supporting details, and conclusion. Also use any of the strategies from Chapter 5 to develop content.

C. Use your group's prewriting to write the first draft. Your first draft should consist of an introduction, a body, and a conclusion and should clearly accomplish your writing purpose. Review the draft and work together to develop an appropriate title.

D. Carefully reread and evaluate the content, structure, and wording of your first draft. Discuss any necessary changes, additions, deletions, and corrections. Using the Checklist for Revising and Editing on page 153 as a guide, work together to revise the first draft. Complete as many revisions as needed.

E. When you are satisfied that your draft is the best work that your group can produce, choose someone to key the revised draft. Make a photocopy for every group member.

F. Carefully reread your revised draft. Using the Checklist for Proofreading on page 105, work together to prepare the final copy. Consult the Writer's Guide that begins on page A 80 to review key points of grammar, punctuation, and capitalization. Have each group member proofread the revised draft independently and use proofreaders' marks from the box on page 105 to mark corrections. Then compare corrections and incorporate all the changes on one draft.

PORTFOLIO

G. Have one group member key the final copy. Proofread the final copy as a group and correct any keyboarding errors. Record the names of all group members on the final copy. Make a photocopy for every group member. Save your final copy in your portfolio.

Assignment 2:
Creating an Essay That Describes a Process

In this assignment you will work independently to plan, write, edit, and proofread the essay that you began developing earlier in this chapter.

A. Review the planning you did in Activity B on page 307, including your prewriting, thesis statement, and outline. Reread the freewriting you did on your topic.

Writing FOCUS CHART

B. Use your prewriting and the questions on the Writing Focus Chart on page 132 to guide you as you plan the first draft of the essay. Use any of the invention techniques you learned in Chapter 2 to develop the introduction, main ideas, supporting details, and conclusion. Also use any of the strategies from Chapter 5 to develop content.

C. Write the first draft of your essay. Your first draft should consist of an introduction, a body, and a conclusion and should clearly accomplish your writing purpose. Review your draft and develop an appropriate title.

D. Share your draft with members of your group or with a peer editor. Use the comments and suggestions from the group or peer editor, in conjunction with the Checklist for Revising and Editing on page 153, to help you make revisions. After sharing essays, work independently to revise your draft.

E. Evaluate the content, structure, and wording of your essay. Using the Checklist for Revising and Editing as a guide, make any necessary changes, additions, deletions, and corrections. Make as many revisions as needed. When you are satisfied, key your revised draft.

F. Carefully reread your revised draft. Using the Checklist for Proofreading on page 105, prepare the final copy. Consult the Writer's Guide that begins on page A 80 to review key points of grammar, punctuation, and capitalization. Use proofreaders' marks from the box on page 105 to mark your corrections.

PORTFOLIO

G. Key the final copy. Look over the final copy and correct any keyboarding errors. Save your final copy in your portfolio.

Assignment 3:
Reading as a Stimulus for Writing

In this assignment you will read a selection and then work independently to plan, write, edit, and proofread an essay that describes a process.

A. Read "How Dictionaries Are Made" on pages A 128-A 130. The writer, S. I. Hayakawa, describes the way dictionary editors gather information about words and their meanings.

B. Use the selection as a stimulus for an essay that describes a process. For example, you might describe a process you are familiar with from your job or from a hobby. Here are several questions to start you thinking.

- What steps are covered in Hayakawa's description of how dictionary editors compile definitions?
- What details, examples, or anecdotes are used to make parts of the process clearer and more interesting?
- When you describe your process, what details about it

might be most interesting to a reader who is unfamiliar with the process?

- What anecdotes can you think of that might illustrate your process in an interesting way?

Use your responses to the preceding questions to help you decide on a specific topic and generate a thesis statement. Decide whether you will describe a process that explains how to do or make something or a process that explains how something works. Freewrite for approximately ten or fifteen minutes on your topic.

C. Share your ideas with members of your group or with a peer editor. Discuss the topic you are considering for your essay. Ask for constructive advice about the topic. Also discuss any problem areas that you foresee.

D. Use your prewriting and the questions on the Writing Focus Chart on page 132 to guide you as you write your first draft. Use any of the invention techniques from Chapter 2 and any of the strategies from Chapter 5 as needed. Your first draft should consist of an introduction, a body, and a conclusion and should clearly accomplish your writing purpose. Review your draft and develop an appropriate title.

E. Share your draft with your group or with a peer editor. Use the comments and suggestions from the group or peer editor, in conjunction with the Checklist for Revising and Editing on page 153, to help you make revisions. After sharing essays, work independently to revise your draft.

F. Evaluate the content, structure, and wording of your draft. Using the Checklist for Revising and Editing as a guide, make any necessary changes, additions, deletions, and corrections. Make as many revisions as needed. When you are satisfied, key your revised draft.

G. Carefully reread your revised draft. Using the Checklist for Proofreading on page 105, prepare the final copy. Consult the Writer's Guide that begins on page A 80 to review key points of grammar, punctuation, and capitalization. Use proofreaders' marks from the box on page 105 to mark your corrections.

H. Key the final copy. Look over the final copy and correct any keyboarding errors. Save your final copy in your portfolio.

USING IRREGULAR VERBS

Grammar Gremlins

Unlike regular verbs, which take an *-ed* or a *-d* ending in the past tense, **irregular verbs** in the past tense change in various ways. Study the following chart of some common irregular verbs.

IRREGULAR VERBS			
Present Tense	Past Tense	Past Participle	Present Participle
be	was, were	been	being
become	became	become	becoming
begin	began	begun	beginning
break	broke	broken	breaking
bring	brought	brought	bringing
buy	bought	bought	buying
catch	caught	caught	catching
choose	chose	chosen	choosing
come	came	come	coming
do	did	done	doing
eat	ate	eaten	eating
fight	fought	fought	fighting
find	found	found	finding
fly	flew	flown	flying
get	got	gotten	getting
give	gave	given	giving
go	went	gone	going
have	had	had	having
know	knew	known	knowing
lay	laid	laid	laying
leave	left	left	leaving
lie	lay	lain	lying
lose	lost	lost	losing
make	made	made	making
ride	rode	ridden	riding
rise	rose	risen	rising
run	ran	run	running
see	saw	seen	seeing
sing	sang	sung	singing
sleep	slept	slept	sleeping
speak	spoke	spoken	speaking
stand	stood	stood	standing
take	took	taken	taking
tear	tore	torn	tearing
think	thought	thought	thinking
throw	threw	thrown	throwing
wear	wore	worn	wearing
win	won	won	winning
write	wrote	written	writing

If you're not sure whether a verb is regular or irregular, check a dictionary. If the past tense and past participle are not shown, the verb is regular.

Activities

A. Complete each sentence by filling in the blanks with the appropriate form of the verbs in parentheses.

1. When we ___Came___ (come) home from a picnic last weekend, I realized I had ___lost___ (lose) my pocket address book.

2. I ___thought___ (think) I had ___left___ (leave) the book in a coffee shop on the way to Benwood State Park.

3. While my husband ___bought___ (buy) our breakfast, I had ___taken___ (take) the book to the phone booth to make a call.

4. Today I ___rode___ (ride) my bike to the coffee shop and ___went___ (go) inside to look for the book.

5. I ___was___ (be) relieved to learn that the owner had ___found___ (find) my address book.

B. The paragraph below contains twelve errors in irregular verb forms. Correct the errors.

Two dogs ~~sleeped~~ *were sleeping* peacefully on the sunny porch. After a while a strange cat come into the yard on silent paws. The minute the dogs ~~seen~~ *saw* the cat, they standed up and ~~give~~ *gave* a low growl. The dogs must have ~~thinked~~ *Thought* that the cat would run from them, but instead the cat let out a fierce yowl. The three animals ~~fighted~~ *faught* long and hard while fur ~~flied~~ *flew*. Then, as suddenly as it had arrived, the cat *or* run away. Both dogs sprawled on the porch, panting and licking their scratches. They ~~was~~ *were* sure they had ~~winned~~ *won*. Then another fierce yowl ~~rised~~ *rose* over the fence. The cat was boasting to its friends!

C. For additional practice in using irregular verbs, see page A 74.

Wrapping it up

Summary

- Use the process strategy to describe how to do or make something or to explain how something works.

- To write a clear explanation of a process, use precise language, include all important details, be concise, present all the steps in the correct order, and, where necessary, give reasons for elements or steps of the process.

- Use appropriate transitional words and phrases to link the steps in a process.

- The purpose of an essay that describes a process is usually to inform, but the purpose may also be to persuade readers that a process is preferable.

- Structure an essay that describes a process using chronological order, to show the sequence in which the steps must be performed or the sequence in which the steps occur.

Thinking it over

- Explain the importance of being able to present a process clearly in daily life. Describe the most useful aspects of the process strategy that you learned in this chapter.

  _____

  _____

  _____

  _____

  _____

  _____

- How will what you have learned in this chapter help you explain processes at work and at school?

_____

_____

_____

_____

_____

_____

_____

_____

_____

_____

IN YOUR
JOURNAL

Review the goals that you set at the beginning of this chapter. In your journal, evaluate your progress toward these goals.

10

EMPLOYING CAUSE AND EFFECT

OBJECTIVES:

Composition

- To explore similarities between analyses of causes and effects in speech and in writing.

- To use the cause/effect strategy to develop essay content.

- To develop cause/effect analyses that present a clear relationship between events.

- To create and revise essays that employ cause and effect.

Grammar

- To eliminate errors in the use of adjectives and adverbs.

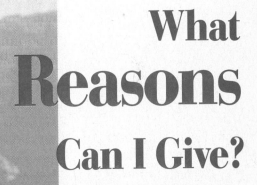

What
Reasons
Can I Give?

A major earthquake can cause massive destruction. People who see the devastation are often left asking "Why?"

Questions that ask why give insight into the *causes* of an *event.* For instance, why did some buildings crumble and others stand during the earthquake? Asking why helps you analyze how an event came to pass.

You might also speculate about events by asking, "What if?" For instance, what if there were a way to predict earthquakes? Questions that ask what if examine a possible *effect,* or result. In this chapter you will learn how to develop essays using cause-and-effect analysis as a way of discovering the relationship between events.

What if I start exercising daily? Why is it important to watch what I drink during pregnancy? What if a B average were required for participation in college sports? We speculate and ask "why" questions and "what if" questions about many things in our lives.

Think of situations in which you have analyzed what caused a situation or what effects resulted from a situation. List specific situations in which you presented causes or effects orally or in writing.

- With friends or relatives:

  _____

  _____

- At work:

  _____

  _____

- At school:

  _____

  _____

For *one* example you listed, consider these questions:

- Why were you analyzing the cause or the effect of a situation?
- How thoroughly did you develop your analysis? What were the strengths and weaknesses of your approach?
- How did your audience respond to your analysis?

IN YOUR JOURNAL

Evaluate your ability to use cause/effect orally and in writing. Then set one or more goals in your journal. Here are some examples:

GOALS:

1. When I examine an event, I will analyze facts carefully to find its causes or its effects.
2. When I describe a cause/effect relationship, I will present that relationship in a clear, logical manner.

EXPLAINING CAUSES AND EFFECTS

GROUP
ACTIVITY

How can you make the connection between an event and its causes or its effects?

A. Each member of your group should choose a topic for which you can analyze the causes and/or effects of a situation. You might consider the causes or effects of getting a college degree, playing in certain sports, or giving up smoking. Think carefully about the topic you choose. What is the connection between the event or issue and its causes or effects? What ideas, facts, and examples can you use for support?

B. Each member of the group should take turns presenting a cause/effect analysis orally to the group.

C. Work together to assess every cause/effect analysis for effectiveness. Identify features that make a cause/effect analysis clear, logical, and useful.

D. Work with your group to create a list of five or more specific guidelines to evaluate the effectiveness of a cause/effect analysis.

E. Evaluate the guidelines your group developed. Work together to improve them. Then write the revised guidelines in the following space.

_____

_____

_____

_____

_____

_____

_____

_____

_____

ANALYZING CAUSES AND EFFECTS

FEATURES OF CAUSE/EFFECT ANALYSES

A **cause/effect analysis** considers what event or series of events (the cause) led to a particular outcome (the effect). Such an analysis examines why something happens and explores important relationships between events. For example, the civil rights movement (the cause) led to laws protecting people's civil rights (the effect). Alternatively, a cause/effect analysis considers what happened or might happen (the effect) as a result of a particular occurrence (the cause). For example, an essay employing cause/effect might suggest that increased violence among youth (the effect) results from violence on television (the cause). An essay employing cause/effect can either begin with the cause and describe the effect, or it can begin with the effect and trace the factors (causes) that brought about that effect.

When you analyze causes and effects in an essay, you may use one of the following approaches to develop your content:

- Analyze the causes of your topic.
- Analyze the effects of your topic.
- Analyze both the causes and the effects.

The approach you choose will depend on your topic, your purpose for writing, and your thesis statement.

IDENTIFYING MORE THAN ONE CAUSE, MORE THAN ONE EFFECT

An event often has several causes and several effects. For example, if you analyze why reading scores have declined in schools in a certain community, you might discover causes such as larger class sizes, increased television viewing and video game playing, and little independent outside reading. If you analyze what a decline in reading scores might lead to, you could cite such effects as shorter attention spans, decreased ability to learn other subjects, less well-developed reasoning skills, and weaker job skills. When you explore the causes or effects of a situation or condition, don't settle for the first cause or effect that comes to mind. Make a careful analysis to determine as many causes and effects as you can.

IDENTIFYING OBVIOUS AND SUBTLE CAUSES

Determining a cause or effect may or may not be a simple or straightforward process. Some causes or effects may be **obvious.** For example, there is no doubt that earthquakes have caused damage in southern California. While an earthquake may be an **obvious** cause of damage, there may be more **subtle**, or less direct, causes for such damage. Possible subtle causes include inadequate building codes, poor road construction, substandard building materials, or inadequate emergency facilities. Similarly, an earthquake can have obvious effects such as damage to buildings as well as subtle effects such as a decline in population as people move to less earthquake-prone areas. A writer must look beyond the obvious causes and effects to more subtle, less direct causes and effects.

AVOIDING PITFALLS OF CAUSE/EFFECT ANALYSIS

To get readers to agree with your analysis of an event and its causes or effects, your cause/effect relationships must not depend on faulty connections. If readers detect a flaw in your reasoning, they will not accept your conclusions. To present convincing cause/effect relationships, avoid these pitfalls: oversimplification, false causes, and errors in logic.

Oversimplification

As you have learned, various factors often combine to bring about a certain effect or effects. When a writer states that only one cause exists for a complex situation, the writer is committing the error of **oversimplification.** A writer may choose to write an essay that focuses on just one important cause, but to present that as the only cause would likely be unrealistic.

False Causes

Sometimes you can misinterpret the clues to the causes of an event and name a **false cause** of that event. For example, suppose you know someone whose cat dies. The person suspects that poisoning is the cause because a neighbor's cat has been killed in a similar way. A veterinarian's examination, however, proves that the *true cause* of the cat's death was kidney failure. Writers analyzing the causes of an event should not jump to conclusions but should do everything possible to find the true causes.

Errors in Logic

Errors in logic can result when causes and effects are based on too little information or on faulty logic. There are several common types of errors in logic.

Conclusions based on too few examples: You have probably often heard a statement such as this: "All auto mechanics are crooks because a friend of mine took his car to a mechanic and was over-charged for a simple repair." This statement presents a conclusion based on only one example. Assuming that one or two examples are evidence of a cause/effect relationship in all such cases is faulty logic and will not convince thoughtful readers. While a writer can present a single example to *illustrate* a cause/effect relationship, the relationship must be supported by more than that one example to be valid.

Conclusions based on coincidence: **Coincidence** is a situation in which events happen at the same time and appear to be connected in some way but aren't. For example, it is a coincidence that a rainstorm often occurs right after you wash your car or your windows. Obviously there is no relationship between the two events merely because they happened near each other in time. When you analyze cause/effect relationships between events, be aware that some events might not be connected, even though they may seem to be because they occurred at the same time or one after the other.

The assumption of only two possible effects: You may have encountered statements such as the following: "Either you vote for candidate X, or our economy will crumble." This statement encourages people to assume that the election can have only two possible results. In reality, few situations are this clearcut. In the matter of an election, there are many issues and choices involved in keeping the economy healthy. When you analyze cause/effect topics, avoid thinking in terms of *either . . . or* relationships that incorrectly assume only one cause or effect.

Test your ability to identify errors in logic by telling what is illogical about the following situations.

- I failed the test because I didn't wear my lucky T-shirt that day. *coincidence*
- All college professors are insensitive because my math professor wouldn't excuse my absence when I had to baby-sit my little brother. *few examples*
- You must buy Speedo Premium gas, or your car won't run. *two possible effect*

USING TRANSITIONS TO LINK CAUSE/EFFECT RELATIONSHIPS

In an essay that provides a cause/effect analysis, use transitional words and phrases such as *because, as a result,* and *therefore* to clarify cause/effect relationships. Transitions can highlight the connection between one event and its cause or effect. Transitions like *moreover* or *in addition* can signal the presentation of additional evidence to support a cause/effect relationship. A transition like *however* can caution readers that some details will contradict or disprove an idea. Consult the chart in Chapter 5, page 193 for transitional words and phrases that can be used to link cause/effect relationships.

UNDERSTANDING CAUSE/EFFECT WRITING TASKS

Many of the cause/effect analyses you write will be in response to school or job-related tasks. It is sometimes difficult to know whether you are being asked to analyze causes or effects or both. How can you tell? Some instructions, such as the following, tell you outright to explain a cause or effect.

- Analyze the *effects* of logging the rainforest on the environment.
- Explain the *causes* of the decrease in the number of lunches sold at Lynn's Cafe in December.
- Analyze the *effects* of the new shopping mall on the city's downtown area.

Other cause/effect tasks will not have instructions that are worded quite so directly. However, clue words such as *why, what if, explain the reasons, what brought about, consequences of, what will happen if, if . . . then . . .* let you know you should analyze causes and effects.

Activity A: Finding Cause/Effect Clue Words

Underline the clue words for cause and effect in the following directions for essay tasks. Then write whether you are being asked to focus on the causes, the effects, or both.

- What are the <u>consequences of</u> the increased divorce rate in the United States?

  effect

- <u>Explain the reasons</u> for the popularity of physical fitness programs and the <u>results of</u> following a fitness program.

  Cause and effect

- <u>What brought about</u> the intense interest in space exploration in the 1950s?

  Cause

FIRST DRAFT: PLANNING AND WRITING ESSAYS THAT EMPLOY CAUSE/EFFECT

The Writing Focus Chart on page 132 can guide you in blending the key elements of writing to create interesting and effective essays that provide a cause/effect analysis. Use the questions on the chart as you consider your purpose, content, structure, audience, and tone.

CHOOSING A TOPIC

How do you select a topic for a cause/effect analysis? First, consider a topic that will not be too overwhelming in size and scope. For example, if you choose a topic such as the causes of the growth in the world's population since 1900, you will need to do a lot of outside research. However, if you choose a topic closer to home, such as the causes and effects of a successful personal relationship, you can draw on your own experience or observations. To help you select a topic, use brainstorming to generate a list of *why* and *what if* questions.

Once you've chosen a manageable topic, decide whether to focus on causes, effects, or both. For example, if you choose a topic such as stress, you may want to narrow it to the causes of stress in everyday life or possibly the effects of stress-reduction practices such as yoga. You may wish to analyze causes, effects, or both causes and effects in your analysis.

ESTABLISHING THE WRITING PURPOSE

Cause/effect analyses are usually written to inform or to persuade. For example, a writer might inform by analyzing the effects that population growth has on city traffic. An essay to persuade might give reasons why research into the development of solar-powered cars should be encouraged as one solution to air pollution.

WRITING A THESIS STATEMENT

After familiarizing yourself with your topic and establishing your writing purpose, write a thesis statement. The thesis statement will help you develop and structure your cause-and-effect analysis. In essays that employ cause/effect, the thesis statement should do one or more of the following:

- Describe the central point you will discuss.
- Explain whether your focus will be on causes, effects, or both.
- State the basic causes or effects and the order in which they will be presented.

The following sentences are examples of thesis statements for essays that employ cause and effect:

> We can work to solve the traffic congestion problem in our community if we look at the main causes: the new mall on Baxter Avenue and the closing of the bus route along Seeley Boulevard.
> If all college dorms were equipped with computers, students would be able to complete writing assignments more efficiently and improve their grades.

You may feel that you don't have enough information yet about the causes and effects related to your topic to write a thesis statement. However, writing a thesis statement at this step helps you focus on a manageable set of ideas that can reasonably be covered in an essay. As you continue your planning, if you decide to eliminate some of the causes or effects you planned to discuss and substitute others, adjust your thesis statement to suit the new focus of your essay.

DEVELOPING THE CONTENT

Once you have determined a topic for your essay and written a thesis statement for it, you can turn to discovering causes or effects. As you learned earlier in the chapter, look for subtle causes as well as obvious causes. Also be careful to avoid oversimplification, false causes, and errors in logic as you are analyzing your topic.

Brainstorming a list of causes or effects may help you uncover additional related causes and effects. Depending on your approach, you can list causes only, effects only, or both causes and effects.

DO YOU WRITE ON A COMPUTER?

Use your computer to brainstorm *why* and *what if* questions for your topic. Key as many items as occur to you, without censoring your thoughts. Then answer your questions. If you decide to change any questions or answers, you can easily revise. Save the file of your brainstormed questions and answers so that you can rearrange and add to them later. Print a copy and highlight or check the words, phrases, and sentences you might want to include in a first draft.

PLANNING THE STRUCTURE

The causes and effects in a cause/effect analysis are usually presented in the body paragraphs of the essay. If you are presenting only causes or only effects, you can devote a separate paragraph to each cause or effect. If you are presenting both causes and effects, you can present the causes in one or more paragraphs and the effects in one or more paragraphs.

You can use the conclusion in one of two ways:

- *To sum up:* Wrap up or review the analysis presented in the body paragraphs.

- *To suggest a solution:* Propose a way to deal with the causes or effects of an ongoing problem or situation such as why a baseball team has never won the World Series.

Using Methods of Organization

Either of the following methods of organization would be effective for structuring an essay that employs cause/effect.

- *Chronological order:* Presenting causes or effects in the order they occurred or will occur is a good structure to use when you are analyzing historical events. For example, when presenting the events that led to a recent Supreme Court decision, you could relate events in the order that they occurred.

- *Order of importance or interest:* Presenting causes or effects in order of importance or interest is a good structure to use when you are attempting to persuade your audience. You can begin with those causes or effects that are least important and end with those that are most important to leave your reader with your strongest point. For example, when arguing to ban smoking in public places by presenting effects of the ban, you could end by stating that the ban would eliminate secondhand smoke, which has been proven in some cases to cause cancer in nonsmokers, from public places.

IN YOUR JOURNAL

Clip or photocopy for your journal examples of interesting selections that employ cause/effect that you come across in newspapers, magazines, or books. Describe the topic and purpose of each example, and explain how the analysis of cause/effect is useful to you as a reader.

Select one essay you particularly like. Then note how the writer has structured the cause/effect analysis. Does the writer use chronological order, order of importance or interest, or a combination of methods to organize the analysis? How does the structure of the piece clarify the content?

Read the following essay, "For All Those Years." As you read, underline the causes and circle the effects the writer describes.

For All Those Years

Nearly half of all marriages end in divorce. This startling statistic makes many people think twice before tying the knot. This statistic also makes one wonder what causes a marriage to succeed. My parents have been married for thirty-three years, and though they've had their ups and downs, they have had a wonderful relationship. Why has their marriage succeeded?

My parents have always expressed their love for each other. Throughout their courtship they did many wonderful things for each other: buying flowers, writing letters, and sending surprises. They've continued these practices throughout their marriage as ways of showing affection.

Another quality of my parents' marriage is that they are flexible about their demands and expectations of each other. When I was four, Dad was laid off from his job. As a result, Mom entered the workforce. Although Dad was soon rehired, Mom enjoyed her job so much that she decided to keep it. Dad was a bit surprised, but he could see it made her happy. If problems arose because of the time demands of their jobs, they worked through those problems—together.

My parents remain committed to each other, even during difficult times. Early in their marriage, Dad was sent overseas. He was a communications specialist in the Vietnam War. Dad wrote home when he could, but he didn't see Mom for nine months. Mom was home alone. Sometimes her single coworkers would encourage her to go out with them and have a good time. When I asked her why she didn't, she told me that she had made a commitment to my father and she was living by that commitment. Meanwhile, thousands of miles away, Dad was living up to the same commitment. When they were reunited, they had nothing to be ashamed of and nothing to be angry with each other about. I have come to believe that their absolute commitment to each other is, more than anything else, what has caused their marriage to work.

I once heard someone say that marriage isn't a fifty-fifty deal. It's ninety-ten on both sides. Could that be the secret of a successful marriage? It seems to describe the one my parents have.

Questions

1. What central point does the writer convey in this essay?

   How the parents of the author had a wonderful life

2. What factors does the writer propose as causes for a successful marriage?

   love for each other, flexible and committed to each other

3. How does the writer achieve unity in the essay? Be specific.

4. How does the writer use chronological order and order of importance or interest to structure the essay? Be specific.

TARGETING A SPECIFIC AUDIENCE

When writing an essay that employs cause/effect, remember not to underestimate your audience's intelligence. Avoid alienating your audience by oversimplifying your causes and/or effects. Oversimplification might cause your audience to distrust your logic or even your motives and become suspicious of your ideas and the evidence you present. You might even offend readers enough so that they will not read your essay with an open mind.

Consider your audience's viewpoint even if you disagree with this viewpoint. For example, you may want to present the negative effects such as pollution, of a local industry. In a small town that heavily relies on this industry for jobs, it would be unwise to ignore the positive effects of the industry. You could point out the way the company strengthens the local economy and, if applicable, mention any ways that the company is trying to minimize pollution. By showing respect to your audience, you will have a better chance of having them listen to your ideas.

The writer of "For All Those Years" on page 332 had a specific audience in mind: young people considering marriage for the first time. The writer wanted them to think deeply about what causes a relationship to succeed. The writer therefore gave an example of a successful marriage and showed what the two people in that marriage did to keep it strong.

Questions

1. Suppose the writer of "For All Those Years" was presenting this cause/effect analysis to couples facing divorce. How might the content and wording of the essay have been changed?

   _____

   _____

   _____

2. If the writer of "For All Those Years" was presenting this cause/effect analysis to older couples who had been married for many years, how might the content and wording of the essay have been changed?

   _____

   _____

SETTING THE TONE

In an essay that employs cause/effect, your tone should be reasonable but convincing. To present an appropriate tone, use **qualifying (limiting) statements** where necessary. Qualifying words and phrases include *sometimes, maybe, probably, most likely, I believe,* or *in my opinion*. These phrases are sometimes necessary to make a statement accurate. For example, in the statement "Another rainy summer will *most likely* cause large-scale flooding in our area," the qualifying phrase *most likely* indicates that no one can absolutely predict that flooding will occur. Since you probably have not discovered every single cause and effect related to your topic, qualifying words and phrases prevent you from making inaccurate or illogical statements.

Questions

1. In "For All Those Years" on page 332, what tone is indicated by the qualifying statement *I have come to believe that their absolute commitment to each other is, more than anything else, what has caused their marriage to work*? Be specific.

_____

_____

2. Locate and describe specific instances in "For All Those Years" where the writer reveals a reasonable, convincing tone.

_____

_____

Activity B: Planning an Essay That Uses Cause/Effect

In this activity you will plan the purpose, content, structure, audience, and tone for an essay that uses cause/effect. Refer to the Writing Focus Chart on page 132 for help in addressing these five key elements. Use separate sheets of paper for your work.

A. Narrow one of the following general topics for an essay that employs cause/effect:

- The causes or effects of an event in your community
- The reasons for the popularity of a certain sport
- The consequences of one action over another

Focus your topic on causes, effects, or both. For example, if you select the general topic "the causes or effects of an event in your community," you could talk about the effects of a permanent flea market that was started on weekends in a local parking lot.

B. Once you have selected and narrowed your topic, establish your writing purpose. Will you write to inform or persuade? Freewrite for ten to fifteen minutes about the topic of your cause/effect analysis. Explore as many ideas, facts, and details as you can about the causes, effects, or both.

C. Based on your prewriting, write a thesis statement.

D. Brainstorm a list of causes and/or effects for your topic. Write as many causes and/or effects as you can think of. Put the list in a logical sequence, eliminating any causes and/or effects that are not important or true.

E. Based on your prewriting, decide how you want to structure your analysis. Decide whether you will use chronological order, order of importance or interest, or a combination of methods to structure your essay. Prepare a conceptual map or an outline of your analysis. Your map or outline should include the causes and/or effects and any details necessary to support or illustrate them.

F. Target a specific audience for your essay. After considering your intended audience, decide what tone is most appropriate for your topic and writing purpose.

PORTFOLIO

Save your work in your portfolio. You will use your prewriting work to create an essay that employs a cause/effect analysis in Assignment 2 on page 341.

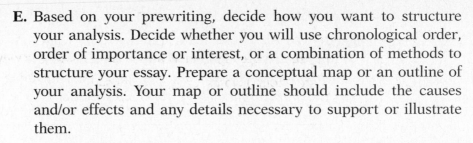

REVISING, EDITING, AND PROOFREADING ESSAYS THAT EMPLOY CAUSE/EFFECT

The Checklist for Revising and Editing on page 153 can guide you in evaluating and revising the first draft of an essay that employs cause/effect. The Checklist for Proofreading on page 105 can help you turn a revised draft into a final copy.

Read the following revised draft of an essay that uses cause/effect, which includes the writer's handwritten revisions. Remember that at this point the writer has not yet corrected errors in grammar, spelling, punctuation, and capitalization. What changes did the writer make to improve the essay?

....

Revised Draft: **I Finally Knew**

I wasn't supposed to hear. ~~I could tell.~~ My mother was

talking to her good friend and I heard her say, "No, her

birth mother never wanted to stay in touch with us." I

was Thirteen when that ^overheard^ remark revealed to me that I was

adopted. ^The news had a dramatic effect on me○^

When I confronted my parents and they admitted the
truth, my initial reaction, of course, was shock. After that I spent about
three days feeling horribly afraid without knowing why
Later I found words for my fear: if I had been adopted, I
might be sent away for any reason, or even for no reason. Then my fear turned
to anger. I was furious with my parents for hiding the
truth from me, and I told them so repeatedly. I was even angryer with the woman who
had given me away.

Learning that I had been born someone else's child
made me suddenly desperate to find out about ~~that~~ my
unknown ~~woman.~~ mother. I demanded that my parents tell me
the womans name, and where I could find her. Although they said they didn't know
my mother's name, they vowed to help me locate her. My parents' behavior amazed me.
Even though I'd ~~behaved badly~~ treated them terribly since finding out about
my adoption, they weren't pushing me away. they still
loved me. Sometime later My parents did help me trace my birth mother,
but I realized that my desire to find her was not as great
as my fear of the meeting. I still haven't gotten in touch with her.

In a way, finding out about my adoption seemed to
~~change me.~~ unravel my personality. I began to wonder what part of me was realy
me. I doubted who I was, who my friends were, and
whether my parents loved me.

I took about a year to come to terms with myself. I also
learned much about my parents. Their patient love
showed me that being a parent involves a lot more than
just giveing birth to a child. They, not some pair of
strangers, were my real parents. I came to realize that the
self I had become was my true self no matter where I had
started out. Now I feel much stronger and more sure of
myself, than most people my age. Most of all, I feel very lucky to have the parents I
have.

On pages 339-340 of this chapter you'll see a rekeyed version of "I Finally Knew" that incorporates the writer's handwritten revisions. You'll use that version to proofread the essay for errors in spelling, punctuation, and so on.

Questions

1. How has the writer improved the effectiveness of this essay? Be specific.

Removed unnecessary detail
Became specific than being vague

2. Why did the writer add a sentence in the introduction?

To be more specific
and to make the introduction
effective

3. Why did the writer move sentences from one part of the fifth paragraph to another?

To arrange them in
chronological or order of
importance

4. What transitions did the writer add to create a smooth flow within and between paragraphs?

When, After that, Sometime later

5. If you were the writer of this essay, what additional revisions would you make in content, structure, and wording?

Read the revised and rekeyed draft of " I Finally Knew" that follows. Proofread the revision, and correct any mistakes in spelling, capitalization, and punctuation as well as any factual, keyboarding, and grammatical errors.

I Finally Knew

I wasn't supposed to hear. My mother was talking to her good friend and I heard her say, "No, her birth mother never wanted to stay in touch with us." I was Thirteen when that overheard remark revealed to me that I was adopted. The news had a dramatic effect on me.

When I confronted my parents and they admitted the truth, my initial reaction, of course, was shock. After that I spent about three days feeling horribly afraid without knowing why Later I found words for my fear: if I had been adopted, I might be sent away for any reason or even for no reason. Then my fear turned to anger. I was furious with my parents for hiding the truth from me, and I told them so repeatedly. I was even angryer with the woman who had given me away.

Learning that I had been born someone else's child made me suddenly desperate to find out about my unknown mother. I demanded that my parents tell me the womans name and where I could find her. Although they said they didn't know my mother's name, they vowed to help me locate her. My parents' behavior amazed me. Even though I'd treated them terribly since finding out about my adoption, they weren't pushing me away. they still loved me. Sometime later, my parents did help me trace my birth mother, but I realized that my desire to find her was not as great as my fear of the meeting. I still haven't gotten in touch with her.

In a way, finding out about my adoption seemed to unravel my personality. I began to wonder what part of

me was realy me. I doubted who I was, who my friends
were, and whether my parents loved me.

　　I took about a year to come to terms with myself. I
came to realize that the self I had become was my true
self no matter where I had started out. I also learned
much about my parents. Their patient love showed me
that being a parent involves a lot more than just giveing
birth to a child. They, not some pair of strangers, were
my real parents. Now I feel much stronger and more sure
of myself than most people my age. Most of all, I feel
very lucky to have the parents I have.

Assignment 1:
Creating an Essay That Employs Cause/Effect
With Your Group

In this assignment you will work with your group to plan, write,
edit, and proofread an essay that employs cause/effect.

A. Choose a topic suitable for a collaboratively written essay. Work
together to narrow the topic and to brainstorm points of
cause/effect. Decide whether your essay will focus on causes,
effects, or both.

B. Working as a group, use the questions on the Writing Focus
Chart on page 132 to guide you as you plan the first draft. Use
any of the invention techniques you learned in Chapter 2 to
develop the thesis statement, introduction, main ideas, supporting details, and conclusion. Also use any of the strategies from
Chapter 5 to develop content.

C. Use your group's prewriting to write the first draft. Your first
draft should consist of an introduction, a body, and a conclusion
and should clearly accomplish your writing purpose. Review the
draft and work together to develop an appropriate title.

D. Carefully reread and evaluate the content, structure, and wording of your first draft. Discuss any necessary changes, additions,

deletions, and corrections. Using the Checklist for Revising and Editing on page 153 as a guide, work together to revise the first draft. Complete as many revisions as needed.

E. When you are satisfied that your draft is the best work that your group can produce, choose someone to key the revised draft. Make a photocopy for every group member.

F. Carefully reread your revised draft. Using the Checklist for Proofreading on page 105, work together to prepare the final copy. Consult the Writer's Guide that begins on page A 80 to review key points of grammar, punctuation, and capitalization. Have each group member proofread the revised draft independently and use proofreaders' marks from the box on page 105 to mark corrections. Then compare corrections and incorporate all the changes on one draft.

PORTFOLIO

G. Have one group member key the final copy. Proofread the final copy as a group, and correct any keyboarding errors. Record the names of all group members on the final copy. Make a photocopy for every group member. Save your copy in your portfolio.

Assignment 2:
Creating an Essay That Employs Cause/Effect

In this assignment you will work independently to plan, write, edit, and proofread the essay you began earlier in this chapter.

A. Review the planning you did in Activity B on page 335, including your prewriting, thesis statement, and outline. Reread the freewriting you did on your topic.

B. Use your prewriting and the questions on the Writing Focus Chart on page 132 to guide you as you plan the first draft of the essay. Use any of the invention techniques you learned in Chapter 2 to develop the introduction, main ideas, supporting details, and conclusion. Also use any of the strategies from Chapter 5 to develop the content.

C. Write the first draft of your essay. Your first draft should consist of an introduction, a body, and a conclusion and should clearly accomplish your writing purpose. Review your draft and develop an appropriate title.

D. Share your draft with members of your group or with a peer editor. Use the comments and suggestions from the group or peer editor, in conjunction with the Checklist for Revising and Editing on page 153, to help you make revisions. After sharing essays, work independently to revise your draft.

E. Evaluate the content, structure, and wording of your essay. Using the Checklist for Revising and Editing as a guide, make any necessary changes, additions, deletions, and corrections. Make as many revisions as needed. When you are satisfied, key your revised draft.

PORTFOLIO

F. Carefully reread your revised draft. Using the Checklist for Proofreading on page 105, prepare the final copy. Consult the Writer's Guide that begins on page A 80 to review key points of grammar, punctuation, and capitalization. Use proofreaders' marks from the box on page 105 to mark your corrections.

G. Key the final copy. Look over the final copy and correct any keyboarding errors. Save your final copy in your portfolio.

Assignment 3:
Reading as a Stimulus for Writing

In this assignment you will read a selection and then work independently to plan, write, edit, and proofread an essay that analyzes the causes and/or the effects of an experience or situation in your life.

A. Read "Probable Cause" by Keith E. Coffee on pages A 130-A 131. In this essay Coffee analyzes the causes and effects of his false arrest.

B. Use the selection as a stimulus for an essay that employs cause/effect. For example, you might analyze the causes of your choosing to go to college or the effects of growing up in your community or the time you made a "wrong" decision. Here are several questions to start you thinking.

- What details from the selection explain the obvious causes of Keith Coffee's arrest? What details explain the subtle causes? What details from the selection illustrate the effects of Keith Coffee's arrest? Have you ever had an experience that left a strong impression on you? What were the causes of this experience? What were the effects? Look beyond the obvious causes or effects of your experience. Are there subtle causes or effects?

Use your responses to the preceding questions to help you decide on a specific topic and generate a thesis statement. Decide whether your essay will focus on causes, effects, or both. Freewrite for approximately ten or fifteen minutes on the topic you select.

C. Share your ideas with members of your group or with a peer editor. Discuss the topic you are considering for your essay. Ask for constructive advice about the topic. Also discuss any problem areas that you foresee.

D. Use your prewriting and the questions on the Writing Focus Chart on page 132 to guide you as you write your first draft. Use any of the invention techniques from Chapter 2 and any of the strategies from Chapter 5 as needed. Your first draft should consist of an introduction, a body, and a conclusion and should clearly accomplish your writing purpose. Review your draft and develop an appropriate title.

E. Share your draft with members of your group or with a peer editor. Use the comments and suggestions from the group or peer editor, in conjunction with the Checklist for Revising and Editing on page 153, to help you make revisions. After sharing essays, work independently to revise your draft.

F. Evaluate the content, structure, and wording of your draft. Using the Checklist for Revising and Editing as a guide, make any necessary changes, additions, deletions, and corrections. Make as many revisions as needed. When you are satisfied, key your revised draft.

G. Carefully reread your revised draft. Using the Checklist for Proofreading on page 105, prepare the final copy. Consult the Writer's Guide that begins on page A 80 to review key points of grammar, punctuation, and capitalization. Use proofreaders' marks from the box on page 105 to mark your corrections.

H. Key the final copy. Look over the final copy and correct any keyboarding errors. Save your final copy in your portfolio.

USING ADJECTIVES AND ADVERBS CORRECTLY

An **adjective** is a word that modifies a noun or a pronoun. Adjectives add descriptive details to sentences and help readers visualize objects, people, and places more precisely. When an adjective modifies a noun, it answers the questions *which, how many,* or *what kind.* In the following examples, the adjectives are in italics.

My *favorite* movie opens with a *big* parade.

(*Favorite* answers the question *which* movie? *Big* answers the question *what kind of* parade?)

Four gray horses pull a coach down a street.

(*Four* answers the question *how many* horses? *Gray* answers the question *what kind of* horses?)

An **adverb** is a word that modifies a verb, adjective, or other adverb. Adverbs, like adjectives, also make descriptions more precise. When an adverb modifies a verb, it answers the questions *where, how,* or *under what conditions.*

Soon the scene switches to a cave that is *nearly* dark.

(*Soon* answers the question *when* does the scene switch? *Nearly* answers the question *how* dark?)

Adverbs frequently (though not always) end in *-ly.* Some adjectives also end in *-ly,* such as *friendly* and *lovely.* Sometimes, writers confuse the two and incorrectly use adjectives to modify verbs.

INCORRECT:
In the movie, Diego gallops *quick* to the rescue.

CORRECT:
In the movie, Diego gallops *quickly* to the rescue.

(*Quickly* answers the question *how* does Diego gallop?)

Activities

A. In the following sentences circle the correct word in parentheses.

1. You can watch many (fine, finely) athletes on television during the Olympic Games.

2. The Winter and Summer Games are an opportunity for couch potatoes to learn about (unusual, unusually) sports such as luge or fencing.

3. You may (sudden, suddenly) find yourself getting interested in these obscure sports.

4. You might start cheering (wild, wildly) because your favorite athlete in the biathlon wins the gold.

B. Identify the word in italics as an adjective or an adverb by writing *adjective* or *adverb* after each sentence. Then write the question the adjective or adverb answers.

1. Some countries *never* seem to win many medals in the Olympics. adverb

Question: _____ where _____

2. Other countries are *impressive* Olympic powers. adjective

Question: _____ what kind _____

3. Some countries, such as Norway, win few medals in the Summer Olympics but produce *countless* champions in the Winter Olympics. adjective

Question: _____ how many _____

C. Read the following paragraph and correct any errors with adjectives or adverbs.

When you make largely purchases such as appliances, you should always plan ahead. Look careful at consumer information that compares one brand with another in terms of quality and price. Make time to shop around at severally stores to get the best possibly price. Don't make decisions too quick. You'll have plenty of time to regret those decisions later.

D. For additional practice in finding and correcting adjective and adverb errors, see page A 75.

WRAPPING IT UP

SUMMARY

- Use the cause/effect strategy to analyze the causes and/or effects of a situation.

- An event can have several causes and effects. Some of these will be obvious, but others may be more subtle.

- To present a convincing cause/effect analysis, avoid pitfalls such as oversimplification, the presentation of false causes, and errors in logic.

- The purpose of an essay that employs cause/effect is usually to inform or to persuade.

- Structure the information in an essay that employs cause/effect in chronological order or in order of importance or interest.

THINKING IT OVER

- Why is it important to analyze causes and/or effects in daily life? Describe two or three of the most useful aspects of cause/effect that you learned in this chapter.

_____

_____

_____

_____

_____

_____

- How can the cause/effect strategy help you in conversations, letters, and debates?

  _____

  _____

  _____

  _____

  _____

  _____

- How will what you have learned in this chapter help you analyze cause/effect situations at work and at school?

  _____

  _____

  _____

  _____

  _____

  _____

IN YOUR JOURNAL

Review the goals that you set at the beginning of this chapter. In your journal, evaluate your progress toward these goals.

OBJECTIVES:

Composition

- To explore similarities between comparisons and contrasts made in speech and in writing.

- To use comparisons and contrasts to develop essay content.

- To write essays that present comparisons and contrasts in a block or point-by-point pattern.

- To create and revise essays that use comparison/contrast.

Grammar

- To eliminate misplaced and dangling modifiers.

How Do I
Make
Comparisons?

When you shop, how do you choose which products to buy? Like the woman in the picture, you probably compare and contrast different brands to see how they are the same and how they differ in terms of price, ingredients, and quality.

Every day you make countless decisions based on comparison and contrast. You make comparisons and contrasts in choosing a major at college, selecting a place to live, deciding where to eat, or picking out a gift for a friend. Just as you use a compare/contrast strategy in your daily life, you can also use this strategy to develop many of the essays you write. In this chapter you will learn how to develop essays that use the compare/contrast strategy.

What shirt should I wear? Should I cook tamales or tacos? Each day we use comparison and contrast to make choices. List specific instances in which you compared or contrasted two items.

- With friends or relatives:

  _____

  _____

- At work:

  _____

  _____

- At school:

  _____

  _____

For *one* example you listed, consider these questions:

- For what purpose were you making this comparison/contrast?
- On what basis did you make your comparison/contrast?
- How thoroughly did you develop your comparison/contrast? What were the strengths and weaknesses of your approach?
- Did you treat the same points about each item equally?
- How did your audience respond to your comparison/contrast?

IN YOUR
JOURNAL

Evaluate your ability to use comparison/contrast orally and in writing. Then set one or more goals in your journal. Here are some examples:

GOALS:
1. When I compare and contrast two things, I will order my ideas logically.
2. I will treat each item I am comparing and contrasting equally.

GROUP
ACTIVITY

If you were comparing and contrasting two people, places, or things, what points about each one would you discuss?

A. Each member of your group will choose a topic to compare and contrast. Consider showing the similarities and differences between two family members, the relative merits of one city over another, or the advantages and disadvantages of two jobs. Think carefully about the two items you are comparing and contrasting. How are they the same and how are they different? What ideas, facts, and examples will you use to support your comparison/contrast?

B. Each member of the group should take turns presenting a comparison/contrast orally to the group.

C. Work together to assess each comparison/contrast for effectiveness. Identify features that make a comparison/contrast clear, logical, and useful.

D. Work with your group to create a list of five or more specific guidelines to evaluate the effectiveness of a comparison/contrast.

E. Evaluate the guidelines your group developed. Work together to improve them. Then write the revised guidelines in the following space.

_____

_____

_____

_____

_____

_____

_____

_____

USING COMPARE/CONTRAST

FEATURES OF COMPARISONS AND CONTRASTS

When you **compare** one thing with another, you identify similarities or common features—how your mother and father are alike, for example, or how the culture of Mexico resembles that of Spain. When you **contrast** one thing with another, you identify differences—how American football differs from soccer, for instance, or how you are different today from the way you were five years ago.

When you compare or contrast two items in an essay, you may use one of the following approaches to develop your content:

- Focus only on the similarities between two things (comparison).

- Focus only on the differences between two things (contrast).

- Focus on both the similarities and the differences between two things (comparison/contrast).

The approach you choose will depend on your topic and your purpose for writing.

COMPARING PARALLEL FEATURES

A comparison/contrast can only be useful if you discuss the same or parallel features about each item. Otherwise, neither you nor your audience will have a basis for determining how the two items are alike and how they are different. Suppose, for example, you discuss two books. If you discuss the plot and characters of one book and the descriptions and setting of the other, you will be unable to compare or contrast these two books in a meaningful way.

TWO PATTERNS FOR COMPARISON/CONTRAST

There are two basic patterns used in the body paragraphs of an essay that uses comparison/contrast: the **block pattern** and the **point-by-point pattern.** Let's take a look at each pattern.

The Block Pattern

One way to structure a comparison/contrast is to present all of your information about the first item (Item A) and then to present all of your information about the second item (Item B). Presenting a block of information about one item at a time works best for short, relatively simple essays. To help readers keep track of your points of comparison/contrast, discuss the same points in the same order for Items A and B.

Suppose you are comparing and contrasting yourself with your roommate in terms of tidiness and study habits. Using the block pattern, you would discuss these two points in the same sequence for both yourself and your roommate. The following outline shows the format that an essay using a block pattern might take.

Block Pattern	
Introduction	
Body Paragraph 1: Item A	Me: my tidiness
Body Paragraph 2: Item A	Me: my study habits
Body Paragraph 3: Item B	My roommate: my roommate's tidiness
Body Paragraph 4: Item B	My roommate: my roommate's study habits
Conclusion	

In a comparison/contrast structured using the block pattern, strong topic sentences and effective use of transitions help to unify the points of comparison of the two items under discussion.

The Point-by-Point Pattern

Another way to structure an essay that uses comparison/contrast is to move back and forth between Item A and Item B on each point of comparison/contrast. You would use the same sequence throughout the essay—first discuss Item A and then Item B.

Suppose you were comparing and contrasting yourself and your roommate using a point-by-point pattern. In each body paragraph you would discuss a point about yourself (Item A) and then the same point about your roommate (Item B).

Alternating between Item A and Item B helps readers keep both items clearly in mind and enables them to follow your comparisons and contrasts easily. The point-by-point pattern is best for longer, more complex essays. The following outline shows the format that an essay using a point-by-point pattern might take.

Point-by-Point Pattern	
Introduction	
Body Paragraph 1: Main Point 1: Item A: Item B:	I am tidier than my roommate. my tidiness my roommate's tidiness
Body Paragraph 2: Main Point 2: Item A: Item B:	I am more studious than my roommate. my study habits my roommate's study habits
Conclusion	

USING TRANSITIONS TO LINK POINTS OF COMPARISON/CONTRAST

WRITER'S TIP

In writing that uses comparison/contrast, transitional words and phrases such as *similarly, moreover, both, on the other hand, however,* or *by contrast* link the two items you are comparing and contrasting and reinforce your points of comparison/contrast. Without transitional words and phrases, writing that presented all the points about Item A and then all the points about Item B would appear to be unconnected. Similarly, writing using the point-by-point pattern would be choppy and monotonous, because transitional words and phrases add variety to your sentence structure. Consult the chart in Chapter 5, page 193, for additional transitional words and phrases that can be used to link points of a comparison/contrast.

UNDERSTANDING WRITING TASKS THAT REQUIRE COMPARISON/CONTRAST

Many of the comparisons and contrasts you write will be in response to school- or job-related tasks. How do you know that you are being asked to compare or contrast two things? Some instructions, such as the following examples, tell you outright to compare and contrast.

- *Compare and contrast* the political philosophies of Martin Luther King, Jr. and Malcolm X.
- *Compare and contrast* two current approaches to handling customer complaints.

Other comparison/contrast writing tasks will not be worded as directly. Clue words such as *similarities and differences, alike and different, advantages and disadvantages, pros and cons, relative merits, longer . . . greater . . . better* let you know that you are being asked to compare and contrast two things.

Activity A: Finding Comparison/Contrast Clue Words

Underline the clue words for comparison/contrast in the following directions.

- Describe the <u>advantages and disadvantages</u> of nuclear versus solar energy.
- Discuss the <u>pros and cons</u> of doing your income taxes yourself.
- Describe the <u>relative merits</u> of eating in a restaurant as opposed to ordering take-out.

Think about examples of comparison/contrast you have read recently. Select one that you found effective. Answer these questions about the comparison/contrast.

DISCOVERY
ACTIVITY

- What two items was the writer comparing and contrasting?

  _____

- What was the purpose of the comparison/contrast?

  _____

  _____

  _____

• Why was the comparison/contrast effective?

_____

_____

_____

FIRST DRAFT: PLANNING AND WRITING ESSAYS THAT USE COMPARISON/CONTRAST

The Writing Focus Chart on page 132 can guide you in blending the key elements of writing to create interesting and effective essays that use comparison/contrast. Use the questions on the chart as you consider the purpose, content, structure, audience, and tone.

CHOOSING A TOPIC

For an essay that uses comparison/contrast, choose a topic that deals with two items that would be interesting or helpful to compare and contrast. There should be some basis for comparison or contrast between the two items; that is, the two items should share certain similarities or differences in some significant way. You can brainstorm or freewrite to discover suitable topics for a comparison/contrast.

When two things are quite similar, you may wish to focus on their differences because their similarities are already obvious. Likewise, when two things are extremely different, you may wish to concentrate on points of similarity. For example, in a comparison/contrast of two different popular magazines, you could explore differences between the magazines in terms of the types of articles they publish and the depth in which they treat their topics. On the other hand, suppose you wanted to compare two leisure-time activities that are very different, such as playing softball and watching professional sports on television. Though seemingly very different, these two activities do have important points of comparison. For example, you might explore ways in which both activities reduce stress and give a feeling of satisfaction. An effective comparison/contrast discovers overlooked or unusual points of similarity or difference.

ESTABLISHING THE WRITING PURPOSE

Once you have chosen a topic, establish your writing purpose. The purpose of essays that use comparison/contrast is usually either to inform or to persuade. If your purpose is to inform, use the comparison/contrast strategy to help your audience understand the relationship between two items. If your purpose is to persuade, use the comparison/contrast strategy to make decisions about two items.

WRITING A THESIS STATEMENT

After familiarizing yourself with your topic and establishing your writing purpose, write a thesis statement. The thesis statement will help you develop and structure your essay.

A thesis statement for an essay that uses comparison/contrast should do the following:

- State the topic of your comparison/contrast.
- Mention the points of comparison/contrast you will discuss.
- Explain whether you will focus on similarities or differences or both.

The following sentences are examples of thesis statements for essays that use comparison/contrast:

> While both swimming and running are excellent forms of exercise, each has advantages that a person planning a physical fitness program should consider.

> Abraham Lincoln of the United States and Benito Juárez of Mexico never met, yet these two great presidents shared many character traits and concerns about human rights.

DEVELOPING THE CONTENT

Once you have selected two items to compare/contrast and have written a thesis statement, decide what points you want to discuss about the two items. Use the invention techniques you learned in Chapter 2, such as brainstorming, to gather points of similarity and difference for a comparison/contrast. Suppose that you have decided to contrast two movies. You might brainstorm to determine how each movie handles the following features differently. Remember, always use parallel points for the two items.

Movie A   *Movie B*

characters   characters

plot   plot

suspense   suspense

special effects   special effects

PLANNING THE STRUCTURE

When you present details in a comparison/contrast, you can use any of the methods of organization you have learned. If you are comparing/contrasting two places or objects, you might use spatial organization. If you are comparing/contrasting two people, you might use chronological organization when presenting details about their lives. The most useful method of organization when writing an essay that uses comparison/contrast is probably order of importance or interest. You can begin with the most important detail or point about each item and work down through less important items (descending approach), or you can start with less important information and build up to the most important detail or point (ascending approach).

To make your comparison/contrast clear, remember to present parallel points about both items that you are comparing/contrasting. Also be sure that you always present features of Item A and Item B in the same order in your comparison/contrast: first A and then B.

As you learned on page 353, you can structure the body of an essay that uses comparison/contrast in either of two basic patterns, the block pattern and the point-by-point pattern. Following are two essays that compare and contrast the same material using the two different patterns.

Read the following essay, "What Makes a Good Job?", which uses the block pattern for comparison/contrast. As you read, underline important points of comparison/contrast.

....

What Makes a Good Job?

When I was in high school, the only considerations I looked for in a job were *which job paid the most* and *which had the best schedule.*

Now that I've had more experience, however, I've found that job satisfaction is an even more important consideration.

The job I took after my freshman year at college was certainly satisfying in terms of pay and schedule. This job, in the office of a vocational center for women, attracted me mainly because the pay was so good. As for the schedule, I never had to arrive earlier than 9 A.M. or leave later than 5 P.M. After about a week in this job, however, I was bored. Since I did not have a social work degree or counseling experience, I was not allowed to work with clients. Instead, my duties were to handle the office's paperwork. I keyboarded and filed correspondence and filled out countless forms. I soon realized that the good pay and the pleasant schedule didn't make up for my general job dissatisfaction. The time seemed to creep by.

When I began my job hunt at the end of my second year in college, I looked less at the pay and schedule of available jobs and more at whether the jobs had any people contact. Luckily, I found what I had been looking for in a job waiting on tables at the local coffee shop. Compared to the office job, waiting on tables did not shine in terms of pay or schedule. Although my average weekly pay was roughly equal to my office salary, the pay varied from week to week because I depended on tips for much of my income. Additionally, my schedule was more hectic than the office schedule had been. The hours were longer, and I worked odd shifts that changed from week to week. Even with the unpredictable pay and hours, however, I enjoyed my job. Juggling different tasks and being on my feet all day were demanding, but time passed very quickly. Moreover, the job gave me ample opportunity to use my skills with people. I loved the contact I had with customers. These favorable working conditions far outweighed the disadvantages of less steady pay and more strenuous work than my old office job.

Now when I look for jobs, I consider three factors: pay, schedule, and job satisfaction. My office job offered good pay and a good schedule but didn't make use of my skills with people and left me dissatisfied. By contrast, although waiting on tables offered less pay and an unpredictable schedule, it was much more satisfying because I got to work directly with people. Working at these two jobs has taught me that job satisfaction is much more important to me than the pay and schedule.

Questions

1. What is the purpose of this essay?

_____

_____

2. What is the writer's thesis statement? Does the writer provide enough specific information to support the central point? Provide specific examples.

_____

_____

_____

3. How is office work like waiting on tables? How are the two jobs different?

SIMILARITIES:

_____

_____

DIFFERENCES:

_____

_____

4. The writer presents a block of information about office work and then a block of information about waitressing. Is this structure effective? Why or why not?

_____

_____

_____

The following version of "What Makes a Good Job?" uses the point-by-point pattern for comparison/contrast. Read the essay, and compare it to the earlier version on pages 358-359.

What Makes a Good Job?

When I was in high school, the only important considerations I looked for in a job were *which job paid the most* and *which job had the best schedule.* Now that I've had more experience, however, I've found that job satisfaction is an even more important consideration.

As I headed into my first "adult" job, I didn't realize how important actually enjoying my job could be. Then, after my freshman year at college, I got a job in the office of a vocational center for women. Since I did not have a social work degree or counseling experience, I was not allowed to work with clients. Instead, my duties involved handling the office's paperwork. I keyboarded and filed correspondence and filled out countless forms. I soon found myself bored. I wanted to work with people, not paper, but this job kept me sitting quietly at my desk all day. The time seemed to creep by.

Because of my disappointment with the office job, during my second year in college, I looked for a job that would have more people contact. Luckily, I found what I had been looking for in a job waiting on tables at the local coffee shop. People skills are very important for waiting on tables. To be a successful waitress, you need to develop a good rapport with your coworkers. Even more important, you must deal with customers in a friendly way. Waiting on tables took advantage of my ability to work well with people. Although I worked hard, the days passed very quickly. I was never bored.

The pay for both the office job and waiting on tables job was adequate, though the salary I earned at the office job was far steadier. In the office job, I received a regular paycheck. As a waitress, I received a small paycheck. The bulk of my pay came as tips, and those tips varied greatly depending on what shift I worked, which tables I was assigned, and how busy the restaurant was. Though my overall waitress pay was roughly equal to what I received for office work, at the end of some days I found myself with less pay than I would have liked.

The schedule of my office job was regular and predictable. I never had to arrive earlier than 9 A.M. or leave later than 5 P.M. On the other hand, waiting on tables was never regular. One week I might work from noon to nine in the evening, and the next I might work from six in the evening to three in the morning. Moreover, the tasks were more physically demanding and less predictable than those of an office job. One minute I was carrying two heavy trays of food, and the next minute I was keeping track of multiple orders at different tables. Although the work was chaotic, I thrived at waiting on tables.

Now when I look for jobs, I consider job satisfaction as well as pay and schedule. When I worked in an office, the pay and schedule were good, but the job didn't make use of my skills with people and left me dissatisfied. By contrast, although waiting on tables paid less dependably and had a more demanding schedule, I found the job much more satisfying because I worked directly with people. Working at these two jobs has taught me that job satisfaction is much more important to me than the pay and schedule.

Questions

1. How do the two versions of "What Makes a Good Job?" differ in terms of purpose and content?

_____

_____

_____

_____

2. How is the structure of the second version different from the structure of the first version on page 358? Be specific.

_____

_____

_____

_____

3. Notice that in the essay that uses the point-by-point pattern (page 360), the writer does not present the three points of schedule, pay, and job satisfaction in the same order as they were presented in the block pattern essay (page 358). What does the varied presentation of these points in the two essays tell you about the flexibility of using the compare/contrast strategy?

_____

_____

_____

4. How does the writer achieve unity in the essay? Be specific.

_____

_____

_____

5. Which version is more effective for an essay on this topic that uses comparison/contrast? Explain your answer.

_____

_____

IN YOUR JOURNAL

Clip or photocopy for your journal examples of interesting comparisons/contrasts you encounter in newspapers, magazines, or books. Describe the topic and purpose of each example, and explain how the comparison/contrast is useful to you as a reader.

Select one comparison/contrast that is particularly effective. Then note how the writer structured the comparison/contrast. Was a block or point-by-point pattern used to present information? How does the structure of the piece clarify the content?

TARGETING A SPECIFIC AUDIENCE

Your intended audience for an essay that uses comparison/contrast will affect what points you will present about your topic in your comparison/contrast. Suppose you are writing an essay contrasting two fitness centers. If you are writing to inform consumers about the differences between the centers, you might focus on the price of membership, the quality of instruction in aerobics classes, and the helpfulness of the instructors. If, on the other hand, you are writing to inform exercise instructors about the advantages and disadvantages of working in one center versus the other, you might focus on wages, working conditions, benefit packages, and so forth.

The feelings and opinions of your intended audience will also affect the way you present your content, particularly if your purpose is to persuade. Suppose you are trying to convince your audience that vegetarian diets are more healthful than diets that include meat. In order to win meat-eaters over to your point of view, you would have to be sure to present a tactful, logical, and balanced comparison/contrast between the two diets. You might begin with an opening sentence such as the following:

> Although I love the taste of a medium-rare cheeseburger, I learned to love a vegetarian diet because of its health benefits.

If you are trying to persuade readers that one thing is better than another, show consideration for your audience so that readers will be open to your point of view.

The writer of "What Makes a Good Job?" had a specific audience in mind: fellow college students. Because this audience might not be familiar with working in an office or restaurant, the writer included specific facts, details, and examples to convey what each work setting was like.

Questions

1. If the writer of "What Makes a Good Job?" was presenting this comparison/contrast to a group of office workers, how might the writer change the content and wording of the essay?

_____

_____

_____

_____

2. If the writer of "What Makes a Good Job?" was presenting this comparison/contrast to a group of restaurant workers, how might the writer change the content and wording of the essay?

_____

_____

_____

_____

DO YOU WRITE ON A COMPUTER?

If you're not sure whether to use a block or point-by-point pattern for comparison/contrast, test *both* approaches on the computer. First, make a conceptual map using the block pattern. If available, use the copy feature of the word processing program to duplicate your map. Rearrange and edit the duplicate until you've created a second map that uses the point-by-point pattern. Print a copy of both maps. Compare the two maps, and use the one that you think is more effective.

SETTING THE TONE

The tone you choose will determine in part how your audience will respond to your essay. When you adopt a specific tone for your essay, be sure that your tone reflects the purpose of your essay. If you were writing an informative essay for a sociology class about differences in infant mortality rates between the United States and Sweden, you would probably use a factual, objective tone instead of a personal tone. If you were trying to persuade consumers that the health care system in Canada is better than the system in the United States, you might use an emotional tone to convince readers to agree with your argument.

In "What Makes a Good Job?" (the first version on pages 358-359) the writer used a personal, upbeat tone to emphasize a preference for one job over another and to present the experiences that led to that preference. If the purpose of the essay had been simply to inform readers about the different tasks involved in office work and waiting on tables, the writer might have used a more neutral tone.

Questions

1. Is the tone of "What Makes a Good Job?" (the first version on pages 358-359) appropriate for reaching an audience of young people with some job experience? Be specific.

   _____

   _____

2. Locate and describe a specific instance in the first version of the essay on pages 358-359 where tone reveals the writer's preference for one job over another.

   _____

   _____

Activity B: Planning an Essay That Uses Comparison/Contrast

In this activity you will plan the purpose, content, structure, audience, and tone for an essay that uses comparison/contrast. Refer to the Writing Focus Chart on page 132 for help in addressing these five key elements. Use separate sheets of paper for your work.

A. Narrow one of the following general topics for an essay that uses comparison/contrast:

- Two movies
- Two cities
- Two foods
- Two cars
- Two animals
- Two types of exercise

For example, if you select the general topic "Two movies," your narrowed topic could be a comparison/contrast of two classic films such as *Gone With the Wind* and *Lawrence of Arabia*.

B. Once you have selected and narrowed a topic, establish your writing purpose. Decide whether your comparison/contrast will focus on similarities or differences, or both. Freewrite for ten to fifteen minutes about the topic of your essay. Explore as many ideas, facts, and examples as you can about the two items you plan to compare/contrast.

C. Based on your prewriting, write a thesis statement.

D. Review the items you chose to compare/contrast. Decide what points you want to discuss about each of these items. Brainstorm a list of similarities and differences between the two items.

E. Based on your prewriting, decide how you want to structure your essay. Decide whether you will use the block pattern or the point-by-point pattern. Prepare an outline that includes important points of comparison/contrast about the items and supporting facts and details.

F. Target an audience for your essay. For example, you might gear your essay toward an audience that is familiar with the two items or experiences you are comparing/contrasting. Alternatively, you might write your comparison/contrast for an audience that is unfamiliar with the topic and might require more explanation. After considering your intended audience, decide what tone is most appropriate for your topic and writing purpose.

PORTFOLIO

Save your work in your portfolio. You will use your prewriting to develop an essay that uses comparison/contrast in Assignment 2 on page 372.

REVISING, EDITING, AND PROOFREADING ESSAYS THAT USE COMPARISON/CONTRAST

The Checklist for Revising and Editing on page 153 can guide you in evaluating and revising the first draft of an essay that uses comparison/contrast. The Checklist for Proofreading on page 105 can help you turn a revised draft into a final copy.

Read the following first draft of an essay that makes use of comparison/contrast, which includes the writer's handwritten revisions. Remember that at this point the writer has not yet corrected errors in grammar, spelling, punctuation, and capitalization. What changes did the writer make to improve the essay?

Revised Draft: **Two Very Different Sons**

I used to think that environment was the all-important factor in ~~deciding~~ *the development of* a person's character, *After the birth of my two sons, however,* I changed my mind. My sons, born a year apart, grew up in the same environment, ~~with me, their single mother,~~ but they have completely different temperments and talents. ~~In the paragraphs that follow, I will talk about how my sons are different.~~

My sons' differing temperments were visible from the outset. My older son Willy learned to speak very early but was slow to walk because he was cautious. He didn't respond well to strangers and would cry if too many people were in the room. *In contrast,* My younger son ben was adventurous and unafraid. As soon as he could stand, he was trying to walk and climb. Even though Ben doesn't speak until he was almost two, he always liked to go up to strangers on the street, in the supermarket, and at the playground.

Not only do my sons have different temperments, they also have My sons showed, early on, radically different artistic talents. I first noticed Willys interest in music one day when I was lisening to the radio. Willy, who was about three, started to run around the apartment, dancing hap-

pyly. I soon realized that Willy enjoyed music of all kinds.

When Willy entered elementary school, he learned to play the recorder.

∧Now he plays the saxophone quite well. His dream is to

become a musician and composer. *Since Ben was a child,*

he has loved to make things with his hands. Ben, how-

ever, has no interest in music. At home, Ben constructed

elaborate fortresses out of blocks. He ∧*also* loved to draw and

paint. ∧*As he grew older,* His paintings won first place in several school art

competitions. Now, at 10, Ben has decided to be a comic

book illustrator when he grows up.

Even though my sons have such different natures, they get along surprisingly

∧ ~~I am always amazed at how well they get along.~~ Willy, *well.*

who are a fast reader and an excellent writer, often helps

Ben with reading and writing homework, areas in which

Ben, who makes friends easily, is great at drawing Willy out of his shell.

Ben is weak. ∧The differences between my sons actually

seem to draw them closer together. I feel very lucky to be

the mother of these two children∧ *who, though so different,*

are so close to each other.

On page 370 of this chapter you'll see a rekeyed version of "Two Very Different Sons" that incorporates the writer's handwritten revisions. You'll use that version to proofread the essay for errors in spelling, punctuation, and so on.

Questions

1. How has the writer improved the effectiveness of this essay? Be specific.

_____

_____

_____

_____

_____

_____

2. Why did the writer delete the phrase *with me, their single mother* in the introduction?

_____

_____

_____

_____

_____

3. Why did the writer change the order of sentences in the second paragraph?

_____

_____

_____

_____

_____

4. What transitions did the writer add to create a smooth flow between points of comparison?

_____

_____

_____

_____

_____

5. If you were the writer of this essay, what additional changes would you make in content, structure, and wording?

_____

_____

_____

_____

_____

_____

Read the revised and rekeyed draft of "Two Very Different Sons" that follows. Proofread the revision, and correct any mistakes in spelling, capitalization, and punctuation as well as any factual, keyboarding, and grammatical errors.

Revised and Rekeyed Draft:

Two Very Different Sons

I used to think that environment was the all-important factor in the development of a person's character. After the births of my two sons, however, I changed my mind. My sons, born a year apart, grew up in the same environment, but they have completely different temperments and talents.

My sons' differing temperments were visible from the outset. My older son Willy learned to speak very early but was slow to walk because he was cautious. He didn't respond well to strangers and would cry if too many people were in the room. In contrast, my younger son ben was adventurous and unafraid. As soon as he could stand, he was trying to walk and climb. Even though Ben doesn't speak until he was almost two, he always liked to go up to strangers on the street, in the supermarket, and at the playground.

Not only do my sons have different temperments, they also have radically different artistic talents. I first noticed Willys interest in music one day when I was lisening to the radio. Willy, who was about three, started to run around the apartment, dancing happyly. I soon realized that Willy enjoyed music of all kinds. When Willy entered elementary school, he learned to play the recorder. Now he plays the saxophone quite well. His dream is to become a musician and composer. Ben, however, has no interest in music. Since Ben was a child, he has loved to make things with his hands. At home, Ben constructed elaborate fortresses out of blocks. He also loved to draw and paint. As he grew older, his paintings won first place in several school art competitions. Now, at 10, Ben has decided to be a comic book illustrater when he grows up.

Even though my sons have such different natures, they get along surprisingly well. Willy, who are a fast reader and an excellent writer, often helps Ben with reading and writing homework, areas in which Ben is weak. Ben, who makes friends easily, is great at drawing Willy out of his shell. The differences between my sons actually seem to draw them closer together. I feel very lucky to be the mother of these two children who, though so different, are so close to each other.

Assignment 1:
Creating an Essay That Uses Comparison/Contrast With Your Group

In this assignment you will work with your group to plan, write, edit, and proofread an essay that uses comparison/contrast.

A. Choose a topic suitable for a collaboratively written essay. Work together to narrow the topic and to brainstorm points of comparison/contrast. Decide whether your essay will focus on comparisons or contrasts, or both.

B. Working as a group, use the questions on the Writing Focus Chart on page 132 to guide you as you plan the first draft. Use any of the invention techniques you learned in Chapter 2 to develop the thesis statement, introduction, main ideas, supporting details, and conclusion. Also use any of the strategies from Chapter 5 to develop content.

C. Use your group's prewriting to write the first draft. Your first draft should consist of an introduction, a body, and a conclusion and should clearly accomplish your writing purpose. Review the draft and work together to develop an appropriate title.

D. Carefully reread and evaluate the content, structure, and wording of your first draft. Discuss any necessary changes, additions, deletions, and corrections. Using the Checklist for Revising and Editing on page 153 as a guide, work together to revise the first draft. Complete as many revisions as needed.

E. When you are satisfied that your draft is the best work that your group can produce, choose someone to key the revised draft. Make a photocopy for every group member.

F. Carefully reread your revised draft. Using the Checklist for Proofreading on page 105, work together to prepare the final copy. Consult the Writer's Guide that begins on page A 80 to review key points of grammar, punctuation, and capitalization. Have each group member proofread the revised draft independently and use proofreaders' marks from the box on page 105 to mark corrections. Then compare corrections and incorporate all the changes on one draft.

G. Have one group member key the final copy. Proofread the final copy as a group, and correct any keyboarding errors. Record the names of all group members on the final copy. Make a photocopy for every group member. Save your final copy in your portfolio.

PORTFOLIO

Assignment 2:
Creating an Essay That Uses Comparison/Contrast

In this assignment you will work independently to plan, write, edit, and proofread the essay you began developing earlier in this chapter.

A. Review the planning you did in Activity B on page 365, including your prewriting, thesis statement, and outline. Reread the freewriting you did on your topic.

B. Use your prewriting and the questions on the Writing Focus Chart on page 132 to guide you as you plan the first draft of the essay. Use any of the invention techniques you learned in Chapter 2 to develop the introduction, main ideas, supporting details, and conclusion. Also use any of the strategies from Chapter 5 to develop content.

C. Write the first draft of your essay. Your first draft should consist of an introduction, a body, and a conclusion and should clearly accomplish your writing purpose. Review your draft and develop an appropriate title.

D. Share your draft with members of your group or with a peer editor. Use the comments and suggestions from the group or peer editor, in conjunction with the Checklist for Revising and Editing on page 153, to help you make revisions. After sharing essays, work independently to revise your draft.

E. Evaluate the content, structure, and wording of your essay. Using the Checklist for Revising and Editing as a guide, make any necessary changes, additions, deletions, and corrections. Make as many revisions as needed. When you are satisfied, key your revised draft.

F. Carefully reread your revised draft. Using the Checklist for Proofreading on page 105, prepare the final copy. Consult the Writer's Guide that begins on page A 80 to review key points of grammar, punctuation, and capitalization. Use proofreaders' marks from the box on page 105 to mark your corrections.

PORTFOLIO

G. Key the final copy. Look over the final copy and correct any keyboarding errors. Save your final copy in your portfolio.

Assignment 3:
Reading as a Stimulus for Writing

In this assignment you will read a selection and then work independently to plan, write, edit, and proofread an essay that compares and contrasts your life with a way of life that is different from yours.

A. Read "Watching China" by Amy Tan on pages A 132-A 134. Amy Tan is a California-born writer whose parents emigrated from China. In this essay she contrasts her life in the United States with that of her relatives in China.

B. Use the selection as a stimulus for an essay that uses comparison/contrast. For example, you might compare and contrast your life with the life of someone who lives in this country but has to struggle harder than you do to meet basic needs, or with the earlier life of a neighbor or relative who came to this country from elsewhere. Here are several questions to start you thinking.

- What details from the selection show most sharply the contrast between Amy Tan's life and the lives of her relatives in China?

- How does Amy Tan use comparison/contrast to examine what she takes for granted in her own way of life?

- Have you ever observed or heard about a way of life that was so different from yours that it shocked you?

- What needs or wishes might you expect to have in common with someone whose daily life is very different from yours?

Use your responses to the preceding questions to help you decide on a specific topic and generate a thesis statement. Decide whether your essay will focus on comparisons or contrasts, or both. Freewrite for ten or fifteen minutes on the topic you select.

C. Share your ideas with members of your group or with a peer editor. Discuss the topic you are considering for your essay. Ask for constructive advice about the topic. Also discuss any problem areas that you foresee.

D. Use your prewriting and the questions on the Writing Focus Chart on page 132 to guide you as you write your first draft. Use any of the invention techniques from Chapter 2 and any of the strategies from Chapter 5 as needed. Your first draft should consist of an introduction, a body, and a conclusion and should clearly accomplish your writing purpose. Review your draft and develop an appropriate title.

E. Share your draft with members of your group or with a peer editor. Use the comments and suggestions from the group or peer editor, in conjunction with the Checklist for Revising and Editing on page 153, to help you make revisions. After sharing essays, work independently to revise your draft.

F. Evaluate the content, structure, and wording of your draft. Using the Checklist for Revising and Editing as a guide, make any necessary changes, additions, deletions, and corrections. Make as many revisions as needed. When you are satisfied, key your revised draft.

G. Carefully reread your revised draft. Using the Checklist for Proofreading on page 105, prepare the final copy. Consult the Writer's Guide that begins on page A 80 to review key points of grammar, punctuation, and capitalization. Use proofreaders' marks from the box on page 105 to mark your corrections.

PORTFOLIO

H. Key the final copy. Look over the final copy and correct any keyboarding errors. Save your final copy in your portfolio.

MISPLACED AND DANGLING MODIFIERS

A **modifier** is a word or group of words that restricts or qualifies the meaning of another word or phrase. The modifiers in the following examples appear in italics.

Mina dreamed of blizzards *almost* all night.

(The word *almost* limits the meaning of "all night.")

Jaleel bought fish food *in a red can*.

(The phrase *in a red can* qualifies "fish food.")

Sometimes writers create unintended meanings or humorous constructions by misplacing modifiers.

MISPLACED MODIFIERS:

Mina almost dreamed of blizzards all night.

(In this sentence *almost* describes "dreamed" instead of "all night.")

Jaleel bought fish food for his goldfish in a red can.

(Were "his goldfish" *in a red can*?)

To avoid misplacing modifiers, position modifiers as close as possible to the word or phrase they describe.

CORRECT:

Jaleel bought fish food in a red can for his goldfish.

Modifying word groups often appear at the beginning of a sentence. When such a word group does not describe the subject of the sentence, the result may be a dangling modifier.

DANGLING MODIFIERS:

Aiming at the target, the bowstring snapped against my arm.

While balancing my checkbook, the doorbell rang loudly.

To correct a dangling modifier, either add the subject to the modifying word group or reword the sentence to make the modifier and subject agree.

CORRECT:

Aiming at the target, I snapped the bowstring against my arm.

The bowstring snapped against my arm when I was aiming at the target.

While balancing my checkbook, I heard the doorbell ring loudly.

While I was balancing my checkbook, the doorbell rang loudly.

Activities

A. Correct the misplaced or dangling modifiers in the following sentences.

1. Jumping out of bed, the covers twisted around Stefan's feet.

2. Stefan ran into the hallway to wake the children wearing only one slipper.

3. When Stefan looked into the refrigerator to make breakfast, he found that he had almost cooked all the eggs yesterday, and there was just one left.

4. Stefan had to call to the car pool driver still in his pajamas and tell the driver to go on without him.

B. Read the following paragraph. Correct any misplaced or dangling modifiers.

One day, when we were young, several bright red trucks surrounded an old oak tree on our block, one with a bright red mechanical bucket. My friends and I thought the oak almost looked like a huge totem pole. Now, however, a woman nearly climbed to the top of the tree to prune its mighty limbs. Then the tree surgeons took huge chain saws from the back of the pickup with sharklike teeth. As the tree surgeons started the saws, we ran screaming down the street with fierce faces. Thinking we had saved the day, the roaring saws were turned off. The tree surgeons didn't leave; instead, one of them told us to watch out for the falling tree.

C. For additional practice in finding and correcting misplaced and dangling modifiers, see page A 76.

WRAPPING IT UP

SUMMARY

- Use a comparison/contrast strategy in an essay to identify how two things are similar or how they are different. An essay that uses comparison/contrast can focus on similarities, differences, or both.

- To create a meaningful comparison/contrast, always choose parallel features for items to compare or contrast.

- Structure the information in an essay that uses comparison/contrast in one of two ways: either present all the information about Item A and then all of the information about Item B (the block pattern), or compare/contrast Items A and B point by point (the point-by-point pattern).

- Use appropriate transitional words and phrases to link the points in a comparison/contrast.

- The purpose of an essay that uses comparison/contrast is usually to inform or to persuade. You may compare/contrast in order to clarify the relationship between two things or to make a choice between two things.

THINKING IT OVER

- Why is it important to make comparisons and contrasts in daily life? Describe two or three of the most useful aspects of comparison/contrast that you learned in this chapter.

  _____

  _____

  _____

  _____

- How can the compare/contrast strategy help you in conversations and in writing?

_____

_____

_____

- How will what you have learned in this chapter help you write comparisons and contrasts at work and at school?

_____

_____

_____

IN YOUR JOURNAL

Review the goals that you set at the beginning of this chapter. In your journal, evaluate your progress toward these goals.

12

USING CLASSIFICATION

OBJECTIVES:

Composition

- To explore similarities between classifications made in speech and in writing.

- To use classification to develop essay content.

- To classify items into categories based on a common feature.

- To create and revise essays that use classification to develop content.

Grammar

- To eliminate unnecessary changes in verb tense.

How Do I
Sort and Group?

Imagine that the books in the library are arranged randomly. How would you find the book you wanted among the thousands on the shelves? Luckily, when you search for books in the library, they are divided and classified in an orderly way.

Classification is a strategy of organization. By sorting and grouping items into categories according to a common feature, we make large topics or tasks more orderly, manageable, and accessible. For example, classified ads in a newspaper are grouped in the categories: "Help Wanted," "Real Estate," "Automobiles for Sale," "Services Available," "Personals," and so on. In this chapter, you will learn how to develop essays in which classification is used to make a central point about a topic.

Jerome explains to a friend that his favorite kinds of foods are fruits, breads, and salads. Tamara prepares a marketing study to analyze her customers in terms of age, occupation, and income. Gaylene writes an English paper about D. H. Lawrence's poetry, essays, and fiction. Edward sorts bolts and washers by size.

Recall situations in which you classified items by placing them into categories, either orally or in writing.

- With friends or relatives: _____

_____

- At work: _____

_____

- At school: _____

_____

For *one* example you listed, consider these questions:

- For what purpose or reason were you classifying information?
- How clear were the categories used?
- Were your categories complete, accounting for all features of the items you were classifying?
- Did any of your categories overlap?
- How did your audience respond to your classification?

IN YOUR JOURNAL

Evaluate your ability to classify items into categories either orally or in writing. Then set one or more goals in your journal. Here are some examples:

GOALS:
1. When I classify, I will sort items into logical categories.
2. I will make sure the categories in my classification do not overlap.

CLASSIFYING ITEMS ORALLY

GROUP ACTIVITY

If you had to classify items into categories, what criteria would you use?

A. Each member of your group will choose a topic that can be divided into categories and classified. You might select one of the following: popular restaurants, fashions, sports, forms of exercise, or television shows.

B. Each member of the group should take turns presenting a classification of something orally to the group.

C. Work together to assess every classification to determine whether it is valid and effective. Identify features that make a classification clear, logical, and useful.

D. Work with your group to create a list of five or more specific guidelines for evaluating the effectiveness of a classification.

E. Evaluate the guidelines your group developed. Work together to improve them. Then write the revised guidelines in the following space.

_____

_____

_____

_____

_____

_____

_____

_____

_____

_____

_____

_____

USING CLASSIFICATION

WHAT IS CLASSIFICATION?

Classification is the division of a topic into smaller groups according to a common feature in order to make a central point. Classification allows us to organize a complicated world and is a natural process. We automatically place items, events, and situations into groups or categories.

Classification gives us a way of specifying characteristics of large groups. For example, your biology instructor will subdivide the large group "animal" into subgroups labeled mammal, fish, bird, reptile, and amphibian. Each subgroup can be further divided and classified, making groups even smaller and more specific. Mammals, for instance, can be divided into carnivores (meat eaters) and herbivores (plant eaters). By classifying information this way, you discover what is common to all members of the category.

Some common groups or categories that you might recognize include the following:

books: fiction and nonfiction
objects: animal, vegetable, and mineral
food groups: fruit, vegetable, meat, dairy, and bread

Other groups or categories, perhaps not so recognizable as the ones above, include the following:

mail: bills, junk mail, personal letters
swimmers: beginners, intermediates, and advanced swimmers
types of laughs: giggles, snorts, silent laughs, hearty laughs

FINDING COMMON FEATURES

Items can be classified into groups only if all the items in a group share one or more common features. For example, a rose, a tulip, a daisy, and an orchid can be grouped together because they are all flowers. A peach, however, could not be grouped into the category of "flowers." To create a classification, you must identify common features that tie together all the items in the category. For example, suppose you wanted to classify stores in a mall because you are designing the store directory that will be on display by each escalator. The most logical and helpful way to classify stores would be to group them according to what they sell: shoes, toys, and so on. All stores that sell shoes, including athletic footwear shops and stores that sell only children's shoes, would share the common feature of selling shoes and would be grouped together.

CREATING CATEGORIES EQUAL IN WEIGHT

Make sure that all categories you create have the same weight. One category should not be able to absorb other categories. For example, if you categorize books, you might create categories such as science fiction, historical novels, and mysteries. It would be inappropriate to include another category for fiction, however. Such a category would include books from the other categories because science fiction, historical novels, and mysteries are subgroups of fiction. The category of fiction can absorb the other categories.

PRESENTING PARALLEL INFORMATION

Information presented in a classification should be parallel. For example, if you present different cooking styles such as Italian, Chinese, American, and French, you must provide the same information about each cooking style. This information may include typical foods of each style. Presenting the same kind of information for each category enables readers to compare the items being classified.

USING TRANSITIONS TO LINK CATEGORIES IN A CLASSIFICATION

When presenting a classification in writing, use transitional words and phrases such as *one such, another,* and *in addition* to clarify the relationships between and among categories. Transitional words and phrases such as *both, similarly,* and *by contrast* are useful for comparing or contrasting the traits of different categories. Consult the chart on page 193 for additional transitional words and phrases that can be used to link categories in a classification.

Think about examples of something you have read recently where the writer classified material by categories. Select one example that you thought was effective. Then answer the following questions.

- What topic was the writer classifying?

  _____

  _____

- What categories did the writer use for the classification?

  _____

  _____

  _____

- What other categories might the writer have used for this topic?

  _____

  _____

  _____

- Why was the classification effective?

  _____

  _____

  _____

UNDERSTANDING WRITING TASKS THAT INVOLVE CLASSIFICATION

You will use classification in many school and job-related writing tasks. In some tasks, instructions may directly ask you to use classification, as in the following sets of instructions.

- Classify the different varieties of orchids.
- Classify countries according to the continent on which each is located.
- Classify vacation hotels by cost and luxury features.
- Classify the types of entry-level positions in the company.

Not all classification tasks, however, may be worded so clearly. Other words that can help you determine that you are being asked to classify items include the following: *divide, group, separate, kinds, types, sort, varieties, categories,* and *parts.*

Activity A: Finding Clue Words That Involve Classification

Underline the clue words that involve classification in the following instructions for writing tasks.

- Describe the varieties of evergreens found in the Southeast.
- What kinds of retirement programs are available to nonworking people?
- Explain the parts of the Executive Branch of the federal government.
- Group cold medications according to side effects.

FIRST DRAFT: PLANNING AND WRITING ESSAYS THAT USE CLASSIFICATION

The Writing Focus Chart on page 132 can guide you in blending the key elements of writing to create an interesting and effective essay that uses classification. Use the questions on the chart as you consider your purpose, content, structure, audience, and tone.

CHOOSING A TOPIC

When you describe a topic by placing it in a category, make sure the topic isn't too broad. Music, for example, is such a broad topic that classifying all its categories would be a huge undertaking. A special branch of music such as rock, classical music, folk music, or jazz would be a more manageable topic, and an even smaller subdivision such as American folk music might be more suitable still.

ESTABLISHING THE WRITING PURPOSE

Most topics can be classified in many different ways. How you classify a topic depends on your purpose because you classify information in order to make a point. For example, if you are examining cars to identify cars that people on a limited budget can afford, you would classify cars by cost. However, if you are a car dealer planning a newspaper ad to sell cars, you would classify cars by make and model. Each classification system allows the writer to make a different *point* about cars.

The purpose of presenting a classification can be to inform or to persuade. For example, an essay that presents information about different colleges or that provides a humorous look at diets will inform readers about the topic. Essays that use classification for informative purposes often help readers make choices about a topic. For example, articles in consumer magazines such as *Consumer Reports* use classification to present information about products. Readers compare data on various brands of a product to decide which brand best suits their needs.

Essays that use classification for a persuasive purpose often present information to persuade readers to consider the writer's viewpoint on a topic. For example, an essay describing ways to volunteer for community service can be written to persuade readers to volunteer for the category of community service that suits their interests.

Creating Categories

Once you've chosen a topic, you will create categories by organizing like elements according to a common feature. Decide how to organize elements of your topic into categories. If your topic is American folk music, for example, you might create categories like traditional, bluegrass, and folk rock. Alternatively, you might create categories such as love songs, work songs, humorous songs, songs of political or social protest, and songs about war. With your categories created, identify common features of each category. For example, traditional folk songs have the following common features: they are usually well over a century old, they may have several versions or variations, and they are usually anonymous.

WRITING A THESIS STATEMENT

After you create categories for a classification and identify common features, write a thesis statement. The thesis statement will help you develop and structure your essay.

A thesis statement for an essay using classification should do one or more of the following:

- State your topic and the categories of classification.
- Present the common features that are the basis of the classification.
- Explain why the classification is important.
- Identify relationships between categories.

The following two examples show the thesis statement, topic, categories, and common features for writing that uses classification:

In order to have a safe, enjoyable swimming experience this summer, you should be aware of whether your swimming skills rank you among beginners, intermediates, or advanced swimmers.

Topic: types of swimmers
Categories: beginners, intermediates, advanced swimmers
Common features:

- beginners—can swim 50 feet, know one front stroke and one back stroke
- intermediates—can swim 75 feet, know crawl stroke, one back stroke, and sidestroke, can tread water and survival float for one minute
- advanced swimmers—can swim 300 feet in good form, know all swimming strokes, can dive, tread water, survival float, and swim underwater

Central point: Swimmers are usually classified as beginners, intermediates, or advanced swimmers according to their level of skill.

When you look in your mailbox, you either groan or smile depending on whether you find bills, junk mail, or personal letters.

Topic: types of mail
Categories: bills, junk mail, personal letters
Common features:

- bills—asking you for money, sent to you as an individual, must be answered as soon as possible
- junk mail—often ask you for money but not because you owe any, often get your name from a mailing list, need never be answered

- personal letters—sent to you as an individual, not usually asking for anything except a reply, answer can be put off but not for too long.

  Central point: The mail you receive is of three basic types: bills, junk mail, and personal letters.

Use your thesis statement as a guide in gathering the facts, details, and examples for each category in your classification.

DEVELOPING THE CONTENT

Once you determine a topic and categories, gather supporting information for each category. Each category should include adequate facts, details, and examples to illustrate the category. For example, for an essay about weatherproof sport clothing you should describe types of weatherproof clothing available in stores. On the other hand, an essay presenting informal categories such as "types of moviegoers" can be illustrated with examples from your observations and experience. Use invention techniques you learned in Chapter 2 to help you gather supporting information. For example, you can brainstorm to come up with a list of common features for each of your categories. You can also ask questions such as the following:

- How are all my categories related to one another?
- What are the qualities and common features of each category?
- What makes this category distinct from the other categories I've set up?
- What details can I use to make this category clear to readers?

As you learned earlier in this chapter, remember to gather parallel information for each category in your classification.

PLANNING THE STRUCTURE

To structure the body of an essay using classification, you will need to decide how to order both the categories and the information within each category. One of the following methods of organization can be used:

- Chronological order
- Order of importance or interest
- Natural order

Let's take a closer look at each of these methods.

Chronological Order

Presenting information in chronological order is effective when you are classifying historical events or periods. For example, when classifying United States history by the wars fought, you can structure the essay in the order that the wars occurred. If you are classifying children by developmental stages, you can begin with the youngest developmental stage, infancy, and move through early childhood, preschool age, school age, and adolescence.

Order of Importance or Interest

Another common approach when using classification is to arrange the information in order of importance or interest, from most to least important or interesting category, or vice versa. This structure is often effective when your purpose is to persuade readers because you can either hook readers' attention at the outset with your strongest point or leave your readers at the conclusion with your strongest point.

Natural Order

An essay that uses classification can also be arranged in a manner that reflects the qualities or traits relating to the topic. For example, in an essay that classifies items by color, you might present items from the darkest to the lightest color, or vice versa.

Read the essay on page 392, "My Path to Adulthood." As you read, underline each of the categories the writer presents.

My Path to Adulthood

As I consider my adult life, I realize how far I've come in balancing the demands of my life. My path to adulthood has led me to become what I once thought I never wanted to be: like my parents. To reach this point, my life has evolved in stages, from a No Way stage through an I Can Handle It stage and a Work Is Everything stage to where I am now, the Healthy Balance stage.

The first stage, the No Way stage, began when I moved away from my parents for the first time. There was "no way" I was going to do things the way my parents had taught me. I was going to dress how I wanted, study when I chose, and eat what I pleased—even chocolate cake for breakfast. Although this stage was brief, it gave me some much-needed freedom.

Next I passed into the I Can Handle It stage where I took responsibility for everything and everyone in my life. I never cut classes. I formed a study group with my friends. (My friends would say I forced them to study!) Whenever a roommate or friend had a problem, I was there to "handle it." I took friends' pets to the vet and babysat on demand. I never said no. After all, "I could handle it." However, the more I handled, the more frazzled I became.

By the time I graduated, I felt pulled apart by my outside commitments. As a result, I resolved to devote my energy to my job—beginning the Work Is Everything stage. During this stage I was often the first to arrive at my office and the last to leave. I volunteered for any office task that needed doing. I never had time for fun or even for rest and rarely went to parties. As for dating, I was usually too busy—or too tired.

At the point of complete collapse, I moved into the "Healthy Balance" stage. Ironically, I entered this stage because of a wonderful talk with my parents, who encouraged me to slow down. I released myself from some of my responsibilities and began to do things like go out with friends. I still worked hard, but I played too.

During this stage I found that I enjoyed spending time with my parents. We actually had a lot in common! In fact, I was very much like my parents. Surprisingly, it has turned out to be a pretty good way to be.

Questions

1. What is the purpose of this essay?

   To inform   The different the stages of life

2. What is the writer's thesis statement?

3. What are the four categories presented in the essay?

   No way stage,   I can handle it stage
   Work is everything stage
   Healthy Balance Stage

4. How does the writer structure the essay? Is this structure effective? Be specific.

IN YOUR JOURNAL

Clip or photocopy for your journal examples of writing using classification that you encounter in newspapers, magazines, or books. Describe the topic and purpose of each example, and identify the categories the writer has created.

Select one essay you particularly like. Describe how the writer has structured the classification. Does the writer use chronological order, order of importance or interest, natural order, or a combination of methods to organize the classification? How does the structure of the piece clarify the content?

TARGETING A SPECIFIC AUDIENCE

For an essay that uses classification, the choice of audience influences how the categories of a topic will be developed. Tell what possible categories you might use for the topic "restaurants," using such common features as cost, type of food served, or location, if you were writing for the following audiences.

- College students:

  _____

  _____

  _____

- Families:

  _____

  _____

  _____

- Single people:

  _____

  _____

  _____

The writer of "My Path to Adulthood" on page 392 had a fairly general audience in mind. The writer felt that the essay would appeal to young adults and parents alike. A different audience might have changed the content and wording of the essay. Suppose the writer of "My Path to Adulthood" was presenting the essay to adults who have difficult relationships with their parents. How might the content and wording of the essay be changed?

SETTING THE TONE

In an essay that uses classification, your tone should be clear and precise. Your language should be concrete and, whenever possible, should contain specific examples.

Though your language should be precise, your tone does not always need to be serious. Classification is often thought of as a formal process, perhaps because classification is widely used by scientists. However, in nontechnical essays that use classification, an informal or even a humorous tone is possible. You can create a lighter tone in several ways. One way is to give your categories humorous names such as the No Way Stage described in the essay on page 392. Another way is to use informal or humorous examples of your categories.

- Suppose you were adding details to "My Path to Adulthood" on page 392 to illustrate one or more of the stages that the writer describes. Give two informal or humorous examples that could be added to the essay.

_____

_____

Use your word processing program to set up categories for a classification in an easy-to-see format. Create a chart, a cluster of lists, or a diagram that shows your categories. See whether you have established parallel features for all your categories. Delete or move information as needed to list parallel features. When you are satisfied with your categories, print a hard copy for reference. Also save your file on your computer or on a disk in case you need to make changes later.

Writing **FOCUS CHART**

Activity B: Planning an Essay That Uses Classification

In this activity you will plan the purpose, content, structure, audience, and tone for an essay that uses classification. Refer to the Writing Focus Chart on page 132 for help in addressing these five key elements. Use separate sheets of paper for your work.

A. Narrow one of the following topics for an essay that uses classification:

- Friends
- Excuses
- Cheaters
- Diets
- Students
- Dreams

For example, if you select the general topic "excuses," your narrowed topic might be "kinds of excuses that never work with instructors."

B. Once you have selected and narrowed a topic, establish your writing purpose. Freewrite for ten to fifteen minutes about the topic you have chosen to classify. Explore different ways you might classify your information to make a point.

C. Create categories for your topic. For example, if your topic is "kinds of excuses that never work with instructors," you might invent humorous categories of excuses such as the Family Disaster excuse and the I Left It at Home excuse. Once you have set up your categories, think about common features for each category. A common feature of the Family Disaster excuse, for example, would be that all such excuses involve emergencies that involve relatives and that prevent assignments from being completed.

D. Based on your prewriting, write a thesis statement.

E. Gather supporting information to illustrate each category. Use brainstorming or questioning to help you gather facts, details, and examples.

F. Based on your prewriting, decide how you want to structure your essay. Determine whether you will use chronological order, order of importance or interest, natural order, or a combination of methods to structure your essay. Prepare a conceptual map or an outline of your essay. Delete any unrelated facts, details, and examples from your map or outline.

PORTFOLIO

G. Target a specific audience for your essay. For example, you might want to address a general audience. Alternatively, you might prefer to address an audience that has experience related to your topic. After considering your intended audience, decide what tone is most appropriate for your topic and writing purpose. Save your work in your portfolio. You will use your prewriting work to develop an essay using classification in Assignment 2 on pages 401-402.

REVISING, EDITING, AND PROOFREADING ESSAYS THAT USE CLASSIFICATION

The Checklist for Revising and Editing on page 153 can guide you in evaluating and revising the first draft of an essay that uses classification. The Checklist for Proofreading on page 105 can help you turn a revised draft into a final copy.

Read the following revised draft of an essay which includes the writer's handwritten corrections. Remember that at this point the writer has not yet corrected errors in grammar, spelling, punctuation, and capitalization. What changes did the writer make to improve the essay?

Revised Draft: **Onward Library Soldiers**

There are students on active study duty at any college library. Some sit at the computors, others gather at study tables, and still others line up at the copy machines. These study troops fall into three categories: the ~~Industri-ous Soldiers~~ the Crammer Cadets, and the Just for Show Officers. *Are active soldiers found in all college library? They*

The Industrious Soldiers work diligently. These soldiers are alert and prepared. They have all the tools they need: papers, pens, textbooks, and sharp minds. They are ready to conquer their enemies: math, chemistry, history, and english. What troopers! *members of the first groups* *to comprehend class material.* *to succeed* *armed for combat and.* *Industrious soldiers fight hard to win.*

The Crammer Cadets are soldiers that the United States military would be appalled to have in their army! Crammer Cadets wait until the last minute, Crammer Cadets also fail to use the resources, such as reference books, computors, library assistants, and tutors. Instead, they cram for exams and to ~~complete their class assignments.~~ Because of poor planning, Crammer Cadets often fail to complete assignments satisfactorily. *make up the second group. They* *to prepare for their classes.* *available to them.* *meet assignment deadlines.* *however,*

The third group, the Just for Show Officers, stand by the study tables, the copy machines, the bathrooms, or the telephones to discuss class assignments or their agendas for the week. These officers are so involved in their discussions that they get almost no work done they also distract everyone else. Nothing irritate an Industrious *are the school socialites. They*

Soldier or a last-minute Crammer Cadet like a Just for
Show Officer.

    The next time youre in the college library, look for
Industrious Soldiers, Crammer Cadets, and Just for Show
Officers. You'll find them at their posts.

On pages 399-400 of this chapter you'll see a rekeyed version of
"Onward Library Soldiers" that incorporates the writer's handwritten revisions. You'll use that version to proofread the essay for errors
in spelling, punctuation, and so on.

Questions

1. How has the writer improved the effectiveness of this essay?

Removed unnecessary stuff, made it precise

2. Why did the writer add a sentence to the introduction?

Make the introduction strong

3. Why did the writer revise the first sentence in the second paragraph?

4. What transitions did the writer add to create a smooth flow
within and between paragraphs?

5. If you were the writer of this essay, what additional revisions
would you make in content, structure, and wording?

Read the revised and rekeyed draft of "Onward Library Soldiers" that follows. Proofread the revision, and correct any mistakes in spelling, capitalization, and punctuation as well as any factual, keyboarding, and grammatical errors.

Revised and Rekeyed Draft:

Onward Library Soldiers

There are students on active study duty at any college library. Some sit at the computers, others gather at study tables, and still others line up at the copy machines. These study troops are active soldiers found in all college librarys. They fall into three categories: the Industrious Soldiers the Crammer Cadets, and the Just for Show Officers.

Members of the first group, the Industrious Soldiers, work diligently to comprehend class material. These soldiers are alert and prepared. They have all the tools they need to succeed: papers, pens, textbooks, and sharp minds. They are armed for combat and ready to conquer their enemies: math, chemistry, history, and english. What troopers! Industrious soldiers fight hard to win.

The Crammer Cadets make up the second group. They are soldiers that the United States military would be appalled to have in their army! Crammer Cadets wait until the last minute to prepare for their classes. Crammer Cadets also fail to use the resources available to them, such as reference books, computors, library assistants, and tutors. Instead, they cram for exams and to meet assignment deadlines. Because of poor planning, however, Crammer Cadets often fail to complete assignments satisfactorily.

The third group, the Just for Show Officers, are the school socialites. They stand by the study tables, the copy machines, the bathrooms, or the telephones to discuss class assignments or their agendas for the week. These officers are so involved in their discussions that they get almost no work done, they also distract everyone else. Nothing irritates an Industrious Soldier or a last-minute Crammer Cadet like a Just for Show Officer.

The next time you're in the college library, look for Industrious Soldiers, Crammer Cadets, and Just for Show Officers. You'll find them at their posts.

Assignment 1:
Creating an Essay That Uses Classification With Your Group

In this assignment you will work with your group to plan, write, edit, and proofread an essay that uses classification.

A. Choose a topic suitable for a collaboratively written essay that uses classification. Work together to narrow the topic, to create categories, and to identify common features.

B. Working as a group, use the questions on the Writing Focus Chart on page 132 to guide you as you plan the first draft. Use any of the invention techniques you learned in Chapter 2 to develop the thesis statement, introduction, main ideas, supporting details, and conclusion. Also use any of the strategies from Chapter 5 to develop content.

C. Use your group's prewriting to write the first draft. Your first draft should consist of an introduction, a body, and a conclusion and should clearly accomplish your writing purpose. Review the draft and work together to develop an appropriate title.

D. Carefully reread and evaluate the content, structure, and wording of your first draft. Discuss any necessary changes, additions, deletions, and corrections. Using the Checklist for Revising and Editing on page 153 as a guide, work together to revise the first draft. Complete as many revisions as needed.

E. When you are satisfied that your draft is the best work that your group can produce, choose someone to key the revised draft. Make a photocopy for every group member.

F. Carefully reread your revised draft. Using the Checklist for Proofreading on page 105, work together to prepare the final copy. Consult the Writer's Guide that begins on page A 80 to review key points of grammar, punctuation, and capitalization. Have each group member proofread the revised draft independently and use proofreaders' marks from the box on page 105 to mark corrections. Then compare corrections and incorporate all the changes on one draft.

PORTFOLIO

G. Have one group member key the final copy. Proofread the final copy as a group, and correct any keyboarding errors. Record the names of all group members on the final copy. Make a photocopy for every group member. Save your final copy in your portfolio.

Assignment 2:
Creating an Essay That Uses Classification

In this assignment you will work independently to plan, write, edit, and proofread the essay you began developing in Activity B earlier in this chapter.

A. Review the planning you did in Activity B on pages 395-396, including your prewriting, thesis statement, and conceptual map or outline. Reread the freewriting you did on your topic.

Writing FOCUS CHART

B. Use your prewriting and the questions on the Writing Focus Chart on page 132 to guide you as you plan the first draft of the essay. Use any of the invention techniques you learned in Chapter 2 to develop the introduction, main ideas, supporting details, and conclusion. Also use any of the strategies from Chapter 5 to develop content.

C. Write the first draft of your essay. Your first draft should consist of an introduction, a body, and a conclusion and should clearly accomplish your writing purpose. Review your draft and develop an appropriate title.

D. Share your draft with members of your group or with a peer editor. Use the comments and suggestions from the group or peer editor, in conjunction with the Checklist for Revising and Editing on page 153, to help you make revisions. After sharing essays, work independently to revise your draft.

E. Evaluate the content, structure, and wording of your essay. Using the Checklist for Revising and Editing as a guide, make any necessary changes, additions, deletions, and corrections. Make as many revisions as needed. When you are satisfied, key your revised draft.

PORTFOLIO

F. Carefully reread your revised draft. Using the Checklist for Proofreading on page 105, prepare the final copy. Consult the Writer's Guide that begins on page A 80 to review key points of grammar, punctuation, and capitalization. Use proofreaders' marks from the box on page 105 to mark your corrections.

G. Key the final copy. Look over the final copy and correct any keyboarding errors. Save your final copy in your portfolio.

Assignment 3:
Reading as a Stimulus for Writing

In this assignment you will read a selection and then work independently to plan, write, edit, and proofread an essay that uses classification.

A. Read "How to Deal With a Difficult Boss" by Donna Brown Hogarty on pages A 134-A 139. In this essay Donna Brown Hogarty classifies the types of bosses employees may confront on the job. She gives advice on how to deal with each type.

B. Use the selection as a stimulus for writing an essay that uses classification. For instance, you might classify the types of professors or teachers you have had as a student. Here are several questions to start you thinking.

- For what purpose does Donna Brown Hogarty present her classification?

- What categories does Donna Brown Hogarty use to classify types of bosses?

- What common features does the writer use for each category?

Use your responses to the preceding questions to help you decide on a specific topic and generate a thesis statement. Freewrite for approximately ten or fifteen minutes on the topic you select.

C. Share your ideas with members of your group or with a peer editor. Discuss the topic you are considering for your essay. Ask for constructive advice about the topic. Also discuss any problem areas that you foresee.

D. Use your prewriting and the questions on the Writing Focus Chart on page 132 to guide you as you write your first draft. Decide what categories you will present, and identify the common feature those categories share. Use any of the invention techniques from Chapter 2 and any of the strategies from Chapter 5 as needed. Your first draft should consist of an introduction, a body, and a conclusion and should clearly accomplish your writing purpose. If you find it useful, make a conceptual map or outline to help you visualize the categories in your classification. Review your draft and develop an appropriate title.

E. Share your draft with members of your group or with a peer editor. Use the comments and suggestions from the group or peer editor, in conjunction with the Checklist for Revising and Editing on page 153, to help you make revisions. After sharing essays, work independently to revise your draft.

F. Evaluate the content, structure, and wording of your draft. Using the Checklist for Revising and Editing as a guide, make any necessary changes, additions, deletions, and corrections. Make as many revisions as needed. When you are satisfied, key your revised draft.

G. Carefully reread your revised draft. Using the Checklist for Proofreading on page 105, prepare the final copy. Consult the Writer's Guide that begins on page A 80 to review key points of grammar, punctuation, and capitalization. Use proofreaders' marks from the box on page 105 to mark your corrections.

H. Key the final copy. Look over the final copy and correct any keyboarding errors. Save your final copy in your portfolio.

UNNECESSARY CHANGES IN VERB TENSE

When you write, avoid switching from present to past tense or past to present tense unnecessarily. To create a logical time order in your writing, be consistent in using verb tenses.

INCONSISTENT:
I rate my favorite shows and chose the best.
Rate is present tense, but *chose* is past tense. Both verbs should be either present or past tense.

CONSISTENT:
Present Tense: I *rate* my favorite shows and *choose* the best.
Past Tense: I *rated* my favorite shows and *chose* the best.

INCONSISTENT:
My father passed the post office but decides to go back.
Passed is past tense, but *decides* is present tense.

CONSISTENT:
Present Tense: My father *passes* the post office but *decides* to go back.
Past Tense: My father *passed* the post office but *decided* to go back.

Activities

A. Each group of sentences contains an inconsistency in verb tense. Cross out one of the verbs, and write above it a verb that makes the tense consistent with the other verbs.

1. When I take my notebook outside to sketch, I find myself absorbed in the scene around me. I used my pencils to record the shapes and colors of the landscape.

2. I capture the jungle-green of the shrubbery. Adding a little more shading, I drew the iron-gray and brown trunks of a tall line of trees.

3. Above them, I use a haze of purple to form the mountains, and I filled in the sky with blue-gray tints.

4. Sketching helps me really see my surroundings. The sketch itself may only be as accurate as my impressions, but the act of making it ~~brought~~ *brings* me closer to the scene.

B. Find and correct seven unnecessary changes in verb tense in the following paragraph.

I had a strange dream yesterday. I dreamed I ~~stand~~ *stood* on a pier near the water. Then a bicycle rolled along the pier toward me. No one is on the bicycle, but the pedals ~~are~~ *were* moving. I jumped out of the way, but the bicycle turned toward me. I ran from the bicycle, and the bicycle chase*d* me along the pier. I ~~must have~~ looked so silly running away from a bicycle! Then another bicycle roll*ed* in front of me. I hopped on that one and started pedaling. My bicycle floated off the pier and into the water. I pedaled at top speed. This cause*d* me to stay afloat. When I woke up, I ~~am~~ *was* making pedaling movements with my legs, and my blankets were on the floor. I needed some rest from my exhausting night's sleep.

C. For additional practice in using verb tenses correctly, see page A 77.

WRAPPING IT UP

SUMMARY

- Use a classification strategy to divide a large topic into smaller segments according to common features to make a central point.
- Items can be classified in a group or category only if all the items share one or more common features. These features tie together all the items in the category.
- All the categories in a classification should be equal in weight.
- A classification should present parallel information about all categories.
- Use appropriate transitional words and phrases to clarify relationships between and among categories in a classification.
- The purpose of an essay that uses classification is usually to inform or to persuade.
- Structure the information in an essay that uses classification using chronological order, order of importance or interest, or natural order.

THINKING IT OVER

- Why is it important to classify information in daily life? Describe three or four of the most useful aspects of classification that you learned in this chapter.

_____

_____

_____

_____

_____

- How can the classification strategy help you in conversations and in writing?

_____

_____

_____

- How will what you have learned in this chapter help you use the classification strategy at work and at school?

_____

_____

_____

IN YOUR JOURNAL

Review the goals that you set at the beginning of this chapter. In your journal, evaluate your progress toward these goals.

13

PROVIDING DEFINITIONS

OBJECTIVES:

Composition

- To explore similarities between providing definitions in speech and in writing.

- To use definitions to develop essay content.

- To use strategies such as examples, description, and comparison/contrast to develop definitions.

- To create and revise essays that provide definitions.

Grammar

- To eliminate nonparallel structures.

How Do I
Tell You
What I Mean?

The audience listening to this comedian can laugh at his jokes because they are familiar with the words and references he uses. The audience shares the comedian's understanding of what those words and references mean. If the comedian used words that the audience interpreted in another way, they probably wouldn't find his jokes funny.

Every day you use terms that you want to be sure are understood in the way that you mean them. Sometimes these terms are unfamiliar to others; other times these terms are used in a special way that is different from the commonly understood meaning. In such cases you define your terms in order to establish a mutually understood meaning. In this chapter you will learn how to develop essays that define a word or term.

To orient new employees, Sarah tells them that *quality control* will be their highest priority and explains what the term means. Students claim that the removal of a controversial advertisement on campus is *censorship*. The dean of students says that removal of the sign is simply in compliance with university regulations. The students and the dean have different interpretations of the term *censorship*.

List specific instances in which you provided a definition to explain the meaning of a word or a term either orally or in writing.

- With friends or relatives:

  _____

  _____

- At work:

  _____

  _____

- At school:

  _____

  _____

For *one* example you listed, consider these questions:

- Why were you giving a definition?
- How thoroughly did you explain the term or idea?
- What were the strengths and weaknesses of your approach?
- How did your audience respond to your definition?

IN YOUR JOURNAL

Evaluate your ability to provide definitions orally and in writing. Then set one or more goals in your journal. Here are some examples:

GOALS:
1. When I provide a definition, I will use appropriate examples to explain the term.
2. I will word definitions carefully.

DEFINING A WORD ORALLY

GROUP ACTIVITY

If someone said, "I'm not familiar with that word; what does it mean?" would you be able to define the word clearly?

A. Each member of your group should choose a word or term to define in a way that makes a point. For example, a term such as *Hollywood* can be defined either as a Los Angeles district or as the center of the American motion picture industry. You may give a definition that goes beyond the standard meaning of the term, explaining that *Hollywood* is often used to indicate an outlook that is glamorous but often superficial. In addition to thinking about the dictionary definition of the word, consider what you think of when you hear this word used.

B. Each member of the group should take turns presenting a definition orally to the group.

C. Work together to assess every definition for effectiveness. Identify features that make a definition clear, logical, and useful.

D. Work with your group to create a list of five or more specific guidelines to evaluate the effectiveness of a definition.

E. Evaluate the guidelines your group developed. Work together to improve them. Then write the revised guidelines in the following space.

_____

_____

_____

_____

_____

_____

_____

_____

_____

GIVING DEFINITIONS

WHAT IS A DEFINITION?

The purpose of providing definitions to develop essay content is to explain the meaning of a word or term in order to make a point. Such an essay will give more than the sentence definition that is found in a dictionary. You might explain your interpretation of a word and tell how it applies to situations you have read about or experienced. In order to clarify this definition and make it convincing to readers, you will supply supporting information such as examples, descriptions or comparison/contrast to provide an **extended definition** of a word or term.

   Some essays that provide definitions are serious efforts to illustrate a certain type of person or a certain trait ("What Makes a Hero?"). Other essays may be humorous ("Packrats: Does One Live at Your House?"). The approach you take will depend on your topic, your purpose for writing, and your thesis statement.

CREATING FORMAL SENTENCE DEFINITIONS

One way to provide a definition is to place the word or term in a defining class of items to which it belongs. For example, *diet cola* could be placed in the larger class of soft drinks while *football fans* could be placed in the larger class of spectators at an event. Another way to provide a definition is to explain what the word or term is like and what it isn't like, such as how football fans differ from other types of spectators. Let's take a look at how to use these strategies to develop definitions.

Placing the Term in a Defining Class

Dictionaries provide definitions that explain the meanings of words or terms by placing them into classes. For instance, you can define an orange as a citrus fruit. In the following diagram, note how the terms *power play*, *ornithology*, and *free verse* have each been placed in a larger defining class.

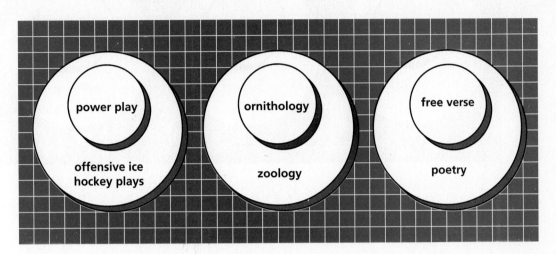

Identifying Distinguishing Features

In addition to placing a word into a class, a definition can also show how the term being defined differs from other members of the class. For instance, the word *orange* is defined as "a citrus fruit (the class) that has a yellow-reddish color and a juicy pulp" (features that differentiate the orange from other members of the class "citrus fruit").

These examples place each term from the diagram above in a defining class and give a distinguishing feature of the term:

A *power play* is an offensive play in ice hockey where one team has an advantage because the other team has a player in the penalty box.

Ornithology is a branch of zoology that deals with birds.

Free verse is a type of poetry that is usually unrhymed and does not have a regular rhythm.

DISCOVERY
ACTIVITY

Create a classification for each of the terms in the following diagram. Place each term in a defining class to which it belongs. Write your answers in the larger circle shown for each term. *Note:* You may have to look up terms in the dictionary.

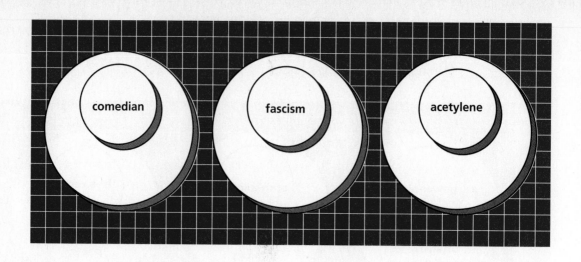

TYPES OF EXTENDED DEFINITION

When you provide a definition in an essay, you can use several methods to extend and clarify the definition.

- Provide a synonym. Use a word or phrase that is similar in meaning to the word being defined and that is more familiar to readers.

> *Farinaceous*, or *grain*, crops are our state's main natural resource.

- Explain what a word *doesn't mean*. This clarifies what the word does mean. You can continue the definition by explaining what the word actually does mean.

> A *deciduous* tree is not an *evergreen* but sheds its leaves during a specific season.

- Describe the origin of a word. Examining the origin of a word often gives insight into an aspect of the word.

> The word *democracy* derives from the Greek word *demos*, meaning "common people."

In providing an extended definition, you will likely use a combination of strategies to develop an appropriate definition for a specific purpose and audience. In an extended definition, you may use one or more of the following strategies:

- Give one or more examples.
- Provide a description.
- Relate a story or anecdote.
- Explain a process.
- Illustrate a cause/effect relationship.
- Compare or contrast with another more familiar term.

An extended definition of the word *orange,* for instance, might discuss specific examples of oranges, such as navel and Valencia, to offer a more detailed picture. An extended definition of *procrastination* might include an anecdote about someone you know who always puts things off until the last minute.

CREATING PERSONAL DEFINITIONS

In many instances you will define words or ideas in generally accepted ways. For example, if you defined *suburbia* as "a residential community outside of a city," most people would probably agree with your definition. If, however, you chose to define *suburbia* in highly personal terms—"Suburbia is a living space where dogs roam free and parents keep their children fenced"—such a definition would fall outside generally accepted ideas. A personal definition challenges readers' preconceived notions about a subject and tries to convince them of something new. The writer, however, needs to supply appropriate supporting evidence to convince readers that the definition is valid.

USING TRANSITIONS TO CLARIFY A DEFINITION

WRITER'S TIP

In an essay that provides definitions, transitional words and phrases can serve many purposes. If you are contrasting two meanings of a term or idea, transitions such as *by contrast* and *however* can stress the differences between the two meanings. If you are giving examples of the way a term or idea can be applied, transitions such as *for example* or *such as* help introduce each example. If you are drawing a conclusion, transitions such as *therefore* and *consequently* signal that conclusion. Consult the chart in Chapter 5, page 193, for transitional words and phrases that can be used to clarify a definition.

UNDERSTANDING WRITING TASKS THAT REQUIRE DEFINITIONS

Responses that require definitions are commonly called for in the subject areas you will study at school and may also be necessary in some job situations. You may be asked for written responses that provide definitions with such requests as the following:

- Define *osmosis*.
- Explain what Freud meant by the term *neurosis*.
- What characteristics define a successful salesperson?

Not all writing tasks that require a definition will use the word *define*. Other clue words that will help you determine if you need to provide a definition include *tell, explain, indicate,* and *reveal*.

Activity A: Finding Definition Clue Words

Underline the clue words in the following directions that ask you to provide a definition.

- Tell what a *microbe* is.
- Explain the meaning of the term *haiku*.
- Indicate what the term *schizophrenia* means.

FIRST DRAFT: PLANNING AND WRITING ESSAYS THAT PROVIDE DEFINITIONS

The Writing Focus Chart on page 132 can guide you in blending the key elements of writing to create interesting and effective essays that provide a definition. Use the questions on the chart as you consider your purpose, content, structure, audience, and tone.

CHOOSING A TOPIC

To select a word or term to define, consider defining a concrete word such as *mammal, freelancer,* or *woofer* that represents a specific object or person. You might also consider defining an abstract word such as *justice, wealth,* or *mathematics* that represents an idea. A good choice for a topic might be a word that is open to a variety of interpretations, such as *truth* or *loyalty*.

Once you've chosen a word or term, decide what class the word belongs to and what features differentiate it from other members of the class. As demonstrated previously, the *orange* in the class of citrus fruit is differentiated from other citrus fruits by its color and texture. Identifying the class a word belongs to and designating its differentiating features is an important first step in writing an extended definition.

ESTABLISHING THE WRITING PURPOSE

The purpose of an essay that uses definitions is usually to inform or to persuade. A straightforward definition of the word *conservation,* for instance, or a humorous definition of *boredom* will inform readers about the meaning of a term. A definition of *political freedom,* for example, can be written to persuade readers to support the writer's viewpoint on issues relating to voting rights and the like.

IN YOUR JOURNAL

Clip or photocopy for your journal examples of effective definitions you encounter in newspapers, magazines, or books. Describe the topic and purpose of each example, and explain how the definition is useful to you as a reader.

Keep a running list of terms or ideas you might want to define as part of an essay. Refer to this list when you're looking for a topic to write about.

WRITING A THESIS STATEMENT

A good way to generate a thesis statement about a word or term you are defining is to look up the word or term in the dictionary. The dictionary can help you think about your topic in a clear, organized way. Remember that if you plan to cite the dictionary definition, do not quote it word for word. Instead, write a **paraphrase**, a restatement of the definition in your own words.

A thesis statement for an essay that provides a definition to develop content should do one or more of the following:

- State the term or idea that you will define.

- Put the term in an appropriate defining class.

- Explain how the term differs from other members of the defining class.

- State why defining the term or idea is useful or necessary.

The following sentences are examples of thesis statements for essays that provide a definition. Each example thesis statement is followed by a list showing the term, its defining class, and its differentiating features.

> Discipline is not a form of punishment but a process of training and learning that helps children and adults.
> Term: discipline
> Defining class: processes of training and learning
> Differentiating features: helps children and adults.

> A garage sale is a rummage sale where people buy other people's unwanted items in large quantities at low prices.
> Topic: garage sale
> Defining class: rummage sales
> Differentiating features: people buy other people's unwanted items in large quantities at low prices.

DEVELOPING THE CONTENT

Once you have chosen a term to define and have identified a defining class and differentiating features for the term, explore strategies you can use to support your thesis statement. Consider which strategies mentioned on page 415 of this chapter are relevant to your chosen term. Use the invention techniques you learned in Chapter 2 to gather details about your term. For example, you might brainstorm as many distinguishing features as you can think of for your topic.

DO YOU WRITE ON A COMPUTER?

If your word processing software has a thesaurus feature, use this electronic word finder to help you identify synonyms for a term. Select or key the word for which you need a synonym and key in the appropriate command. The computer will then display a list of possible synonyms. You can select each synonym to see whether it has other synonyms that will help you develop your definition. Consult a dictionary to be sure that the synonyms you select have the exact shade of meaning that you intended for your original term.

PLANNING THE STRUCTURE

In an essay that provides a definition to develop content, the structure will depend on the strategy or strategies you've chosen to develop your definitions. You may use any of the following methods or a combination of methods to structure a definition.

- *Example Paragraphs:* Devoting a separate paragraph to each example is an effective way to develop a definition. For instance, an extended definition of *heroism* might devote one paragraph each to a different type of heroic behavior.

- *Order of Importance or Interest:* Arranging information in order of least to most important or interesting information or vice versa is effective when your purpose is to persuade readers. For example, an extended definition of *psychological manipulation* might produce the strongest effect on readers by presenting the most shocking example last.

- *Chronological Order:* Use chronological order when defining terms that involve a process or that illustrate cause and effect. By "beginning at the beginning" and working step-by-step toward the end, readers progress naturally through the topic. An extended definition of a concept like *religious conversion* could be structured in such a step-by-step pattern. Terms such as *boycott* that involve cause and effect also lend themselves to time order. First explain the cause and then the effect.

- *Block or Point-by-Point Pattern:* Comparing or contrasting your personal definition of *happiness* with a generally accepted definition of *happiness* could be structured in the block pattern, presenting your personal definition of happiness and then comparing it with the generally accepted definition. A personal definition of a *couch potato* as a student of popular culture could be structured using the point-by-point pattern, alternating features of the standard definition of couch potato with features of your definition.

Read the following essay, "Bookworms Are for Real." As you read, underline the defining class that establishes the definition for the term and number the differentiating features in the margin.

Bookworms Are for Real

Bookworm is the name given to the larva (wormlike early stage) of several kinds of moths or beetles that feed on the binding and paste of books. Human bookworms, unlike their worm counterparts, feed on the words and ideas contained in books. Human bookworms probably got their not-so-attractive name because of the one trait they share with wormy bookworms—the fact that they spend most of their time around books. The lowly name given to book lovers is a hint of the way they are often viewed by others.

Many people think of bookworms as passive, dull, even lazy—a lot like a real worm. The only reason they move is to turn a page. People who view bookworms as passive don't realize how rapidly bookworms' minds are moving and how far these "passive" folk are traveling. Through their reading, bookworms encounter other cultures, witness events that took place hundreds of years ago, and gain insight into controversial issues.

Because reading is such an individual pastime, human bookworms often seem as solitary as their worm namesakes. Unfortunately, many nonreaders assume that because bookworms spend so much time alone, they are disconnected and antisocial. Many human bookworms, however, are not at all isolated, disconnected, or antisocial. Though bookworms may spend large amounts of time glued to the pages of a book, they are connected to the universe in extremely responsible ways. Many bookworms use what they have learned from books to do a lot of good in the world. Some do volunteer work. Others choose careers they have read about, such as medicine or teaching, that help improve people's way of life.

Like the creatures they were named for, bookworms don't seem to lead very glamorous lives. Don't be too hasty in judging bookworms by their appearance, though. For one thing, bookworms are usually interested in more than one subject and therefore are more interesting to talk to than someone who focuses on only one special interest. Spending a little time coaxing a bookworm to talk instead of read might not be as boring as you think. After all, as any bookworm could tell you, you can't judge a book by its cover.

Questions

1. What is the purpose of this essay?

To define "Bookworm"
Inform or explain the readers about
Main characteristics of human bookworms

2. What is the writer's thesis statement? Does the writer provide enough specific information to support the central point? Cite specific examples.

_____

_____

_____

3. What defining class and differentiating features does the writer identify in the essay?

Defining class - Human Bookworms
Differentiating feature - Human bookworm
from other types of Bookworm

4. How does the writer structure the essay? Is this structure effective? Be specific.

Example paragraphs

_____

_____

5. How does the writer achieve unity in the essay? Be specific.

_____

_____

_____

TARGETING A SPECIFIC AUDIENCE

You need to consider your audience very early in the process of developing a definition. Knowing your audience will help you determine your choice of topic (what will most interest these particular readers?) and the differentiating features you discuss (what is this audience likely to know about the topic?). Consider how familiar your readers are likely to be with the topic and what preconceived notions they might have. If the term is specialized, you may need to provide more supporting information to be clearly understood. If the term is controversial, you may need to cite reliable sources to convince readers to accept your definition.

The writer of "Bookworms Are for Real" on pages 420-421 assumed the term *bookworm* would be familiar to be most readers. However, since the original meaning of *bookworm*, an actual worm-like creature, would probably not be familiar to readers, the writer provided this definition. The writer also assumed that most readers would likely have preconceived notions about bookworms and presented material that contradicted the usual notion of bookworms as dull or antisocial people. If the writer of "Bookworms Are for Real" was presenting this definition to a group of booklovers, how might the content and wording of the essay be changed?

SETTING THE TONE

The tone of an essay that provides a definition can be serious or humorous, depending on the term you choose to define. When writing about topics that readers might be sensitive about, you might begin with a neutral tone that presents convincing facts and ideas in a straightforward manner and save personal emotions for later in the essay. Remember, your goal is to interest readers in the topic.

When you define a term, be aware of the feelings or emotions associated with the word or term. Doing so will help you take into account how the word is used by your intended audience in actual speech and writing.

Think about these closely related words: *women*, *girls*, *ladies*, *dames*, and *chicks*. What would happen if a male politician addressed a group of women voters as dames or chicks? He would undoubtedly lose their vote because of the negative connotations these words carry.

Questions

1. Is the tone of "Bookworms Are for Real" serious or humorous? Give specific examples from the essay to support your answer.

   _____

   _____

2. Select two or three words in "Bookworms Are for Real" that have emotional associations connected with them. Describe these associations.

   _____

   _____

   _____

   _____

Activity B: Planning an Essay That Provides a Definition

In this activity you will plan the purpose, content, structure, audience, and tone for an essay that provides a definition. Refer to the Writing Focus Chart on page 132 for help in addressing these five key elements. Use separate sheets of paper for your work.

A. Choose one of the following general terms for an essay that provides a definition, or select a word or term of your choosing.

- A good sport
- A social butterfly
- Generosity
- Beauty
- Happiness
- Wisdom

Place the term in a defining class. For example, the term "good sport" could go in the defining class of "likable people."

B. Brainstorm as many distinguishing features as you can for your term. Put a check mark next to those features that are within the defining class you chose for your topic.

C. Establish your writing purpose. Also think about the point you will be making with your definition. Freewrite for ten to fifteen minutes about your topic.

D. Based on your prewriting, write a thesis statement.

E. Select one or more of the following strategies to develop additional information about the term: description, narration, example, process, cause/effect, and comparison/contrast. Briefly state how you will use each strategy.

F. Based on your prewriting, decide how you want to structure your essay. Decide whether you will use example paragraphs, order of importance or interest, chronological order, the block pattern, or the point-by-point pattern. Prepare an outline of your essay.

G. Target a specific audience for your essay. You might address an audience that is unfamiliar with the word or term, or you might address an audience that is familiar with the standard definition but will find *your* definition unusual or unexpected. After considering your intended audience, decide what tone is most appropriate for your topic and writing purpose.

PORTFOLIO

Save your work in your portfolio. You will use your prewriting work to develop an essay that provides a definition in Assignment 2 on pages 429-430.

REVISING, EDITING, AND PROOFREADING ESSAYS THAT PROVIDE DEFINITIONS

The Checklist for Revising and Editing on page 153 can guide you in evaluating and revising the first draft of an essay that provides a definition. The Checklist for Proofreading on page 105 can help you turn your revised draft into a final copy.

Read the following revised draft of an essay that provides a definition. Remember that at this point the writer has not yet corrected errors in grammar, spelling, punctuation, and capitalization. What changes did the writer make to improve the essay?

Revised Draft: **Dingers**

Roger Maris hit more dingers in one season than anyone else in major league baseball. Hank Aaron hit more
of them in his major league carear than any other player

in the history of the game. ~~Nolan Ryan, another all-time champ, was more famous for his pitching skills.~~ *During baseball season every year,* Baseball

fans sit in the bleachers at major league parks waiting for

the Announcer to shout that another dinger has ~~been~~ *just* *put their team ahead* hit. What is all the excitement about? *What exactly is a dinger ?*

~~The term~~ *a* dinger is more commonly known as a home

run ~~a play that happens when~~ *In this play* a batter hits a baseball off *The dinger is probably the most exciting play in baseball* the playing feild and over the fence. When a batter digs

his cleats into the dirt, crouchs in his stance, and takes a

full cut at the perfect pitch, the fans go wild.

Unlike fly balls or line-drive singles, Dingers happen only occasionally. Perhaps three or

four times in a game, players will hit a dinger *out of the park.* Rarely will

any single a player hit more than one, *per game.* Sometimes, nobody hits any

at all. *For that reason,* The dinger is well appreciated by fans. Even those

cheering for the opposing team. Whoever hits a dinger

automatically scores one run. If there are runners on

base, those players also score. The most exciting ~~score~~ *kind of home run* is

the "grand slam," which happens when a player hits a

dinger with the bases loaded. *The result : four runs with one swing of the bat.*

Fans worship players who can swing the bat and knock baseballs out of the park. The more dingers a player hits

during a season, the more popular the player becomes. ~~It is a sign of power and control.~~ The ability to hit dingers

consistently has made players ~~famous.~~ *into national heroes.* The excitment of

this baseball play causes fans to cheer wildly and to send

the names of players into the history books, where they

will live forever.

On pages 426-427 of this chapter you'll see a rekeyed version of "Dingers" that incorporates the writer's handwritten revisions. You'll use that version to proofread the essay for errors in spelling, punctuation, and so on.

Questions

1. How has the writer improved the effectiveness of this essay? Be specific.

   Removed unnecessary details. Became Specific. Improved the content.

2. Why did the writer delete the sentence about Nolan Ryan in the introduction?

3. Why did the writer change the order of sentences in the fifth paragraph?

4. What transitions did the writer add to create a smooth flow from one detail to the next?

5. If you were the writer of this essay, what additional revisions would you make in content, structure, and wording?

Read the revised and rekeyed draft of "Dingers" that follows. Proofread the revision, and correct any mistakes in spelling, capitalization, and punctuation as well as any factual, keyboarding, and grammatical errors.

Revised and Rekeyed Draft:

Dingers

Roger Maris hit more dingers in one season than anyone else in major league baseball. Hank Aaron hit more of them in his major league career than any other player in the history of the game. During baseball season every year, baseball fans sit in the bleachers at major league parks waiting for the Announcer to shout that another dinger has just put their team ahead. What is all the excitement about? What exactly is a dinger?

A *dinger* is more commonly known as a home run. In this play a batter hits a baseball off the playing feild and over the fence. The dinger is probably the most exciting play in baseball. When a batter digs his cleats into the dirt, crouchs in his stance, and takes a full cut at the perfect pitch, the fans go wild.

Unlike fly balls or line-drive singles, dingers happen only occasionally. Perhaps three or four times in a game, players will hit a dinger out of the park. Rarely will any single player hit more than one per game. Sometimes, nobody hits any at all. For that reason, the dinger is well appreciated by fans, Even those cheering for the opposing team.

Whoever hits a dinger automatically scores one run. If there are runners on base, those players also score. The most exciting kind of home run is the "grand slam," which happens when a player hits a dinger with the bases loaded. The result; four runs with one swing of the bat.

The more dingers a player hits during a season, the more popular the player becomes. Fans worship players who can swing the bat and knock baseballs out of the park. The ability to hit dingers consistently has made players into national heroes. The excitment of this baseball play causes fans to cheer wildly and to send the names of players into the history books, where they will live forever.

Assignment 1:

Creating an Essay That Provides a Definition With Your Group

In this assignment you will work with your group to plan, write, edit, and proofread an essay that provides a definition.

A. Choose a term such as *courage*, *success*, *friend*, or *hero* that is suitable as a topic for a collaboratively written essay that provides a definition. Freewrite for ten to fifteen minutes about how you would explain the meaning of the term. Discuss your freewriting with members of your group.

B. Working as a group, use the questions on the Writing Focus Chart on page 132 to guide you as you plan the first draft. Use any of the invention techniques you learned in Chapter 2 to develop the thesis statement, introduction, main ideas, supporting details, and conclusion. Also use any of the strategies from Chapter 5 to develop content.

C. Use your group's prewriting to write the first draft. Your first draft should consist of an introduction, a body, and a conclusion and should clearly accomplish your writing purpose. Review the draft and work together to develop an appropriate title.

D. Carefully reread and evaluate the content, structure, and wording of your first draft. Discuss any necessary changes, additions, deletions, and corrections. Using the Checklist for Revising and Editing on page 153 as a guide, work together to revise the first draft. Complete as many revisions as needed.

E. When you are satisfied that your draft is the best work that your group can produce, choose someone to key the revised draft. Make a photocopy for every group member.

F. Carefully reread your revised draft. Using the Checklist for Proofreading on page 105, work together to prepare the final copy. Consult the Writer's Guide that begins on page A 80 to review key points of grammar, punctuation, and capitalization. Have each group member proofread the revised draft independently and use proofreaders' marks from the box on page 105 to mark corrections. Then compare corrections and incorporate all the changes on one draft.

PORTFOLIO

G. Have one group member key the final copy. Proofread the final copy as a group, and correct any keyboarding errors. Record the names of all group members on the final copy. Make a photocopy for every group member. Save your final copy in your portfolio.

Assignment 2:
Creating an Essay That Provides a Definition

In this assignment you will work independently to plan, write, edit, and proofread the essay that you began developing earlier in this chapter.

A. Review the planning you did in Activity B on pages 423-424, including your prewriting, thesis statement, and outline. Reread the freewriting you did on your topic.

B. Use your prewriting and the questions on the Writing Focus Chart on page 132 to guide you as you plan the first draft of the essay. Use any of the invention techniques you learned in Chapter 2 to develop the introduction, main ideas, supporting details, and conclusion. Also use any of the strategies from Chapter 5 to develop content.

C. Write the first draft of your essay. Your first draft should consist of an introduction, a body, and a conclusion and should clearly accomplish your writing purpose. Review your draft and develop an appropriate title.

D. Share your draft with members of your group or with a peer editor. Use the comments and suggestions from the group or peer editor, in conjunction with the Checklist for Revising and Editing on page 153, to help you make revisions. After sharing essays, work independently to revise your draft.

E. Evaluate the content, structure, and wording of your essay. Using the Checklist for Revising and Editing as a guide, make any necessary changes, additions, deletions, and corrections. Make as many revisions as needed. When you are satisfied, key your revised draft.

PORTFOLIO

F. Carefully reread your revised draft. Using the Checklist for Proofreading on page 105, prepare the final copy. Consult the Writer's Guide that begins on page A 80 to review key points of grammar, punctuation, and capitalization. Use proofreaders' marks from the box on page 105 to mark your corrections.

G. Key the final copy. Look over the final copy and correct any keyboarding errors. Save your final copy in your portfolio.

Assignment 3:
Reading as a Stimulus for Writing

In this assignment you will read a selection and then work independently to plan, write, edit, and proofread an essay that provides a definition of an everyday term.

A. Read "Pair—or—Less Situation" by Suzann Ledbetter on pages A 139-A 140. As you read this humorous selection, think about other terms that don't mean exactly what they appear to mean at first glance.

B. Use the selection as a stimulus for writing an essay that provides a definition. For instance, you might choose to write about a word like *proud* that takes on other meanings; you might choose to examine a pair of words such as *raise* and *raze* that have similar sounds but different meanings; or you might choose to discuss a particular figure of speech such as *pulling your leg* that might sound odd to someone who interprets the meaning literally. Here are several questions to start you thinking.

- What details does the writer use to show the logic of her argument about how illogical the meaning of the word *pair* is?

- What language or details does the writer use to set a humorous tone?

- Do you know someone who learned English as a second language who found humor in certain words or phrases because of the odd meanings they carried?

- How could you use a dictionary or other word book to help you come up with ideas for your essay?

Use your responses to the preceding questions to help you decide on a specific topic and generate a thesis statement. Freewrite for approximately ten or fifteen minutes on the topic you select.

C. Share your ideas with members of your group or with a peer editor. Discuss the topic you are considering for your essay. Ask for constructive advice about the topic. Also discuss any problem areas that you foresee.

D. Use your prewriting and the questions on the Writing Focus Chart on page 132 to guide you as you write your first draft. Use any of the invention techniques from Chapter 2 and any of the strategies from Chapter 5 as needed. Your first draft should consist of an introduction, a body, and a conclusion and should clearly accomplish your writing purpose. If you find it useful, make a conceptual map or diagram to help you visualize the content and structure of your essay. Review your draft and develop an appropriate title.

E. Share your draft with members of your group or with a peer editor. Use the comments and suggestions from the group or peer editor, in conjunction with the Checklist for Revising and Editing on page 153, to help you make revisions. After sharing essays, work independently to revise your draft.

F. Evaluate the content, structure, and wording of your draft. Using the Checklist for Revising and Editing as a guide, make any necessary changes, additions, deletions, and corrections. Make as many revisions as needed. When you are satisfied, key your revised draft.

G. Carefully reread your revised draft. Using the Checklist for Proofreading on page 105, prepare the final copy. Consult the Writer's Guide that begins on page A 80 to review key points of grammar, punctuation, and capitalization. Use proofreaders' marks from the box on page 105 to mark your corrections.

H. Key the final copy. Look over the final copy and correct any keyboarding errors. Save your final copy in your portfolio.

Grammar Gremlins

Parallelism involves expressing parallel, or equivalent, elements using the same grammatical form. For instance, the words *run*, *swim*, and *jump* are parallel (all three words take the same form—the present form of the verb) while the words *sing*, *shouting*, and *play* are not parallel (shouting has an *-ing* form while *sing* and *play* do not). Parallelism applies not only to words but also to phrases and clauses.

(handwritten margin notes:) and / or / Either-or / Not only / but / then / also / or / and

All items in a series should be parallel. This includes words—such as nouns, verbs, and adjectives—as well as phrases and clauses.

I have found wildflowers <u>in the park</u>, <u>along the sidewalk</u>, and <u>throughout the woods</u>.

(The underlined phrases are all prepositional phrases in a series.)

On a cold day, the engine <u>grinds</u>, <u>sputters</u>, and then <u>roars</u> into life.

(The underlined clauses are all verbs in a series.)

The book reminded me of a time <u>when sailing ships cruised the oceans</u>, <u>when horses and buggies clattered along cobblestone streets</u>, and <u>when the fastest way to travel from coast to coast was by rail</u>.

(The underlined clauses are all adverbial clauses in a series.)

An awkward sentence is formed when parallel elements are not presented in parallel grammatical form.

NONPARALLEL STRUCTURES:
The astronomer <u>focused the telescope</u>, <u>panned the sky</u>, and after several minutes, <u>was identifying distant star clusters</u>.

(The underlined phrases are not parallel because *was identifying* has an *-ing* form while *focused* and *panned* do not.)

PARALLEL STRUCTURES:
The astronomer <u>focused the telescope</u>, <u>panned the sky</u>, and after several agonizing minutes, <u>identified distant star clusters</u>.

(The underlined phrases are parallel because *focused*, *panned*, and *identified* all take the past form of the verb.)

Use parallel structures when pairing two ideas. Balance single words with single words, clauses with clauses, and phrases with phrases. The correlative conjunctions *not only . . . but also* and *both . . . and* are often used to pair ideas. The underlined elements in the following sentences are parallel.

The store brought to the city not only <u>many beautiful imports from Africa</u> but also <u>a new way of seeing the world</u>.

The package for the baby contains not only <u>tiny booties and mittens</u> but also <u>handmade bonnets</u>.

<u>Don't bank on the false promises of others</u>; <u>bank on your own ingenuity</u>.
Both <u>the mayor</u> and <u>the fire chief</u> have spoken to the scout troops.

NONPARALLEL STRUCTURES:

Parents can treat teenagers as adults by <u>giving them several options to choose from</u> rather than <u>to give them ironclad rules to follow</u>.

(The underlined phrases are not parallel because *giving* is an *-ing* form and *to give* is an infinitive.)

PARALLEL STRUCTURES:

Parents can treat teenagers as adults <u>by giving them several options to choose from</u> rather than <u>giving them ironclad rules to follow</u>.

(The underlined phrases are parallel because *giving* has an *-ing* form in each phrase.)

Activities

A. Revise the following sentences to correct any nonparallel structures. Use proofreaders' marks to make corrections.

1. Small fishermen are in danger of losing their livelihoods because of overfishing, pollutant levels rising, and harsh competition from larger fishing fleets.

2. Family fishermen with one boat, fishing cooperatives having several larger boats, and large industrial fishing fleets compete for the dwindling fish population.

3. There is a decline in both the overall catch of fish and fishermen are noticing a decline in the quality of fish caught.

4. Sometimes, when fishermen do make a good catch, they find not only are the fish younger and smaller but also carrying sores and mutations from toxic pollutants.

5. Small fishermen are important both to the local economy and they are important to the national economy.

B. Read the following paragraph. Correct any nonparallel structures. Use proofreaders' marks to make corrections.

Camouflage is used by animals not only to hide from predators that might attack them, but also for concealing themselves from potential prey they want to attack. Different patterns of color and shapes have the effect of disrupting a creature's outline, changing with the background environment and to imitate other objects or animals. Some insects or amphibians look like parts of plants or even are trying to match other animals. An unmoving walking stick insect on a tree, in a bush, or walking on a plant looks like just any other twig to a hungry bird. The viceroy butterfly mimics the shape and has imitated the coloration of the poisonous monarch butterfly. Animals have even inspired people to make use of camouflage: soldiers put on green army uniforms not only to break up their outlines, but also for blending in with the surroundings. Camouflage is the costume shop of nature and for survival, an animal's best disguise.

C. For additional practice in finding and correcting nonparallel structures, see page A 78.

Wrapping It Up

Summary

- Use a definition to establish the meaning of a word in order to make a point. To define a word, put the word in a defining class and distinguish it from other members of the class.
- Your purpose in writing an essay that provides a definition is usually to inform or to persuade.
- Structure an essay that provides a definition by using example paragraphs, chronological order, order of importance or interest, the block pattern, or the point-by-point pattern.

Thinking It Over

- Why is being able to define terms and ideas an important skill?

  _____

  _____

- How can the definition strategy help you in conversations and in writing?

  _____

  _____

IN YOUR JOURNAL

Review the goals that you set at the beginning of this chapter. In your journal, evaluate your progress toward these goals.

14

PRESENTING ARGUMENTS

OBJECTIVES:

Composition

- To explore similarities between arguments used in speech and in writing.

- To use the argument strategy to develop essay content.

- To write essays that present clear, logical arguments.

- To create and revise essays that present arguments.

Grammar

- To use negative expressions correctly.

How Do I Argue Effectively?

Why do we favor one person's viewpoint over another's? We tend to agree with a person because his or her arguments are logical and emotionally satisfying. When presenting an argument, people use facts, examples, expert opinions, and emotional appeals to support their ideas. Speakers or writers who do this successfully will convince people to believe them.

When you present an argument, are you able to support your ideas successfully? Do you convince your audience to agree with you? In the same way you use an argument to convince someone to agree with you or to follow a course of action, you can use arguments to develop essays. In this chapter you will learn how to develop essays that argue for or against an issue or that convince readers to take a specific action.

How can I convince the university to improve parking facilities? Can I convince my friends that some kinds of music are not suitable for young children? When you express a viewpoint on an issue, you try to persuade someone to do something or to agree with you.

List specific instances in which you presented an argument either orally or in writing.

- With friends or relatives:

  _____

  _____

- At work:

  _____

  _____

- At school:

  _____

  _____

For *one* example you listed, consider these questions:

- Why were you presenting this argument?
- How thoroughly did you develop your argument?
- What were the strengths and weaknesses of your approach?
- Did you support your ideas with relevant facts and examples?
- How did your audience respond to your argument?

IN YOUR JOURNAL

Evaluate your ability to present an argument orally and in writing. Then set one or more goals in your journal. Here are some examples:

GOALS:

1. When I develop an argument, I will support my point of view with logic, facts, and expert opinions.
2. In my argument I will consider opposing points of view.

PRESENTING AN ARGUMENT ORALLY

GROUP ACTIVITY

If you were trying to convince someone to agree with you, what arguments would you use?

A. Each member of your group will select an issue to present an argument about, such as the following:

- Should college athletes be tested routinely for steroids?
- Should the legal drinking age be lowered to age 18?
- Should gay couples be allowed to adopt children?
- Should doctors be allowed to help in the suicide of terminally ill people?

Think carefully about the issue you are arguing for or against. What facts, examples, and expert opinions will you use to support your argument?

B. Each member of the group should take turns presenting a side of an issue orally to the group. Some group members may choose to argue a side of an issue that they disagree with. This is called "playing devil's advocate." Any group members playing devil's advocate should present arguments as though they agree with those arguments.

C. Work together to assess every argument for effectiveness. Identify specific features that make an argument clear, logical, and convincing.

D. Work with your group to create a list of five or more specific guidelines to evaluate the effectiveness of an argument.

E. Evaluate the guidelines your group developed. Work together to improve them. Then write the revised guidelines in the following space.

_____

_____

_____

_____

EXPRESSING OPINIONS

TYPES OF ARGUMENTS

An essay that presents an argument is designed to influence people to believe something or to behave in a specific way. There are two basic types of arguments. One type is designed to convince the audience to accept a particular point of view. Essays that present this type of argument often deal with political or social issues: for example, whether the government should provide universal health care to all citizens. Arguments of this type can also deal with lighter subjects: for example, whether the local newspaper should publish comic strips. A second type of argument is designed to convince readers to take a specific course of action. Essays that present this type of argument might urge a boycott of certain products.

USING SUPPORTING EVIDENCE

A writer uses evidence to convince an audience of the central point of an argument. **Evidence** consists of facts, expert opinions, and logic. **Facts** are items of information that can be proved. **Opinions** are beliefs that may or may not be based on facts; **expert opinions** are beliefs on a subject held by someone who is considered knowledgeable on that subject. **Logic** is a type of reasonable thinking that builds to a conclusion.

The following sentences are examples of each type of evidence.

Fact: Cesar Chavez was born near Yuma, Arizona.

Opinion: Cesar Chavez was one of the most important human rights activists of the twentieth century.

Expert opinion: According to authors Dana Catharine de Ruiz and Richard Larios, the activist Cesar Chavez was instrumental in improving conditions for migrant farm workers.

Logic: If workers believe they are being treated fairly, they are more likely to be productive. Creating decent, fair working conditions for employees can therefore be cost-effective because it results in higher productivity.

Sometimes research is necessary to provide solid evidence to support the arguments presented in an essay. For example, suppose you plan to argue in favor of abolishing the death penalty. First you would need to find out what the existing federal and state laws on capital punishment are as well as the financial and social effects of the death penalty. The evidence you uncover in your research might include the following facts:

- Sentencing a convicted criminal to death does not save the state money, because a convicted criminal is allowed many appeals of the guilty verdict and in fact may spend more than ten years on death row. Court costs to the state for one such criminal may reach a million dollars.

- Studies by government agencies such as the Department of Justice have shown no unusual rise in violent crime in states that have abolished the death penalty.

- In states with the death penalty, such as California, the rate of violent crime has still risen.

- The overwhelming proportion of criminals sentenced to death in the United States are nonwhite and poor.

- Around 2,000 prisoners are currently under sentence of death in the United States. Some of these prisoners have been on death row for over six years.

Use the facts that best support your viewpoint to make your case. Remember, few issues in life are clearcut. If the right solution to every problem was always obvious, people of good conscience would always agree with one another. Your job as a writer is to state your viewpoint as convincingly as possible.

USING EMOTIONAL APPEALS

In addition to evidence such as facts, expert opinions, and logic, you also can use emotional appeals to influence your audience. If you were arguing against the death penalty, for example, you might use statements such as the following:

- Most other industrialized countries do not have a death penalty. Countries with a death penalty include many totalitarian nations and less industrially developed nations. Should the United States model itself after countries that have a death penalty?

- Putting people to death for capital crimes is not the way civilized people should deal with wrongdoers.
- If an innocent person is sent to prison, you can get that person out if you later find evidence of that person's innocence. What happens if, *after* someone is executed for murder, you find evidence of that person's innocence?

REFUTING THE OPPOSING VIEWPOINT

One effective way to present an argument is to bring up points that work against the argument and then to **refute,** or disprove, those points. Suppose you are arguing in favor of capital punishment. You know that people who are against capital punishment point out that the death penalty does not save the state money because court costs for years of appeals may reach a million dollars. You might refute this point by saying that the cost of keeping thousands of convicted murderers in prison for life—which could be up to thirty or forty years—can be just as high.

AVOIDING PITFALLS THAT WEAKEN AN ARGUMENT

Several common errors in the presentation of supporting evidence can result in an argument that appears convincing on the surface but that will be discounted by a thoughtful reader. You should avoid the following in an argument:

- **Vague Generalizations**. A **generalization** is a statement meant to apply to all examples of something. Many generalizations are not valid because they could not possibly apply to every specific example. For instance, the generalization "College athletes are more interested in sports than in studying" is not true in all cases. However, a generalization such as "All athletes at our college must fulfill certain grade requirements," is specific, not vague, and can be proved. If you make a statement that can be proved but that has exceptions, **qualify,** or limit, the statement by adding words such as *usually, most,* or *often.*

- **Personal Attack**. Criticizing someone with whom you disagree based on some personal trait instead of an action or behavior is both unpleasant and illogical. In the 1860s, many people who disagreed with President Lincoln's handling of the Civil War also criticized his appearance and his "backwoods" manners. Neither of these criticisms had any bearing on Lincoln's actions as president and were not valid evidence of his fitness or unfitness to be president.

- **Group Defense**. To convince readers to agree with your argument you might write: "If you believe in the principles of our group, you will support us in our fight to ban rock concerts from the college amphitheater." Careful readers will realize that asking for support on the basis of the group is not a defense of the actual issue. Such readers may actually be alienated by this approach to persuasion.

- **Bandwagon Approach**. The idea behind the bandwagon approach is to get people to believe that they should "jump on the bandwagon" by adopting the viewpoint that many people share about an issue. An example of this approach is the phrase, "Almost everyone agrees that this president is wrong about raising taxes; why shouldn't you?" In fact, "almost everyone" probably doesn't agree about this or any other issue. An additional reason for avoiding the bandwagon approach is that thoughtful readers will realize the truth of an idea is not related to the idea's popularity. Even if most people share a certain belief, that doesn't make the belief accurate.

- **False Authority**. Using the opinion of someone who is well known but who is not an expert on the topic of your argument does not provide useful support for an argument. For example, suppose you want to include an expert opinion in an essay about opposing foreign aid to a particular country. You read that a rock star has made public statements urging our government not to send aid to that country. Unless the singer has a reason to be an expert on that country (perhaps he is a native of that country), his opinion lends no weight to your argument.

- **Slanted Language**. Using words that carry an emotional shading can be very effective in arguments. Be careful, however, to back such words with evidence. Otherwise your arguments may sound overly emotional and inaccurate. The statement "Wasteful governments *rob* people" can make you sound biased. On the other hand, if this statement is used together with examples of government waste and dollar amounts of the cost, such words can be a call for government reform.

- **False Cause and Effect**. Be careful about making false connections between two events in a cause/effect relationship. The statement "By electing Mike Reaver as state senator, we ensured that local street crime would rise" is an example of a false connection between two events. More likely, the rise resulted from a number of causes, not just Mike Reaver's work or voting record. (For more information on cause/effect relationships, see Chapter 10.)

- **Either-Or Statement**. Avoid statements that predict only two possible outcomes for a situation. An example is the statement "Either we settle the dispute, or war will result." Usually matters are more complicated than such either-or statements allow.

An awareness of the pitfalls that weaken an argument can make you a more effective writer. This awareness can also make you a better reader and listener. Evaluating supporting evidence for validity helps you to analyze advertisements, speeches by political candidates, and material in newspapers and magazines.

Think about examples of arguments you have read recently. Select one that you found effective. Then answer the following questions about the argument.

DISCOVERY
ACTIVITY

- What were the two opposing viewpoints on the issue?

  _____

  _____

  _____

- What was the purpose of the argument?

  _____

  _____

  _____

- Why was the argument effective?

  _____

  _____

  _____

USING TRANSITIONS TO LINK THE EVIDENCE IN AN ARGUMENT

In writing an essay that presents an argument, use transitional words and phrases both within and between paragraphs to develop the logic of your argument and lead the reader to your conclusion. Transitions such as *for one thing*, *in addition,* and *another* signal that you are about to present a new point. Transitions such as *however* and *on the other hand* alert readers that you will present contradicting evidence. Transitions such as *therefore* and *in conclusion* point to results or conclusions. Consult the chart in Chapter 5, page 193, for transitional words and phrases that can be used to link the evidence in an argument.

UNDERSTANDING WHEN YOU MAY NEED TO PRESENT AN ARGUMENT

Many of the arguments you present will be in response to school- or job-related tasks. Among your class assignments and job-related writing tasks may be ones such as these that direct you to present an argument:

- *Should* all cities set up mass transit systems? *Persuade* readers of your opinion on this issue.

- *State and defend your opinion* on whether communities should be allowed to set curfews for people under the age of 16.

- *Present a proposal* in favor of installing a new computer system in our office.

Sometimes it is difficult to detect when you are being asked to present an argument. Clue words such as *must, ought to, pros and cons, belief, favor, support, oppose, abolish, for, against,* and *reasons* let you know that your response should present an argument.

Activity A: Finding Clue Words for Arguments

Underline the clue words in the following directions for writing tasks that indicate that you need to present an argument.

- Testing of nuclear weapons should be abolished.

- Are airbags effective in saving lives?

- Do you support or oppose a higher cigarette tax to pay for a national health care plan? Give your reasons.
- Should all teenagers join Students Against Drunk Driving?

FIRST DRAFT: PLANNING AND WRITING ESSAYS THAT PRESENT ARGUMENTS

The Writing Focus Chart on page 132 can guide you in blending the key elements of writing to create interesting and effective essays that present an argument. Use the questions on the chart as you consider your purpose, content, structure, audience, and tone.

CHOOSING A TOPIC

When you are writing an essay to present an argument, choose an issue for which two opposing viewpoints exist. For an argument to be effective, a difference of opinion is needed. If possible, choose a topic about which you feel strongly. Your topic should be one you know about either from personal experience or observation or one you can research. If you must do research, be sure that you can find sufficient supporting information.

Remember that topics for arguments can deal with issues in any area. A local issue, such as whether a nearby movie theater should be demolished to make way for a parking lot, is just as suitable as an issue of national or global importance, such as whether all nations need to enact better environmental laws.

ESTABLISHING THE WRITING PURPOSE

Once you have chosen a topic, establish your writing purpose. The purpose of an essay that presents an argument is usually to persuade or to convince. Your purpose might be simply to persuade your audience to understand or share your viewpoint. Alternatively, your purpose might be to convince your readers to take some sort of action. In the process of persuading readers you will be informing them about the factors that influence an issue or position.

WRITING A THESIS STATEMENT

After familiarizing yourself with your topic and establishing your writing purpose, write a thesis statement. The thesis statement will help you gather evidence to support your argument.

A thesis statement for an essay that presents an argument should do one or more of the following:

- Provide a clear, specific statement of your viewpoint.
- State the main ideas you will use to support your argument.
- Tell why the topic is important.

Avoid vague thesis statements such as the following:

> Pornography should be banned.

> Some people shouldn't have dogs as pets.

The preceding thesis statements are too general; the audience has no idea of the direction in which each argument will develop. The following thesis statements give more details about the issue that the essay will cover.

> Sexually explicit pornographic magazines should not be displayed on newsstands where they can be seen by children.

> People who live in apartments shouldn't keep large dogs because it's unfair to dogs to make them live in such cramped quarters.

A well-focused thesis statement lets readers know what viewpoint will be presented. Also, a clear, logical thesis statement shows readers that the writer has given careful thought to the issue. Even readers who disagree with your viewpoint will be more likely to give it fair consideration if your intention is clear.

DEVELOPING THE CONTENT

Once you have selected a topic on which to present an argument and have written a thesis statement, decide what reasons you will give for attacking or defending an issue.

Brainstorming is a particularly helpful way of gathering ideas when preparing an argument. For example, you might brainstorm a list of two columns, labeling one "Pro" and the other "Con," and list arguments in favor of your viewpoint and against your viewpoint. If you have trouble filling in the column that applies to the position you plan to take in your argument, this might be a hint that your position cannot be adequately supported. Likewise, if you fill in very strong arguments in the column applying to the opposing position, plan ways to refute this opposing viewpoint in your argument.

Your content will consist of supporting evidence—facts, opinions, expert opinions, and logic—for your points. Some of this material can come from your personal experience and observations, but you may also need to do research.

DO YOU WRITE ON A COMPUTER?

Brainstorming a list of pros and cons on a computer can save you time because you can easily rearrange your points and evidence as many times as necessary. Once you set up the "Pro" column and the "Con" column of your list, you can move points around on your list to reflect the order in which you plan to introduce them in your essay. You can also key ideas that occur to you about each point. Print a copy of your list to refer to as you write your first draft.

PLANNING THE STRUCTURE

The introduction of your essay explains why the topic is important and states what argument will be presented. The body paragraphs present the evidence to support the thesis statement. The conclusion ties the essay together by summing up the points and perhaps suggesting a solution to the issue.

Essays that present an argument are usually structured in order of importance or interest. An argument can be arranged in ascending order, beginning with the least important reason and building up to the most important reason. This structure locates the strongest point of the essay at the end, to leave readers with the most important point. Arranging your argument in descending order also has advantages. If you sense that your audience might be against your position, you can begin with your strongest point. This approach captures your readers' attention right away and might surprise them into a favorable reaction.

Using an Outline to Structure Your Argument

An outline will help you arrange the points in an argument and will show whether you are missing any crucial evidence. Your outline should clarify the points you will make in your argument and the support you will provide for each point. Your outline might look like the following:

Topic:
Introduction
      Thesis Statement
      Background of Problem
Body
      Point 1
            Support for point 1
      Point 2
            Support for point 2
      Point 3
            Support for point 3
Conclusion
      Recommendations:
      Restatement of central point

Read the following essay, "There's No Excuse for Not Voting." As you read, underline the evidence that the writer uses to support the argument.

There's No Excuse for Not Voting

A low voter turnout weakens the representative nature of our government. Though every American citizen 18 years or older has the right to vote, a large percentage of Americans do not vote. In recent presidential elections, as few as 55 percent of eligible voters cast ballots. This low number compares with a voter turnout of at least 80 percent in many other democratic countries. People who don't vote usually have excuses: their vote won't make a difference, they don't trust politicians, or they don't have time to vote.

Those who argue that one vote doesn't count might be surprised to find how often a few votes have swayed an election. In the presidential elections of 1960, 1968, and 1976 the outcome was determined by a margin of less than 3 percent. In some local elections, the outcome hinges on a few hundred votes and one percentage point.) One vote may not seem like much, but if hundreds of people take this attitude, the number of nonvoters becomes significant.

Many people don't vote because they distrust politicians. This line of reasoning misses the point. There will be politicians whether we vote for them or not. When we take part in the process, we send a message to elected officials that we are watching them and that we expect them to act on our behalf. Our votes are a link between our wishes and the actions of elected officials.

Some people claim they are too busy to vote, but this claim has little value. For the benefit of those who have a full work day, polling places remain open for long hours—in most states from 6 or 7 A.M. to 9 P.M. Polling places are usually within easy distance of people's homes. Elderly or disabled voters can usually rely on car pools run by local volunteers for transportation. Voters who will be away during elections can even mail in absentee ballots. In addition, the voting process itself takes only a few minutes. Finding the time to vote doesn't call for that great a sacrifice.

Voting is so crucial that we should all work to make this a country of voters. Our forebears risked their lives to gain this precious right for us. People should view voting as not just a privilege but an obligation. Voting is the part we play in maintaining a government that works for the people.) 3   2

Questions

1. What is the purpose of this essay?

   To persuade or convince readers to vote.

2. What is the writer's thesis statement? Does the writer provide enough evidence to support the central point? Be specific.

   _____

   _____

   _____

3. What facts and emotional appeals does the writer use?

   _____

   _____

   _____

4. This writer presents arguments *against* voting and uses evidence to refute each argument. Is this structure effective for presenting an argument in favor of voting? Explain.

_____

_____

_____

5. How does the writer achieve unity in the essay? Be specific.

Every paragraph is related to thesis statement.

IN YOUR JOURNAL

Clip or photocopy from newspapers, magazines, or books examples of writing that presents an argument. Describe the topic and purpose of each example, and explain how you found the argument effective or useful to you as a reader.

Select one example that was particularly effective. Describe how the writer has structured the argument. How does the structure help prove the point the writer is making?

TARGETING A SPECIFIC AUDIENCE

The kind of evidence or statements you include in your argument will depend on how closely your views coincide with those of your audience. If your audience is likely to disagree with your viewpoint, use appeals and information that are most likely to bring this audience into agreement with you. For example, suppose you are trying to limit the use of animals for dissection in biology classes, and you are writing to an audience of pre-med students. If you state that anyone who has ever dissected an earthworm is a monster, you would be unlikely to win your audience over. You might instead suggest that in many instances computer images can substitute for live-animal experiments.

If you are proposing something to an audience that will likely agree with your viewpoint, you will devote less space to arguing why something should or should not be done. Suppose, for example, you want to persuade fellow students to petition your college for more on-campus parking. Many students would probably agree with you. Instead of devoting the bulk of your essay to arguing why increasing on-campus parking spaces is a good idea, you could devote more space to persuading students to accept your proposal for convincing the administration to enact this change.

Regardless of the topic and the audience, you should be fair, thorough, and reasonable if you hope to persuade the audience to support your argument.

The writer of "There's No Excuse for Not Voting" on pages 449-450 had a specific audience in mind: people of voting age. The writer assumed that these people would have a certain amount of knowledge about the American political system. The writer also assumed that while many people do not vote, these people are not likely to be opposed to voting. The writer therefore appealed to the audience's better nature. If the writer of "There's No Excuse for Not Voting" was presenting this essay to a group of people who had never before voted or registered to vote, how might the writer have changed the content and wording of the essay?

SETTING THE TONE

The tone you set will determine in part how your audience responds to your argument. Be sure that your tone reflects the purpose of your essay. You might choose a factual, objective tone, or you may prefer a more emotional tone. Remember that readers are more likely to respond favorably to an argument when the writer acknowledges the concerns of people holding the opposing viewpoint.

Suppose you were writing an essay arguing that your local government wastes tax dollars on unneeded expenditures. You might use any one of the following tones:

- An objective tone, presenting facts that speak for themselves
- An emotional tone, presenting examples designed to rouse your audience to anger
- A humorous tone, presenting examples or anecdotes that illustrate the wasteful practices you are criticizing

In "There's No Excuse for Not Voting" on pages 449-450, the writer began with an emotional appeal, used a reasonable tone to refute the excuses for not voting, and continued with an emotional tone for the conclusion. The tone of the essay clearly shows that the writer is not neutral on the issue of low voter turnout.

Questions

1. Is the tone of "There's No Excuse for Not Voting" in keeping with the intended audience? Be specific.

_____

_____

_____

2. Locate and describe a specific instance in the essay where tone reveals the writer's purpose.

_____

_____

_____

Activity B: Planning an Essay That Presents an Argument

In this assignment you will plan the purpose, content, structure, audience, and tone for an essay that presents an argument. Refer to the Writing Focus Chart on page 132 for help in addressing these five key elements. Use separate sheets of paper for your work.

A. Narrow one of the following general topics for an essay that presents an argument:

- Violence on television
- A problem in your community
- Families and divorce
- Something all people should do
- Gossip about celebrities
- Something no one should do

   For example, if you select the general topic "something all people should do," your narrowed topic might be "Everyone should spend at least two hours a week doing volunteer work."

B. Once you have selected and narrowed a topic, establish your writing purpose. Decide whether your argument will be an attempt to get readers to agree with your opinion or an attempt to convince them to take some action. Freewrite for ten to fifteen minutes about the topic of your argument. Explore as many ideas, facts, and examples as you can about the issue you have chosen.

C. Based on your prewriting, write a thesis statement.

D. Gather ideas for your argument. Brainstorm a list of points in favor of and against your position. Also gather supporting evidence from your personal experiences, from your observations, and from your research.

E. Based on your prewriting, decide how you want to structure your essay. Prepare an outline that includes the points you are planning to make and the supporting evidence you will present.

F. Target a specific audience for your essay. For example, you might gear your essay toward an audience that is familiar with your topic but might disagree with your viewpoint. Alternatively, you might wish to address an audience that might agree with your view but might disagree with the recommendations you plan to make. After considering your audience, decide what tone is most appropriate for your topic and writing purpose.

PORTFOLIO

Save your work in your portfolio. You will use your prewriting work to develop an essay that presents an argument in Assignment 2 on page 460.

REVISING, EDITING, AND PROOFREADING ESSAYS THAT PRESENT ARGUMENTS

The Checklist for Revising and Editing on page 153 can guide you in evaluating and revising the first draft of your essay. The Checklist for Proofreading on page 105 can help you turn your revised draft into a final copy.

Read the following revised draft of an essay that presents an argument. Remember that at this point the writer has not yet corrected errors in grammar, spelling, punctuation, and capitalization. What changes did the writer make to improve the essay?

Revised Draft: **Are American Athletes Overpaid?**

American athletes have ofen been accused of being overpaid. ^For example, Famous ballplayers sign contracts that guarantee them millions of dollars. ^for one year's work ○ They may earn additional millions for product endorsements. *Nevertheless,* Athletes do deserve their salaries, a conclusion that can be supported by ana-lyzeing the reasons for their high earnings and consider- *comparing their careers to those of other entertainers* ing the nature of their careers.

Athletes gets high salaries mainly because of market demand for their services. ~~It is the public that buys the tickets.~~ demand for athletes is high because tens of millions of sports fans watch televised and live games, why shouldn't athletes get a fair proportion of the earnings *from those games*? The same holds true for product endorsements. If the public is willing to respond to an advertisement starring a famous athlete by buying the advertised product, the athlete as well as the *manufacturer of the product* ~~company~~ should benefit. Athletes bring in big *profits* ~~bucks~~ for several brands of sneakers for example only because people ~~go out to~~ purchase the *brands* ~~item~~ worn by their sports heroes. *Public demand, not the athletes, is the main determining factor in athletes' high earnings.*

Athletes are entertainers, and many other types of entertainers are highly paid. Some actors earn over $7 *Talk show hosts earn multimillion-dollar salaries each year.* million for a single movie. Since high Salaries are the norm for the entertainment business, why should the salaries of athletes be an exception?

Finally, Consider the nature of an athlettic career. Unlike the members of most other professions, athletes usually begin their "job training" as children. Injuries can end the career of a basketball or football player in five years or less. They must practice and develop for many years before they can begin to play professionally, and unlike *however,* other professionals, the athletes ~~are limited in the num~~ *usually have short careers.* ~~ber of years they can make these large salaries.~~ In most sports even an athlete who never suffers an injury loses *or earlier* the physical edge by the age of 35 and must quit. Athletes therefore have a limited number of years in which they can earn such large salaries.

Athletes are like any other worker's in our society.

They earn what their services are worth to others ⊙ In addition⌃

⌃They work hard at their jobs, and they provide spectators

thrilling experience ⊙

with a ~~good time~~. When the matter is seen from that

⌃

angle, American athletes' earnings seem completely fair.

On pages 457-458 of this chapter you'll see a rekeyed version of "Are American Athletes Overpaid?" that incorporates the writer's handwritten revisions. You'll use that version to proofread the essay for errors in spelling, punctuation, and so on.

Questions

1. How has the writer improved the effectiveness of this essay? Be specific.

   Used specific details instead of being vague.
   Used Transitions. Removed unnecessary details

2. Why did the writer add the phrase "comparing their careers to those of other entertainers" in the introduction?

   To make the thesis statement specific

3. Why did the writer change the order of sentences in the fourth paragraph?

   To arrange in the order.

4. What transitions did the writer add to create a smooth flow within and between paragraphs?

   Nevertheless, Since

5. If you were the writer of this essay, what additional revisions would you make in content, structure, and wording?

Read the revised and rekeyed draft of "Are American Athletes Overpaid?" that follows. Proofread the revision, and correct any mistakes in spelling, capitalization, and punctuation as well as any factual, keyboarding, and grammatical errors.

Revised and Rekeyed Draft:

Are American Athletes Overpaid?

American athletes have ofen been accused of being overpaid. For example, famous ballplayers sign contracts that guarantee them millions of dollars for one year's work. They may earn additional millions for product endorsements. Nevertheless, athletes do deserve their salaries, a conclusion that can be supported by analyzeing the reasons for their high earnings, comparing their careers to those of other entertainers, and considering the nature of their careers.

Athletes gets high salaries mainly because of market demand for their services. demand for athletes is high because tens of millions of sports fans watch televised and live games, why shouldn't athletes get a fair proportion of the earnings from those games? The same holds true for product endorsements. If the public is willing to respond to an advertisement starring a famous athlete by buying the advertised product, the athlete as well as the manufacturer of the product should benefit. Athletes bring in big profits for several brands of sneakers for example only because people purchase the brands worn by their sports heroes. Public demand, not the athletes, is the main determining factor in athletes' high earnings.

Athletes are entertainers, and many other types of entertainers are highly paid. Some actors earn over $7 million for a single movie. Talk show hosts earn multimillion-dollar salaries each year. Since high Salaries are the norm for the entertainment business, why should the salaries of athletes be an exception?

Finally, consider the nature of an athlettic career. Unlike the members of most other professions, athletes usually begin their "job training" as children. They must practice and develop for many years before they can begin to play professionally. Unlike other professionals, however, athletes usually have short careers. Injuries can end the career of a basketball or football player in five years or less. In most sports even an athlete who never suffers an injury loses the physical edge by the age of 35 or earlier and must quit. Athletes therefore have a limited number of years in which they can earn such large salaries.

Athletes are like any other worker's in our society. They earn what their services are worth to others. In addition, they work hard at their jobs, and they provide spectators with a thrilling experience. When the matter is seen from that angle, American athletes' earnings seem completely fair.

Assignment 1:
Creating an Essay That Presents an Argument With Your Group

In this assignment you will work with your group to plan, write, edit, and proofread an essay that presents an argument.

A. Choose a topic suitable for a collaboratively written essay that presents an argument. Work together to narrow the topic and to brainstorm points of argument. Decide whether your essay will focus on convincing your audience to agree with you on an issue or on persuading readers to take a specific action.

B. Working as a group, use the questions on the Writing Focus Chart on page 132 to guide you as you plan the first draft. Use any of the invention techniques you learned in Chapter 2 to develop the thesis statement, introduction, main ideas, supporting details, and conclusion. Also use any of the strategies from Chapter 5 to develop content.

C. Use your group's prewriting to write the first draft. Your first draft should consist of an introduction, a body, and a conclusion and should clearly accomplish your writing purpose. Review the draft and work together to develop an appropriate title.

D. Carefully reread and evaluate the content, structure, and wording of your first draft. Discuss any necessary changes, additions, deletions, and corrections. Using the Checklist for Revising and Editing on page 153 as a guide, work together to revise the first draft. Complete as many revisions as needed.

E. When you are satisfied that your draft is the best work that your group can produce, choose someone to key the revised draft. Make a photocopy for every group member.

F. Carefully reread your revised draft. Using the Checklist for Proofreading on page 105, work together to prepare the final copy. Consult the Writer's Guide that begins on page A 80 to review key points of grammar, punctuation, and capitalization. Have each group member proofread the revised draft independently and use proofreaders' marks from the box on page 105 to mark corrections. Then compare corrections and incorporate all the changes on one draft.

G. Have one group member key the final copy. Proofread the final copy as a group, and correct any keyboarding errors. Record the names of all group members on the final copy. Make a photocopy for every group member. Save your final copy in your portfolio.

Assignment 2:
Creating an Essay That Presents an Argument

In this assignment you will work independently to plan, write, edit, and proofread the essay you began developing earlier in this chapter.

A. Review the planning you did in Activity B on pages 453-454, including your prewriting, thesis statement, and outline. Reread the freewriting you did on your topic.

B. Use your prewriting and the questions on the Writing Focus Chart on page 132 to guide you as you plan the first draft of the essay. Use any of the invention techniques you learned in Chapter 2 to develop the introduction, main ideas, supporting details, and conclusion. Also use any of the strategies from Chapter 5 to develop content.

C. Write the first draft of your essay. Your first draft should consist of an introduction, a body, and a conclusion and should clearly accomplish your writing purpose. Review your draft and develop an appropriate title.

D. Share your draft with members of your group or with a peer editor. Use the comments and suggestions from the group or peer editor, in conjunction with the Checklist for Revising and Editing on page 153, to help you make revisions. After sharing essays, work independently to revise your draft.

E. Evaluate the content, structure, and wording of your essay. Using the Checklist for Revising and Editing as a guide, make any necessary changes, additions, deletions, and corrections. Make as many revisions as needed. When you are satisfied, key your revised draft.

F. Carefully reread your revised draft. Using the Checklist for Proofreading on page 105, prepare the final copy. Consult the Writer's Guide that begins on page A 80 to review key points of grammar, punctuation, and capitalization. Use proofreaders' marks from the box on page 105 to mark your corrections.

G. Key the final copy. Look over the final copy and correct any keyboarding errors. Save your final copy in your portfolio.

Assignment 3:
Reading as a Stimulus for Writing

In this assignment you will read a selection and then work independently to plan, write, edit, and proofread an essay that presents an argument.

A. Read "No Books, No Brains, No Chance" by Sheryl McCarthy on pages A 141-A 142. Sheryl McCarthy is a newspaper columnist who writes about current issues. In this essay she argues for the value of a good education and explores some of the serious consequences for individuals and for society when students drop out of high school.

B. Use the selection as a stimulus for writing an essay that presents an argument. For example, you might persuade readers of the value of a planned exercise program or of a healthy diet. You might argue that smokers are being treated justly (or unjustly) when they are forbidden to smoke in public buildings. Here are several questions to start you thinking.

- How does the writer use facts, expert opinions, and logic to present her argument?

- Has the writer presented primarily an emotional or a logical argument? Why do you think so?

- What conclusion does the writer reach?

- About what current issues do you have strong feelings? Can you identify causes or recommended solutions?

- How might you persuade an audience of readers that your ideas and viewpoint have merit?

Use your responses to the preceding questions to help you decide on a specific topic and generate a thesis statement. Freewrite for approximately ten or fifteen minutes on the topic you select.

C. Share your ideas with members of your group or with a peer editor. Discuss the topic you are considering for your essay. Ask for constructive advice about the topic. Also discuss any problem areas that you foresee.

D. Use your prewriting and the questions on the Writing Focus Chart on page 132 to guide you as you write your first draft. Use any of the invention techniques from Chapter 2 and any of the strategies from Chapter 5 as needed. Your first draft should consist of an introduction, a body, and a conclusion and should clearly accomplish your writing purpose. If you find it useful, make a conceptual map or outline to help you visualize the content and structure of your essay. Review your draft and develop an appropriate title.

E. Share your draft with members of your group or with a peer editor. Use the comments and suggestions from the group or peer editor, in conjunction with the Checklist for Revising and Editing on page 153, to help you make revisions. After sharing essays, work independently to revise your draft.

F. Evaluate the content, structure, and wording of your draft. Using the Checklist for Revising and Editing as a guide, make any necessary changes, additions, deletions, and corrections. Make as many revisions as needed. When you are satisfied, key your revised draft.

G. Carefully reread your revised draft. Using the Checklist for Proofreading on page 105, prepare the final copy. Consult the Writer's Guide that begins on page A80 to review key points of grammar, punctuation, and capitalization. Use proofreaders' marks from the box on page 105 to mark your corrections.

H. Key the final copy. Look over the final copy and correct any keyboarding errors. Save your final copy in your portfolio.

USING NEGATIVE EXPRESSIONS CORRECTLY

Grammar Gremlins

To convey a negative idea in a sentence, use only one negative expression. If you use two negative expressions in the same sentence, you create a **double negative**, which has a *positive* meaning.

CORRECT (ONE NEGATIVE):
I hope your daughter will *not* lose interest in science.
I hope your daughter will *never* lose interest in science.
I hope your daughter will *not* ever lose interest in science.

INCORRECT (TWO NEGATIVES):
I hope your daughter will *not never* lose interest in science.

CORRECT:
We *don't* need to buy anything else.
We need to buy *nothing* else.

INCORRECT:
We *don't* need to buy *nothing* else.

The words *neither...nor* are considered to form one negative expression.

CORRECT:
Su Lin will attend *neither* the party *nor* the conference.

INCORRECT:
Su Lin will *not* attend *neither* the party *nor* the conference.

Be careful not to create a double negative when you use words such as *hardly* and *scarcely*.

CORRECT:
Victor could *hardly* lift the suitcase.

INCORRECT:
Victor could *not hardly* lift the suitcase.

Activities

A. Change or delete one or more words in each sentence to eliminate the double negative. Use proofreaders' marks to make your corrections.

1. A hologram is a three-dimensional image that is ~~not~~ neither a photograph nor a sculpture.

2. Holograms look real, but you can't ~~never~~ touch them.

3. At science museums, visitors ~~can't~~ hardly believe that their hands go right through the holograms on display.

4. I ~~don't~~ know nothing as frustrating as trying to grab a holographic dollar bill.

5. Don't ~~never~~ be surprised if someday holograms are used in place of sculptures.

B. Correct the five double negatives in the following paragraph. Use proofreaders' marks to make your corrections.

> An old-fashioned amusement park is not ~~nothing~~ like the popular theme parks of today. Once they were places for summertime fun that offered rides on wooden carousels, inhuman tests of strength, curious stage shows, and just a hint of danger. One couldn't help but get lost in the seamy carnival atmosphere. However, in 1955 the first theme park, Disneyland, opened, and things haven't ~~never~~ been the same. The old amusement park's Ferris wheel can't ~~hardly~~ compete with the high-tech rides, movie-based attractions, and imported wild animals of some of today's theme parks. Although customers of the late 1800s never had ~~no~~ chance to compare the two, some of these people might say that the theme park's appeal isn't nothing but Hollywood glamour and expert marketing.

C. For additional practice in using negative expressions, see page A79.

WRAPPING IT UP

SUMMARY

- Present an argument in an essay to convince readers to agree with your viewpoint or to persuade them to take a specific course of action.
- Use evidence such as *facts, expert opinions,* and *logic* to convince an audience of the central point of an argument. This evidence might result from personal experience, observation, or research. Emotional appeals in an argument can influence an audience.
- If needed, present and refute opposing viewpoints in order to support your viewpoint in an argument.
- Include only accurate and appropriate evidence in an argument.
- Structure the points in an argument in a logical order, from least important point to most important point, or vice versa.

THINKING IT OVER

- Why is it important to be able to present arguments effectively in daily life? Describe two or three of the most useful aspects of presenting arguments that you learned in this chapter.

_____

_____

_____

_____

_____

_____

- How will what you have learned in this chapter help you present arguments in writing at work and at school?

_____

_____

_____

_____

_____

_____

_____

_____

Review the goals that you set at the beginning of this chapter. In your journal, evaluate your progress toward these goals.

Appendix

The essays you have written throughout this book will help you prepare for and take essay tests in school. In general, **essay tests** are designed to test your knowledge of large issues and concepts. They require you to **synthesize**—compress and combine—information that you've learned. Here's an example of an essay question:

Question: Compare and contrast the characters Ishmael and Queequeg in *Moby Dick.*

To answer the question, you need to know the characters and events in Moby Dick thoroughly so that you can explain how these key characters are alike and how they are different. Here's how a possible answer might begin:

Answer:

> *Ishmael and Queequeg are two very different characters, but they share certain qualities. When the two men meet . . .*

Your essay will be evaluated on how completely and accurately you answer the question and follow the directions. For this reason, you must understand exactly what you are being asked to do before you begin writing. As with other essay assignments, the directions or questions for essay tests include clue words that will help you know what to do. The chart on page A 3 lists some of those clue words and their meanings.

PREPARING FOR ESSAY TESTS

The best way to prepare for essay tests is to do so actively. Two strategies for preparing for essay tests are to predict possible questions and to rehearse answers to the questions you predict.

Clue Words in Essay Tests

Compare: Write about the similarities and differences between two or more people, places, or things.

Contrast: Write about the differences between two people, places, or things.

Criticize or *Critique:* Write an evaluation, expressing your opinion and supporting your opinion with facts, examples, and descriptions.

Define: Write the exact meaning of a term. The meaning you write should be specific to the course you are taking. Include examples to make your definition clear.

Describe: Write in detail, giving information about appearance, behavior, qualities, and purpose.

Discuss: Write in detail, describing the positive and negative aspects or identifying opinions pro and con regarding the subject.

Enumerate: Write a list of parts, key points, causes, effects, or benefits. Begin by identifying how many items there are, then write about each one, beginning with "First . . ." or using numerals.

Evaluate: Write about the advantages and disadvantages, pros and cons of situations, events, or issues. Cite experts and give your own opinion, supported by facts, examples, and other details.

Illustrate: Write a detailed description, explaining how a process or system works or how an event happened. Your description should include examples.

Outline: Write a list of the main parts and important details. You may need to ask your instructor whether you should create an outline with roman numerals and letters or whether you should write your description in paragraph form.

Prove: Write the facts that explain why a statement is true. These facts are usually ones that have been presented in class or in your textbook.

State: Write as clearly and precisely as possible.

Summarize: Write a clear, condensed description, including only the most important points.

Trace: Write a description of development over time, from the earliest events to the latest.

PREDICTING QUESTIONS

A good way to predict test questions is to recognize clues from your instructor. If the instructor relies heavily on the textbook for explanations and discussion, test questions are likely to be based on text-book content. On the other hand, if the instructor relies heavily on lecture notes and outside readings, test questions are likely to be based on lecture material and other assigned readings.

During lectures, notice when the instructor emphasizes certain points by displaying them on the board or a chart or by repeating them. Notice clue words the instructor uses such as *most important*, *significant*, *key*, and so on. Information that is emphasized in this way is likely to appear on a test.

In addition, study material from quizzes or from questions the instructor asks in class. Such material is likely to appear in a slightly different form on a test.

REHEARSING WITH OUTLINES

Based on the questions you predict will be on the test, you can rehearse and prepare outlines to develop an essay response. You rehearse information when you think about it, reread it, talk about it, and recite it aloud. Rehearsing increases your ability to remember information from your notes. One good way to rehearse is to recite material aloud in 15- to 25-minute sessions. Schedule your test preparation so that you have enough time to rehearse orally.

For each question, prepare a brief outline of the topic, including the main ideas, supporting details, and examples you would include in an essay. After preparing the outline, test your ability to recall the information by following these steps:

1. Cover the outline with another sheet of paper.

2. Slide the paper down to reveal a topic or main idea.

3. Try to recall the supporting details for the topic or main idea.

4. Check your recall by revealing the details.

PORTFOLIO

Activity: Identifying Possible Essay Test Questions

Imagine that you just learned that you will have an essay test in one of your courses. Consider clues you've picked up from the instructor and information from both your textbook and lecture notes. On a separate sheet of paper, identify five essay questions that could appear on the test. Save your work in your portfolio.

TIPS FOR TAKING ESSAY TESTS

Use the following strategies to improve your chances of doing well on an essay test:

1. *Pay attention to all instructions.* Your instructor may give you directions before you begin the test, such as when to begin, how much time you have, and what to do with the completed test.

2. *Preview the test unless you are instructed not to do so.* Previewing the test gives you an idea of what to expect.
   - Note the sections and the kinds of test items.
   - Notice the number of items and points in each section.
   - Read each question and make sure you understand the instructions for each section.

3. *Budget your time.* After you have previewed the test, decide how much time to spend on each section. Allocate time according to point values. If you have to write two essays in 50 minutes and each essay is worth 50 points, spend 25 minutes on each essay. Check the time periodically to make sure you are budgeting your time.

4. *Plan each essay on a separate sheet of paper.* Jot down all your ideas and organize them in a list, outline, or map. Then use this plan to guide your writing.

5. *Begin each essay answer by writing a thesis statement that says exactly what you will do.* Use clue words in the test instructions to help phrase your thesis statement, as in the following example:

   > *Question:* Enumerate the primary parts of the human circulatory system.

   > *Thesis Statement: The four main parts of the human circulatory system are the heart, arteries, capillaries, and veins.*

   Notice how a specific number—four—replaces the key word *enumerate.* To complete the answer, you would describe each part of the human circulatory system.

6. *Provide adequate supporting evidence.* Support your thesis statement with specific ideas, facts, examples, and details.

7. *Write neatly.* If you make corrections, make them neatly. A neat appearance can improve your grade.

8. *Check your answers.* Make sure your essays have unity, support, and coherence. Then proofread your essays carefully.

Assignment:
Answering Essay Test Questions

In this assignment you will work to plan and answer questions for an essay test.

A. Review the list of essay questions you created for the activity on page A 4.

B. Choose one of the essay questions to answer. Plan your essay by jotting down your ideas and then organizing them into a list, outline, or map.

C. Draft your answer. Instead of keying your essay, write it neatly. Begin by writing a thesis statement that uses clue words in the test question. Support your thesis statement with specific ideas, facts, examples, and details.

D. Evaluate the content, structure, and wording of your answer. Carefully check the facts you have included.

E. Proofread your answer and make corrections neatly. Save your answer in your portfolio.

PORTFOLIO

In many of your classes, you will need to write summaries of written and oral material. A **summary** (sometimes called an **abstract** or **précis**) is a concise presentation that gives key information about an article, an event, a TV program or movie, or an oral presentation. Effective summaries help a reader or listener quickly understand the main purpose, content, and structure of an original work.

Summaries take many forms and appear in a variety of situations. They can be brief (as short as one sentence) or lengthy (several pages long). Summaries may be oral or written and will always be based on some longer, more complex material. You may be asked to write a one-paragraph summary of a 30-minute educational video, a two-page summary of the events in a 500-page novel, or a one-page summary of the key events in a two-week internship you completed. Whether a summary is based on a book, a videotape, a lecture, or a personal experience, the basic goal is the same: to compress a broad range of information into a few well-chosen words.

Summarizing involves a combination of reading, study, and writing skills. To write an effective summary, you must identify the main ideas and key details in the original work. You must also translate the original information into your own words. Putting complex information into your own words helps you understand and remember the main ideas of the original work.

SUMMARIZING WRITTEN INFORMATION

If you are asked to write a summary of a written work, begin by previewing the text. To preview an article, look at the title, subtitle, introductory and final paragraphs, headings and subheadings, and any words that stand out in special type (boldface or italics). To preview a book, look at the title, table of contents, preface, first and last chapters, chapter openers and summaries, and any photographs and illustrations.

After previewing the text, read the work thoroughly. As you read, jot down or highlight main ideas and key details. Pay special attention to topic sentences, defined terms, examples, and lists of items (called *enumerations*); these features often contain important information. You may want to turn headings into questions and read to find the answers; this technique helps you read more carefully.

As soon as you finish reading, write a sentence that expresses the central point of the work. Then reread key sections, jotting down important ideas and significant details.

SUMMARIZING ORAL OR ONE-TIME-ONLY INFORMATION

When you are asked to summarize oral or "one-time-only" situations such as lectures, speeches, videotapes, and events, you must take a different approach from that used to summarize written information. Take notes as the lecture, speech, or other event unfolds. Jot down words, phrases, or brief sentences that indicate key points. Many speakers use verbal cues such as repetition to alert you to key points. Listen carefully to openings and closings of speeches and conversations; they often contain the central point and main ideas. When you summarize events, try to compare your account of what happened with the perceptions of someone else who was present. Incorporate important points from the other person's account that you may have missed. Afterward, write a sentence that conveys the central point or dominant impression of the oral presentation or event. This sentence will help you structure the contents of your summary.

ESTABLISHING THE WRITING PURPOSE

The purpose of a summary is always to inform. For this reason, a summary should always present the central point and main ideas of the original source in an objective, impersonal way. Don't include personal comments and opinions in a summary.

IDENTIFYING AND CONDENSING THE CONTENT

Your task in a summary is to identify and condense existing information. Use the invention techniques of questioning, outlining, and mapping to pinpoint and organize those main ideas from an original source that should be included in your summary.

PLANNING THE STRUCTURE

Most summaries begin by stating the purpose and central point of the original source. If you are summarizing a written work, such as a book or an article, your first sentence should identify the author, title, publisher, date of publication, and central point of the work. In summarizing oral information, such as a speech or an interview, give similar background information: the title of the talk (if there was one), the speaker, the purpose or topic of the talk, the location, and the date. In summarizing an event (a day on an internship or a situation you observed), mention the nature of the event (including the date and location) and explain who was involved. Here are two examples of opening sentences for summaries:

- In Toni Morrison's Nobel Prize acceptance speech (Stockholm, Sweden, 1993), she used a folktale to talk about the importance of language.

- The growth of television home-shopping shows as a profitable business is the subject of Don L. Boroughs's article "Purchasing Power" in the January 31, 1994 issue of *U.S. News & World Report*.

The most logical way to structure a summary is to follow the structure of the original work. For example, you might present the main ideas in the same order that the writer or speaker did, or you might structure your summary in order of importance, from the least to the most important idea. The structure of your summary should also reflect the emphasis the writer or speaker placed on specific points. If a writer discusses three main ideas but spends one page on the first idea, three pages on the second, and nine pages on the third, you should discuss the third idea at some length. To be concise, you may also combine ideas from the original source.

Once you have analyzed the structure of the original work, use an outline or map to organize the main ideas and key details to include in your summary.

TARGETING A SPECIFIC AUDIENCE

Assume that readers know little if anything about the original work you are summarizing. Always include enough information to convey the central point and main ideas of the original work. Some of the summaries you write will be for your own use, so *you* will be the audience. For example, you might write a summary of a difficult textbook section to understand the material better, or you might write a summary of your lecture notes to help prepare for an exam. Whether you are writing a summary for yourself or another audience, word your summaries so that they are clear and comprehensive.

SETTING THE TONE

Depending on your content and on the tone of the original work, the tone you adopt may be informal (a description of your internship to a mentor) or very formal (a summary for a report). If you summarize a humorous article, you should use an informal tone to indicate to the reader that the article was humorous. Similarly, if you summarize a serious article, you should use a factual, objective tone to reflect the substance of the original work. You may also include a phrase or sentence in your summary that refers directly to the tone of the original. Here is an example:

> George Will's essay "Printed Noise" is a lighthearted criticism of the cutesy names given to many food products to make them sound more tempting.

Although you want to keep your summaries brief, make sure you mention the key characteristics of the original work.

The language you use for a summary should reflect but not copy or imitate the wording of the original. The wording you use should always be your own. If you use another writer's words and try to pass them off as your own, you will be **plagiarizing**. If you quote directly from the original source, do so sparingly. Don't use more than two quotations in a single paragraph of your summary. When you quote somebody else's words, always enclose the quoted material within quotation marks, as in the following example:

> In *The Plug-In Drug,* Marie Wynn's analysis of the effects of television watching on children, Wynn describes the "trance-like nature" of young children's behavior as they watch television.

The following example is a summary of a newspaper article. As you read the summary, note in the margin how the writer has structured the summary, and circle the sentence or sentences that express the central point of the original article.

Summary

In the article "Secrets of Long Life From 2 Who Ought to Know" (*The New York Times,* September 23, 1993), journalist Melinda Henneberger presents Sadie and Bessie Delany, two African-American women who have collaborated with a writer on a book about themselves and their eventful lives. The Delany sisters, both over 100 years of age, were born to a former slave who later became the first African-American bishop of the Episcopal Church in the United States. Sadie and Bessie Delany, who never married and have lived together all their lives, carried on the family tradition of achievement in the face of prejudice. Bessie Delany became New York State's second female African-American dentist, and Sadie Delany became New York City's first African-American high school home economics teacher. The sisters wrote their book, *Having Our Say: The Delany Sisters' First Hundred Years* (Kodansha Publishing, 1993), along with Amy Hill Hearth to share their lives with others. Melinda Henneberger recounts her visit with the sisters, during which the women give tips for a long healthy life (which include yoga and garlic); detail a daily routine that includes doing their own cooking and watching television news programs; share reminiscences of the joys and difficulties of life for African Americans through the twentieth century; and tell how their newfound celebrity has affected their lives today by bringing interviewers and television crews to their home. Henneberger shows through the Delanys' words that a strong character can overcome the obstacles of racism, poverty, and even old age.

TIPS FOR PREPARING SUMMARIES

Use the following strategies to prepare effective summaries:

- Check headings, subheadings, and words in special type for key details.
- Search introductions and conclusions and the topic sentences of each paragraph to identify main ideas.
- Listen carefully to opening and closing statements in oral presentations to identify main ideas.
- Note statements that are emphasized or that are repeated throughout a written work or a discussion—such statements reveal key details about the topic.

Activity: Planning a Summary

PORTFOLIO

Select a written work that you would like to summarize. Choose a book, an article, a poem, a short story, or a textbook chapter. Preview and read the work you have selected. After you finish reading, identify the following features of the original work: the central point, main ideas and key details, the structure, and the tone. Use separate sheets of paper for your work, and save your work in your portfolio.

Assignment:
Creating a Summary

In this assignment you will work to plan, write, edit, and proofread a summary.

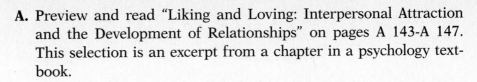

A. Preview and read "Liking and Loving: Interpersonal Attraction and the Development of Relationships" on pages A 143-A 147. This selection is an excerpt from a chapter in a psychology textbook.

B. Use the questions on the Writing Focus Chart on page 132 to guide you as you plan a summary of the selection. Identify and condense the central point and main ideas of the excerpt. Use mapping and outlining to structure your summary.

C. Use your prewriting to write the first draft of your summary. Your first draft should cover the central point and main ideas in the original work.

D. Use the Checklist for Revising and Editing on page 153 to help you make revisions. After revising your summary, key a revised draft. Use the Checklist for Proofreading on page 105 and consult the Writer's Guide that begins on page A 80 to prepare the final copy. Use proofreaders' marks from the box on page 105 to mark your corrections. Then key the final copy and correct any keyboarding errors. Save your final copy in your portfolio.

In many of your college courses, you will be asked to write a **report** on a book, article, speech, or other written or oral information. Sometimes such reports are called **reaction papers, book reports, evaluations, themes,** or **reviews.** Whenever your instructor asks you to both summarize and respond personally to written or oral source material, you must do a report.

ESTABLISHING THE WRITING PURPOSE

The purpose of a report is twofold: to inform and to persuade. The first part of a report includes a summary of important points in an original work. As with all summaries, the purpose of this part is strictly to inform. The second part of a report presents personal reactions to an original work. In the latter part of a report, you present personal opinions, observations, and judgments. Your goal is to convince readers to agree with your evaluation of the original work.

DEVELOPING THE CONTENT

The first part of a report will be your summary of an original work. Use the techniques described on page A 9 for identifying and condensing content for a summary.

The second part of a report is similar to the body of an essay. Use the same invention techniques you use to gather content for an essay to discover content for your personal reactions. In particular, ask yourself questions such as the following to help generate ideas for a report:

- How is the work related to the focus of the course?

- How does the work mirror the important social, political, religious, and philosophical issues of today?

- How is the work relevant to me personally? Does the work address issues that apply to my life? What are those issues, and why are they important to me?

- How complete, accurate, inspiring, and well-organized is this work? Would I recommend this work to others? Why or why not?

Use these questions and the invention techniques used to develop essays to gather ideas, details, and examples for your report.

PLANNING THE STRUCTURE

In the first part of a report, your summary may be one or two paragraphs. The second part of your report (which may be two or more paragraphs) should present your reaction to the work. Your conclusion should evaluate the work or make a recommendation. The structure you choose for the second part of a report will depend on the work you are discussing and the point you are trying to make. For example, if you were doing a report on a historical novel about the Civil War, you might compare and contrast the Civil War period with present times. If you were writing a report on Sandra Cisneros's *House on Mango Street*, you might focus on three aspects of her writing: her use of language, the integrity of her characters, and the relevance of her stories.

TARGETING A SPECIFIC AUDIENCE

When planning and writing a report, consider your audience's response to the information you present. Even though your personal reaction is an important part of a report, you must support your responses with adequate evidence. Although you are being asked for a personal reaction, you must focus on the work, not on yourself. To clarify the distinction, compare the following personal reactions to a poem:

Vague: I really liked Emily Dickinson's poem "I heard a Fly buzz — when I died." The poem was very moving. I enjoyed reading it aloud . . .

Better: I am impressed by how much mystery, beauty, and emotion Emily Dickinson compacts into the short poem "I heard a Fly buzz —when I died." Her description of the fly's "Blue—uncertain stumbling Buzz" is vivid and unusual . . .

In the first statement the writer focuses on personal reactions to the poem and not on the poem. No support is given to explain why the poem is moving or enjoyable to read aloud. In the second statement the writer focuses on specific features in the poem and uses a quote to support the statement. Remember, use quotes sparingly in the summary section of a report; use quotes from the original work in the second part of a report to support your reaction to the work.

SETTING THE TONE

The tone you adopt in a report will depend on the original work and your reaction to it. The first part of your report should be written in a neutral, factual tone. The second part of your report will express your personal feelings about the work. If you were reporting on a magazine article about urban violence and you wanted to convey how serious and upsetting the material was, you would use an emotional, serious tone. If you were reporting on one of Shakespeare's comedies, you might adopt a more lighthearted, witty tone.

Read the following report on Louise Erdrich's short story "The Leap." As you read, do the following: circle the sentence or sentences that summarize the central point of the story, note in the margins how the writer has structured the report, and underline evaluations and recommendations the writer makes.

Report on "The Leap"

Louise Erdrich's short story "The Leap" (*Harper's*, 1990) centers on a woman's relationship with her mother. The mother was a trapeze performer, Anna of the Amazing Avalons. While Anna was performing with her first husband, Harold, a fluke accident occurred. A bolt of lightning struck the main pole of the big-top tent while the two acrobats were in mid-air. Harry fell to his death, but Anna was able to save herself by grabbing onto a supporting wire as she fell. Her badly burned hands kept the scar of that accident, but Anna lived. While recuperating in the hospital, Anna met the man who would become her second husband. This man was the doctor who nursed her back to health.

The narrator of "The Leap" is Anna's daughter. Later in the story, the daughter tells of an event that took place when she was seven years old. Anna, who had long since retired from the trapeze world, courageously used her aerial skills to save her daughter when the daughter was trapped in their burning house. The trapeze accident and Anna's later rescue of her daughter are the two main events that structure this compelling story.

My enjoyment of "The Leap" is largely based on my appreciation of Erdrich's ability to create dramatic situations. The Flying Avalons are portrayed in highly romantic terms: "They loved to drop gracefully from nowhere, like two sparkling birds, and blow kisses as they threw off their plumed helmets and high-collared capes" (200). As performers, Harry and Anna blew mock kisses to each other after being blindfolded for their act. They acted as if they were "never again to meet" (200). This staged gesture increases the drama of the story when it turns out that they actually never do see each other alive again. Similarly, when Anna saves her daughter from the burning house, she climbs up and then leaps from a tree to the window where the daughter is trapped. Erdrich depicts the rescue in vivid detail: as the daughter looks out the window, she sees that her mother was "hanging by the backs of her heels from the new gutter we had put in that year, and she was smiling. I was not surprised to see her, she was so matter of fact" (203). The precise description of the event, combined with the mother's calm confidence in her physical ability, made me appreciate the full drama of the situation.

Another aspect of the story that I found interesting is Erdrich's ability to weave certain details throughout the story to reveal the personalities of the characters. The fact that Anna was a blindfolded trapeze artist is used to show the depth of her character later when Anna has actually become blind. As the narrator states in the story: "My mother lives comfortably in extreme elements. She is one with the constant dark now, just as the air was her home, familiar to her, safe, before the storm that afternoon" (200).

I am also impressed by Erdrich's ability to show the dramatic changes that can occur in a person's life. After Anna's trapeze accident, the doctor, her future husband, taught her how to read. Thinking about this fact later, the daughter asks, "I wonder if my father calculated the exchange he offered: one form of flight for another. For after that, and for as long as I can remember, my mother has never been without a book" (202). Now that Anna is blind, reading is less available to her. The daughter comes home, then, to rescue her mother much as Anna had rescued her earlier. "I came home to read to my mother, to read out loud, to read long into the dark if I must, to read all night" (202).

Not only is "The Leap" a carefully constructed, well-balanced story, it is also emotionally touching. The love and loyalty that mother and daughter share is shown in how carefully they take care of each other. The themes of flight, danger, and safety are carefully woven together. I was inspired by the leaps of imagination and love that the story's characters take and would recommend this story to others.

Activity: Planning a Report

PORTFOLIO

Select a written work for which you would like to do a report. You might choose a biography, a memoir, a novel, a short story, a poem, or an article. Write a short summary of the written work you have chosen. Then use the invention techniques that you learned in Chapter 2 to gather ideas for the personal reaction part of a report on this work. Use the questions on pages A 14–A 15 as a starting point. Write your summary and personal reactions on a separate sheet of paper. Save your notes in your portfolio. You will have an opportunity to use your notes in the following assignment.

Assignment:
Creating a Report

In this assignment you will work to plan, write, edit, and proofread the report you began developing in the preceding activity.

A. Review the planning you did in the activity. Freewrite about the work you have selected. Write down ideas and opinions that occur to you. Include issues, details, examples, and quotes from the original work that seem important to you.

B. Use your prewriting and the questions on the Writing Focus Chart on page 132 to guide you as you write the first draft of a report on the selection. Your first draft should contain an objective summary of the selection as well as a fully developed personal reaction to the work.

C. Use the Checklist for Revising and Editing on page 153 to help you make revisions. After revising your report, key a revised draft. Use the Checklist for Proofreading on page 105 and consult the Writer's Guide that begins on page A 80 to prepare the final copy. Use proofreaders' marks from the box on page 105 to mark your corrections. Then key the final copy and correct any keyboarding errors. Save your final copy in your portfolio.

When you apply for jobs, you will use your summarizing and writing skills to prepare an effective résumé and application letter. You will use your résumé and application letter to introduce yourself to potential employers.

WRITING RÉSUMÉS

A **résumé** is a brief summary of your work experience and educational background. The purpose of a résumé is to persuade potential employers to grant you an interview, not a job. Well-written résumés enable employers to quickly assess your qualifications for a particular job and decide whether they want to interview you.

THE PARTS OF A RÉSUMÉ

The sample résumé on page A 21 shows one acceptable format for a résumé. Although there are many ways to organize a résumé, most résumés contain the following standard parts:

- *Heading.* Your name, address, and home and work telephone numbers.

- *Objective.* A statement of your job goal or the type of work you are seeking.

- *Work experience.* A listing of your job history, presented in reverse time order, beginning with your most recent job.

- *Education.* Information about your education, presented in reverse time order. Include the type of college degree you earned and the year you received it.

- *Other.* Include any aspects of your background that could interest a potential employer, such as special skills, community service, professional activities, military service, and special interests.

John F. Sparks
1510 Tousle Avenue
Chicago, IL 60639-3047
Home: 312-555-1815   Work: 312-555-6003

OBJECTIVE

Seek responsible position where strong analytical and computer skills are needed to solve complex business problems.

EXPERIENCE

TRAFFIC SUPERVISOR   July 1993-Present
Graphic Improvements, Chicago, Illinois
Responsible for tracking orders and maintaining computer system. Trouble-shoot problems as they occur. Directly handle client queries.

- Created revised work-flow procedures that reduced average time needed to fill customer orders by approximately two hours.
- Made bill-tracking spreadsheet to more easily account for income.
- Trained staff on use of new computer system.

ASSISTANT DEPARTMENT MANAGER   March 1992-July 1993
Regal Department Store, Chicago, Illinois

- Recommended procedure to get merchandise price-marked and out of receiving a half-day earlier than previous standard.
- Tripled sales in open-stock housewares as a result of improved stocking schedule.

STOCK CLERK   June 1990-March 1992
Regal Department Store, Chicago, Illinois

- Handled customer sales, designed displays, and inventoried stock.
- Promoted to Assistant Department Manager based on ability to maximize potential sales by controlling inventory levels.

EDUCATION

LaSalle University (Chicago, Illinois), September 1990-May 1994, B.S. in accounting, minor in computer science

- Received strong foundation in business practices and in the decision-making process.
- Gained comprehensive knowledge of spreadsheet software (Lotus) and graphics software (Adobe Illustrator and Quark Xpress).

SPECIAL SKILLS AND ACTIVITIES

- Speaking knowledge of Spanish
- Volunteer work for Big Brothers of America

TIPS FOR PREPARING RÉSUMÉS

Use the following strategies to prepare an effective résumé:

- Keep your résumé brief. Especially for people who are new to the workforce or have limited work experience, one page is usually best.

- List your job experience and educational background in reverse time order, beginning with your most recent job or schooling.

- Use active verbs that demonstrate your ability to take charge and make improvements, such as *achieved, completed, created, conducted, launched, managed, started, strengthened, supervised, trained, won,* and *wrote.*

- For each job, give the dates of employment, the name and address of the company, your job title, specific achievements, and skills you acquired.

- For your education, list any honors, special school projects, and activities that might interest a potential employer.

- Include your grade point average only if you have a B average or higher.

- If you are currently working toward a college degree, note this and present an estimated date of completion. For example: "Working toward a degree in English at the University of Arizona; will receive a B.A. degree in June 1997."

- Describe measurable achievements such as *Exceeded sales quota by 16 percent* or *Won employee of the month award.*

- Do not include the following items on your résumé: age, height, weight, race, ethnicity, or marital status; your current salary or salary expectations; or the names, addresses, and phone numbers of references.

- Avoid using the personal pronouns *I* and *my.*

- Use phrases, not sentences, in your descriptions.

- Make sure your résumé has a neat and uncluttered appearance.

- Print your résumé on quality 8½- by 11-inch paper.

- Proofread your résumé carefully to correct errors in spelling, punctuation, and grammar.

Remember that a résumé is an advertisement for yourself, a way of selling your unique skills and qualities to a potential employer. Present yourself in a positive light, but don't exaggerate or lie about your achievements. Outright lies on a résumé can cost you a job, and most interviewers will easily see through exaggerations.

Activity A: Developing a Résumé

PORTFOLIO

To develop a résumé, gather information about your work experience and educational background. First, jot down as much information as possible about your job history. For now, include all the jobs you've ever performed. Next, gather information about your educational background and any other special skills or activities that might make you attractive to a potential employer. Use a separate sheet of paper to plan the contents of your résumé. Save your notes in your portfolio. You will have a chance to work on your résumé in the assignment on page A 26.

WRITING APPLICATION LETTERS

The résumé you send to a potential employer should always be accompanied by an application letter. The purpose of an **application letter** is to introduce yourself to a potential employer and create an interest in the unique abilities you have to offer. Like a résumé, an application letter should be concise. The letter should highlight those aspects of your background that make you uniquely suited to a particular job.

THE PARTS OF AN APPLICATION LETTER

An application letter should contain the following parts:

- *Return address and date line.* Key your address and the date (month, day, and year) about two inches from the top of the page.
- *Opening.* The opening of the letter includes the inside address (the name and address of the person to whom you are writing) and the

salutation (or greeting). The salutation, for example, "Dear Ms. Valens: " should be followed by a colon. If you are responding to a box number in the classified ads of a newspaper, use the following inside address format and salutation:

Box X124
New York Times
New York, NY 10108

Dear Sir or Madam:

- *Body.* In the body of the letter, begin by stating the specific job you are applying for and where you learned about the job. Then explain in a paragraph or two who you are and what skills and training you have to offer. Conclude by expressing your willingness to interview for the job.
- *Closing.* The closing of your letter should include a parting phrase like *Sincerely* or *Sincerely yours* followed by a comma and your name and signature.
- *Enclosure notation.* At the left margin, two lines below your name, key the word *Enclosure*. This is a reminder to the recipient that the letter contains an enclosure—in this case, your résumé.

TIPS FOR PREPARING APPLICATION LETTERS

Use the following strategies to prepare an effective application letter to accompany a résumé:

- Make sure your letter is neat.
- Use an acceptable letter format (one acceptable format is shown on page A 25).
- Print your letter on quality 8½- by 11-inch paper (preferably the same kind of paper you used for your résumé).
- Proofread your letter carefully to correct errors in spelling, punctuation, and grammar.

1510 Tousle Avenue
Chicago, IL 60639-3047
June 9, 1995

Ms. Deborah Spillfelter
Vice President, Print Services
Fusk and McCloud Advertising Agency
510 South Wacker Drive
Chicago, IL 60640-2519

Dear Ms. Spillfelter:

Your advertisement in the June 4 issue of the <u>Chicago Tribune</u> for a client services administrator described the ideal candidate as "a person with creativity and drive." I offer these qualities and my problem-solving and communication skills for the position with your agency.

Trafficking positions in two high-pressure environments, a large department store and a small but busy graphics business, required expert coordination in the flow of merchandise and information as well as interaction with customers and staff members.

Initiating new procedures at Regal Department Store resulted in shortened price-marking time and increased efficiency of the stocking schedule. Implementing revised work-flow procedures at Graphic Improvements led to a 15 percent increase in the client base and increased the productivity of eight staff members.

Efforts in both positions required the willingness to look at long-standing procedures with creativity and energy. Accounting coursework and computer expertise enabled me to explore cost-effective trafficking alternatives.

After you review information about my education, experience, and skills on the enclosed résumé, please call me to arrange a time to discuss the client services administrator position and my qualifications. You may reach me at 312-555-6003 during the day or at 312-555-1815 after 6 p.m.

Sincerely,

John F. Sparks

John F. Sparks

Enclosure

Activity B: Planning an Application Letter

In your local newspaper locate an ad for a job for which you would like to apply. Based on what you have learned about application letters, write the rough draft of a letter that you would send along with your résumé to this potential employer. Freewrite your letter on a separate sheet of paper. Save the letter in your portfolio. You will have an opportunity to write your letter in the following assignment.

Assignment:
Creating a Résumé and an Application Letter

In this assignment you will work to plan, write, edit, and proofread the résumé you began developing in the activity on page A 23 and the application letter you began developing in the preceding activity.

A. Review the planning you did in Activity A. Use your prewriting and the questions on the Writing Focus Chart on page 132 to guide you as you write the first draft of a résumé. Your first draft should include the following standard features: your name, address, and telephone number; work experience; educational background; any other special skills and honors that are relevant to your job application.

B. Review the planning you did in Activity B. Use your prewriting and the questions on the Writing Focus Chart on page 132 to guide you as you write the first draft of an application letter. Your first draft should include the following: a return address and date line, an inside address, a salutation, a body, a closing, and an enclosure notation.

C. Use the Checklist for Revising and Editing on page 153 to help you make revisions. After revising your résumé and your application letter, key a revised draft of each. Use the Checklist for Proofreading on page 105 and consult the Writer's Guide that begins on page A 80 to prepare the final copy of each document. Use proofreaders' marks from the box on page 105 to mark your corrections. Then key the final copy of each document and correct any keyboarding errors. Save your final copy of each document in your portfolio.

This chapter will show you how to use effective research, note-taking, and outlining techniques to gather, arrange, and format the contents of a research paper.

A **research paper** is a long piece of writing (usually at least 1,500 words) that draws on the writings and research of others to explain or make a central point about a topic. Unlike essays based on personal experience, research papers are based on information you find in books, articles, encyclopedias, interviews, recordings, and other sources.

Here are the basic steps involved in writing a research paper. Some of the steps will be familiar to you from the work you have done on essays:

1. Select a topic and gather general information.

2. Narrow the topic, establish a writing purpose, and write a thesis statement.

3. Do research and take notes.

4. Develop the content and outline the structure.

5. Target an audience and set the tone.

6. Write the research paper and use appropriate citations.

SELECTING A TOPIC

As with essays, the first step in writing a research paper is to select and narrow your topic. When selecting a research topic, consider the following questions:

- What topics interest me?
- Are there any topics I've studied in a class that I would like to know more about?
- How long is my paper supposed to be?
- Will I be able to locate a variety of sources about the topic?

USING THE LIBRARY TO GATHER INFORMATION

In the essay writing process, you typically gather information after you have written a thesis statement. When you plan a research paper, however, you need to gather preliminary information before you create a thesis statement. Investigating your topic at the library will let you know whether enough information is available for a research paper. Your investigation might also steer you toward an aspect of the topic that you would never have considered otherwise.

The library is traditionally the place to find books on all subjects. Books are only one resource in a modern library, however. The library also contains **periodicals** (journals, magazines, and newspapers) and microfilm and microfiche collections. Until you become familiar with the location of all the resources in your campus library, ask the reference librarian to explain them to you. You can usually find the reference librarian at a desk near the reference section or the library catalog section.

The following sections discuss resources commonly found in college libraries.

PRINTED CATALOGS

Many libraries have a **card catalog** that contains information on 3-inch-by-5-inch cards, with three cards for each book: author, title, and subject. On the author card, the author's name appears first, and the card is filed alphabetically by the last name of the author. On the title card, the title of the book appears first, and the card is filed alphabetically by the first word of the title. On the subject card, the subject or topic of the book appears first, and the card is filed alphabetically by the first word of the topic. The illustration on page A 29 shows sample author, title, and subject cards.

In some libraries this information is found in multivolume sets. One set of volumes includes information arranged alphabetically by the last names of the authors; a second set includes information arranged alphabetically by the titles of the books; a third set contains information arranged alphabetically by subject.

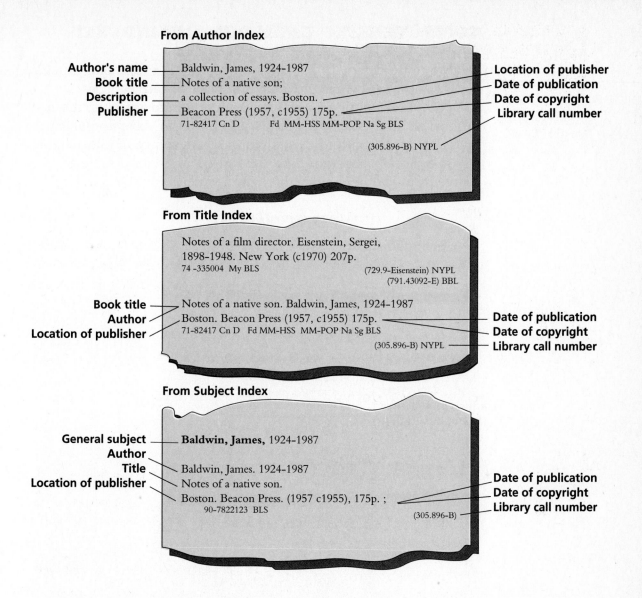

From Author Index

Author's name — Baldwin, James, 1924–1987
Book title — Notes of a native son;
Description — a collection of essays. Boston. — Location of publisher
Publisher — Beacon Press (1957, c1955) 175p. — Date of publication
71-82417 Cn D   Fd MM-HSS MM-POP Na Sg BLS — Date of copyright — Library call number

(305.896-B) NYPL

From Title Index

Notes of a film director. Eisenstein, Sergei,
1898-1948. New York (c1970) 207p.
74 -335004 My BLS   (729.9-Eisenstein) NYPL
                                      (791.43092-E) BBL

Book title — Notes of a native son. Baldwin, James, 1924–1987
Author — Boston. Beacon Press (1957, c1955) 175p. — Date of publication
Location of publisher — 71-82417 Cn D   Fd MM-HSS MM-POP Na Sg BLS — Date of copyright
                                      (305.896-B) NYPL — Library call number

From Subject Index

General subject — **Baldwin, James,** 1924–1987
Author —
Title — Baldwin, James. 1924–1987
Location of publisher — Notes of a native son.
Boston. Beacon Press. (1957 c1955), 175p. ; — Date of publication
90-7822123 BLS — Date of copyright
(305.896-B) — Library call number

For your preliminary research, you will find the subject listings most useful. Think of key words that might express your topic. For example, if you are considering writing about how television affects teenagers' behavior, you might look up these topics: *television, teenagers,* and *adolescence.* Whenever you look up a subject, see whether the listing provides any cross-references. A **cross-reference** is a notation that refers to related information listed elsewhere. A listing for "teenagers" might say "See also *adolescence.*"

COMPUTERIZED CATALOGS AND INDEXES

To keep up to date with advances in information technology, many libraries now use computer catalogs in place of card catalogs.

A **computer catalog** lists recent sources of information published in journals and other periodicals as well as in recently published books. Suppose you find a listing for a recent source of information, but your library does not have the source. You can usually get the source from another library through the interlibrary loan service.

From Computerized Catalog

Title Search —— Search: T= Notes of a Native Son
Heading + Notes of a Native Son
Matched Items = 4

NYPL (Call No. :305.896-B)
HSS A Bl Br Cl Cs D F Fw Hg Hl Ht Hu
In J Lm Ss Ts W Y ** Ba Be Ct Ea Ew Fd Fr
Fx X Mh Mr Pk Sv Tm Wk ** Nb Pr St *A

Author —— Baldwin, James, 1924-1987
Title —— Notes of a Native Son/ By James Baldwin.
Location of publisher —— Boston, Beacon Press, 1957, c1955 175p.
Date of publication —— 1. United States-Race relations.
2. Afro-Americans-Civil Rights.
3. Afro-Americans-Social Conditions to 1964.
4. Baldwin, James.

Author search —— Search: A= Baldwin, James
Heading = Baldwin, James, 1924-1987
Matched Items = 22

NYPL (Call No. :305.896-B)
HSS B Cs Hf In Kp S Sc Ts ** Cp Fx Pm
Rd Tg Tm Wf Wk Wo ** Gk Nd Pr Sg **

Baldwin, James
Notes of a Native Son.
Boston, Beacon Press (1957, c1955)
175p. Essays.Published also by Dial Press,
1963 and by Bantam Books, 1964.
Copyright renewed 1983
1. Afro-Americans.
2. United States-Race relations

Subject search —— Search: S= African-American Essayists
Heading = African-American Essayists
Matched Items = 63

A major advantage of the computer catalog is that it can make the same information available at many workstations—even in different buildings—simultaneously. An electronic system is also fast, easy to use, and easy to update.

In addition to computer catalogs, libraries also have computer indexes or data bases. These resources provide you with current articles on a variety of subjects. The indexes are specialized, such as *Psychlit* (Psychology) and *ERIC* (Education), and are constantly being updated. Use them if your library subscribes to them. If computer indexes are not available, use the bound-book form of the index.

With the computer index, you key your topic and the computer searches for the information. If you use an index in book form, you simply select your topic alphabetically. You may need help from the reference librarian if you can't find anything using your wording of the topic. For example, if you were researching the heroism of ordinary people during crises in modern society, this topic might be listed under the headings *Heroism* or *Altruistic Behavior*. The following illustration shows a sample from an electronic catalog system. Such systems are user-friendly. They provide clear, simple directions for finding the information you want.

```
077 BOBST LIBRARY GEAC LIBRARY SYSTEM- ALL*CHOOSE SEARCH
What type of search do you wish to do?
    1.  TIL - Title, journal title, series title, etc.
    2.  AtT - Author, illustrator, editor, organization, etc.
    3.  A-T - Combination of authors and title.
    4.  SUB - Subject heading assigned by library.
    5.  NUM - Call number, ISBN, ISSN, etc.
    6.  BOL - Boolean search on title, author and subject.
    7.  LIM - Limit your search to a portion of the catalog.
  Enter number or code:          Then press SEND


077 BOBST LIBRARY GEAC LIBRARY SYSTEM- ALL*CHOOSE SEARCH
    Start at the beginning of the subject and enter as
    many words on the subject as you know below.
    When you can, be specific.
        Ex:  Molecular biology    (Not biology)
```

THE SHELF LOCATION OF A BOOK

Books in the library are usually in shelves called stacks. A library's books are arranged in either open stacks—shelves to which you will have access—or closed stacks—shelves to which only the librarians have access. If you need a book that is located in closed stacks, you must usually fill out a slip requesting the librarian to get the book for you. If you need a book that is located in open stacks, you will be able to find the book for yourself.

A card catalog or computer catalog will tell you where to find a book in the library. The location of the book is indicated by a call number. The **call number** gives the general category or subject area of a book plus an identification number for the specific book. Libraries use one of two classification systems, the Dewey decimal system or the Library of Congress system. The Dewey decimal system classifies books according to a number system, while the Library of Congress system classifies books according to a system of letters and numbers.

Each system includes numerous subdivisions for each class of information. Under the Dewey decimal system, for example, if you looked up the category of History (900-999), you would find subdivisions such as American History (973). American History is further divided into such subcategories as the American Revolution (973.3) and the American Civil War (973.7).

Activity A: Using Your Library's Catalog System

PORTFOLIO

Use the catalog system in your college library to find three books on a topic that interests you. If you can't find at least three books on your research topic, revise the topic or select a new one. List the information the catalog gives you about each book, including the author, title, place of publication, copyright date, and a brief description of the book. If you are using a computer catalog, print out the information about each book. Use separate sheets of paper for your work, and save your work in your portfolio. You will continue to work on your topic in Activity B on page A 33.

PERIODICALS

Journals, magazines, and newspapers are published at regular time intervals—daily, weekly, monthly, or quarterly. That's why they're called **periodicals**. All periodicals are usually located in the same section of the library. The most recent issues are usually located on shelves, organized alphabetically by title. Past issues are bound into book format or are put on microfiche or microfilm. A special device is used to read periodicals on microfiche or microfilm.

Periodicals are indexed and cataloged separately from books. The main catalog for periodicals is *The Reader's Guide to Periodical Literature*. This is a general index of a variety of magazine and journal articles on a wide range of topics. Under specific topics in the *Reader's Guide*, you'll find the titles of articles about particular topics, along with the names and dates of periodicals where these articles appear.

The *Reader's Guide* is fairly easy to use. When you find an article you need, note the title of the article, the title of the periodical, the date published, and the page numbers of the article.

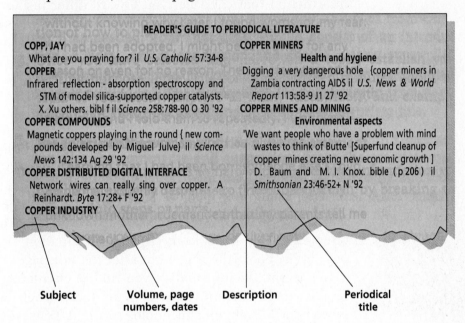

READER'S GUIDE TO PERIODICAL LITERATURE

COPP, JAY
What are you praying for? il *U.S. Catholic* 57:34-8
COPPER
Infrared reflection - absorption spectroscopy and STM of model silica-supported copper catalysts. X. Xu others. bibl f il *Science* 258:788-90 O 30 '92
COPPER COMPOUNDS
Magnetic coppers playing in the round { new compounds developed by Miguel Julve} il *Science News* 142:134 Ag 29 '92
COPPER DISTRIBUTED DIGITAL INTERFACE
Network wires can really sing over copper. A Reinhardt. *Byte* 17:28+ F '92
COPPER INDUSTRY

COPPER MINERS
  Health and hygiene
Digging a very dangerous hole {copper miners in Zambia contracting AIDS il *U.S. News & World Report* 113:58-9 Jl 27 '92
COPPER MINES AND MINING
  Environmental aspects
'We want people who have a problem with mind wastes to think of Butte' [Superfund cleanup of copper mines creating new economic growth] D. Baum and M. I. Knox. bible (p 206) il *Smithsonian* 23:46-52+ N '92

Subject   Volume, page numbers, dates   Description   Periodical title

Activity B: Using the *Reader's Guide*

PORTFOLIO

In the *Reader's Guide*, find citations for at least three articles related to the research topic you worked on in Activity A on page A 32. If you can't locate at least three articles, revise your topic or select a new one. List the information the *Reader's Guide* provides about each article, including the author and title of the article, name of the periodical, volume, page number, publication date, and a brief description of the article. Use separate sheets of paper for your work, and save your work in your portfolio. You will continue to work on the topic for your research paper in Activity C on page A 49.

REFERENCE BOOKS

Most libraries have a large collection of books that readers can use only in the library. These are called **reference books.** These reference materials are expensive or popular and, for these reasons, are not available for circulation outside of the library.

Libraries contain both general and specialized references. General references include multivolume encyclopedias and one-volume dictionaries that are organized alphabetically by subject or title. Encyclopedia articles often have cross-indexing and bibliographic information that can steer you toward other resources when you're researching a topic. Specialized references include **subject encyclopedias** or **dictionaries** for various fields of study, including music, education, philosophy, and sociology.

CIRCULATING BOOKS

Circulating books are books that you can check out of the library. You can find them by using the computer catalog or card catalog. From the catalog, write down the information you'll need to find the book: the call number, author, and title. Also write the publishing and copyright information to cite the book later as a source in your research paper. Double-check this information on the copyright page of the book (the page right after the title page).

In general, the information you find in circulating books may not be absolutely current, especially for topics such as "the women's movement," "computer technology," or "AIDS research," for which new information develops all the time. For a topic such as "the history of the civil rights movement during the 1960s," however, timeliness is less of an issue.

MISCELLANEOUS RESOURCES

Many libraries have videotapes of documentaries, art performances, and classic films. Some libraries have various kinds of information available on CD-ROM (Read-Only Memory). The music sections of some libraries have audio tapes, records, and CDs of musical performances, plays, and poetry. These items may be important parts of your research. For a complete list of resources available through your library, ask your librarian.

NARROWING THE TOPIC

Your preliminary research will give you enough information so that you can narrow your topic. Although a research paper is somewhat longer than an essay, you still need to make your topic specific enough to be covered thoroughly in your paper. For example, if you originally selected the topic of recycling, you might narrow the topic and deal with businesses that currently use recycled materials to manufacture new products such as road surfacing material and packaging.

ESTABLISHING THE WRITING PURPOSE

Most often your writing purpose for a research paper will be to explain a central point about your topic or to present a persuasive argument or opinion about your topic. For example, if a writer simply presented information about the effectiveness of various treatments for drug addiction, the writing purpose would be to inform. If the writer decided, based on the research, to argue for or against certain treatments, the writing purpose would be to persuade.

WRITING A THESIS STATEMENT

Like an essay, a research paper should convey a central point or dominant impression to the reader. The central point of a research paper should be expressed in a thesis statement that does one or more of the following:

- Introduces the research topic.
- Presents a central point about the topic.
- Lists at least two specific ideas or points the paper will cover.

Sometimes after you have begun researching a topic, your instructor may ask you to write a brief research proposal. A **research proposal** describes what you hope to explore in your paper, based on your findings in your preliminary library research. Writing a research proposal helps you focus your topic and pinpoint the aims of your research. As you continue to look for source material in the library, use your thesis statement and research proposal to guide you in your search.

Here is a thesis statement and research proposal that one writer prepared as a guide to finding source material:

Thesis Statement: The difference between a hero and an inactive bystander depends partly on the situation, but the decision to act is most often triggered by factors within the person's nature.

Research Proposal: In this research paper I will investigate the heroic behavior of individuals during some recent disasters. I will explore personality traits that such heroes seem to have in common. My paper will draw on original news accounts from newspapers and magazines, interviews with rescuers, and studies of the nature of heroism.

DOING RESEARCH AND TAKING NOTES

Once you decide on your specific topic and writing purpose and create your thesis statement, you can begin your detailed research. To develop content for a research paper, you will have to gather information about your topic from a variety of materials such as books, articles, government reports, scientific studies, recordings, and videotapes. The amount and type of sources you need will vary depending on your topic and thesis statement. For some topics, you may need anywhere from six to fifteen sources. Consult pages A 28-

A 35 for guidelines on using a library to locate research sources.

You may use both primary and secondary sources for your research. **Primary sources** are original works by a writer, such as novels, poems, stories, diaries, letters, autobiographies, and scientific studies. **Secondary sources** are works about an original source or person, such as critical evaluations, reviews, biographies, encyclopedias, and textbooks.

As you research your topic, focus on current journals that give the most recent information. This is because college instructors usually give more importance to citations from the most current sources than to those from sources with earlier publication dates. If you are researching an aspect of the war in Bosnia, for instance, you would not want to limit yourself to information from a book that was published in 1993—too many events have occurred since then. You would want to locate the most recent books and articles on the topic.

As you read books and periodicals with information on your topic, you need to evaluate each source. This means taking notes on important passages, statistical data, quotations, and bibliographic material. If the book is a reference book or a periodical that you can't check out of the library, you'll need to take notes at the library. If the book is a circulating book, you can check out the book and take notes wherever you please.

Most writers prefer to write notes on index cards. When you take notes on a source, follow these general guidelines:

- Prepare a separate card for each source. Write on one side only.
- Identify the author and title of the source at the top of the card.
- Record quotations, statistics, and bibliographic information carefully. Check your notes against the original source to be sure they're accurate.

The notes you take for a research paper will fall into the following categories:

- Bibliographic notes
- Direct quotations
- Paraphrases
- Summaries

Let's take a look at each of these categories.

BIBLIOGRAPHIC NOTES

For each source you intend to use in your research paper, prepare a bibliographic note that lists the author, title, city of publication, publisher, copyright date, and call number. To prepare a bibliographic note for an article, note the author, title, journal, volume number, publication date, and page numbers. The information on your bibliographic notes will help you cite sources within and at the end of your paper. The following example shows a bibliographic note for a book and an article:

> Cullinan, Bernice E.
>   Literature and the Child New York: Harcourt Brace
> Jovanovich, 1989.
>
> Simic, Charles
>   "Fried Sausage." Ohio Review. 1993: 143-145.

DIRECT QUOTATIONS

As you research your topic, record notes of phrases, sentences, and passages that would make effective quotations in your paper. Write the name of the source, followed by the exact wording of the quotation, including the original punctuation. Use **ellipsis marks,** three spaced periods, to indicate any omitted words or sentences. If the words you delete come in the middle of a sentence, use three spaced periods; if the omission comes at the end of a sentence, add a fourth spaced period (the fourth period indicates the end of the sentence). Put the page number of the original source after the quotation. The following example shows a direct quotation recorded on a note card.

Faulkner, William. Light in August
"Memory believes before knowing remembers. Believes longer than recollects, longer than knowing even wonders. Knows remembers . . . a corridor . . . (111)."

PARAPHRASES

When you restate another writer's words in your own words, you are **paraphrasing**. You must use your own words and sentence structure while maintaining the content and intent of the original source. As with direct quotations, you need to acknowledge the author and page number of any material you paraphrase. If you use any phrases from the original source in your paraphrase, enclose this material in quotes. Here is an example of an original passage and a paraphrased note.

Original:
Contrary to the popular notion that Americans are pill poppers, seeking relief at the first twinge of discomfort or depression, research strongly suggests that they are actually *under*-medicated for severe pain. —Melinda Henneberger (*New York Times*, Apr. 3, 1994, E5)

Paraphrase:

Henneberger, Melinda. "It Pains a Nation of Stoics to Say 'No' to Pain." (New York Times, Apr. 3, 1994)

Do Americans really take pain medication too frequently and without sufficient cause? Melinda Henneberger says that research reveals the opposite: Many Americans in extreme pain don't receive adequate pain relief (E5).

SUMMARIES

Sometimes you may need to summarize information you read. Summary notes give you an overview of important points in sources that you may not want to discuss in depth. (Refer to Enrichment Chapter B for information on writing summaries.) If you write a summary about an entire work, simply record the name of the author and the title of the source at the top of the note card. If you write a summary of a particular section or page, record the page number(s) as well. Here is an example of a short summary note.

Kenyatta, Jomo. Facing Mt. Kenya
This book, by the man who later became the first president of Kenya, describes the lifeways of the Gikuyu (Kikuyu) people. Kenyatta discusses the organization of Gikuyu society and describes typical forms of work. Kenyatta also describes Gikuyu traditions and compares traditional Gikuyu society with European society.

DEVELOPING THE CONTENT AND PLANNING THE STRUCTURE

The information you have gathered from your research will form the basis for the content of your research paper. As you decide what main ideas you will present in your paper, sort through your research material for facts, details, examples, and other information that can be cited to support each main idea. Weed out note cards that do not fit into the framework of your paper. Put these cards away in case you need to use them later.

Make sure you have all the supporting information that you need. If you find that you need additional facts, details, or examples to support any of your main ideas, do additional research to locate this material.

Once you have arranged a balanced, comprehensive amount of research material that supports the ideas you will present in your paper, decide how to structure the material effectively. Presenting ideas in order of importance or interest is the most common structure for research papers. Consider what method of organization or combination of methods would best suit your topic and content. For example, if you were writing a research paper that examined Eleanor Roosevelt's work with the United Nations, you might choose to structure your content in chronological order.

Like an essay, a research paper should begin with your thesis statement and an engaging introduction, and end with a sense of closure. Use the same techniques you use in essays to introduce your topic: begin with a quotation, a question, an anecdote, or an interesting fact. Because a research paper covers more ground than an essay, you may need more than one paragraph to introduce your research topic. Likewise, you may need several paragraphs at the end of your paper both to review the points you've made and to make a final point, recommendation, or judgment.

Once you have decided how to structure your paper, put your notes in that sequence. Based on your notes, prepare a formal outline of your research paper. On page A 52 you will find one writer's formal outline for a research paper. Use this example to guide you as you prepare your outline.

Targeting an Audience and Setting the Tone

Many of the research papers you write will be for instructors or professionals who specialize in a particular subject area. Consider what your audience knows about your topic when you cite particular quotations, facts, statistics, and examples in your paper.

When planning and writing a research paper, look for information that casts a new light on your topic or presents known aspects of your topic in a unique way. If your topic is a current issue, include the most up-to-date information in your paper. Distinguish carefully between facts and statistics that are common knowledge and facts and statistics that are specialized information. If you mention a date such as New Year's Day, no citation is required because this information is common knowledge. However, if you were presenting U.S. unemployment statistics for 1994, you would have to cite the source of your figures.

As you plan and write, remember that your tone—the wording you use to paraphrase and connect research data—will help to unify the content and purpose of your paper. Even though you are paraphrasing, summarizing, and quoting other writers in your paper, your own voice or wording should come across to the reader. Usually, research papers adopt a somewhat formal or objective tone. Depending on your topic and writing purpose, you may use pronouns such as *we*, *they*, or *one*, rather than *I* and *my*, in order to convey a more neutral, impersonal tone.

Writing the Research Paper and Using Appropriate Citations

Because your research paper relies heavily on other writers' work, you must acknowledge every source you use. You must provide an in-text **citation** (the author and page number) for each quotation, paraphrase, and bit of special statistical data included in the paper. You must also provide a "Works Cited" list at the end of the paper that lists information about the sources you used.

There are many ways to style in-text and end-of-paper citations.

Two style manuals commonly used in college courses are *The MLA Handbook for Writers of Research Papers* and the *Publication Manual of the American Psychological Association*. *The MLA Handbook* is most often used for research papers in the humanities (English, philosophy, art history, comparative literature), while the *APA Manual* is commonly used for research papers in the social sciences (psychology, anthropology). The *MLA* style is one of the simplest ways to format citations. Information on styling citations in this chapter is based on *The MLA Handbook*. Consult your instructor before you prepare citations to see if a particular style manual is required.

STYLING IN-TEXT CITATIONS

In-text citations should include the author and page number of the original quotation, paraphrase, or statistic. When using an in-text citation, give the author's name either in the sentence or in parentheses at the end of the sentence. Here are two examples of in-text citations formatted according to the *MLA* style:

"In a national public opinion poll sponsored by Mayday, 92 percent of 1,000 Americans polled at random said they felt pain is an inevitable part of life" (Henneberger E5).

Melinda Henneberger says "patients shun strong medicine because they fear addiction, although studies have concluded that very few of them—less than 1 percent in hospital settings—become psychologically addicted to pain medication" (E5).

On pages A 51-A 66 you'll see a research paper with citations that follow the style of *The MLA Handbook*.

Tips for Styling In-Text Citations ≈≈≈≈

Follow these general guidelines for styling in-text citations within the body of your paper:

- If you include the author's name in the sentence, use the full name. In the citation, put the author's last name in parentheses followed by the page number. Do *not* put a comma between the author's name and the page number.
- Place the parenthetical citation after the quote, paraphrase, or statistic but before the period that ends the sentence.

- If you are using two or more sources by the same author, include an abbreviated title in the in-text citations. Place the abbreviated title after the author's name and before the page number. For instance, if your paper contained quotes from two books by Galway Kinnell, you could distinguish between the two books as follows: (Kinnell, *Book of Nightmares*, 10) and (Kinnell, *When One Has Lived*, 15).

- If you alter direct quotations by deleting words or by adding words of your own, clearly indicate this by correct use of ellipsis marks and brackets. Use three spaced periods (an ellipsis) for deletions within a sentence and four spaced periods for deletions at the end of a sentence. If you add an explanatory phrase within a direct quotation, enclose your words in brackets (see the example in the research paper on page A 59).

- For direct quotations that are four or more lines long, begin the quotation on a new line. Indent the quotation ten spaces from the left margin, and double-space the quotation. Omit quotation marks for indented material. An example occurs on page A 59 in the research paper.

Styling the "Works Cited" List

At the end of a research paper you must provide a list of works you cited in your paper. Preparing a "Works Cited" list is easy if you keep bibliographic notes on sources as you plan and write your paper. If you have prepared bibliographic notes carefully, simply put the notes in alphabetical order. Then prepare your "Works Cited" list according to an acceptable style manual.

The following examples show you how to reference various kinds of sources in your "Works Cited" list. Each example has been styled according to *The MLA Handbook*.

Book by one author

Richardson, Joan. <u>Wallace Stevens: The Later Years, 1923-1955</u>. New York: William Morrow, 1988.

Always include the full title of a book, including any subtitle. Place a colon between the title and subtitle.

Two or more books by one author

Bellow, Saul. <u>Dangling Man</u>. New York: Vanguard, 1944.
—. <u>Seize the Day</u>. New York: Viking, 1956.

A book by two or more authors

Davidson, James West, and Mark Hamilton Lytle. <u>After the Fact: The Art of Historical Detection</u>. New York: Alfred A. Knopf, 1982.

The first author's name should be reversed, but the other authors' names should be listed in regular order (with the first name first and the last name last).

An edited book

Pack, Robert, Sydney Lea, and Jay Parini, eds. <u>The Breadloaf Anthology of Contemporary Poetry</u>. New Hampshire: UP New England, 1985.

Note that abbreviations can be used for publishers' names (*U* for *University* and *P* for *Press*).

A revised or later edition

Holt, Hamilton. <u>The Life Stories of Undistinguished Americans As Told by Themselves</u>. 2nd ed., New York: Routledge, 1990.

For a revised or later edition, use these abbreviations: *2nd ed., 3rd ed., 4th ed.,* or *Rev. ed.*

A chapter in a book

Kunitz, Stanley. "I'm Not Sleepy." <u>Interviews and Encounters With Stanley Kunitz</u>. New York: Sheep Meadow P, 1993. 185-192.

A magazine article

Bishop, Elizabeth. "The Art of Losing." The New Yorker Mar. 28, 1994: 82-89.

Include the day, month, and year of the article. Except for May, June, and July, abbreviate the month. For articles in scholarly journals, you should also include the number of the volume or issue: for example, *Journal of Social Issues* 37 (1981): 7-12.

A newspaper article

Sudetic, Chuck. "Bosnian Serbs Are Accused of More 'Ethnic Cleansing.'" The New York Times Apr. 2, 1994, late ed., p. 6.

If the article is in a special edition or section of the paper, include the edition after the date and the section before the page number (for example, *late ed., sec. A:10*).

An editorial or letter to the editor

"Mideast Peace, Back on Track." Editorial. The New York Times Apr. 1, 1994, sec. A:26.
Schumack, Ray. "Public Relations Lures Largely for Glamour." Letter. The New York Times Apr. 6, 1994, late ed., p. 18.

An encyclopedia article

Galloway, I. H. "Brazil." World Book Encyclopedia. 1989 ed.

For articles in well-known encyclopedias or dictionaries, don't cite the editor of the reference book. Include the author of the article, if there is one.

A pamphlet

Thompson, Dorothy Burr. An Ancient Shopping Center: The Athenian Agora. Princeton: American School of Classical Studies, 1971.

Provide the same information for a pamphlet as you would for a book.

A movie or videotape

> House of the Spirits. Dir. Bille August. With Meryl Streep, Jeremy Irons, Glenn
> Close, Winona Ryder, Antonio Banderas. Miramax, 1994.

Include the title, director, distributor, and year. If appropriate, provide additional information such as the actors or the size and length of the film. For example, cite the size and length after the year: 1993. 16 mm, 55 min.

A TV or radio program

> "Paul Simon: Born at the Right Time," American Masters. PBS. WNET, New
> York. Apr. 2, 1994.

For TV and radio programs, include the network (for instance, PBS), the local station that broadcast the program (such as WNET), the city, and the broadcast date.

A Recording

> Holiday, Billie. "Pennies from Heaven." The Legacy. Columbia, CD, AAD 47725,
> 1991.

Begin the citation with the name of the performer or composer. Give the title of the song or piece of music, followed by the album title and manufacturer. If the recording is on an audio tape or a compact disk, indicate this before citing the catalog number and year the recording was issued.

An interview

> Brooks, Gwendolyn. Interview. By Nicole Blackman. New York Quarterly.
> 1993, 19-23.
> Cuomo, Mario. Personal Interview. Apr. 24, 1994.

Begin the entry with the name of the person who was interviewed. For published or recorded interviews, give the title (if there is one) or indicate "Interview." Also provide publication or broadcast information. If you conducted the interview yourself, list the name of the person interviewed, and include the phrase "Personal Interview" or "Telephone Interview," followed by the date.

Tips for Styling a Works Cited List ≈≈≈

Follow these general guidelines for styling a "Works Cited" list:

- Include only those sources you actually cited in your paper.
- Alphabetize your sources by the author's last name.
- If the source doesn't have an author, alphabetize by the first important word of the title (omit words such as *The*, *A*, and *An*).
- If you used more than one work by the same author, key the author's name for the first citation only. For subsequent entries, key three hyphens followed by a period (---.) in place of the author's name.
- Double-space your citations. After the first line, indent five spaces for the rest of each entry. Underline titles of books, magazines, newspapers, films, and so forth, but do not underscore end punctuation.

PREPARING THE TITLE PAGE

At the beginning of your research paper, provide a title page that includes the following:

- Your name
- The course name and number
- Your instructor's name
- The date
- The title of your paper

The heading and title of your paper can be keyed either on a cover sheet (see the example on page A 51) or at the top of the first page. If you key the heading information at the top of the first page, follow this format:

Saskia Paschen
English 230
Professor Klass
10 May 1994

       The Green Man and Sir Gawain

Activity C: Planning a Research Paper

In this activity you will continue to plan the research paper you began to work on in Activities A and B on pages A 32 and A 33. Refer to the Writing Focus Chart on page 132 for help in addressing the elements of purpose, content, structure, audience, and tone. Use separate sheets of paper for your work.

A. Use the topic you selected and began to research in Activities A and B on pages A 32 and A 33. Establish the purpose of your research paper.

B. Write a thesis statement and a brief research proposal for a paper on your topic. In your proposal, include the kinds of sources you hope to use and describe at least three aspects of your topic you plan to investigate in your paper.

C. At the library, read and take notes on several books and articles you found on your topic. Based on your reading, prepare at least four note cards: a bibliographic note, a direct quotation, a paraphrase, and a summary.

D. When you have accumulated research information on your topic, use the same strategies you use to develop essays to develop your content.

E. Target an audience for your research paper. After considering your intended audience, decide what tone is most appropriate for your topic and writing purpose.

Save your work in your portfolio. You will use your work to create a research paper in the following assignment. Before you complete the following assignment, read the research paper beginning on page A 51.

Assignment:
Creating a Research Paper

In this assignment you will work to plan, write, edit, and proofread the research paper you began developing in Activity C on this page.

A. Review the planning you did in Activity C, including your thesis statement, research proposal, and research notes.

B. Use your prewriting and the questions on the Writing Focus Chart on page 132 to guide you as you plan the first draft of your research paper. Prepare a formal outline of your topic, similar to the one on page A 52.

C. Write the first draft of your research paper. Your first draft should have a heading and title, in-text citations, and a "Works Cited" list. The citations should be styled according to *The MLA Handbook* as explained on pages A 42-A 48.

D. Evaluate the content, structure, and wording of your draft. Using the Checklist for Revising and Editing on page 153 as a guide, make any necessary changes, additions, deletions, and corrections. If necessary, modify your outline or do additional research. Make as many revisions as needed. When you are satisfied, key your revised draft.

E. Carefully reread your revised draft. Using the Checklist for Proofreading on page 105, prepare the final copy. Consult the Writer's Guide that begins on page A 80 to review key points of grammar, punctuation, and capitalization. Proofread all in-text citations against the "Works Cited" list. Make sure the spellings of authors' names and titles are consistent throughout, and that you have a full bibliographic entry in the "Works Cited" list for every source you have cited in the body of your paper. Use proofreaders' marks from the box on page 105 to mark your corrections.

PORTFOLIO

F. Key the final copy. Look over the final copy and correct any keyboarding errors. Save your final copy in your portfolio.

RISING TO THE OCCASION:
HEROISM AND ALTRUISM

by
Laurel M. Dodge

Psychology 110
Dr. Joel Morgan

March 3, 1995

Outline

Thesis Statement: The difference between a hero and an inactive bystander depends partly on the situation, but the decision to act is most often triggered by factors within the person's nature.

I. Occurrence of heroism in recent events
   A. Heroic behavior of people who put themselves at risk to help others
   B. Definition of altruism
   C. Altruistic behavior displayed by rescuers during two recent events
      1. Los Angeles earthquake of 1994
      2. Los Angeles riots of 1992

II. Acts of heroism
   A. Los Angeles earthquake, January 17, 1994
      1. Background information about earthquake
      2. Specific incidents of heroism
         a. Rescues at Northridge Meadows apartment complex
         b. Rescues at trailer park in Fillmore
      3. Statements by rescuers
   B. Los Angeles riots, April 29, 1992
      1. Background information about causes of riots
      2. Specific incidents of heroism
         a. Rescue of truck driver Reginald Denny
         b. Rescue of motorist Takao Hirata
      3. Statements by rescuers

III. Speculations on the nature of heroism
   A. Personality traits of heroes
   B. Examples of altruism during the Los Angeles earthquake and riots
      1. Rescuers have strong sense of self
      2. Have empathy for those in danger
      3. Have sense of duty
         a. Duty to fulfill personal standards
         b. Duty to a moral, ethical, or religious code
         c. Duty to the community
      4. Act in spite of fear

IV. Conclusion
   A. Heroes exhibit altruistic behavior
   B. Generosity of spirit or altruism can be fostered in individuals

Number each page in the upper right-hand corner. Your last name should also appear.

Allow a margin of about one inch all around your text. Double-space the text.

People in modern society are often considered to be alienated from others and wrapped up in their own lives. How, then, can we explain the many instances of ordinary people who spontaneously reach out to help others, often at great risk, in times of crisis? The difference between an inactive bystander and a hero often depends on factors like opportunity, physical strength, and skill. However, the decision to act is most often triggered by factors within the person: an individual code of behavior; a sense of moral, ethical, or religious obligation; or a sense of duty to the community.

Altruism is the term used to define helping behavior that has little or no evident benefit for the helper. Such behavior includes actions ranging from a small helpful gesture (giving up one's seat on a bus) to rescues that risk the life of the rescuer.

Events such as the Los Angeles earthquake in January 1994 and the Los Angeles riots in April 1992 led to many incidents of heroic behavior. Again and again, people risked injury or death to come to the aid of neighbors and even strangers. These people were not trained rescue workers paid to respond in emergency situations. They were ordinary people who were bystanders at a disaster or emergency.

On January 17, 1994, at 4:31 A.M. Pacific Standard Time, an earthquake registering 6.6 on the Richter scale struck near Los Angeles (Mintz 3). The epicenter of the quake was in the suburban town of Northridge, in the densely populated San Fernando Valley just northwest of Greater Los Angeles (Roberts 26). The quake damaged or destroyed buildings, collapsed bridges, buckled roads in the vast Los Angeles freeway system, damaged electrical generators, and ruptured gas lines and water mains (Ramirez A20, Browne A18, Fritsch A18). Rescue workers reacted quickly, but for people trapped in collapsed or burning buildings, instant aid was necessary. In many such cases, this aid came from ordinary citizens whose only advantage as rescuers was the fact that they were already on the scene.

One scene of such aid was Northridge Meadows, a three-story apartment complex. Located virtually on the epicenter of the quake, the complex was so badly damaged that three stories were compressed into

---

Use parentheses to set off in-text citations.

two (Johnson A19). Most of the residents who could get out pulled themselves from the rubble and made for the relative safety of the open. Some, however, stayed and began the search for their neighbors, despite the risk of another quake that could make the building collapse even further (Gleik 35, Howlett 3A).

Resident Joseph Tyler helped rescue his next-door neighbor by kicking in her door and helping her crawl out of the wreckage. Robert Horton found a ladder and with the aid of three other men helped dozens of people climb to safety (Gleick 35). Erik Pearson climbed to safety but returned to help evacuate neighbors (LaGanga A17). Mike Kubeisey entered the apartments of several elderly residents who were too scared to leave their homes. He escorted them out through the only remaining exit from their apartments—the windows (Kolbert A19).

Others performed similar deeds elsewhere in the area. In a mobile home park in Fillmore, Charles Radcliffe ran among the trailers to evacuate elderly neighbors. He managed to rescue one woman just before her mobile home burned to the ground (LaGanga A17).

Many of these people tried afterwards to express their emotions or explain why they did what they did. Charles Radcliffe, who saved so many at the mobile home park, said, "I just wanted to make sure everyone got out OK. . . . It all happened so quick. I didn't really even think about it. It just seemed like the right thing to do" (LaGanga A17). Erik Pearson, a rescuer at Northridge Meadows, expressed regret that he couldn't do more. "I lost one person," he said. "There was a little old lady in the back. Two beams fell on her. I told her to hold on, I'd be right back with a ladder. By the time I got back, she'd passed away" (LaGanga A17). Others were frank about revealing their fear. Mike Kubeisey, who escorted elderly residents to safety at Northridge Meadows, said, "They were scared. I was scared. There was water and blood everywhere. I thank God I'm standing here" (Kolbert A19).

In a natural disaster, people within a community often discover closer ties, and this sense of belonging and shared crisis often brings out the best in people. Other disasters, such as crime or civil strife, are less likely to unite community members and encourage altruistic behavior.

Use ellipsis marks to indicate words that have been left out of a direct quotation.

One of the most extreme examples of such an event in recent years was the April 29, 1992, Los Angeles riots. These riots were brought on by the not-guilty verdict against four white police officers on trial for the beating of African-American motorist Rodney King. The worst rioting took place in South Central Los Angeles, the site of the original confrontation between the police officers and King. For more than 48 hours, rioters broke doors and windows, looted shops, and set fire to buildings (Ellis 26). The only witness to many of these attacks was a news helicopter that hovered overhead (Church 20). The helicopter's televised footage of the beating of truck driver Reginald Denny at the intersection of Florence and Normandie Avenues motivated several residents from the riot-torn community to become rescuers.

Denny's beating was telecast as it was happening. After seeing the event unfold on television, Lei Yuille and her brother Pierre drove to the scene. Bobby Green also saw the beating on TV and drove three miles to the intersection. At the intersection Green himself was attacked, but, as he said in a later interview, "The only thing on my mind was to get Reggie out of there." Green and Lei Yuille helped drive Denny to a hospital with the aid of Titus Murphy and Terri Barnett, who had also arrived at the intersection after seeing the beating on television. Except for Murphy and Barnett, who knew each other, none of the rescuers had ever met one another or Denny before (Treen 91-92).

Gregory Alan-Williams heard on a radio news program that rioters were beating motorists at Florence and Normandie. Alan-Williams drove over at once. He arrived to see Takao Hirata being attacked in his stalled car. Alan-Williams and another bystander, Jorge Gonzalez, rushed to aid Hirata. Gonzalez was knocked down and beaten by rioters, but Alan-Williams was able to drag Hirata out into the street until he found someone who would take him to the hospital (Treen 92-93, Alan-Williams 86-87).

Later, these rescuers were asked why they had left the safety of their homes or cars to face a hostile mob in order to rescue strangers. Speaking of Reginald Denny, Bobby Green said, "He was a truck driver, just like me. That could have been me laying down there. I would want or heroic response. When Bobby Green said, "He was a truck driver, just like me. . . . All truck drivers should stick together" (Treen 91-92), Green identified with his fellow truck driver and therefore could feel some of what Reginald Denny must have been feeling.

Charles Radcliffe, who saved so many at the mobile home park during the earthquake, said, "I knew a lot of them [the elderly residents of the park] would not be able to see without their glasses and I knew they would be shaken up" (LaGanga A17). Radcliffe's ability to empathize with his neighbors caused him to think of a detail that would not have crossed the minds of most bystanders. His awareness of the difficulty the elderly residents would have escaping was one of the main factors that motivated him to act.

Gregory Alan-Williams, one of Takao Hirata's rescuers, was able to envision a future where he might be in Hirata's place. Gregory Alan-Williams told interviewers, "I said to myself 'If I don't help this man, when the mob comes for me, there will be nobody there for me.' If I stood there and watched this man be murdered, then what sort of justice could

Use single quotation marks to show dialogue within a direct quotation.

I ask for myself" (Treen 93)? Being able to imagine oneself in someone else's situation is one way people can experience the feelings of others.

Most of the heroes profiled here referred to a sense of duty of one sort or another that inspired their actions. Phrases like "It had to be done," "Somebody had to do something," and "It was the right thing to do," used by various of the rescuers, all seem to show a personal sense of duty or responsibility even in the face of despair (Gibbs 37).

Some heroes see their duty as one to themselves, a means of measuring up to the expectations they have for themselves. Others see their duty as one to a religious, moral, or ethical code. Such a code defines some actions as right and just. Performing these actions are thus a believer's duty. Researcher Shalom Schwartz has shown that "people who have a sense of moral obligation to the victim are more likely to help than those who do not" (Shotland 52). Still other heroes may see their duty as one to the community. These people think of themselves as part of a larger whole and feel compelled to act in the interests of that larger whole.

In Gregory Alan-Williams's book he cites religion as one of the major influences on his life. He also mentions that the teachings of loved ones instilled in him a moral code, and that his encounters with enemies also taught him lessons about personal responsibility (Alan-Williams 12-13). Alan-Williams has a well-developed moral and ethical code under which he feels obligated to act to improve a challenging or difficult situation. Under this moral and religious code, it would have been wrong for Alan-Williams to do nothing. Charles Radcliffe, the earthquake rescuer at the Fillmore trailer park, also seemed to refer to a moral or a religious code when he said, "It all happened so quick. . . . It just seemed like the right thing to do" (LaGanga A17).

Lei Yuille, another of Denny's rescuers, has a strong guiding sense of justice. She has stated that she "saw a wrong being done against someone who was innocent" (Treen 91). Her comment that she saw an "innocent" person being wronged and her actions to correct that wrong reveal that she has a sense of responsibility both to her community (and its rules of justice) and to a higher code of justice.

Like many of the other earthquake rescuers, Erik Pearson reveals devotion to his community. Pearson's main reaction to his deeds was not satisfaction about having saved several people but remorse about the one woman he had not been able to save. This reaction seems to reveal that Pearson felt as if he had failed in his duty to his neighbors (community) even though he had made a heroic effort (LaGanga A17).

Heroes aren't fearless. Both Mike Kubeisey and Joseph Tyler, rescuers at the Northridge Meadows apartment complex, were open about expressing past and present fear relating to the quake. Kubeisey admitted that he was as scared as those he rescued (Kolbert A19). Tyler, while narrating his actions to a reporter, stopped midsentence in distress as another aftershock struck (Gleick 34-35).

What is important is that these heroes acted in spite of the fear. They also acted in spite of all they had to lose. Jorge Gonzalez, a third-year law student, had risked years of effort to help Gregory Alan-Williams attempt a rescue of Takao Hirata. Due to the beating he received in his heroic attempt to help, Gonzalez barely made it through

his law school finals (Alan-Williams 196-197). Another hero, Bobby
Green, had a wife and four children, yet he still acted to drive riot
victim Reginald Denny to safety. The altruistic behavior seen in the acts
of these people is clear: they helped strangers at considerable cost to
themselves.

There is some evidence that altruism can be fostered in people.
Social psychologist Jane Pilavin has suggested that teaching helping
behavior and emergency response in schools may increase the likelihood
of a helping response later in life (Shotland 54). A sense of self is
developed by a positive upbringing, support from family and the
community, and a lifestyle that gives people a sense of control over their
lives. Empathy is partly inborn but may be nurtured by parents and
fostered by experience, role-playing, and imagination. A sense of
responsibility can be developed by parents, teachers, community, and
religion. If attention is focused on these aspects of child-rearing and
individual development, we may find many more people prepared to be
heroes (Feldman 511-512).

Works Cited

Alan-Williams, Gregory. <u>A Gathering of Heroes: Reflections on Rage and Responsibility</u>. Chicago: Academy Chicago Publishers, 1994.

Browne, Malcolm W. "California Says Its Renovation Plan Limited Damage to Highway Bridges." <u>The New York Times</u> Jan. 18, 1994: A18.

Church, George J. "The Fire This Time." <u>Time</u> May 11, 1990: 18-25.

Ellis, David. "L.A. Lawless." <u>Time</u> May 11, 1992: 26-29.

Feldman, Robert S. <u>Understanding Psychology</u>. New York: McGraw-Hill, 1989.

Fritsch, Jane. "Quake Revealed Flaws in 'Safe' Structures' Design." <u>The New York Times</u> Jan. 20, 1994: A18.

Gibbs, Nancy. "Aftershock." <u>Time</u> Jan. 31, 1994: 26-37.

Gleick, Elizabeth. "Terror at Northridge Meadows." <u>People</u> Jan. 31, 1994: 32-35.

Howlett, Debbie. "Under Blue Skies, Dark Days Lie Ahead." <u>USA Today</u> Jan. 19, 1994: 3A.

Johnson, Dirk. "With 16th Body Found, Grim Vigil Is Complete." <u>The New York Times</u> Jan. 19, 1994: A19.

Kolbert, Elizabeth. "Airborne in Bed: A Building Collapses, Leaving 15 Dead." <u>The New York Times</u> Jan. 18, 1994: A1 and A19.

LaGanga, Maria L. "Acts of Valor from Simple to Supreme." <u>The Los Angeles Times</u> Jan. 18, 1994: A3 and A17.

Mintz, Phil. "A City Left Shaken." <u>New York Newsday</u> Jan. 18, 1994: 2-13, 18-19.

Ramirez, Anthony. "Gas and Electric Services Are Disrupted for Millions of Customers." <u>The New York Times</u> Jan. 18, 1994: A20.

Roberts, Steven V. "Breaking Point." <u>U.S. News & World Report</u> Jan. 31, 1994: 26-36.

Shotland, R. Lance. "When Bystanders Just Stand By." <u>Psychology Today</u> June 1985: 50-55.

Treen, Joe. "Heroes in the Hood." <u>People</u> May 18, 1994: 90-93.

GRAMMAR GREMLINS: ADDITIONAL ACTIVITIES

RECOGNIZING SENTENCE FRAGMENTS

For instruction, see the Grammar Gremlins in Chapter 1, page 32.

A. Each group of sentences contains at least one sentence fragment. Circle the sentence fragments.

1. Summerville Cafe was voted the best new restaurant for this year. Several unique entrées. Has excellent service.

2. The chef's specialty is a vegetarian dish. Artichoke and black olive pizza with a white sauce. Will fill you up in no time.

3. Accommodating hours. Summerville Cafe is open for lunch at 11 A.M. Remains open until 11 P.M.

4. The atmosphere is friendly and warm. A fireplace for cool nights. A diner can stretch out in the spacious booths.

5. The price range varies depending on what you order. Sandwiches can be ordered for lunch or dinner at a reasonable price. More expensive entrées such as lobster and steak. Desserts are expensive. But delicious!

B. Read the following paragraph. Circle the sentence fragments.

Seeing the Rocky Mountains for the first time is a breathtaking experience. Form a 5,000-mile range from Mexico to Alaska. The Rocky Mountains reach their greatest width, 300 miles, in Colorado and Utah. In Colorado alone, there are 54 peaks over 14,000 feet high. The tallest, Mt. Elbert. It reaches up to 14,419 feet. Pikes Peak, in central Colorado, perhaps the most famous peak in the Rockies. This mountain boasts a height of 14,110 feet. The Rockies are not all mountains. In between the majestic peaks you'll find large plateaus, flatlands covered with brush, and semi-arid deserts. There are many cities and towns nestled in areas all over the mountain range. Popular place for tourists.

ELIMINATING SENTENCE FRAGMENTS

For instruction, see the Grammar Gremlins in Chapter 2, page 78.

A. Each of the following groups of sentences contains at least one sentence fragment. Correct a fragment either by combining the fragment with another word group or by rewriting the fragment as a complete sentence.

1. My first day as a college student was certainly memorable. If not particularly enjoyable. I had arrived on campus three days before classes were to begin, so I had plenty of time to find my way around. Need lots of practice learning my way around a new place.

   My first day as a college student was not particularly enjoyable but certainly memorable. I had arrived on campus 3 days before class were to begin, so that I plenty of time to find my way around. Learning my way around a new place needed lots of practice.

2. During those three days, my roommate and I walked from our dorm room to the buildings where our classes were to be held. Did quite well, only getting lost once.

   We went quite well getting lost only once.

3. Then the day came when I had to make the trek to my first class alone. Started out feeling confident. As I walked down the street. I began to question which way I needed to go.

   I started out feeling confident but as I walk down the street I began to question which way I needed to go.

4. It wasn't long. I had no idea where I was. Embarrassed. Would I have to reveal my status as a mere freshman by asking how to get to Galloway Hall? I would, and I did.

   I got It wasn't long before I had no idea where I was. Embarrased as I had to reveal my status as a mere freshmen by asking how to get to Galloway hall.

5. Tried not to show how stupid I felt. Asked directions to Galloway Hall. The guy I spoke with smiled and then chuckled as he pointed to a building about five feet away. I felt like a fool.

   I tried not to show how stupid I felt. I asked directions to Galloway hall. The guy ---

B. Read the following paragraph. Eliminate any sentence fragments you find. Either combine a fragment with another word group to form a complete sentence, or rewrite a fragment as a complete sentence.

Does anybody like mosquitoes? They ~~are~~ such pests! ~~that~~ They always seem to bite *you* more than anyone else you're with. When mosquitoes are not biting you, ~~They~~ can be interesting to learn about. Mosquitoes have been around for at least 200 million years. You may think of mosquitoes living in forests and damp swampy regions, but they are even more common in the Arctic. Big eaters. ~~even~~ Will double or even triple their weight with one meal of blood. The female mosquito ~~takes~~ blood to make her eggs.

Run-on Sentences

For instruction, see the Grammar Gremlins in Chapter 3, page 110.

A. Correct the following run-on sentences by making two separate sentences or by using a comma and a conjunction. Use the proofreaders' marks on page 105 to make corrections.

1. Martin had been looking forward to a fishing trip with his father for weeks the day finally arrived.

2. Martin heard his father's footsteps on the stairs he'd been awake for an hour just waiting for his dad's call.

3. His father made coffee ~~and~~ Martin scrambled some eggs.

4. His father said that a good breakfast was an important factor in catching lots of fish they ate quickly and gathered their gear and were on their way. ~~Then they're~~

5. It was the middle of summer; the lake was so still that the water seemed frozen.

B. Read the following paragraph. Correct any run-on sentences.

A familiar name in American history is Sojourner Truth she was an African-American woman who fought to end slavery and obtain equal rights for all women. She was born a slave in 1797 her original name was Isabella Baumfree. She ran away when her master lied about letting her go she became free in 1828 when the state of New York made slavery illegal. Baumfree changed her name to Sojourner Truth after believing ~~that~~ God told her to preach love and justice. She traveled through New England and made speeches demanding that slavery be ended she visited the White House and spoke with President Lincoln. After the abolition of slavery, Sojourner Truth continued to speak out she made speeches against the unfair treatment of women. Sojourner Truth continued her fight until her death in 1883.

MORE ABOUT RUN-ON SENTENCES

For instruction, see the Grammar Gremlins in Chapter 4, page 158.

A. Correct the following run-on sentences by using a semicolon or by subordinating a lesser idea. When using a subordinate clause, you will have to decide which clause to subordinate.
   1. Serena had to call her mother the meeting would take much longer than she expected.
   2. The soccer club was meeting for the second time this week; they were having trouble deciding on when to hold their annual fund-raiser.
   3. Serena was the club's president, she needed to preside over the entire meeting.
   4. A vote would eventually have to be taken, everyone seemed to feel strongly about this issue.
   5. Only one date could be chosen some members would be disappointed.

B. Read the following paragraph. Correct any run-on sentences. Use at least one semicolon and restructure at least one sentence to include a subordinate clause.

Americans love basketball and football, soccer is the world's most popular sport. There are soccer leagues in North America, South America, Europe, Africa, and Asia. Often, soccer games will attract over 100,000 people to watch the fast-moving competition. The World Cup games are held every four years teams from many countries compete. Millions of fans watch the World Cup games on television thousands of others attend the games. Soccer is gaining in popularity in the United States many high schools and colleges now have soccer teams.

SUBJECT-VERB AGREEMENT

For instruction, see the Grammar Gremlins in Chapter 5, page 201.

A. Underline the subject in each sentence. Circle the form of the verb in parentheses that correctly agrees with the subject.

1. My favorite movie (is, are) *Philadelphia*.
2. Tom Hanks (play, plays) a young lawyer who is fired from a prestigious law firm for having AIDS.
3. The partners in the firm (claim, claims) that Hanks' character failed to do his job.
4. There (is, are) many scenes set in a courtroom in this movie.
5. At the heart of the film (is, are) two characters who learn to respect each other: Hanks' character and the lawyer he hires to sue the company on his behalf.

B. Read the following paragraph. Correct any mistakes in subject-verb agreement using proofreaders' marks from page 105.

Video cameras makes home movies easy and fun. A video camera at family gatherings turn family members into movie stars. On a video camera is buttons allowing you to zoom in for close-ups or take wide-angle shots. There is video cameras in all price ranges. Video cameras are different from movie cameras because they use videotape instead of film. One nice feature of videotapes are that videotapes do not have to be developed. You can view your movie on your television right after recording the action. Videotape is also reusable, unlike film. You can tape over the same videotape a number of times.

MORE ABOUT SUBJECT-VERB AGREEMENT

For instruction, see the Grammar Gremlins in Chapter 6, page 230.

A. Underline the subject(s) in each of the following sentences. Circle the verb in parentheses that agrees with the subject(s).

1. My two dogs and one cat (has, have) interesting personalities.
2. Everybody (love, loves) the dogs, but few people pay much attention to the cat at first.

3. Either the dogs or I (greet, greets) visitors at the door.
4. Meanwhile, nobody (seem, seems) to notice the cat as she sits in her quiet corner.
5. Finally, one of the dogs (go, goes) over to the cat to "show" her to the visitors.

B. Read the following paragraph. Correct any mistakes in subject-verb agreement.

Nearly everyone worry about outdoor pollution, but indoor pollution is also a problem. Indoor pollution includes fumes from household cleaners or fresh paint as well as cigarette smoke. Neither your home nor your office are entirely safe from indoor pollution. One problem is that many new apartments or office buildings has double-thick windows to cut heating and cooling costs. These windows keep air from seeping out, but they also allows fumes to build up inside. Nobody know how to solve the problem completely, but some people have found ways to improve air quality. Many people now use gentler household cleaners. A painter or a repair worker open all windows while using any product giving off fumes. In some communities, smoking is prohibited in public buildings. Indoor pollution is a problem that everyone need to help solve.

PRONOUNS AND ANTECEDENTS

For instruction, see the Grammar Gremlins in Chapter 7, page 259.

A. In each group of sentences, there are two pronouns that do not agree with their antecedents or that are unclear. Circle the pronouns. Then rewrite the sentences to correct any errors.

1. The class had its history final exam today. Only Nina and Tim finished his before time was called. It was the hardest one yet.

_____

_____

_____

2. The history exam consisted of 25 multiple-choice questions and 5 essay questions. They were tricky. Few students in the class were comfortable with his answers.

_____

_____

_____

_____

3. The students were worried although the instructor, said, "I covered everything on the exam in my lectures." They did not feel well prepared. Evvie, who is the top history student, and Rita, who is close behind, worried about her results.

_____

_____

_____

_____

_____

B. Read the following paragraph. Circle any pronouns that do not agree with their antecedents or that are unclear. Either change the pronoun or reword the sentence to make it correct.

The Nobel Prizes have existed since 1901, when people first received it for physics, chemistry, medicine, literature, and peace. An economics prize was added in 1969. The Swedish inventor Alfred Nobel founded them. The medals and the money accompanying it are awarded in Stockholm, Sweden. The only exception is the Peace Prize, which is presented in Oslo, Norway. No one can submit their own name for a prize. For instance, a scientist or economist must have their name suggested by other experts. Many winners share his or her awards. For instance, in 1903, Marie Curie, Pierre Curie, and Antoine Becquerel won for his discovery of radioactivity. Everyone does not always accept their award. Boris Pasternak, who won the literature prize in 1958, was forced by his country, the Soviet Union, to refuse the award. Many people thought it was unfair.

USING REGULAR VERBS

For instruction, see the **Grammar Gremlins** in Chapter 8, page 288.

A. Complete each sentence by filling in the blank with the appropriate form of the regular verb in parentheses.

1. After her car accident, Rebecca _____stayed_____ (stay, past tense) in the hospital for three weeks.

2. Because of her injuries, several doctors _____were consulting_____ (consult, past participle) on her condition.

3. Next week, Rebecca _____will be starting_____ (start, present participle) physical therapy on an outpatient basis.

4. The many visitors _____helped_____ (help, past tense) keep Rebecca's spirits high.

5. We know she is feeling better because she _____is talking_____ (talk, present participle) about getting back to work.

B. Read the following paragraph. Correct any errors in verb forms.

After twenty years of living with my parents or with room-mates, I finally move^d into my own apartment. It's been great. I haven't washed the dishes or clean^ed my room yet. All last week I stay^ed awake until midnight. Of course, I've suffer^ing the next day at work, but it's been worth it. I imagine I'll get over this stage of newfound freedom, but for the moment, I am enjoy^ing it.

USING IRREGULAR VERBS

For instruction, see the **Grammar Gremlins** in Chapter 9, page 316.

A. Complete the following sentences by filling in each blank with the appropriate form of the irregular verb in parentheses.

1. Our team has finally _____become_____ (become) champions.

2. During the final baseball game fans _____saw_____ (see) lots of excitement.

3. The other team scored early on, and we _____found_____ (find) ourselves one run behind.

4. Finally in the last inning our team _____got_____ (get) hot!

5. Mark _____began_____ (begin) the inning with a home run that tied the game, and then Alfonso _____breaked____ (break) the tie with another home run.
_____broke_____

B. Read the following paragraph. Correct any errors in verb forms.

For centuries, people have ~~knowed~~ songs and folktales about the colorful hero Robin Hood. They know that he ~~taked~~ [took] from the rich and ~~gived~~ [gave] to the poor. They also know about the time he ~~standed~~ [stood] on a bridge and ~~fighted~~ [fought] with Little John to get across a river. Although Little John ~~winned~~ [won] the fight, he was impressed with Robin Hood's courage, and the two men ~~become~~ [a] friends. Famous writers have even ~~write~~ [written] about Robin Hood. People are still not sure, though, whether Robin Hood ever actually existed. ~~Been~~ [Was] there a man behind the myth? For years, scholars have [been thinking] ~~thinked~~ that a real Robin Hood did exist in England in the 1200s. Their theories ~~are~~ [were] based on ballads that date back to the 1300s.

USING ADJECTIVES AND ADVERBS CORRECTLY

For instruction, see the Grammar Gremlins in Chapter 10, page 344.

A. In the following sentences, circle the correct word in parentheses.

   1. In the summer of 1990, Susan Hendrickson (accidental, **accidentally**) found a dinosaur bone belonging to a Tyrannosaurus rex.

   2. Ms. Hendrickson, who worked for the Black Hills Institute in Hill City, South Dakota, was (eager, **eagerly**) digging for duck-billed dinosaurs.

   3. Instead, she spotted a different and (**unusual**, unusually) bone sticking out of a hill.

   4. She (quick, **quickly**) showed the bone to the head of the institute who identified it as belonging to a Tyrannosaurus rex.

   5. A crew (eventual, **eventually**) uncovered the rest of the giant dinosaur.

B. Identify the word in italics as an adjective or adverb by circling *adjective* or *adverb* following each item. Then write the question the adjective or adverb answers.

   1. My son takes forever getting himself ready for school *each* morning.   *adjective* **adverb**
   Question: _____

2. He looks *carefully* in his closet to find the perfect outfit to wear, often changing his mind several times before selecting an outfit. (adjective) adverb

Question: _____

3. Once he's selected the *perfect* outfit, my son hurries to get dressed for school. (adjective) adverb

Question: _____

C. Read the following paragraph and correct any errors in the use of adjectives or adverbs.

Many colleges require that all students learn a foreign language before graduating. This is not an easily thing to do. Learning a second language takes day practice and hard work. You must spend many hours in the language lab, listening close to tapes of native speakers. Some foreign language instructors speak no English in their classes. During the first few weeks, you feel as though you don't understand a singly thing. Then you'll begin slowly to pick up certain words. The key to learning a language is daily practice.

Misplaced and Dangling Modifiers

For instruction, see the Grammar Gremlins in Chapter 11, page 376.

A. Correct the misplaced or dangling modifiers in the following sentences.

1. Tourists enjoy visiting the Biltmore Estate in Asheville, North Carolina, which was built by George W. Vanderbilt during 1890-1895.

2. The property includes the Biltmore House, which was inhabited by the Vanderbilt family with 255 rooms.

3. While walking through the Biltmore House, the mansion can overwhelm any visitor by its sheer size.

4. You will almost see 300 beautifully decorated rooms.

5. Strolling around the estate, the magnificent gardens will impress you.

B. Read the following paragraph. Correct any misplaced or dangling modifiers.

Reluctantly, Nathan's collection of books was sold to a book dealer. Having lost money recently, many of Nathan's most treasured items had to be sold. Nathan almost hated to see all his books go. As a young boy, his grandfather would read the books as Nathan sat in his lap. The memories were special ones and looking at the books always brought them back. While watching the books being carried away, the sadness overcame Nathan. What other hardships must he endure?

UNNECESSARY CHANGES IN VERB TENSE

For instruction, see the Grammar Gremlins in Chapter 12, page 404.

A. Each group of sentences contains an inconsistency in verb tense. Cross out one of the verbs, and write above it a verb that makes the tense consistent with the other verbs.

1. Are you looking for a new job? You might consider going into the animal recapturing business. The job sometimes required ~~required~~ *s* you to recapture animals that have escaped from zoos. Other times you might have to capture wild animals that have entered people's homes.

2. People in the animal recapturing business catch cougars, monkeys, and snakes. They ~~didn't~~ *don't* find it unusual to catch alligators or pythons.

3. If you're going to capture a large animal, such as a cougar or other cat, a tranquilizer ~~was~~ *is* used.

4. You ~~had~~ *have* to be carefully trained if you're going to enter this trade. The work can be dangerous.

5. Of course, if you're not particularly fond of snakes, rodents, and other such creatures, you can chóse a totally different profession.

B. Find and correct the six unnecessary changes in verb tense in the following paragraph.

My spring break turned out to be nothing like my plans. I expect*ed* to spend a relaxing week reading books, swimming at the beach, and visiting friends. Instead, I spend most of the time star-

ing at the ceiling flat on my back in my bedroom. I came down
with a terrible case of the flu, which lasts until it was time to
return to school. On top of that, I develop a stiff neck. I am miserable all week. Monday morning after spring break, I don't feel
rested and rejuvenated. Instead, I was ready for a vacation from
my vacation.

Using Parallel Structures

For instruction, see the Grammar Gremlins in Chapter 13, page 432.

A. Revise the following sentences to correct any nonparallel structures.

1. Mark Twain, a favorite American author, wrote novels, gave
   lectures, and he went on world tours.

2. His stories took you to small towns on the Mississippi River,
   and he wrote a story about a man who wakes up in England
   during the days of King Arthur.

3. Twain is a favorite of adult readers, but also children like him.

4. Twain wrote *The Prince and the Pauper*, the story of two boys
   who look exactly alike. One boy, Edward, is wealthy, and poor
   Tom has no money.

5. During his last years, Twain was not a happy man. His wife
   and daughter died, he lost a lot of money, and he was suffering from ill health.

B. Read the following paragraph. Correct any nonparallel structures.

The opening ceremony of the 1994 Winter Olympics was
breathtaking. The ceremony featured colorful costumes, the
music was beautiful, and inspiring speeches. The audience was
captivated by the performers as they sang songs of ancient Norway and were performing traditional dances. The only thing
equal to the beauty of the ceremony was the scenery around the
arena. The athletes from each country also took part in the ceremony. They looked not only impressive in their uniforms but also
you could tell they were excited. The result was both a memorable ceremony and a start to the Games that was exciting.

USING NEGATIVE EXPRESSIONS CORRECTLY

For instruction, see the Grammar Gremlins in Chapter 14, page 463.

A. Read each sentence. If a sentence has a double negative, change or delete one or more words to eliminate the double negative. If the sentence does not contain a double negative, write *correct.*

1. When the police officer stopped me, I ~~didn't have~~ *had* neither a driver's license nor proof of insurance.

2. I had left the house in such a hurry, I didn't carry my purse or wallet. *Correct*

3. My mother had called me and was so anxious for my help, I wasn't thinking about nothing ~~else~~ except getting in the car and going.

4. Of course, that isn't ~~no~~ excuse for not taking my driver's license.

5. The police officer didn't listen to ~~none of~~ my excuses. He issued me a ticket.

B. Find and correct the five double negatives in the following paragraph.

I ~~don't~~ never want to ride on that roller coaster again. After much begging, my roommate finally convinced me to go on that ride. After the first 30 seconds, I didn't ~~never~~ think I'd walk on solid ground again. Once we started, ~~however,~~ I didn't have no other choice but to close my eyes and wait it out. The ride kept going faster and faster, and my stomach kept getting more upset. I didn't think I'd make it to the end without passing out. I won't ~~never~~ trust my roommate's opinion about such things again! In fact, I will not be caught nowhere near a fairgrounds with my roommate.

WRITER'S GUIDE

GRAMMAR FUNDAMENTALS

Grammar is the study of how words work together. Grammar includes such elements as whether a word is a verb or an adjective, when the ending -ed is needed on a verb, and what words must be included in a sentence to make the sentence complete. Because language is a method of communi-cation among people, it depends on shared knowledge of grammar rules to preserve clarity. Knowing the rules of grammar helps all writers and speakers of a language communicate their ideas precisely and effectively.

LIST OF GRAMMAR TERMS

Grammar has a vocabulary all its own. Some grammar terms you may seldom hear and never use. Others you will encounter quite often. The following list represents a selected group of common grammar terms that are useful to know. Many of these terms are explained in the appropriate Grammar Gremlins in this text. To review, refer to the pages indicated. Grammar terms not explained elsewhere are defined here.

active voice verb form whose subject carries out the action of the verb. Example: The truck rumbled down the old dirt road. Compare *passive voice*.

adjective a word that modifies or describes a noun or a pronoun. See also the *adjective* section in "Parts of Speech" (page A 83) and the Grammar Gremlins for Chapter 10 (page 344).

adverb a word that modifies or describes a verb, adjective, or other adverb. See also the *adverb* section in "Parts of Speech" (page A 83) and the Grammar Gremlins for Chapter 10 (page 344).

antecedent the word for which a pronoun stands. See also the *pronoun* section in "Parts of Speech" (page A 82) and the Grammar Gremlins for Chapter 7 (page 259).

clause a group of words that contains a subject and a verb. An **independent**, or **main**, **clause** expresses a complete idea and can stand alone as a sentence. A **dependent**, or **subordinate**, **clause** does not express a complete idea and cannot stand alone as a sentence.
Example:

independent clause

Emily majored in philosophy

dependent clause

while she was at college.

conjunction a word or phrase that connects words or group of words. See also the *conjunction* section in "Parts of Speech" (page A 83) and the Grammar Gremlins for Chapters 3 (page 110), 4 (page 158), 6 (page 230), and 7 (page 259).

direct quotation the exactly quoted words of a speaker or writer, usually enclosed in quotation marks. Example: "I'll meet you in the lobby," said Mr. Perez. Compare *indirect quotation*.

fragment a word group that is not a complete sentence because it does not express a complete idea. See also the Grammar

Gremlins for Chapters 1 (page 32) and 2 (page 78).

gerund a verb form that ends in *-ing* and functions as a noun. Example: *Reading* is Evan's favorite pastime.

indirect quotation a restatement of a speaker's or writer's words. Example: Mr. Perez said that he would meet us in the lobby. Compare *direct quotation*.

infinitive the simple verb form preceded by *to*. Example: The class decided *to donate* money to the building fund.

interjection a word that expresses emotion and is usually grammatically separate from the rest of a sentence. See also the *interjection* section in "Parts of Speech" (page A 83).

modifier a word or group of words that limits or qualifies the meaning of another word or phrase. See also the Grammar Gremlins for Chapters 10 (page 344) and 11 (page 376).

noun a word that names a person, place, thing, or idea. See also the *noun* section in "Parts of Speech" (page A 82).

object the person or thing that receives the action of a verb. Example: The dog dug a *hole*.

participle a verb form that may be combined with helping verbs to form different tenses or that may function alone as an adjective. **Present participles** end in *-ing*. **Past participles** of regular verbs end in *-ed* or *-d*. See also the Grammar Gremlins for Chapters 8 (page 288) and 9 (page 316).

passive voice verb form whose subject is acted upon. Example: The prize was claimed by the winner. Compare *active voice*.

phrase a word group of two or more words that does not express a complete idea.

preposition a connecting word that relates a noun or pronoun to another word (or words) in a sentence. See also the *preposition* section in "Parts of Speech" (page A 83).

pronoun a word that stands for a noun. See also the *pronoun* section in "Parts of Speech" (page A 82) and the Grammar Gremlins for Chapter 7 (page 259).

run-on sentence two (or more) separate sentences that have been run together as one sentence. See also the Grammar Gremlins for Chapters 3 (page 110) and 4 (page 158).

sentence a group of words that contains a subject and a verb and expresses a complete idea. See also "Sentence Basics" (page A 84) and the Grammar Gremlins for Chapters 1 (page 32) and 2 (page 78).

subject the doer of the action in a sentence or the person, place, or thing that the sentence is about. See also "Sentence Basics" (page A 84) and the Grammar Gremlins for Chapters 1 (page 32), 2 (page 78), 5 (page 201), and 6 (page 230).

tense the form of a verb that positions action at some point in past, present, or future time. See also the Grammar Gremlins for Chapters 8 (page 288) and 9 (page 316).

verb a word or phrase that expresses action or state of being. See also the *verb* section in "Parts of Speech" (page A 83); "Sentence Basics" (page A 84); and the Grammar Gremlins for Chapters 1 (page 32), 2 (page 78), 5 (page 201), 6 (page 230), 8 (page 288), 9 (page 316), and 12 (page 404).

Activity A: Identifying Grammar Elements

Identify the number of the item or items in which examples of the following grammar elements appear. Then label the elements within each numbered item. *Note:* You may find an element more than once.

Active voice __4, 8, 10_____

Passive voice _____9_____

Direct quotation ___7___

Indirect quotation ___2___

Phrase ___1___

Fragment ___1___

Run-on sentence ___5___

Gerund ___10___

Infinitive ___4___

Participle ___3___

Adjective ___2___

Object ___8___

1. The computer on the low table.
2. Martin said that a blue car arrived at noon.
3. Are you coming to the seminar that is scheduled for next Tuesday?
4. She wanted to write.
5. Charlie took a long walk he needed the exercise.
6. Most of the audience left after the first act.
7. "I saw him!" shouted Sally.
8. Susan opened the front door.
9. The presents were opened by the new mother.
10. Swimming is not difficult to learn.

PARTS OF SPEECH

Every word has a **part of speech**, or speech category. A word's part of speech is based on how it is used in a sentence. These are the eight speech categories in English:

noun   adverb
pronoun   preposition
verb   conjunction
adjective   interjection

A **noun** names a person, place, thing, or idea. A **common noun** refers to any of a group or class of persons, places, things, or ideas. A **proper noun** names a specific person, place, thing, or idea. Proper nouns are normally capitalized while common nouns are not. Compare these common nouns and proper nouns:

Common Nouns	Proper Nouns
female	Lauren
writer	Alice Walker
continent	Asia
monument	Mount Rushmore
religion	Buddhism

A **pronoun** is a word that stands for a noun. The word for which the pronoun stands is called its **antecedent**. In the following sentence, *she* is a pronoun that stands for the noun *Mariel*, its antecedent.

When *Mariel* looked up, *she* saw Tim.

A **verb** is a word or phrase that expresses action or state of being. The verbs in the following sentences appear in italics.

The Braves *won* the pennant.
The playwright *wrote* a new play.
Our house *is* two blocks from the park.
The senior class *is traveling* to Seattle.
The trip *could have been* longer.

An **adjective** modifies or describes a noun or a pronoun.

defective cord   *vacant* building
Japanese art   *two* puppies
She is *excited*.   The winds are *strong*.

An **adverb** modifies or describes a verb, adjective, or other adverb.

Our friends visited *recently*. (*Recently* modifies the verb *visited*.)
Jean felt *slightly* ill. (*Slightly* modifies the adjective *ill*.)
Alan shut the door *very* quickly. (*Very* modifies the adverb *quickly*.)

A **preposition** is a connecting word that relates a noun or pronoun to another word (or words) in a sentence. In the following sentence, the preposition *in* relates the noun *students* to the word *library*.

The students studied *in* the library.

Library is the **object** of the preposition *in*. A word group that begins with a preposition—*in the library*—is called a **prepositional phrase**.

Here are some of the most common prepositions:

above	by	out
across	for	over
after	from	through
against	in	to
at	into	under
before	of	with
between	on	

A **conjunction** is a word or phrase that connects words or groups of words.

Coordinating conjunctions connect words or word groups that are of essentially equal importance. Here are some common coordinating conjunctions:

and	so	yet
for	or	nor
but		

Marie *and* the supervisor get along very well.
Use a pen *or* a dark pencil when completing the form.
Loud *but* pleasant music was heard in the streets.

Subordinating conjunctions connect a dependent clause to a main clause. In the following sentences, the subordinating conjunction *unless* connects *we raise tuition* to *the college will have to close*.

The college will have to close *unless* we raise tuition.
Unless we raise tuition, the college will have to close.

Here are some common subordinating conjunctions:

after	that
although	though
as	unless
because	until
before	when
even though	where
if	while
since	who

Correlative conjunctions are used in pairs to connect related elements. Here are some correlative conjunctions:

both . . . and	neither . . . nor
not only . . . but also	whether . . . or
either . . . or	

Both Martha *and* Sam will participate in the final ceremony.
The report was *not only* objective *but also* complete.

An **interjection** is a word that expresses emotion. Interjections usually are grammatically separate from the rest of a sentence.

Hey! Stop that man.
Yes, I'll volunteer to help with the campaign.

Activity B: Identifying Parts of Speech

Identify the parts of speech of the italicized words in the following sentences. Write your answers in the blanks provided.

1. *No*, don't put it there. ___Interjection___
2. *They* took tickets at the door. ___Pronoun___
3. Maria *promised* to take the children to the beach this weekend. ___Verb___
4. Ed tagged along *with* the group. ___preposition___
5. The *Rocky Mountains* were breathtaking. ___Proper noun___
6. We ate popcorn *and* watched a movie. ___Co-ordinating conjuction___
7. It didn't start raining until *after* we got home. ___Subordinating Conjuction___
8. *Leslie* owes Katina $25. ___Proper noun___
9. The *shabby* farm house had to be torn down. ___Adjective___
10. Although Robert was angry, he spoke *quietly*. ___adverb___

Activity C: Distinguishing Between Common and Proper Nouns

In the blanks provided, write whether the nouns in italics are common or proper.

1. Ellen spoke to the *neighbor* next door. ___Common___
2. Our visit to *Canada* was great fun. ___Proper___
3. Some television *advertisements* are very convincing. ___Common___
4. *Lake Superior* has some beautiful beaches. ___Proper___
5. The three new *representatives* arrived in Washington on Friday. ___Common___

Activity D: Identifying Pronouns and Antecedents

In the following sentences, underline the pronouns and circle the antecedents.

1. The clown chose one child and brought her up to the stage.
2. Mario wrote the report after he collected the information.
3. The spectators were excited as they watched the skater enter the rink.
4. Chris called after he finished his homework.
5. Elaine asked whether she needed to bring anything to the meeting.

SENTENCE BASICS

A **sentence** is a group of words that contains a subject and a verb and expresses a complete idea. The **subject** is the doer of the action or the person, place, or thing that the sentence is about. The **verb** shows action or state of being. A sentence may have a **compound subject** (more than one subject) or a **compound verb** (more than one verb).

In the following sentences, the subjects are underlined once and the verbs twice.

<u>Emma</u> <u><u>thanked</u></u> everyone for helping.

The <u>ice cream</u> <u><u>melted</u></u> and <u><u>dripped</u></u> down her hand.

The new <u>sofa</u> and <u>chair</u> <u><u>arrived</u></u> today.

The <u>cat</u> <u><u>jumped</u></u> on the window sill and <u><u>leaped</u></u> out the window.

<u>Mary</u> <u><u>is</u></u> late again.

That <u>compact disc</u> <u><u>sounds</u></u> terrific.

To identify the subject of a sentence, ask yourself: *Whom or what is the sentence about?* To identify an action verb, ask yourself: *Which word tells what the subject does?*

Another hint for recognizing verbs is to remember that verbs show time through their tense. Notice how the verbs change in each of the following pairs of sentences.

Present Tense: Al *sits* in that row every day.
Past Tense: Al *sat* elsewhere last term.

Present Tense: I *hear* music playing at night.
Past Tense: I *heard* music playing late last night.

Some sentences contain verbs that consist of more than one word.

I *am collecting* money for the fundraising drive.

José *has* often *collected* money for the drive in the past.

He *should have collected* at least $100.

I wonder how much money I *will collect* for the drive.

In the preceding examples, the words in italics are the verbs. Each sentence has a **helping verb** to help form the main verb of the sentences. These are the most commonly used helping verbs:

can	should	has
could	was	have
do	were	might
did	are	must
had	may	will
is	shall	would

Sentence Structure

Sentences have four basic structures.

A **simple sentence** expresses only one complete idea.

The job will start in two weeks.

A **compound sentence** is made up of two independent ideas or main clauses joined by a coordinating conjunction.

Michael is fishing today, and Marie is playing tennis.

Caution: Do not confuse a compound sentence with a simple sentence that contains either a compound subject or a compound verb.

Simple Sentences:
Esther and Clayton met in a math class. (compound subject)
Tyler stood in line and bought a ticket. (compound verb)

Compound Sentence:
Maria made pizza for dinner, and she served apple pie for dessert. (two independent ideas)

A **complex sentence** is made up of one main clause and one subordinate clause joined by a subordinating conjunction.

While I was sleeping, the dog got into the linen closet.

A **compound-complex sentence** is made up of at least two main clauses and at least one subordinate clause.

When you come to the party, bring your tape player with you, or we'll have no music for dancing.

See also the *clause* entry in the List of Grammar Terms (page A 80) and the *conjunction* section in "Parts of Speech" (page A 83).

Kinds of Sentences

A sentence may make a statement, ask a question, express a command or request, or make an exclamation. All sentences start with a capital letter and end with a period, question mark, or exclamation point.

Statement: The buses along this route run every half hour.

Question: When will you be ready to meet me in the lobby?

Command/Request: Please walk the dog, and feed the cat.

Exclamation: I can't believe the way our team played!

When a sentence takes the form of a command or request, the subject may not be stated. Instead, the subject may be understood to be *you*, as in the preceding example of command/request.

Activity E: Identifying Subjects and Verbs

In the following sentences, underline the subjects once and the verbs twice.

1. A trip to San Francisco would be great!
2. Rosa and Emily will arrive later.
3. The waves rolled gently across the beach and carried shells onto the sand.
4. The reporter spoke with the victim, and then he wrote his story.
5. During the storm, James lit candles in two rooms.
6. Four deer ran through the woods.
7. The instructor extended the deadline for the assignment.
8. The colt whinnied and neighed at the sight of its mother.
9. Todd bought his first car.
10. I fell on the ice yesterday.

Activity F: Identifying Sentence Structures

In the blanks provided, write whether the sentences are simple, compound, complex, or compound-complex.

1. That horse will never win the race. _____Simple_____

2. Susan will take ballet this year, but she will also continue taking tap and jazz lessons. _____Compound_____

3. When Nancy finishes college, she will travel to Mexico, and then she will begin graduate school. _____Compound-Complex_____

4. If you have completed the prerequisites, you can take Professor Grant's class this quarter. _____Complex_____

5. Joe picked up Harry, so I stayed at home and worked. _____Compound_____

PUNCTUATION

Punctuation marks have many functions. They set off separate ideas to make them easier to read. End punctuation marks give clues as to whether a sentence makes a statement, asks a question, gives a command, or makes an exclamation. They even indicate where a speaker's voice might go up, go down, or pause when reading sentences aloud.

See also the section "Kinds of Sentences" on page A 86.

COMMA

A comma indicates a pause within a sentence rather than a full stop, as a period does. Commas can set off or separate many types of words or phrases.

- **Use commas to set off words and word groups that are *not* essential to the meaning or completeness of a sentence.**

  We have no doubt that you will make an excellent treasurer. (If you omitted the words *no doubt*, the sentence would lose its meaning.)

  She will explain everything soon, no doubt. (If you omitted the words *no doubt*, the sentence would still be complete, and its meaning would be clear.)

  As shown in the preceding examples, the word group *no doubt* is essential to the first sentence but not to the second.

  A nonessential word group may appear at the beginning or end of a sentence.

  After all, you are the first person to complete this course.

  You are the first person to complete this course, after all.

  A nonessential word group may also appear inside a sentence. When a nonessential word group interrupts the sentence flow, set it off with *two* commas.

  She will, no doubt, explain everything.

  This shop, in my opinion, sells the best coffee in town.

  Mr. Shelton, my father's best friend, is my godfather.

  My boss, who lives near me, is in my car pool.

  Max, my new puppy, has fur as soft as velvet.

  Often (though not always) you can distinguish an essential word group from a nonessential one by reading the sentence to yourself *without* that word group. If the remaining words no longer form a complete sentence or no longer make sense, the words you've omitted are essential and should not be set off with commas.

  Nonessential, one comma: The check is in the mail, *I assure you*.

  Nonessential, two commas: The check is, *I assure you*, in the mail.

  Essential: I assure you that the check is in the mail.

  Nonessential word groups may add facts and details. If that information is simply extra or unnecessary, however, the word group is still considered nonessential and should be set off with one or more commas.

  Carmen Diaz, my aunt's friend, will be visiting her for two weeks this summer.

  My aunt, who lives in a large house, loves having visitors.

  My aunt's friend and *who lives in a large house* may be interesting pieces of information, but they are nonessential to the completeness of the sentences.

  Arnold Begay, a student in our class, won the essay contest. (*A student in our class* is nonessential because the student is identified by name.)

A student from our class won the essay contest. (*From our class* is necessary for completeness because without these words we wouldn't know *which* student won.)

- **Use a comma to set off introductory word groups.**
Opening the refrigerator, Brandon looked for a snack.
When you arrive, phone and let us know.
After the storm ended, everyone pitched in to clean up.
As a result of the accident on the expressway, several students arrived late.

- **Use a comma to set off transitional words and phrases that appear at the beginning of a sentence.** A transitional word or phrase signals a relationship between one sentence and another or between one idea and another.
In fact, filming was completed ahead of schedule.
Nevertheless, you must complete your paper by Friday.

- **Use two commas to set off nonessential transitional words and phrases that appear inside a sentence.**
Dr. Ling informs us, however, that the therapy is experimental.
I found out, furthermore, that the fitness center will be closed for repairs for two weeks.

Note: For additional information concerning transitional words and phrases, see Chapter 5 (page 193).

- **Use commas to separate items in a series.** A series consists of three or more words or word groups.
The dress is red, green, and gold.
Don't forget your tennis racket, your snack, and a change of clothes.
We will travel through Wyoming, Nebraska, Iowa, and Illinois.

The agenda includes touring the city until noon, eating lunch, and seeing an afternoon show.
Ellen volunteered to set up the event, Tony said he'd chaperon, and Ezra agreed to clean the room.
She looked for her keys under the sofa, behind the television, and in the desk.

Do not use a comma if all the items in the series are connected by *and* or *or*.
Paige painted the siding and the trim and the woodwork.
You can choose to ride your bike or take a bus or walk.

Do not use a comma if only two items appear in a series.
My favorite Texas cities are Austin and San Antonio.
Rudy will pick you up or call by 7 P.M.

- **Use a comma between two independent clauses that are connected by *and*, *but*, *or*, or *nor*.**

independent clause   independent clause
The door opened, *and* I went in.

independent clause independent clause
Alan ran, *but* Tim walked.

Caution: Do not use a comma alone between two independent clauses. Doing so would create a run-on sentence. Use a comma with *and*, *but*, *or*, or *nor* to join two independent clauses.

In a sentence with one subject and two verbs, you do not need a comma. Compare the following examples:

One Independent Clause:
subject   verb   verb
Monty delivered his paper and returned home.

Two Independent Clauses:

subject   verb   subject verb

Monty delivered his paper, and he returned home.

See also the *Sentence Structure* section in "Sentence Basics" (page A 85.)

- **Use a comma to separate two (or more) adjectives that both modify the same noun.**
  a cold, refreshing glass of lemonade

- **Use commas to set off the name of a state or country that appears directly after the name of a city.**
  Beatrice visited relatives in Portland, Maine, and Toronto, Canada.

- **Use commas to set off the year when it appears directly after the month and day.**
  On June 5, 1994, Don graduated from college.

Do not use a comma for only the month and year.

Her brother was born in March 1965.

- **Use commas to set off a direct quotation (the exact words of a speaker or writer) from the rest of a sentence.**
  "I'm not ready to go to bed," the child complained.

  "You must pass this test," the instructor reminded us, "or you will not get credit for the course."

Do not use a comma to set off an indirect quotation (a restatement of a speaker's or writer's words). Compare these examples:

Tanya said, "This stir-fry tastes great." (direct quotation)

Tanya said that the stir-fry tasted great. (indirect quotation)

Note: For rules concerning the use of quotation marks, see "Quotation Marks" (page A 91).

Activity A: Using Commas, Part 1

In the following sentences, insert commas as needed. Commas will not be needed in every sentence.

1. Austin Texas is a lively friendly city.
2. After sanding the furniture you need to apply the finish.
3. Her first choice was Chicago without a doubt but she also loved Dallas.
4. Before leaving for work John read the morning paper fed the dog and called the day care center.
5. "If the weather is bad" said Mrs. Jordan "we'll have to postpone our trip to Colombia South America until July 1."
6. Mandy said that the flight was delayed for two hours.
7. Kendra was born in January 1965.
8. The new student is friendly bright and creative.
9. Ms. Wong explained "After you open the contents of the package you must be careful not to disturb the mixture."
10. You can learn about daily events on television and in the paper and on the radio.

Activity B: Using Commas, Part 2

Insert commas as needed in the following paragraph.

The track meet was a great success. The teams arrived promptly, nobody was injured, and everyone seemed to have a great time. Only one minor mishap occurred. The starting gun, of all things, failed to work. Mr. Evans called a sporting goods shop, and the shop sent a new gun over right away. After that, the competition went ahead with no problems. Mrs. Rainsford said that this track meet was one of the best meets she had ever attended. Even George Poirier, the head coach, was overheard saying, "This is a great track meet!"

APOSTROPHE

Apostrophes can lead to errors because many words that use an apostrophe are the near-doubles of words that do not use an apostrophe (*it's* and *its*, for example). Be especially careful when you think you may need to use an apostrophe.

- **Use an apostrophe in contractions to indicate the omission of a letter or letters.**

  do + not = don't (*o* omitted)
  we + have = we've (*ha* omitted)

  can + not = can't (*no* omitted)
  it + is = it's (*i* omitted)

  we + are = we're (*a* omitted)
  she + will = she'll (*wi* omitted)

  let + us = let's (*u* omitted)
  could + not = couldn't (*o* omitted)

  who + is = who's (*i* omitted)
  I + am = I'm (*a* omitted)

- **Use an apostrophe to make nouns show possession. For singular nouns not ending in *s*, *x*, or *z*, add an apostrophe plus *s*.**

  Kathy's car
  the mouse's tail
  somebody's book

- **For most singular nouns ending in *s*, *x*, or *z*, add an apostrophe plus *s*. Exceptions include words that would sound awkward when pronounced with the extra *s*.**

  the box's lid   Chris's omelet
  Liz's garden   Tess's apartment
  but: Massachusetts' capital

- **For plural nouns already ending in *s*, add just an apostrophe.**

  the girls' coats   the rabbits' hutch
  the Jensens' pool

- **For plural nouns that do not end in *s*, add an apostrophe plus *s*.**

  the deer's paths   the men's hats
  the mice's ears

  Do not use an apostrophe with possessive pronouns.

  This key is *yours* to keep, and that key is *ours*. The rest of the keys are *theirs*.
  Caution: Do not confuse *it's*, meaning "it is," with the possessive pronoun *its*.

  It's time for us to go. (apostrophe used in a contraction)
  The company will have *its* picnic in July. (no apostrophe—possessive pronoun)

Activity C: Using Apostrophes

Insert an apostrophe or an apostrophe plus *s* in appropriate places in the following sentences.

  1. My teams mascot, a lion, was printed on my T-shirt.

2. We watched as the children's balloons floated into the air.

3. Butterflies' wings can be very beautiful.

4. We found deer's footprints in the mud.

5. The hippopotamus' nose stuck out of the water.

6. It's not a scary movie.

7. Katie's car was stolen from the parking lot last week.

8. We've got a new shipment arriving in the morning.

9. The fox's tail was a bushy plume.

10. This students' records are incomplete.

Activity D: Using Apostrophes in Contractions

In the space provided, rewrite the italicized expressions as contractions, using apostrophes to indicate the omission of letters.

1. *He will* have to do research for his report. ___He'll___

2. I *would not* go there in the spring during the rainy season. ___Wouldn't___

3. Our class *is not* participating in the opening ceremony. ___isn't___

4. *I have* been meaning to call you all week. ___I've___

5. They *should not* be allowed to use those parking spaces. ___shouldn't___

QUOTATION MARKS

The most important use of quotation marks is to signal a reader that certain phrases or sentences are direct quotations of a speaker or writer. Quotation marks can also be a useful way to set off some titles of spoken or written works.

• **Use quotation marks to enclose a direct quotation—the exact words of a speaker or writer.**

"Don't forget your lunch," Brandon reminded me.

My father calls his car his "road warrior's chariot with seat belts."

Do not use quotation marks with an **indirect quotation**—a restatement of a speaker's or writer's words.

May said, "You'll be able to see the full moon tonight." (direct quotation)

May said that we would be able to see the full moon tonight. (indirect quotation)

Use two pairs of quotation marks when a direct quotation is interrupted by words other than those of the speaker or writer. Use a comma before and after the interrupting words.

"I love reading," said Melinda, "and my favorite books are mysteries." (The words *said Melinda* are not part of the quotation.)

When a quotation consists of two or more consecutive sentences, use only one pair of quotation marks.

The archaeologist said, "This site was discovered only five years ago. The ruins date back to the 1400s. Many items from the site will be displayed in the museum for the community to see next month."

• **Always place commas and periods inside the closing quotation mark.**

"Look on page four," said Fred, "and

you'll find the article about the senator's visit."

- **Always place semicolons and colons outside the closing quotation mark.**
  Thea said, "I never agreed to that"; then she left the room.
- **Place question marks and exclamation points inside the closing quotation mark if they are part of the quotation itself. Place question marks and exclamation points outside the closing quotation mark if they are part of the sentence as a whole.**
  Penny asked, "How do I get to the roller coaster?" (Only the quotation itself is a question.)
  Did Ben Franklin say, "Three may keep a secret, if two of them are dead"? (The whole sentence, not the quotation, is a question.)

- **Use quotation marks to enclose the titles of parts or sections of a longer published work, such as chapters of a book or articles in a newspaper or magazine.**
  You'll enjoy the article "Watching Your Children Grow," by Dr. William Peterson.
  Chapter 2, "The History of Rhetoric," is hard to understand.

- **Use quotation marks to enclose the titles of essays, short stories, reports, poems, lectures, and songs.**
  "The Harbor" is a short, simple poem by Henry Wadsworth Longfellow.
  My favorite song is "Send in the Clowns."

  Note: For additional rules concerning titles, see "Underscores" (page A 95) and "Capitalization" (page A 95).

Activity E: Using Quotation Marks

Insert quotation marks where they are needed in the following sentences.

1. Gloria Estefan is performing next month, said Rosa, and I plan to go to the concert.
2. Turn down the music! demanded Jordan. It's hurting my ears.
3. Hannah told us that the trip should take around four hours.
4. Her article, Living in Memphis, was printed in the Sunday edition of the paper.
5. When is the movie starting? asked Alex.
6. Hasn't everyone heard the famous line from *Hamlet*, The play's the thing?
7. The reporter announced, There will be a special report at 2 P.M.
8. Anna continued to listen to Puff the Magic Dragon, I thought I'd go crazy!
9. Mrs. Barton gave Rebecca an A for her report, Opening the Door.
10. I said that I was ready to give my presentation.

COLON

A colon is used to signal or set apart information that expands on, defines, or explains material mentioned earlier in the sentence.

- **Use a colon to end a clause containing a preparatory expression such as *the following*, *as follows*, *here are*, and *these*, that refers to a series of items that follows. Use a colon even if the preparatory expression is implied, not stated.**

The order of speakers is as follows: Nancy Saunders, James Chen, and Henry Yazzie. (stated preparatory expression)

The children's exhibit will be touring these three cities: New York, Chicago, and Houston. (stated preparatory expression)

Robin has had some interesting jobs: zoo worker, stagehand, and cartoonist. (implied preparatory expression)

- **Use a colon to introduce or emphasize a single word or phrase.**
  Her answer was simple: no.

The key to successful singing is simple: practice every day.

- **Use a colon to introduce an explanation.**
  She revealed the solution: the chemicals, when mixed, created a reaction.

- **Use a colon to separate hours and minutes when expressing time and to represent the word *to* when stating proportions.**
  Her flight leaves at 6:24 P.M.
  The ratio of water to rice should be 2:1.

Activity F: Using Colons

Insert colons where they are needed in the following sentences.

1. I included three references: Ms. Temple, Ms. Raebur, and Mr. Nickelson.
2. The following workshops are canceled: "Improving Your Grammar," "Writing for Children," and "Selling Your Writing."
3. Our team was outnumbered 4:1.
4. We all laughed at his reason for not turning in his paper: the dog ate it.
5. Robin gets home from campus around 3:45 P.M.
6. Elaine plays two instruments: the clarinet and the oboe.
7. Brad's cat Lady won the blue ribbon for a good reason: she was the only cat who didn't try to scratch the judge.

SEMICOLON

A semicolon signals a pause that is stronger than a comma but weaker than a period.

- **Use a semicolon to divide two independent clauses that are not connected by a coordinating conjunction (*and, but, or,* or *nor*).**
  Thomas is unavailable to see clients today; Paula will take his appointments.
  My old car finally broke down; I'm buying a new one soon.

- **Use a semicolon between independent clauses that are linked by a transitional word or phrase.**

Marcus studies very hard; however, calculus is still very difficult for him.

The weather was awful; nevertheless, the cyclists were out in full force.

Molly is a talented musician; in fact, she plays both classical and jazz piano.

- **Use a semicolon to separate items in a series if some of the items already contain commas.**

We flew over Augusta, Maine; Boston, Massachusetts; and Miami, Florida.

Activity G: Using Semicolons

Insert semicolons where needed in the following sentences.

1. The preparations for the party are complete; nonetheless, you need to go over the list one more time.

2. On our musical tour we will try to visit the cities of Austin, Texas; Nashville, Tennessee; and Chicago, Illinois.

3. I can't be late; I have a noon appointment.

4. Catherine loves baseball; in fact, she has a great collection of baseball cards.

5. The luncheon will begin at 12:30 P.M.; the first speaker will follow at 1:30 P.M.

6. What is the connection between Salem, Oregon; Bethlehem, Pennsylvania; and Moab, Utah?

7. My cousin has twins; my neighbor has triplets.

8. I enjoy watching movies; however, I don't own a VCR.

DASH

Dashes do not have many specific uses of their own but are usually used in place of commas, semicolons, colons, or parentheses for dramatic emphasis. Dashes are most effective when used sparingly. Writing that is too full of dashes loses its impact. When you are tempted to use dashes, therefore, consider other punctuation marks before making your final decision.

- **Use a dash to set off a word or word group that you want to emphasize. If the word or word group to be emphasized appears within the sentence, use a dash before and after the word or word group to set it off.**

Warm apple pie—it makes my mouth water. (in place of a colon)

Vegetables are healthy—especially when they are steamed. (in place of a comma)

We traveled to St. Louis—it's a great, old city. (in place of a semicolon)

The dam—I can't believe it—has broken! (in place of commas or parentheses)

Katie—our new neighbor—lives by herself. (in place of commas)

Caution: Do not confuse dashes with hyphens. When keying, key the hyphen twice (--) to indicate a dash.

PARENTHESES

Parentheses are one of the few punctuation marks always used in pairs. Parentheses always enclose a word or phrase.

- **Use parentheses to enclose material that is extra, or nonessential, to the meaning of a sentence.**
  Father bought a gallon of strawberry ice cream (which I can't resist) at the store.

My grandmother (she's 91) took a trip to Hawaii.

Richard Nixon (1913-1994) served two terms as vice president before running for President.

Ascorbic acid (Vitamin C) is found in citrus fruit.

UNDERSCORES

Underscores are used to call attention to certain words or phrases.

- **Underscore the titles of long published works, such as books, magazines, and newspapers.**

  <u>Huckleberry Finn</u>   <u>Time</u>

  <u>The New York Times</u>

  Note: If you are using electronic equipment with the capability of printing italic type, use italics rather than underscores.

- **Underscore the titles of movies, television and radio shows, plays, operas, record albums, and paintings.**

  <u>My Fair Lady</u>   <u>60 Minutes</u>

  <u>The Tempest</u>   <u>Meet the Beatles</u>

  <u>Today</u>   <u>Jurassic Park</u>

  Note: For additional rules concerning titles, see "Quotation Marks" (page A 91) and "Capitalization" (on this page).

Activity H: Using Dashes, Parentheses, and Underscores

Insert dashes, parentheses, and underscores where needed in the following sentences.

1. We saw the movie Batman Forever last weekend.
2. The plane was supposed to arrive at 3 P.M. it's already 45 minutes late.
3. Charles Dunwoody our mayor gave the opening address.
4. A PAC political action committee can greatly influence our politicians.
5. Stubborn it's his middle name.
6. The book Everything Is Somewhere contains geography quizzes.
7. Add grated cheese about 1 cup to the macaroni.
8. I have a subscription to my favoirte magazine, Sports Illustrated.
9. Calvin bought a raffle ticket he won the grand prize.
10. The hemlock tree an evergreen has needle-shaped leaves.

MECHANICS

Mechanics are stylistic details that are used only in written language. They have no effect on spoken sentences but make a piece of writing look polished and professional.

CAPITALIZATION

Capital letters are used to call attention to names and other important words.

- **Capitalize the first word of a sentence.**
  My uncle spent two weeks hiking in Canada.

- **Capitalize the first word of a direct quotation.**
  Martha said, "Don't forget to pack your toothbrushes and toothpaste for the two-week camping trip."

- **Capitalize proper nouns—nouns that name a *specific* person, place, thing, or idea. Also capitalize the word *I*.**

Tuesday	Arizona
September	Mars
Albania	Grand Canyon
Walnut Street	Sears Tower
Exxon Corporation	Civil War
Thurgood Marshall	Mother's Day
Nobel Peace Prize	Cornell University

  Do not capitalize common nouns—nouns that refer to any of a group or class of persons, places, things, or ideas.

supervisor	corporation
college	month
country	state
agency	love

  Also do not capitalize names of animals, plants, sports, or the four seasons.

baseball	dolphin
golf	ivy
tiger	summer
maple tree	spring

  Do capitalize any proper nouns, or adjectives derived from proper nouns, that form part of the name of an animal or plant.

African daisy	*King Charles* spaniel
Irish wolfhound	*Bengal* tiger
Chinese cabbage	*Douglas* fir

- **Capitalize adjectives that are derived from proper nouns.**

Indian corn	*Elizabethan* drama
French door	*Chinese* food
Aztec ruins	*African* music

- **Capitalize the names of races, nationalities, and languages.**

Haitian	Native American
Canadian	Korean

- **Capitalize a person's title when it appears before the person's name.**

Doctor Spock	*King* Hussein
Prime Minister Major	*Professor* Chavez

Do not capitalize such titles when they are used simply as common nouns.

The debate was between a doctor and a professor.

Several heads of state, including a queen and a president, attended the ceremony.

- **Capitalize words that indicate family relationships when they appear alone or before a person's name.**

  Don't let *Mom* and *Dad* find out about their surprise party.

  Both *Grandma* Little and *Aunt* Molly were able to visit.

  Do not capitalize family titles when they are used simply as common nouns.

  Claire has no living grandparents, aunts, or uncles.

  Also do not capitalize family titles when they follow a possessive word such as *my*, *his*, *her*, or *their*.

  My aunt, my grandmother, and my seven cousins all live in the same town.

  His mother and his two uncles are sister and brothers.

- **Capitalize specific course titles.**

  Biology 301   Math 101

  Do not capitalize the names of general subjects.

  This year I'm taking biology and math.

- **In titles of written works and works of art, capitalize the first and last words, all major words including verbs, and all words of four or more letters.**

  Music of the Night

  "And They Lived Happily Ever After for a While"

  "To Build a Fire"

  "When There Is a Mouse in the House"

  A Visit to William Blake's Inn

  Note: For additional rules concerning titles, see "Quotation Marks" (page A 91) and "Underscores" (page A 95).

Activity A: Using Capitalization

Using proofreaders' marks from page 105, indicate the words that need to be capitalized or made lowercase in the following sentences.

1. Turn left on magnolia drive, and you'll see the park.
2. my Aunt's favorite neighborhood restaurant is golden plum, which serves wonderful italian cuisine.
3. my favorite season is spring because of the beautiful Dogwood trees.
4. dr. martin said, "we rarely see any cases of german measles or mumps anymore."
5. We celebrate doctor martin luther king's birthday in january of every year.
6. My favorite class this year has been Physics.
7. I am a Lawyer in the state of alabama.
8. Many years ago I visited the washington monument in Washington, d.c.
9. our high school, merriwether high, was commended for its work in environmental studies and in mathematics.
10. the manager attended the meeting.

NUMBERS

Numbers are usually written either as words or as figures.

- **Spell out numbers from one through ten. Use figures for numbers above ten.**

two children	25 years
seven computers	250 miles
ten people	150,000 votes
eight friends	19 pages

- **Treat numbers in the same sentence or paragraph consistently. If you use figures for some numbers, use figures for all, even those that are usually written as words.**

Taylor University has approximately 30,000 students, but just 10 of them will win the Anderson Award this year.

- **Use figures to express dates, times, percentages, decimals, street and box numbers in addresses, and parts of a book.**

May 6, 1994	17.5 yards
11:35 A.M.	2791 Henry Street
50 percent reduction	page 102

- **Spell out a number that begins a sentence.**

Twenty-five people were waiting at the gate by daybreak.

ABBREVIATIONS

An **abbreviation** is a shortened, or abbreviated, form of a word. In general, avoid abbreviating words in formal writing except for certain commonly used titles, organization names, technical terms, and the like.

- **Most abbreviations end with a period.**

Mr. Paulson	A.M., P.M.	Ph.D.
Ms. Narita	Al Wayne, Jr.	Prof. Drew

- **An acronym is a specialized abbreviation that is usually made up of the first initials of each word in a name or phrase. Acronyms are usually written with capital letters and no periods.**

NASA	EPA	YWCA	IRS
CIA	VCR	USC	CBS
UNICEF	FDIC	MADD	SWAT

Activity B: Using Numbers and Abbreviations

Using proofreaders' marks from page 105, correct any errors in numbers or abbreviations in the following sentences.

1. She celebrates her birthday on June twenty-five. *25*

2. The store gave her a ten percent discount on the sweater. *10*

3. I have a year's membership at the Y.M.C.A. *YMCA*

4. I can't believe we have to be there at five-thirty A.M.! *5:30*

5. You'll need a box that measures seven inches by 9 inches. *7*

6. Parker Weathers, Junior, is following in his father's footsteps. *Jr.*

7. I can't believe we were assigned to read all the way to page one-hundred and seven. *107*

8. 10 cars entered the race. *Ten*

9. Mister Gonzalez lives at twenty-one North Peachtree Drive. *Mr.* *21*

10. Our daughter was born on October thirty-one, nineteen eighty-nine. *31, 1989*

WORD USE

USING THE DICTIONARY

A dictionary is one of a writer's most useful tools. If you learn the features of a dictionary, you will be better able to make it work for you as a writing and vocabulary tool.

A dictionary contains several sections of specialized information. The front section usually contains information on how the dictionary is set up. For example, this section may contain a list of abbreviations used in the dictionary entries. Sections at the back of the dictionary might include such features as a biographical dictionary, a dictionary of place names, and a list of common symbols. The most important source of information, however, is the word entries themselves. In addition to supplying the correct spelling and meaning of words, the word entries provide much other information.

A Dictionary Entry

The entry on page A 99 is from *Merriam Webster's Collegiate Dictionary, Tenth Edition*. After the entry is an analysis of its features.

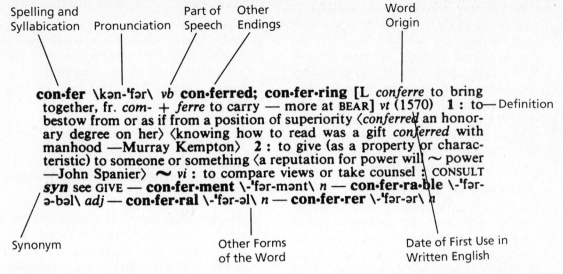

Spelling and Syllabication • Pronunciation • Part of Speech • Other Endings • Word Origin • Definition • Synonym • Other Forms of the Word • Date of First Use in Written English

con·fer \kən-'fər\ *vb* **con·ferred; con·fer·ring** [L *conferre* to bring together, fr. *com-* + *ferre* to carry — more at BEAR] *vt* (1570) **1 :** to bestow from or as if from a position of superiority ⟨*conferred* an honorary degree on her⟩ ⟨knowing how to read was a gift *conferred* with manhood —Murray Kempton⟩ **2 :** to give (as a property or characteristic) to someone or something ⟨a reputation for power will ~ power —John Spanier⟩ ~ *vi* : to compare views or take counsel **:** CONSULT *syn* see GIVE — **con·fer·ment** \-'fər-mənt\ *n* — **con·fer·ra·ble** \-'fər-ə-bəl\ *adj* — **con·fer·ral** \-'fər-əl\ *n* — **con·fer·rer** \-'fər-ər\ *n*

- *Spelling* The spelling of the word is the standard American English spelling. Sometimes an alternative spelling (often a British spelling) may appear after the first spelling. The first spelling is always the preferred one.

- *Syllabication* A multisyllable word is shown broken into its separate syllables. The syllables may be separated by dots. The **syllabication** helps you to pronounce the word and also hyphenate it correctly if you need to break the word at the end of a line of text. The syllabication also shows whether an expression is written as one word (like *roundhouse*), as a hyphenated word (like *round-the-clock*), or as two words (like *round steak*).

- *Pronunciation* The preferred pronunciation is given first, followed by alternate pronunciations. Pronunciation symbols can vary somewhat from dictionary to dictionary. Most dictionaries supply a pronunciation key every few pages. Notice the placement of the accent mark or marks in the pronunciation of a word. These accent marks tell you which syllable to stress when you say the word aloud.

- *Part of Speech or Speech Category* Usually the part of speech is written as an abbreviation. The part of speech tells you how the word is used in a sentence. The following list shows the typical abbreviations for parts of speech:

n	noun
vb	verb
vt	transitive verb—a verb that takes an object
vi	intransitive verb—a verb that does not take an object
adj	adjective
adv	adverb
prep	preposition
conj	conjunction
interj	interjection

A word can belong to more than one speech category, sometimes with a change in pronunciation. For example, the noun *present*, accented on the first syllable, means "gift." The verb *present*, accented on the second syllable, means "to give to someone." Some dictionaries show these two words as two different entries; others include alternate definitions within the same entry.

- *Other Endings* Some words undergo a change in spelling, depending on how they are used in a sentence. For example, nouns change spelling to show number (*shoe, shoes, goose, geese*). Verbs change spelling to show tense or number (*chat, chatting, chatted; bring, brought*). Adjectives change spelling to show comparison (*hot, hotter, hottest; breezy, breezier, breeziest*). These grammatical forms of words are called **inflectional forms**.

- *Word Origin or Etymology* The word origin helps you understand a word's meaning and sometimes how the word came to have several meanings. In the case of the word *confer*, the word originated in Latin (L). One can see how the meaning of the Latin word *conferre*, "to bring together," could have developed into meaning "to compare views or take counsel," and one can see how the earlier Latin word *ferre*, "to carry," could have developed into meaning "to bestow" or "to give."

- *How the Word Is Used* Sometimes an entry will supply a phrase or sentence showing how the word is used in **context**, or with other words in a sentence. Such context phrases or sentences can be useful as vocabulary builders.

- *Date of First Use in Written English* Some dictionaries cite the first recorded date that a word was used in writing in the English language. Some entries will show a number such as *14c* (meaning "fourteenth century") rather than an exact date.

- *Definition* Many words have more than one definition. If you're not sure which meaning a word has in a certain context, reread the context, substituting meanings until one makes sense.

- *Synonym* A synonym is a word that has a similar meaning to another word. Some dictionaries give synonyms for certain words. The synonym can help you understand the meaning of the entry word. For instance, if you looked up the word *consult*, you would find this meaning: "to deliberate together." This meaning is similar to one meaning of the word *confer* ("to compare views or take counsel").

- *Other Forms of the Word* By adding different **suffixes,** or endings, a word can function as other parts of speech. Many dictionaries provide the spelling, syllabication, and speech category of these variations of the entry word.

Activity A: Using the Dictionary

Use a dictionary to answer the following questions.

1. What is a synonym for *constant*?

   invariable

2. Can *recoil* be used as a noun?

   No

3. What is the word origin of *entourage*?

4. What is an alternative spelling for *theater*?

   theatre

5. What are the plural forms of *hippopotamus*?

   es

6. What syllable is stressed in *granola*?

_____*l*_____

7. What are the inflectional forms of *swim*?

_____swam, swum_____

8. How many syllables does *raconteur* have?

_____2_____

9. Where can you divide *mesmerizing*?

_____mes—mer—_____

10. What are the other forms of *regulate*?

_____regulated, regulating_____

IMPROVING YOUR SPELLING

You can improve your spelling with a little practice. The following steps will help you.

- **When you are not sure how to spell a word, look it up in a dictionary.** Do this as part of the proofreading step whenever you complete a writing assignment.

- **If you use a word processor or electronic typewriter with a spelling verification function, use this function every time you write.** Remember, though, that a spelling verification function won't detect errors such as writing *to* for *too*, because *to* is also a correctly spelled word. Use your dictionary as a final check.

- **Begin keeping a word list of your own.** On this list, write words you know you often misspell. Keep this list where you can easily refer to it, and study it regularly. If you can, come up with clues that help you remember the correct spelling of words. For instance, you can remind yourself that *separate* is spelled with an *a* by remembering that it means "apart."

- **Learn basic spelling rules.** The following rules will give you a start. Exceptions to spelling rules exist, but you can learn these exceptions separately, perhaps by adding them to your word list.

Words Ending in Silent *E*

1. If a word ends in silent *e*, drop the *e* when adding a **suffix** (word ending) that begins with a **vowel** (*a, e, i, o,* or *u*) or with *y*.

live	living	blue	bluish
shade	shady		

Exception: like   likeable

2. If a word ends in silent *e*, keep the *e* when adding a suffix that begins with a **consonant** (a letter that is not a vowel).

bore	boredom
appease	appeasement
use	useful
care	careless

3. If a word ends in *-ce* or *-ge*, keep the *-e* when adding a suffix beginning with *a* or *o*.

outrage   outrageous
manage   manageable

4. If a word ends in *-ie*, change the *ie* to *y* when adding *-ing*.

lie   lying
vie   vying
Exception: dye   dyeing

Words Ending in *Y*

1. If a word ends in a consonant and *y*, change the *y* to *i* when adding most suffixes.

heavy heavier   funny funniest
fifty fiftieth
Exception: shy   shyly

2. If a word ends in a vowel and *y*, do not change the *y* to *i* when adding a suffix.

buy   buyer   gray   grayish
joy   joyful
Exceptions: pay   paid   lay laid
              say said

Words with *EI* and *IE*

This rhyme will help you with most words in this category:

I before E
Except after C
Or when sounded like *ay*
As in *neighbor* and *weigh*.

1. The usual spelling is *ie*.

chief   priest
grief   shield
yield   thief
brief   retrieve

2. The spelling is *ei* following *c*.

receive   ceiling
perceive   conceive
deceive   receipt
conceit   conceited

3. The spelling is *ei* in words that sound like *ay*.

neighbor   freight
weight   reign
eight   sleigh

4. Here are a few exceptions to the rules given in the rhyme:

either   speices
weird   seize
science   heir
neither   leisure
foreign   sufficient
ancient   caffeine
height   conscience
their

Adding Prefixes and Suffixes

1. If a **prefix** (beginning element of a word) ends with the same letter that begins the **root word** (core element of a word), include both letters.

illegible   misspelled
unnatural   illogical

2. If a suffix begins with the same letter that ends the root word, include both letters.

carefully   artificially
stubbornness   morally
suddenness   locally

3. Double the final consonant when adding a suffix if *all* the following conditions are true:

- The suffix begins with a vowel.
- The word ends in a single consonant (except *w*, *x*, or *y*).
- The ending consonant is preceded by a single vowel.
- The word has one syllable *or* is a multisyllable word that has the accent on the last syllable.

hit	hitting
propel	propeller
expel	expelled
pop	popping
beg	beggar
tag	tagged
drop	dropping
repel	repellent
admit	admittance

4. Do not double the final consonant in the following conditions:

- The suffix begins with a consonant (exception: see Rule 2 of this "Adding Prefixes and Suffixes" section).

red	redness	ship	shipment
loyal	loyalty		

- The word ends in *w*, *x*, or *y*.

slow	slowly	box	boxer
pay	payee		

- The word ends in two consonants.

divert	diverted	talk	talking
instruct	instructor		

- The ending consonant is preceded by two vowels.

plead	pleaded
cartoon	cartoonist
green	greenish

- The word has several syllables, but the accent is *not* on the last syllable.

cancel	canceling
labor	laborer
vocal	vocalist

The following words are exceptions to Rules 3 and 4 of this "Adding Prefixes and Suffixes" section.

bus	buses
program	programmed
sidestep	sidestepped
outfit	outfitted
kidnap	kidnapping

Adding Suffixes With Commonly Confused Spellings (*ant/ent, ance/ence, ize/ise, sion/tion,* and *ceed/cede*)

The English language contains several pairs of suffixes that are spelled similarly, including *ant* and *ent*, *ance* and *ence*, *ize* and *ise*, *sion* and *tion*, and *ceed* and *cede*. These confusing suffix pairs can cause difficulties in spelling words correctly. Since there are so many exceptions and so few rules in these suffix pairs, look each word up in a dictionary until you are sure of the spelling.

Activity B: Identifying Root Words, Prefixes, and Suffixes

For each of the following words, identify the root word and the prefix or suffix.

	Root Word	Prefix	Suffix
1. immoral	moral	in	
2. activate	active		ate

	Root Word	Prefix	Suffix
3. unable	able	un	
4. misspell	spell	mis	
5. blameless	blame		less
6. unpleasant	pleasant	un	
7. trainer	train		er
8. disarm	arm	dis	
9. filler	fill		er
10. suddenness	sudden		ness

Activity C: Adding Prefixes and Suffixes

For each of the following root words, add the prefix or suffix.

1. il + logical = _illogical_

2. desire + able = _desireable_

3. travel + ed = _traveled_

4. pay + ed = _payed_

5. begin + ing = _begining_

6. il + legal = _illegal_

7. mis + diagnose = _misdiagnose_

8. obey + ed = _obeyed_

9. need + ed = _needed_

10. stop + age = _stopage_

Using a Spelling List

The following list contains commonly used words that are often misspelled.

ability	accommodate	acquire
absence	accompany	across
accept	accuracy	address
accident	ache	adequately
accidentally	acknowledgment	advertise

advice
advise
against
aggravate
aggressive
amateur
analysis
analyze
annual
answer
anxious
apparent
appreciate
approximately
argument
athlete
attendance
auxiliary
balance
bargain
basically
being
benefited
bicycle
bottle
breath
breathe
business
calendar
candidate
career
careful
careless
category
certain
choose
citizen
clothes
column
comfortable
commercial
committee
competition
completely
concede
condition
connote
conscience

conscious
definite
describe
difference
disappoint
distance
doubt
education
efficient
eighth
embarrass
emphasize
entrance
environment
exaggerate
exhaustible
familiar
fascinate
February
financial
forty
government
guidance
handkerchief
harassment
height
illegal
imitation
immediately
important
independent
instead
intelligent
interest
interfere
interruption
irresistible
jewelry
judgment
kindergarten
knowledge
leisure
library
lightning
likely
lonely
maintain
maintenance

manageable
marriage
material
mathematics
meant
miscellaneous
mortgage
necessary
nickel
ninety
obedient
occasion
occurrence
omission
opinion
opportunity
outrageous
pamphlet
parallel
particular
personnel
physical
plausible
pleasant
possess
precede
preferable
preference
privilege
probably
procedure
proceed
proceeding
prohibit
pursue
quarter
recede
recognize
recommend
refer
reference
renowned
representative
resistance
resource
restaurant
ridiculous
safety

sandwich	strength	twelfth
satellite	succeed	unanimous
scarcely	successful	unique
scissors	supersede	unusual
secretary	surprise	usually
separate	technique	vacuum
several	temperature	valuable
severely	tenant	view
similar	theory	villain
simultaneous	thorough	vinyl
sincerely	tomorrow	visitor
sophomore	tragedy	Wednesday
straight	traveler	withhold

Activity D: Correcting Commonly Misspelled Words

For each of the following words, write the correct spelling. Refer to a dictionary as needed.

1. adolesent _adolescent_
2. grammer _Grammar_
3. cemetary _~~cementing~~ cemetery_
4. desendant _descendant_
5. delemma _dilemma_
6. writting _writing_
7. rythm _____
8. visable _visible_
9. expecially _especially_
10. disipline _discipline_

Activity E: Correcting Misspellings

Using proofreaders' marks from page 105, correct the spelling errors in the following paragraph.

Martha went to the school counslor _counselor_, Mrs. Ware, to get some advise on how best to interveiw for a job. The first thing Mrs. Ware told Martha was to be preparred by knowing what the job intailed. She also told Martha to look profesional by dressing apropriately and staying calm. Mrs. Ware said that even tho inter-

appropriately,

though

veiwing for a job can cause anziety, Martha should stay relaxed and respond to the questions honestly. "If you don't know an anser, it's best to admit this rather than tring to make something up," said Mrs. Ware.

COMMONLY CONFUSED WORDS

Some words are so close in appearance that you may easily confuse one word for another. Here is a list of some commonly confused words. Notice that many of these word sets are **homophones**, or words that sound alike but are spelled differently. Become familiar with the listed words. Remember that your dictionary is also a useful tool to help you master these words. As with other spelling problems, you may want to create a list of the commonly confused words about which you feel least secure.

accept   to receive or agree to
except   other than
   I offered Dee the tools, and she *accepted* them.
   I *accept* the job your company has offered me.
   Everyone *except* Jonathan knows how to swim.

adapt   to adjust or become adjusted to new circumstances
adopt   to take up and use as one's own
   You can *adapt* this pattern to make a vest.
   Susan has *adopted* Marianna's style of dressing.

advice   suggestions or recommendations
advise   to recommend
   I question the *advice* Peter just gave you.
   I *advise* you to avoid that busy intersection.

affect   to change or to influence (verb)
effect   to bring something about (verb) *or* a result (noun)
   Newspapers can *affect* how we think about political issues.

   The new president has *effected* changes in company policy.
   The new working hours have had a major *effect* on staff efficiency.

all ready   fully prepared
already   before now
   We are *all ready* to move into our new house.
   Before I could put on my coat, Tom had *already* left.

all right
IMPORTANT: Although some dictionaries list the word *alright*, this spelling is not usually accepted as correct. The preferred spelling of this expression is *all right*.
   The doctor said that everything was *all right*.
   All right, you can come with me!

all together   all at once
altogether   in all
   The soldiers marched *all together*.
   Altogether, I earned 57 dollars.

capital   the city where a state or national government resides
capitol   the building where a legislature meets
   Springfield is the *capital* of Illinois.
   Our state *capitol* building is located on Main Street.

desert   a land area with very little rainfall
dessert   a sweet dish eaten at the end of a meal
   Surprisingly, many flowers grow in the *desert*.
   I ordered strawberry cheesecake for *dessert*.

every day   each day

everyday   ordinary; usual

>I have to go to English class *every day* at 8 A.M.
>
>I can use my *everyday* dishes in the microwave.

farther   more distant in space

further   more distant in time or degree

>Stand *farther* back so I can get you both in the picture.
>
>The second novel taes place *further* back in the past.

its   belonging to it

it's   the contraction of *it is*

>The puppy played with *its* toy outside.
>
>*It's* about time we all got together.

loose   too large, not tight

lose   to misplace

>This skirt is too *loose* around my waist.
>
>Did you *lose* your receipt again?

passed   went by without stopping

past   in the time before now

>Julia *passed* the store on the way to work.
>
>The painful memories are now in the *past*.

personal   concerning a particular person; private

personnel   employees

>That information is too *personal* to share.
>
>The *personnel* office has a record of your vacation days.

principal   main; someone in charge of a school

principle   a rule or standard of behavior

>Oil is the *principal* resource of many countries.
>
>Hannah Longfellow is the *principal* of Monroe High School.
>
>A strong work ethic is a matter of *principle*.

quiet   silent, making little noise

quit   to stop completely; to leave a job

quite   extremely

>Living in the country is so *quiet*.
>
>Michael *quit* his job after only two weeks.
>
>The weather in the spring is *quite* pleasant.

raise   to lift something else

rise   to move from a lower to a higher position without the help of outside power

>Don't forget to *raise* the flag after sunrise.
>
>We enjoy watching the sun *rise* over the ocean.

stationary   at a fixed point; not moving

stationery   writing materials or supplies

>The train stood *stationary* while we waited for repair workers.
>
>Maria's new *stationery* includes paper and envelopes.

than   a word used to compare

then   at that time; next

>I can run faster *than* my brother.
>
>We ate a good breakfast, and *then* we were on our way.

there   at that spot

their   belonging to them

they're   a contraction of *they are*

>Our friends should be meeting us *there*.
>
>*Their* lawn looks so green.
>
>*They're* performing a concert in San Antonio next month.

threw   past tense of *to throw*

thorough   complete; careful

through   in one side and out the other; ended

>Jason *threw* the ball to his father.
>
>Judith prepared a *thorough* report on the Vietnam War.
>
>When I was *through* with my dinner, I walked *through* the woods.

to   in the direction of

too   also; excessively

two   the number after one

>I traveled *to* Australia last summer.
>
>Are you *too* young to go to the dance, *too*?
>
>I have *two* cats.

your   belonging to you

you're   a contraction of *you are*

>You'll find *your* coat on the hook behind the door.
>
>*You're* invited to attend the opening session tomorrow night.

Activity F: Correcting Commonly Confused Words

Circle the word in parentheses that makes each sentence correct.

1. Because my sister is out of town, I will (accept, except) the award for her.
2. Columbia is the (capital, capitol) of South Carolina.
3. I shouldn't have eaten that (desert, dessert). Now I'm absolutely stuffed!
4. Put this document in a safe place so you don't (loose, lose) it.
5. All office (personal, personnel) are to attend the meeting with the president next Monday.
6. I received a new box of (stationary, stationery) for my birthday.
7. You may need to let your tea cool since it is still (quiet, quit, quite) hot.
8. If you have any questions about how the school is run, just ask the (principal, principle).
9. If (your, you're) not ready in time, just call us.
10. The article on discipline gives some good (advice, advise).

Activity G: Correcting Errors in Word Usage

Circle the word in parentheses that makes each sentence correct.

1. Your new house is much larger (than, then) your old one.
2. (All together, Altogether) our school has 56 first graders.
3. If you have completed (your, you're) form, place it in the blue basket.
4. The inspector made a (thorough, through) check of the house.
5. I interviewed the homeowner and (than, then) wrote the newspaper article about the fire.
6. The fans watched the winner (raise, rise) the trophy high above her head in triumph.
7. She (accepted, excepted) the award for the outstanding essay.
8. A skinned knee seems like an (everyday, every day) occurrence on the playground.
9. If you look over (there, their), you'll notice our new fountain.
10. In the (passed, past), shopping malls were not as common as they are today.

Activity H: Selecting Correct Words

Circle the correct word in each pair in parentheses in the paragraph that follows.

Buying a new house can be a stressful activity. If (your, you're) considering buying a house, be prepared. (Its, It's) best to (accept, except) that (there, their) will be some anxious times and things may not go smoothly. (There, Their) are some things you can do, however, to reduce stress. You can begin by doing a (thorough, through) background check on the property. For example, you can find out how much the current owner paid for the house and what improvements, if any, that the owner made in the (passed, past). This information, which is available at the county courthouse, can (affect, effect) how much you'll want to pay for the house. (Than, Then) you can make an appointment with the local building inspector. The inspector can (advice, advise) you on the condition of the house and what improvements still need to be made. Finally, talk (to, too) your banker to learn how much your monthly mortgage payments would be and what to expect for additional costs. Putting this information (altogether, all together) will make buying a house a less stressful undertaking. Instead of wasting your energy worrying, you will be able to look forward to living in (your, you're) new home.

STYLE

DEVELOPING YOUR VOCABULARY

Excellence in writing is directly tied to a good vocabulary. The larger your vocabulary, the better able you will be to choose just the right words for whatever you want to say. This does not mean that you need to use complex, multisyllable words in every sentence you write. Rather, you should know a range of words—simple ones, elaborate ones, technical ones, descriptive ones—so that you will always be able to use the words that best suit what you are writing. The following techniques will help you develop your vocabulary.

Use a vocabulary list or studybook. Many vocabulary-builder lists and books are available. One of the best vocabulary sources is a good dictionary, which contains all the words you would ever want to learn, along with definitions and example sentences.

Whatever vocabulary source you use, study it often. Either look through it in a quiet moment or set a specific goal, such as learning one new word a day. When you learn a new word, be sure you learn how it is used. Nothing makes a sentence more awkward than a word that doesn't belong.

Read as much as you can. Reading can help you improve your writing. The more you see words used in context, the more likely they are to become part of your vocabulary. Set aside a half hour or more every day to read. Here are some reading suggestions:

- **Read a newspaper every day.** If you live in or near a big city, you will have access to one or more major newspapers, such as *The Los Angeles Times, The Washington Post,* or *The New York Times,* as well as local newspapers. Often these newspapers are available in other regions in public libraries. Getting your news from a newspaper instead of only from television will give you an opportunity to absorb, think about, and review the language used to communicate the news.

- **Read a weekly newsmagazine such as *Time* or *Newsweek* regularly.** Many libraries subscribe to these magazines. Because these magazines quote a variety of people in interviews, including politicians, scientists, entertainers, and ordinary people from many countries, you will be exposed to different types of language styles.

- **Read other magazines in your areas of interest.**

- **Read fiction and nonfiction books.** Choose books that look interesting so that you can develop the habit of reading for enjoyment as well as to learn. If you have children, read their books aloud to them. Both you and your children will benefit from this activity.

When you read, look for articles, features, chapters, or even letters to the editor that say something in a way that you find interesting. Examine the way the writer combines words. If any words are unfamiliar to you, try to determine their meanings from the context. See the following section for more information on context clues. Use a dictionary to confirm the meaning of each new word.

Use Context Clues. The surrounding words in a sentence or paragraph you are reading can provide clues to the meaning of an unfamiliar word. Several kinds of context clues can help you figure out the meaning of an unfamiliar word.

- Your own experience

    Sally has an *insatiable* appetite for potato chips; she can eat a whole bag by herself.

In the preceding sentence, you can use your experience of the habit-forming nature of junk food to infer that *insatiable* probably means "unending" or "unable to be satisfied."

- Comparison or contrast clue

    My nephew has an *aversion* to spicy foods, but he especially likes sweet-tasting foods such as fruit.

In the preceding sentence, the phrase "but he especially likes sweet-tasting foods such as fruit" helps you infer that *aversion* probably means "dislike."

- Synonym clue

    Ms. Carson bought some colorful *remnants* at the fabric store; she will use these pieces for a quilt.

In the preceding sentence, the word *remnants* is used in such a way that you can infer that it means "small fabric pieces."

- Direct definition clue

    She felt *ambivalent* about the issue; she just couldn't make up her mind which side to support.

In the preceding sentence, the word *ambivalent* is defined by the phrase that follows it, "couldn't make up her mind."

Keep a vocabulary list. Collect vocabulary words that you want to master. Make an entry for each word. The following details should go into each entry:

- The word itself

- The pronunciation of the word (use dictionary symbols, including syllable divisions and accent marks, to show this information)

- The word's meaning or meanings

- The word's part of speech

- One sentence that shows the use of each meaning

Activity A: Enhancing Your Vocabulary

From the following list, select at least five words to study. Use your dictionary to determine the pronunciation of the word, one definition of the word, and the related part of speech. Write a sentence using the word correctly.

deflect	turbulence	mutation
nuance	ascend	denounce
introspection	sonorous	mellifluous
tenacious	lucid	tangible

1. Word: _____ deflect _____
   Pronunciation: _____ di flekt' _____
   Definition: _____ turn from a course _____
   Part of speech: _____ transitive verb, intransitive verb _____
   Sentence using word: _____

   _____

2. Word: _____ ascend _____
   Pronunciation: _____ a send' _____
   Definition: _____ to move upward _____
   Part of speech: _____ Intransitive verb _____
   Sentence using word: _____

   _____

3. Word: _____ lucid _____
   Pronunciation: _____ loo'sid _____
   Definition: _____ easily understood _____
   Part of speech: _____ adjective _____
   Sentence using word: _____

   _____

4. Word: _____ turbulence _____
   Pronunciation: _____ tur'byə lence _____
   Definition: _____ characterized by disturbance, disorder, etc _____
   Part of speech: _____ adjective _____
   Sentence using word: _____

   _____

5. Word: _____ *mutation* _____

Pronunciation: _____ *mu-ta'tion* _____

Definition: _____ *a change or alteration* _____

Part of speech: _____ *Intransitive verb* _____

Sentence using word: _____

_____

EFFECTIVE WORD CHOICE

Writing seems easy if you just dash off the first word that comes into your mind and speed on. For your writing to be effective, however, you must spend the time and effort to evaluate what you have written to see whether anything can be said in a better way. No one can give you a rule book that will help you find the perfect word for every situation. You will develop that skill naturally as you gain more practice in writing. You can, however, apply the following guidelines to almost any type of writing.

Be concise. When you first write your thoughts, you're usually thinking more about expressing your ideas than about finding just the right language. The first draft of a piece of writing, therefore, may tend to be wordy. When you revise your writing, be sure your sentences are concise. Look at the following examples:

Wordy: If you ever get a chance to do volunteer work in your community, you should do it because it can be very rewarding.

Concise: Doing volunteer work can be very rewarding.

Be precise. Vague language gives readers no more than a general idea of what you are trying to tell them. Many words, especially nouns, verbs, and adjectives, are all-purpose words that don't always fit your thoughts. Check your writing to make sure that you use sharp, precise words to communicate your ideas effectively. This does *not* mean that you must always use a more elaborate word instead of a simple one. Sometimes you can make your writing more precise by using a simple word or by adding descriptive details.

Vague: The mountains were very high.

Precise: The mountains loomed above us, breathtakingly high.

Precise: The treeless mountains, veined with last winter's unmelted snow, were so high that their sharply angled peaks seemed to pierce the clouds.

Avoid slang. Slang expressions are usually unsuitable in formal writing such as essays for class. An exception to this rule is if you are writing a story in which you want to reproduce someone's natural speaking style. At other times, avoid using expressions like the following in your writing:

that's cool	number-crunching
flew the coop	all washed up
let's boogie	take a snooze

Avoid trite expressions. Some expressions have been used so often that they now sound boring instead of vivid. These expressions are often called **clichés**. They may be the first words you think of when you want to express an idea. Take time, however, to think of another, more original way to state your idea. The following clichés are a small sample of the many in existence.

drop me a line
we're all in the same boat
first and foremost
top of the line
keep a stiff upper lip
time flies
she's way off base
he's head and shoulders above the rest

Avoid pretentiousness. Many inexperienced writers (and a few experienced ones) believe elaborate language is preferable to plain language: if a one-syllable word is good, a four-syllable word must be better. In fact, the opposite is often true. Sentences filled with multisyllable words often sound pompous. They may even sound inaccurate because we are more likely to misuse a fancy word than a simple one. Actually, some of the most memorable writers in history, including Abraham Lincoln, Emily Dickinson, and Ernest Hemingway, preferred simple language. Think of elaborate words as spices. If you use more spice than food, your meals taste overwhelming. On the other hand, if you use just a touch of spice, you bring out the flavor of your food.

Pretentious sentence: As per the memorandum delivered Tuesday last, all vacation requests will be expedited.

Simpler, more effective sentence: The memo sent last Tuesday says that all vacation requests will be processed quickly.

Activity B: Achieving Effective Word Choice

Rewrite the following sentences to achieve effective word choice.

1. When Tom approached the podium to deliver his speech, he was so overcome with nervousness that he stuttered and stammered and his voice shook terribly.

   _____

   _____

2. It goes without saying that Maria is the best candidate for the position.

   _____

   _____

3. The house on the corner was beautiful.

   The corner home was beautiful.

   _____

4. Your interview may be unpleasant, but just keep a stiff upper lip.

   _____

   _____

5. I'm afraid you're out of the running.

   _____

   _____

6. Her excessive use of language drove us all crazy.

   _____

   _____

7. All of our decisions were overturned by a hypercritical administrator.

_____

_____

8. The movie was scary.

_____

_____

9. She couldn't believe her eyes when she saw her daughter's performance in the play.

_____

_____

10. Time flies when you're working hard.

_____

_____

ACHIEVING SENTENCE VARIETY

Good writing depends partly on the words you choose and partly on the way you combine your words. The basic unit of combination in any writing is the sentence. You can make your writing more attractive to readers if you pay attention to the length and construction of each sentence. If several sentences in a row all use the same pattern, your writing becomes monotonous. When you reread your writing, consider varying sentence patterns in any of the following ways.

Vary the beginnings. Does each sentence begin with the same word, such as _the_ or _he_? Does each sentence begin with the subject and then state the verb? Here are some ways to modify this pattern:

- Begin some sentences with a transitional word such as _Next_ or _As a result_.

- Begin some sentences with a prepositional phrase such as _After the morning session_ or _Because of her dedication_.

- Rearrange the word order of some sentences.

Monotonous beginnings: She was late for school. She quickly dressed. She brushed her hair and teeth. She ate breakfast. She gathered her books. She rushed out the door.

Varied beginnings: She was late for school. Quickly she dressed and then brushed her hair and teeth. She gathered her books in between nibbles of breakfast. Then she rushed out the door.

For more information on transitional words and phrases, see Chapter 5, pages 192-194.

Vary the length. If every sentence is short and choppy or long and involved, the reader will soon become bored and lose track of what you are saying. Examine your writing to be sure you include a variety of sentence lengths.

- If your sentences are all long and involved, break some of them apart. Look especially for sentences such as the following:

- Sentences with independent parts joined by a semicolon.
- Sentences with independent parts joined by *and*, *but*, *or*, or *nor*.
- Sentences beginning or ending with subordinating thoughts and containing subordinating conjunctions such as *as*, *before*, *because*, *if*, *since*, or *when*.

All long sentences: A symphony orchestra is a large orchestra that includes the following instrument families: strings, woodwinds, brass, and percussion. Much of the music played by a symphony orchestra is classical, music written long ago, but many symphonies play modern melodies from movies or the theater or orchestral versions of hit tunes by popular musicians. The size of the orchestra can change according to the music it plays; some pieces require only a chamber orchestra, others call for a full orchestra, and still others demand additional soloists such as a pianist.

Varied sentence length: A symphony orchestra is a large orchestra. It includes the following instrument families: strings, woodwinds, brass, and percussion. Much of the music played by a symphony orchestra is classical, music written long ago. Many symphonies, however, also play modern melodies from movies or the theater. They may even play orchestral versions of hit tunes by popular musicians. The size of the orchestra can change according to the music it plays. Some musical pieces require only a chamber orchestra while others call for a full orchestra. Still other pieces demand additional soloists such as a pianist.

- If your sentences are all short and choppy, combine sentences to vary your sentence lengths. The following methods are examples of how you can combine sentences:
- Join two independent thoughts using *and*, *but*, *or*, or *nor*.
- Join one independent thought with a subordinating thought using subordinating conjunctions such as *as*, *before*, *because*, *if*, *since*, or *when*.
- Create a longer sentence containing a series of nouns, verbs, or adjectives to replace several parallel sentences that have a repetitious rhythm.

All short sentences: I love to swim in the summer. I also love to read. Bike riding is also fun. I love being outdoors. Summer seems so relaxing. The longer days are the reason. They make me feel as if I have more time. The sun goes down too early in the winter. I just want to hibernate.

Varied sentence length: I love to be outdoors swimming, reading, and riding my bike during the summer. Summer seems so relaxing because of the longer days. They make me feel as if I have more time. In the winter, the sun goes down too early, and I just want to hibernate.

Activity C: Achieving Sentence Variety

Rewrite the following paragraphs to achieve sentence variety.

1. The salesperson wouldn't leave. He talked for hours. I thought I'd go crazy. I tried to stop him. Nothing seemed to work. I finally bought something. Then he left.

_____

_____

_____

_____

2. Your vacation will be delightful since you'll be visiting many of the major cities in New England including Portland, Maine; Burlington, Vermont; Concord, New Hampshire; and Boston, Massachusetts. You'll first fly into Boston and stay for three days, after which you'll take a bus up through the Green Mountains in Vermont and tour several Vermont farms. While in Portland, you'll spend time on the beach sunning, fishing, and looking for shells, and then you'll eat at one of the city's finest seafood restaurants.

_____

_____

_____

_____

_____

_____

3. Mother is driving down. She plans to arrive tomorrow just before lunchtime. She'll stay for a week. She wants to visit several of her friends in the neighborhood. She has also asked me to reserve theater tickets for her. She wants to see at least one play while she's here.

_____

_____

_____

_____

_____

_____

4. I signed up for English 102. I've already completed English 101, I enjoy English very much. I love literature, I even love writing papers. I hope to become a high school English teacher eventually.

I signed up for English 102. I've already completed English 101, and I enjoy English very much. I love writing papers and literature are my favourite and even love writing papers. Eventually I hope to become a high school english teacher.

5. Whenever I sit down to talk on the phone, it never fails that my young daughter seems to have some emergency or important request that takes my immediate attention, so she interrupts me, taps on my shoulder, and even pulls at my arm, and with that kind of behavior going on, it's no wonder that I'm unable to hold any kind of satisfying conversation and that I have to end the conversation sooner than I would like.

_____

_____

_____

_____

_____

_____

_____

_____

_____

_____

_____

_____

Don't Expect Me To Be Perfect

Sun Park

(See Reading as a Stimulus for Writing on page 77.)

1 I am a 16-year-old Korean-American. My family has been in the United States for six years now. I'll be a junior next fall.

2 When I first came to the States, it took two years before I could speak English fluently. By the time I started middle school, I realized that most of my fellow students had never met many kids like me before. They had this idea, probably from TV and movies, that all Asians are nerds and all Asians are smart. It's true that some are. I know many smart people. But what about those Asians who aren't so smart? Having a reputation for brains is nice, I guess, but it can also be a pain. For instance, sometimes when my classmates do not know something, they come to me for the answer. Often I can help them. But when I can't they get these weird expressions on their faces. If I were a genius, I would not mind being treated like one. But since I am not, I do.

3 The problem isn't just limited to the classroom. My mother and father expect an awful lot from me, too. Like so many Korean parents, and many ambitious American parents, they're very competitive and can't help comparing me with other kids. Mine always say to me, "So and so is so smart, works so hard and is so good to his or her parents. Why can't you be more like him or her?" Because I am the oldest kid in my family, they expect me to set a good example for my younger sisters and relatives. They'd rather I concentrate on schoolwork than dating. They want me to be No. 1.

4 Most of the time I want to do well, too. I'm glad to take all honors classes. But now that I am at those levels, I have to be on my toes to keep doing well. The better I do, the more pressure I seem to place on myself. Because my parents want me to be perfect—or close to perfect—I find myself turning into a perfectionist. When I do a project and make one little error, I can't stand it. Sometimes I stay up as late as 2 A.M. doing homework.

5 I don't think I would be like this if my parents weren't motivating me. But I don't think they know what pressure can do to a teenager. It's not that they put me down or anything. They have plenty of faith in me. But to tell the truth, sometimes I really like to be lazy, and it would be nice just to take it easy and not worry so much about my grades all the time. Maybe my parents know this. Maybe that's why they encourage me to be better. Well, it still drives me crazy when they compare me with others. I wonder if those smart kids have parents like mine.

6 Sure, I'm proud of who I am, and I love my parents very much. But then there are times I just feel like taking a break and going far away from parents and teachers. Of course that's impossible, but it's always nice to dream about it.

Easy Job, Good Wages ≈≈≈≈≈≈≈≈≈≈≈≈

Jesus Colon

(See Reading as a Stimulus for Writing on page 156.)

This happened early in 1919. We were both out of work, my brother and I. He got up earlier to look for a job. When I woke up, he was already gone. So I dressed, went out and bought a copy of the *New York World* and turned its pages until I got to the "Help Wanted Unskilled" section of the paper. After much reading and rereading the same columns, my attention was held by a small advertisement. It read: "Easy job. Good wages. No experience necessary." This was followed by a number and street on the west side of lower Manhattan. It sounded like the job I was looking for. Easy job. Good wages. Those four words revolved in my brain as I was travelling toward the address indicated in the advertisement. Easy job. Good wages. Easy job. Good wages. Easy . . . 1

The place consisted of a small front office and a large loft on the floor of which I noticed a series of large galvanized[1] tubs half filled with water out of which I noticed protruding the necks of many bottles of various sizes and shapes. Around these tubs there were a number of workers, male and female, sitting on small wooden benches. All had their hands in the water of the tub, the left hand holding a bottle and with the thumb nail of the right hand scratching the labels. 2

The foreman found a vacant stool for me around one of the tubs of water. I asked why a penknife or a small safety razor could not be used instead of the thumb nail to take off the old labels from the bottles. I was expertly informed that knives or razors would scratch the glass thus depreciating[2] the value of the bottles when they were to be sold. 3

I sat down and started to use my thumb nail on one bottle. The water had somewhat softened the transparent mucilage[3] used to attach the label to the bottle. But the softening did not work out uniformly somehow. There were always pieces of label that for some obscure reason remained affixed to the bottles. It was on those pieces of labels tenaciously fastened to the bottles that my right hand thumb nail had to work overtime. As the minutes passed I noticed that the coldness of the water started to pass from my hand to my body giving me intermittent body shivers that I tried to conceal with the greatest effort from those sitting beside me. My hands became deadly clean and tiny little wrinkles started to show especially at the tip of my fingers. Sometimes I stopped a few seconds from scratching the bottles, to open and close my fists in rapid movements in order to bring blood to my hands. But almost as soon as I placed them in the water they became deathly pale again. 4

---

[1]**galvanized:** iron or steel coated with zinc to prevent rust
[2]**depricating:** lowering
[3]**mucilage:** glue or adhesive

But these were minor details compared with what was happening to the thumb of my right hand. For a delicate, boyish thumb, it was growing by the minute into a full blown tomato colored finger. It was the only part of my right hand remaining blood red. I started to look at the workers' thumbs. I noticed that these particular fingers on their right hands were unusually developed with a thick layer of corn-like surface at the top of their right thumb. The nails on their thumbs looked coarser and smaller than on the other fingers—thumb and nail having become one and the same thing—a primitive unnatural human instrument especially developed to detach hard pieces of labels from wet bottles immersed in galvanized tubs.

After a couple of hours I had a feeling that my thumb nail was going to leave my finger and jump into the cold water of the tub. A numb pain imperceptibly began to be felt coming from my right thumb. Then I began to feel such pain as if coming from a finger bigger than all of my body.

After three hours of this I decided to quit fast. I told the foreman so, showing him my swollen finger. He figured I had earned 69 cents at 23 cents an hour.

Early in the evening I met my brother in our furnished room. We started to exchange experiences of our job hunting for the day. "You know what?" my brother started, "early in the morning I went to work where they take labels off old bottles—with your right hand thumb nail . . . Somewhere on the west side of lower Manhattan. I only stayed a couple of hours. 'Easy job . . . Good wages . . .' they said. The person who wrote that ad must have had a great sense of humor." And we both had a hearty laugh that evening when I told my brother that I also went to work at the same place later in the day.

Now when I see ads reading, "Easy job. Good wages," I just smile an ancient, tired, knowing smile.

Enough Bookshelves
Anna Quindlen

(See Reading as a Stimulus for Writing on page 199.)

The voice I assume for children's bad behavior is like a winter coat, dark and heavy. I put it on the other night when my eldest child appeared in the kitchen doorway, an hour after he had gone to bed. "What are you doing down here?" I began to say, when he interrupted: "I finished it!"

The dominatrix[1] tone went out the window and we settled down for an old-fashioned dish about the fine points of *The Phantom Tollbooth*. It is the

---

[1]**dominatrix:** a woman who tries to exert unquestioned authority over others

wonderful tale of a bored and discontented boy named Milo and the journey he makes one day in his toy car with the Humbug and the Spelling Bee and a slew of other fantastical characters who change his life. I read it first when I was ten. I still have the book report I wrote, which began "This is the best book ever." That was long before I read *The Sound and the Fury* or *Little Dorrit*, the Lord Peter Wimsey mysteries or Elmore Leonard. I was still pretty close to the mark.

All of us have similar hopes for our children: good health, happiness, interesting and fulfilling work, financial stability. But like a model home that's different depending on who picks out the cabinets and shutters, the fine points often vary. Some people go nuts when their children learn to walk, to throw a baseball, to pick out the "Moonlight Sonata" on the piano. The day I realized my eldest child could read was one of the happiest days of my life.   3

"One loses the capacity to grieve as a child grieves, or to rage as a child rages: hotly, despairingly, with tears of passion," the English novelist Anita Brookner writes in *Brief Lives*, her newest book. "One grows up, one becomes civilized, one learns one's manners, and consequently can no longer manage these two functions—sorrow and anger—adequately. Attempts to recapture that primal spontaneity[2] are doomed, for the original reactions have been overlaid, forgotten."   4

And yet we constantly reclaim some part of that primal spontaneity through the youngest among us, not only through their sorrow and anger but simply through everyday discoveries, life unwrapped. To see a child touch the piano keys for the first time, to watch a small body slice through the surface of the water in a clean dive, is to experience the shock, not of the new, but of the familiar revisited as though it were strange and wonderful.   5

Reading has always been life unwrapped to me, a way of understanding the world and understanding myself through both the unknown and the everyday. If being a parent consists often of passing along chunks of ourselves to unwitting—often unwilling—recipients, then books are, for me, one of the simplest and most surefire ways of doing that. I would be most content if my children grew up to be the kind of people who think decorating consists mostly of building enough bookshelves. That would give them an infinite number of worlds in which to wander, and an entry to the real world, too; in the same way two strangers can settle down for a companionable gab over baseball seasons past and present, so it is often possible to connect with someone over a passion for books.   6

(Or the opposite, of course: I once met a man who said he thought *War and Peace* was a big boring book, when the truth was that it was only he who was big and boring.)   7

I remember making summer reading lists for my sister, of her coming home one day from work with my limp and yellowed paperback copy of *Pride and Prejudice* in her bag and saying irritably, "Look, tell me if she   8

2**spontaneity:** behavior that arises from natural impulses marries Mr. Darcy, because if she doesn't I'm not going to finish the book." And the feeling of giddiness I felt as I piously said that I would never reveal an ending, while somewhere inside I was shouting, yes, yes, she will marry Mr. Darcy, over and over again, as often as you'd like.

You had only to see this boy's face when he said "I finished it!" to know that something had made an indelible mark upon him. I walked him back upstairs with a fresh book, my copy of *A Wrinkle in Time*, Madeleine L'Engle's unforgettable story of children who travel through time and space to save their father from the forces of evil. Now when I leave the room, he is reading by the pinpoint of his little reading light, the ship of his mind moving through high seas with the help of my compass. Just before I close the door, I catch a glimpse of the making of my self and the making of his, sharing some of the same timber. And I am a happy woman. 9

A Pothole from Hell
Mark Goldblatt

(See Reading as a Stimulus for Writing on page 228.)

Three weeks ago, the apartment building next to mine commissioned some kind of underground maintenance. Workmen with hardhats, foul mouths and jackhammers showed up for four consecutive mornings. At precisely 7 A.M., they started to batter the concrete sidewalk into submission. 1

They dug a deep trench that ran from the lawn next door out into the street and raised an eight foot high mound of dirt, as if to testify to the seriousness of their mission. The fourth day, they filled in the trench with the dirt and left. 2

What remained is a pothole. 3

Let me explain, first of all, that this is not your run-of-the-mill pothole. This is epic, a pothole from hell. I measured it: six feet by four and a half feet; its basin lies 14 inches beneath street level. If this were Hawaii, we'd be barbecuing pigs in it. 4

It cannot be straddled by the widest sedans nor skimmed by the speediest sportsters. By night, the sparks from chassis flash like roman candles. It is beneath my window, so I hear it claim its victims for hours on end. 5

I have made a study of the frequencies. These are more consistent than you might guess: two impacts a minute during the morning rush, one a minute for most of the afternoon, three a minute at the height of the evening rush. And I have even developed a hypothesis about why the evening is worse than the morning: coffee spills. 6

What happens, I think, is that the jolt dislodges those supposedly spillproof decanters of coffee affixed to dashboards. The resulting coffee spill, in turn, serves to remind the driver the following morning to avoid the pot- 7 hole. By contrast, the bat-out-of-hell mentality of quitting time contributes to the sudden surge at evening rush.

But indeed the pothole has become for me much more than a mere study in physics and sociology. It has come to represent a source of justice, a kind of (dare I say?) divine intervention in the workaday world. 8

You see, the street I live on is intended for a single lane of traffic in each direction. The neighborhood lies between two schools, where cars are required to slow down at all times. Yet few do. Now, at no cost to the police, the pothole has become an administrator of swift and sudden retribution for minor violations. 9

There is a space to avoid the pothole, about eight feet between its western ridge and the yellow median, if you see it in time—which you can unless you are speeding. Or unless, and this is perhaps the most perfect justice, you are trying to pass on the right of a car travelling at a reasonable speed. That is the path of severest axle damage and probably severest psychological damage as well. 10

Perhaps it is unconscionable to take such satisfaction in the grief of others. Yet the pothole has brought together the citizens of this community more than any event since the last blackout. By the dozens, we congregate on the sidewalk: old and young, male and female, black and white. We watch. We wince. 11

We do not root for or against particular cars. When hubcaps go flying, we are careful to note where they roll; we direct the drivers to them with looks of consolation. We are not a mean people. 12

Sooner or later, of course, the pothole will be repaired. That is the way of city life and it is right. For if the pothole were to last too much longer, drivers would learn to avoid the street. Local businesses would suffer. Property values would go down. 13

One morning I am going to wake up and the pothole will be gone. For that reason, I am determined to appreciate it while I can. This Friday night, my date and I are going to phone for a pizza. We are going to dine *al fresco*,[1] on the fire escape, looking down upon the scene like gods, watching the justice of the world unfold. 14

And if the pizza arrives stuck to the lid of the box, like gods we will understand why. 15

[1]*al fresco:* outdoors

Only Daughter
Sandra Cisneros

(See Reading as a Stimulus for Writing on page 257.)

Once, several years ago, when I was just starting out my writing career, I was asked to write my own contributor's note for an anthology I was part of. I wrote: "I am the only daughter in a family of six sons. *That* explains everything." 1

Well, I've thought about that ever since, and yes, it explains a lot to me, but for the reader's sake I should have written: "I am the only daughter in a *Mexican* family of six sons." Or even: "I am the only daughter of a Mexican father and a Mexican-American mother." Or: "I am the only daughter of a working-class family of nine." All of these had everything to do with who I am today. **2**

I was/am the only daughter and *only* a daughter. Being an only daughter in a family of six sons forced me by circumstance to spend a lot of time by myself because my brothers felt it beneath them to play with a *girl* in public. But that aloneness, that loneliness, was good for a would-be writer—it allowed me time to think and think, to imagine, to read and prepare myself. **3**

Being only a daughter for my father meant my destiny would lead me to become someone's wife. That's what he believed. But when I was in the fifth grade and shared my plans for college with him, I was sure he understood. I remember my father saying, "*Que bueno, ni'ja*, that's good." That meant a lot to me, especially since my brothers thought the idea hilarious. What I didn't realize was that my father thought college was good for girls—good for finding a husband. After four years in college and two more in graduate school, and still no husband, my father shakes his head even now and says I wasted all that education. **4**

In retrospect,[1] I'm lucky my father believed daughters were meant for husbands. It meant it didn't matter if I majored in something silly like English. After all, I'd find a nice professional eventually, right? This allowed me the liberty to putter[2] about embroidering my little poems and stories without my father interrupting with so much as a "What's that you're writing?" **5**

But the truth is, I wanted him to interrupt. I wanted my father to understand what it was I was scribbling, to introduce me as "My only daughter, the writer." Not as "This is only my daughter. She teaches." *Es maestra*—teacher. Not even *profesora*. **6**

In a sense, everything I have ever written has been for him, to win his approval even though I know my father can't read English words, even though my father's only reading includes the brown-ink *Esto* sports magazines from Mexico City and the bloody *¡Alarma!* magazines that feature yet another sighting of *La Virgen de Guadalupe*[3] on a tortilla or a wife's revenge on her philandering[4] husband by bashing his skull in with a *molcajete* (a kitchen mortar made of volcanic rock). Or the *fotonovelas*, the little picture paperbacks with tragedy and trauma erupting from the characters' mouths in bubbles. **7**

My father represents, then, the public majority. A public who is uninterested in reading, and yet one whom I am writing about and for, and privately trying to woo. **8**

---

[1]**in retrospect:** as I look back
[2]**putter:** to move or act aimlessly
[3]***La Virgen de Guadalupe:*** The Virgin Mary as she is revered in Mexico
[4]**philandering:** engaging in many love affairs

When we were growing up in Chicago, we moved a lot because of my   9
father. He suffered bouts of nostalgia. Then we'd have to let go our flat,
store the furniture with mother's relatives, load the station wagon with
baggage and bologna sandwiches and head south. To Mexico City.

We came back, of course. To yet another Chicago flat, another Chicago   10
neighborhood, another Catholic school. Each time, my father would seek
out the parish priest in order to get a tuition break, and complain or boast:
"I have seven sons."

He meant *siete hijos*, seven children, but he translated it as "sons." "I   11
have seven sons." To anyone who would listen. The Sears Roebuck
employee who sold us the washing machine. The short-order cook where
my father ate his ham-and-eggs breakfasts. "I have seven sons." As if he
deserved a medal from the state.

My papa. He didn't mean anything by that mistranslation, I'm sure. But   12
somehow I could feel myself being erased. I'd tug my father's sleeve and
whisper: "Not seven sons. Six! and *one daughter*."

When my oldest brother graduated from medical school, he fulfilled my   13
father's dream that we study hard and use this—our heads, instead of
this—our hands. Even now my father's hands are thick and yellow, stubbed
by a history of hammer and nails and twine and coils and springs. "Use
this," my father said, tapping his head, "and not this," showing us those
hands. He always looked tired when he said it.

Wasn't college an investment? And hadn't I spent all those years in col-   14
lege? And if I didn't marry, what was it all for? Why would anyone go to
college and then choose to be poor? Especially someone who had always
been poor.

Last year, after ten years of writing professionally, the financial rewards   15
started to trickle in. My second National Endowment for the Arts Fellow-
ship. A guest professorship at the University of California, Berkeley. My
book, which sold to a major New York publishing house.

At Christmas, I flew home to Chicago. The house was throbbing, same   16
as always; hot *tamales* and sweet *tamales* hissing in my mother's pressure
cooker, and everybody—my mother, six brothers, wives, babies, aunts,
cousins—talking too loud and at the same time, like in a Fellini film,
because that's just how we are.

I went upstairs to my father's room. One of my stories had just been   17
translated into Spanish and published in an anthology of Chicano writing,
and I wanted to show it to him. Ever since he recovered from a stroke two
years ago, my father likes to spend his leisure hours horizontally. And
that's how I found him, watching a Pedro Infante movie on Galavisión and
eating rice pudding.

There was a glass filmed with milk on the bedside table. There were sev-   18
eral vials of pills and balled Kleenex. And on the floor, one black sock and
a plastic urinal that I didn't want to look at but looked at anyway. Pedro
Infante was about to burst into song, and my father was laughing.

I'm not sure if it was because my story was translated into Spanish, or   19
because it was published in Mexico, or perhaps because the story dealt

with Tepeyac, the *colonia* my father was raised in and the house he grew up in, but at any rate, my father punched the mute button on his remote control and read my story.

I sat on the bed next to my father and waited. He read it very slowly. As 20 if he were reading each line over and over. He laughed at all the right places and read lines he liked out loud. He pointed and asked questions: "Is this So-and-so?" "Yes," I said. He kept reading.

When he was finally finished, after what seemed like hours, my father 21 looked up and asked: "Where can we get more copies of this for the relatives?"

Of all the wonderful things that happened to me last year, that was the 22 most wonderful.

Introductions to New York
Bob Blaisdell

(See Reading as a Stimulus for Writing on page 286.)

Just a year ago I began teaching basic writing composition at the Borough of Manhattan Community College. My students were from all over the world—in one class 20 of 25 were foreign born—and from all over New York. We shared knowledge of about five cultural figures: Presidents Bush and Clinton, Michaels Jackson and Jordan, and Madonna. A reference to anyone else would elicit puzzled expressions. 1

What topics of conversation and writing could we possibly share? Well, 2 we could all tell stories. They wrote about their families, neighborhoods, homelands, food, love, death—the fundamentals, of course, of literature— and they wrote ungrammatically, unidiomatically, unpretentiously and unusually beautifully and freshly about all of those subjects.

A phenomenon very familiar to New Yorkers was the subject of two of 3 the essays.

On Nov. 2, at night, three men entered a candy store in Manhattan. They 4 took all the money and shot twice at the person who was working there. The person who had been shot was asking help of the people who were walking in the busy street.

Everybody ignored him. 5

Fortunately he was saved, saved by a lady passing by. This lady, who was 6 good at heart, took him inside the store and called the police. The police arrived and instead of taking him to the hospital right away, they were asking him questions. They were waiting for an ambulance.

The doctors had to take out one of his kidneys. They saved him. Every- 7 body was surprised, because this poor employee was in a critical state.

After removing his kidney the doctors didn't care about him much. 8 Maybe because he was a poor Indian. The police closed the file the next day. Nobody wanted to help him anymore except his boss, my father. This is what he told my father.

"When they came in, I had no doubt that they are thieves. I came out of the counter because I didn't want them to steal anything. They showed me the gun. I held the gun and started to push them outside the store. When I reached the door, I saw blood coming out of my body. I don't know when they shot me. When I saw my blood I got nervous and fell right there. They went inside the store and took out all the money. Nobody came to help me except this kind young lady." 9

My father paid him his weekly salary until he became healthy again. 10

—Preeti Kumar, 19, who was born in India and lives in Queens.

Like other big cities in the world, people in New York City are always in a hurry. Everyone is in a race against time. I think it is not a good excuse for being cold-blooded. 11

Last week I saw a scene that astonished me. I was taking a train to uptown to visit my friend. On the platform I saw a woman with worn clothes walking unsteadily. Suddenly, she fainted. 12

I saw other people just keep walking; they kept getting on and off the train as if nothing happened. Then I saw the woman waking up for a while; her eyes were full of hopelessness and puzzled as if they complained about being abandoned. After a while she stood up herself and then got on a train. 13

I just wondered why others didn't try to help this woman. Even a short sentence like, "Are you O.K.?" was good enough. 14

At my friend's home, I talked about this event to him and complained a lot about others' behavior in the station. My friend looked at me and said, "What did you do at that time? Just looking?" 15

I looked at him and said nothing. On my way home, I was astonished that, like others on the platform, I was selfish and cold-blooded, too. 16

—Siu Poon, 22, who was born in Hong Kong and lives in Manhattan.

How Dictionaries Are Made
S. I. Hayakawa

(See Reading as a Stimulus for Writing on page 314.)

It is widely believed that every word has a correct meaning, that we learn these meanings principally from teachers and grammarians (except that most of the time we don't bother to, so that we ordinarily speak "sloppy English"), and that dictionaries and grammars are the supreme authority in matters of meaning and usage. Few people ask by what authority the writers of dictionaries and grammars say what they say. I once got 1 into a dispute with an Englishwoman over the pronunciation of a word and offered to look it up in the dictionary. The Englishwoman said firmly, "What for? I am English. I was born and brought up in England. The way I speak *is* English." Such self-assurance about one's own language is not uncommon among the English. In the United States, however, anyone who is willing to quarrel with the dictionary is regarded as either eccentric[1] or mad.

Let us see how dictionaries are made and how the editors arrive at definitions. What follows applies, incidentally, only to those dictionary offices where first-hand, original research goes on—not those in which editors simply copy existing dictionaries. The task of writing a dictionary begins with reading vast amounts of the literature of the period or subject that the dictionary is to cover. As the editors read, they copy on cards every interesting or rare word, every unusual or peculiar occurrence of a common word, a large number of common words in their ordinary uses, and also the sentences in which each of these words appear, thus:

pail

The dairy *pails* bring home increase of milk

Keats, *Endymion*, I, 44-45

That is to say, the context of each word is collected, along with the word itself. For a really big job of dictionary-writing, such as the *Oxford English Dictionary* (usually bound in about twenty-five volumes), millions of such cards are collected, and the task of editing occupies decades. As the cards are collected, they are alphabetized and sorted. When the sorting is completed, there will be for each word anywhere from two or three to several hundred illustrative quotations, each on its card.

To define a word, then, the dictionary-editor places before him the stack of cards illustrating that word; each of the cards represents an actual use of the word by a writer of some literary or historical importance. He reads the cards carefully, discards some, rereads the rest, and divides up the stack according to what he thinks are the several senses[2] of the word. Finally, he writes his definitions, following the hard-and-fast rule that each definition *must* be based on what the quotations in front of him reveal about the meaning of the word. The editor cannot be influenced by what *he* thinks a given word *ought* to mean. He must work according to the cards or not at all.

The writing of a dictionary, therefore, is not a task of setting up authoritative[3] statements about the "true meanings" of words, but a task of *recording*, to the best of one's ability, what various words *have meant* to authors in the distant or immediate past. *The writer of a dictionary is a historian, not a lawgiver.* If, for example, we had been writing a dictionary in 1890, or even as late as 1919, we could have said that the word "broadcast" means "to scatter" (seed, for example), but we could not have decreed that from

2

3

4

5

[1]**eccentric:** odd
[2]**senses:** meanings
[3]**authoritative:** coming from an expert

1921 on, the most common meaning of the word should become "to disseminate[4] audible[5] messages, etc., by radio transmission."[6] To regard the dictionary as an "authority," therefore, is to credit the dictionary-writer with gifts of prophecy which neither he nor anyone else possesses. In choosing our words when we speak or write, we can be *guided* by the historical record afforded us by the dictionary, but we cannot be *bound* by it, because new situations, new experiences, new inventions, new feelings are always compelling us to give new uses to old words. Looking under a "hood," we should ordinarily have found, five hundred years ago, a monk; today, we find a motorcar engine.

[4]**disseminate:** spread
[5]**audible:** that can be heard
[6]**transmission:** the sending of a signal

Probable Cause ～～～～～～～～～～～～
Keith E. Coffee

(See Reading as a Stimulus for Writing on page 343.)

Prior to my arrest, I had not considered jail a possibility for me. First, I obey the law. Second, I am married and the father of a young son, own two new cars and a new home and have a management position with a major supermarket chain. Somehow I thought all this placed me beyond the pale of incarceration[1]—that somehow I had power over my condition. But I found out I was not beyond being arrested for being Black in the white suburb where I lived. An oversimplification, maybe, but true.   1

I was arrested in the driveway of my apartment complex by a police officer who had spotted a set of automobile rims in the hatch of my car. I had just purchased the rims from a friend—who had himself bought them from a major retail outlet—and was returning from his home with my wife and son when the officer pulled me over. He was a short, well-constructed white man who asked me a few questions, then for a receipt for the rims. Since I did not have one, I was later told there was "probable cause" for the officer to believe the rims in my possession were stolen. (Had he required it, I also could not have produced a receipt for the basketball shoes or wedding band that I was wearing at the time). It was then that I was told to step out of my vehicle: I was under arrest.   2

I was handcuffed and placed in the backseat of the officer's patrol car, while my wife, who was holding our infant son, watched. Their presence   3

[1]**incarceration:** being in jail

kept me from having any verbal or physical confrontation[2] with the officer regarding my arrest—and so did his presence. Here was a man, to my thinking, with a gun, who could kill me with impunity.[3]

I knew that any resistance on my part could result in another mother grieving for her son, another grieving widow and another child without a father. 4

My own powerlessness is a difficult subject to entertain. Men, especially 5 young, socially aware, politically active African-American men of the nineties, are no longer supposed to be powerless victims before the prejudice of society. Today, should our rights be violated, our reaction is to resist with all available vigor. Yet my arrest brought me face-to-face with powerlessness. There were feelings of isolation and violation as we rode to the police station; there were shame and humiliation in being escorted by two officers, each holding me by the arm, to a booking room; and there was the indignity of being searched (again), then told not only to remove my shoes, but also my wedding band. None of this, however, was as punishing as having to endure my own impotence,[4] my complete inability to keep an iron door from slamming shut behind me, given that I had done nothing wrong.

I can imagine no other condition like being in jail. I was forbidden 6 access to those I love. There was no wife or son, or family. Nor was there any sense of my having control over my own destiny. I sat resigned to the fact that my fate was now in the hands of someone else. My participation was limited to sitting and watching the minutes pass like hours, and hoping that God could hear my prayers for release.

Some seven hours later my supplications[5] were answered. My wife and 7 brother posted my bail. Two days later I was informed that I could come down to the station and pick up my property. All charges had been dropped; no case could be made.

Since my release, I have sought legal advice. An attorney told me that I 8 might challenge the officer's assumption of "probable cause" when he arrested me and file suit, but this would be expensive and time consuming, with my chance of winning being almost nonexistent. Still, the choice was mine. I have, instead chosen to forget my powerlessness, my time in jail.

But in trying to forget my own incarceration, I have to forget the young 9 African-American men I see in the backseats of police cars, or forget men like Rodney King, whose beating last March by Los Angeles police officers was videotaped. I must forget that their crime might only be that of being young and Black and male—forget moreover, that for them there may be no money for bail, no way out. For me, there is the sound of a cell door closing that looms large in my memory. With that sound I am reminded of the powerlessness of a previous condition—slavery.

[2]**confrontation:** fight
[3]**impunity:** without fear of being punished for a deed
[4]**impotence:** powerlessness
[5]**supplications:** pleading

Watching China

Amy Tan

(See Reading as a Stimulus for Writing on page 373.)

1   I am an ignorant observer of the situation in China, unversed[1] in politics, a citizen of the United States, where "inalienable[2] rights" have been a fact of life from the day I was born.

2   But over the past months, I have been watching the televised coverage of events in Beijing,[3] often stopping what I was doing in mid-bite, mid-page, or mid-sentence.

3   Because I am also Chinese, China is the motherland I inherited from my ancestors. When the demonstrations were first televised, I would scan the students' determined faces, my chest pounding, thinking I might recognize someone in a crowd of 100,000. All Chinese are family to one another in some unexplainable way. And I know there were other Chinese Americans who proudly watched as the students pushed forward one historic moment after another.

4   Two weeks after the demonstrations began, I received a letter from one of my half-sisters, who lives in Beijing. I quickly read through the usual chitchat: her congratulations on my new book, how hard my niece is studying, how healthy everyone is. And then I found what I was looking for: a brief mention of "things changing" and "the situation is steady" and "please don't worry." Nothing more.

5   The next day, I listened to the news again. Martial law had been declared. My sister's quiet words reminded me of how careful I should be in talking or writing about China.

6   I had considered not writing this at all. And then I realized: it is precisely this feeling of restraint that is at the heart of the student movement. How could I not write?

7   One night, I winced when one broadcaster mispronounced Beijing as "bee-zhing." "Bay-JING." I corrected him. "This is China you're talking about." At the same time, I was painfully aware of my own ignorance about China. My parents came to America in 1949 in the midst of an earlier revolution: my mother was forced to leave behind three other daughters, my half-sisters. If my parents had lacked the gold ingots[4] to buy passage, if they had waited just a few more months, I would perhaps not be here today in a comfortable home in San Francisco, watching China on television and writing about what I see and feel. One night, at the beginning of the student movement, I watched Dan Rather arguing with a Chinese official over his right not to have his satellite plug pulled.

---

[1] **unversed:** not knowledgeable
[2] **inalienable:** cannot be taken away
[3] **events in Beijing:** pro-democracy demonstrations in China's capital city that were violently crushed by the Chinese government in 1989
[4] **ingots:** bars

"I have a contract," he insisted. **8**

The Chinese official scanned the document, unmoved. "The situation **9** described in this document has changed," he replied dryly.

How much we Americans take our freedoms for granted. We already **10** have the rights: freedom of expression, contracts and legal departments to protect them, the right to put differences of opinion to a vote. We put those rights in writing, carry them in our back pockets all over the world, pull them out as proof. We may be aliens[5] in another country, but we still maintain that our rights are inalienable.

I try to imagine what democracy means to people in China, who dream **11** of it. I don't think they are envisioning electoral colleges,[6] First Amendment rights, or civil lawsuits. I imagine that their dreams of democracy begin with a feeling in the chest, one that has been restrained for so long it grows larger and more insistent, until it bursts forth with a shout. Democracy is the right to shout, "Listen to us."

That is what I imagine because I was in China in 1987. I saw glimpses of **12** another way of life, a life that could have been mine. And along with many wonderful things I experienced in my heart, I also felt something uncomfortable in my chest.

In Shanghai in 1987, I attended the wedding of my niece. After the cere- **13** mony, she and her husband went home to the three-room apartment shared with her mother, father, and brother. "Now that you're married," I said with good humor, "you can't live at home anymore."

"The waiting list for government-assigned housing is sixteen years," **14** replied my niece's husband. "We will both be forty-eight years old when we are assigned our own place."

My mouth dropped. He shrugged. **15**

While on a boat trip down the Huangpu River, I asked a tour guide how **16** she had chosen her career. She told me matter-of-factly that people in China did not choose careers. They had jobs assigned to them.

She saw my surprised expression. "Oh, but I'm lucky. So many people **17** can't get any kind of good job. If your family came from a bad background—the bourgeoisie[7]—then, no college. Maybe only a job sweeping the streets." At a family dinner in Beijing, I learned that my sister's husband could not attend our get-together. He was away at his job, said my sister.

"When will he return?" I asked. My mother explained that his job was in **18** a city thousands of miles away. He had been living apart from my sister for the past ten years. "That's terrible," I said to my sister. "Tell him to ask for a transfer. Tell him you miss him."

"Miss, not miss!" my mother sniffed. "They can't even ask." **19**

One of my sisters did ask. Seven years ago, she asked for a visa[8] to leave **20** China. Now she lives in Wisconsin. A former nurse, she now works six days

---

[5]**aliens:** foreigners
[6]**electoral colege:** the government body that officially elects the U.S. president
[7]**bourgeoisie:** business and professional people
[8]**visa:** a document that allows someone to travel to another country

a week, managing a take-out Chinese restaurant. Her husband, trained as a surgeon, works in the kitchen. And recently I've met others who also asked, a waiter who was once a doctor in China, a taxi driver who was formerly a professor of entomology,[9] a housekeeper who was an engineer. Why did they ask to leave? I found it hard to understand how people could leave behind family, friends, their motherland, and jobs of growing prestige.[10]

My sister in Wisconsin helped me understand. After my novel was pub- 21
lished, she wrote me a letter. "I was once like you," she said. "I wanted to write stories as a young girl. But when I was growing up, they told me I could not do so many things. And now my imagination is rusted and no stories can move out of my brain."

My sister and I had the same dream. But my brain did not become 22
rusted. I became a writer. And later, we shared another dream, that China and our family were on the verge of a better, more open life. We did not imagine that the blood that is thicker than water would be running through the streets of Beijing. We did not believe that one Chinese would kill another. We did not foresee that an invisible great wall would rise up, that we would be cut off from our family, that letters would stop, that the silence would become unbearable.

These days I can only imagine what has happened to my family in 23
China. And I think about the word democracy. It rolls so easily off my English-speaking tongue. But in Beijing it is a foreign-sounding word, so many syllables, so many clashing sounds. In China, democracy is still not an easy word to say. Many cannot say it.

Hope then. 24

[9]**entomology:** the study of insects
[10]**prestige:** high status

How To Deal With a Difficult Boss
Donna Brown Hogarty

(See Reading as a Stimulus for Writing on page 403.)

Harvey Gittler knew his new boss was high-strung—the two had worked 1
together on the factory floor. But Gittler was not prepared for his co-worker's personality change when the man was promoted to plant manager.

Just two days later, the boss angrily ordered a standing desk removed 2
because he'd seen a worker leaning on it to look up an order. He routinely dressed down employees at the top of his lungs. At one time or another he threatened to fire virtually everyone in the plant. And after employees went home, he searched through trash cans for evidence of treason.

For many workers, Gittler's experience is frighteningly familiar. Millions 3
of Americans have temperamental bosses. In a 1984 Center for Creative Leadership study of corporate executives, nearly 75 percent of the subjects reported having had at least one intolerable boss.

"Virtually all bosses are problem bosses, in one way or another," says   4
psychologist Mardy Grothe, co-author with Peter Wylie of *Problem Bosses: Who They Are and How To Deal With Them*. The reason, he says, lies in lack of training. Most bosses were promoted to management because they excelled at earlier jobs—not because they have experience motivating others.

Uncertain economic times exacerbate[1] the bad-boss syndrome.[2] "There   5
is an acceptance of getting results at any price," says Stanley Bing, a business executive and author of *Crazy Bosses*. "As a result, the people corporations select to be bosses are the most rigid and demanding, and the least able to roll with the punches."

Bad bosses often have a recognizable *modus operandi*.[3] Harry Levinson,   6
a management psychologist in Waltham, Mass., has catalogued problem bosses, from the bully to the jellyfish to the disapproving perfectionist. If you're suffering from a bad boss, chances are he or she combines several of these traits and can be dealt with effectively if you use the right strategy.

The Bully

During his first week on the job, a new account manager at a small   7
Pennsylvania advertising agency agreed to return some materials to a client. When he mentioned this at a staff meeting, the boss turned beet red, his lips began to quiver and he shouted that the new employee should call his client and confess he didn't know anything about the advertising business, and would *not* be returning the materials.

Over the next few months, as the account manager watched co-workers   8
cower under the boss's browbeating,[4] he realized that the tyrant fed on fear. Employees who tried hardest to avoid his ire[5] were most likely to catch it. "He was like a schoolyard bully," the manager recalls, "and I've known since childhood that, when confronted, most bullies back down."

Armed with new-found confidence and growing knowledge of the ad   9
business, he matched his boss's behavior. "If he raised his voice, I'd raise mine," the manager recalls. True to type, the boss started to treat him with grudging respect. Eventually, the young man moved up the ranks and was rarely subjected to his boss's outbursts.

Although standing up to the bully often works, it *could* make matters   10
worse. Mardy Grothe recommends a different strategy: reasoning with him after he's calmed down. "Some bosses have had a problem with temper control all their lives, and are not pleased with this aspect of their personality," he explains. Want a litmus test?[6] If the boss attempts to compensate for his outburst by overreacting and trying to "make nice" the next day, says Grothe, he or she feels guilty about yesterday's bad behavior.

---

[1]**exacerbate:** to make something worse
[2]**syndrome:** a distinctive or characteristic pattern of behavior
[3]***modus operandi:*** Latin for "way of doing things"
[4]**browbeating:** bullying
[5]**ire:** anger
[6]**litmus test:** a term used in chemistry that has come to mean a sure way to detect or evaluate
  something

Grothe suggests explaining to your boss how his temper affects you. For **11** instance, you might say, "I know you're trying to improve my performance, but yelling makes me less productive because it upsets me."

Whatever strategy you choose, deal with the bully as soon as possible, **12** because "once a dominant/subservient relationship is established, it becomes difficult to unshackle,"[7] warns industrial psychologist James Fisher. Fisher also suggests confronting your boss behind closed doors whenever possible, to avoid being disrespectful. If your boss continues to be overbearing, try these strategies from psychologist Leonard Felder, author of *Does Someone at Work Treat You Badly?*

- To keep your composure while the boss is screaming, repeat a calming **13** phrase to yourself, such as "Ignore the anger. It isn't yours."

- Focus on a humorous aspect of your boss's appearance. If she's got a **14** double chin, watch her flesh shake while she's yammering.[8] "By realizing that even the most intimidating people are vulnerable, you can more easily relax," explains Felder.

- Wait for your boss to take a breath, then try this comeback line: "I want **15** to hear what you're saying. You've got to slow down."

Finally, never relax with an abusive boss, no matter how charming he or **16** she can be, says Stanley Bing. "The bully will worm his or her way into your heart as a way of positioning your face under his foot."

The Workaholic

"Some bosses don't know the difference between work and play," says **17** Nancy Ahlrichs, vice president of client services at the Indianapolis office of Right Associates, an international outplacement firm. "If you want to reach them at night or on a Saturday, just call the office." Worse, such a boss invades your every waking hour, making it all but impossible to separate your own home life from the office.

Ahlrichs advises setting limits on your availability. Make sure the boss **18** knows you can be reached in a crisis, but as a matter of practice go home at a set time. If he responds angrily, reassure him that you will tackle any project first thing in the morning. Get him to set the priorities, so you can decide which tasks can wait.

If you have good rapport[9] with the boss, says Mardy Grothe, consider **19** discussing the problem openly. Your goal is to convince him that just as he needs to meet deadlines, you have personal responsibilities that are equally important.

The Jellyfish

"My boss hires people with the assumption that we all know our jobs," **20** says a woman who works for a small firm in New England. "Unfortunately, he hates conflict. If someone makes a mistake, we have to tiptoe around instead of moving to correct it, so we don't hurt anyone's feelings."

---

[7]**unshackle:** become free of
[8]**yammering:** talking loudly or angrily
[9]**rapport:** a good relationship

Her boss is a jellyfish. He has refused to establish even a rudimentary[10]   21
pecking order in his office. As a result, a secretary sat on important correspondence for over a month, jeopardizing a client's tax write-offs. Because
no one supervises the firm's support staff, the secretary never received a
reprimand, and nobody was able to prevent such mishaps from recurring.
The jellyfish simply can't take charge, because he's afraid of creating conflicts.

So *"you* must take charge," suggests Lee Colby, a Minneapolis-based   22
management consultant. "Tell the jellyfish: 'This is what I think I ought to
be doing. What do you think?' You are taking the initiative, without step-
ping on your boss's toes."

Building an indecisive supervisor's confidence is another good strategy.   23
For example, if you can supply hard facts and figures, you can then use
them to justify any course you recommend—and gently ease the jellyfish
into taking a firmer stance.

The Perfectionist

When Nancy Ahlrichs was fresh out of college, she landed her first full-   24
time job, supervising the advertising design and layout of a small-town
newspaper. On deadline day, the paper's crotchety general manager would
suddenly appear over her shoulder, inspecting her work for errors. Then
he'd ask a barrage of questions, ending with the one Ahlrichs dreaded
most: "Are you sure you'll make the deadline?"

"I never missed a single deadline," Ahlrichs says, "yet every week he'd   25
ask that same question. I felt belittled by his lack of confidence in me."

Ironically, the general manager was lowering the staff's productivity. To   26
paraphrase[11] Voltaire, the perfect is the enemy of the good. According to
psychiatrist Allan Mallinger, co-author with Jeanette DeWyze of *Too Perfect: When Being in Control Gets Out of Control*, "the perfectionist's overcon-
cern for thoroughness slows down everyone's work. When everything has
to be done perfectly, tasks loom larger." The nit-picking boss who is behind
schedule becomes even more difficult, making subordinates ever more miserable.

"Remember," says Leonard Felder, "the perfectionist *needs* to find some-   27
thing to worry about." To improve your lot with a perfectionist boss, get
her to focus on the big picture. If she demands that you redo a task you've
just completed, mention your other assignments and ask her to prioritize.
Often, a boss will let the work you've completed stand—especially when
she realizes another project may be put on hold. If your boss is nervous
about a particular project, offer regular briefings. By keeping the perfectionist posted, you might circumvent[12] constant supervision.   28

Finally, protect yourself emotionally. "You can't depend on the perfectionist for encouragement," says Mallinger. "You owe it to yourself to get a
second opinion of your work by asking others."

---

[10]**rudimentary:** basic
[11]**paraphrase:** restate or change the words somewhat
[12]**circumvent:** get around

The Aloof Boss

When Gene Bergoffen, now CEO of the National Private Truck Council, worked for another trade association and asked to be included in the decision-making process, his boss was brusque and inattentive. The boss made decisions alone, and very quickly. "We used to call him 'Ready, Fire, Aim,'" says Bergoffen. **29**

Many workers feel frozen out by their boss in subtle ways. Perhaps he doesn't invite them to key meetings or he might never be available to discuss projects. "At the core of every good boss is the ability to communicate expectations clearly," says Gerard Roche, chairman of Heidrick & Struggles, an executive search firm. "Employees should never have to wonder what's on a boss's mind." **30**

If your boss fails to give you direction, Roche says, "the worst thing you can do is nothing. Determine the best course of action, then say to your boss: 'Unless I hear otherwise, here's what I'm going to do.'" **31**

Other strategies: When your boss does not invite you to meetings or include you in decision making, speak up. "Tell her you have information that might prove to be valuable," suggests Lee Colby. If that approach doesn't work, find an intermediary who respects your work and can persuade the boss to listen to your views. **32**

To understand your boss's inability to communicate, it's vital to examine his work style. "Some like hard data, logically arranged in writing," says Colby. "Others prefer face-to-face meetings. Find out what makes your boss tick—and speak in his or her language." **33**

Understanding your boss can make your tenure[13] more bearable in a number of ways. For instance, try offering the boss two solutions to a problem—one that will make him happy and one that will help you to reach your goals. Even the most intractable[14] boss will usually allow you to solve problems in your own way—as long as he's convinced of your loyalty to him. **34**

No matter which type of bad boss you have, think twice before going over his head. Try forming a committee with your colleagues and approaching the boss en masse. The difficult boss is usually unaware of the problem and often is eager to make amends. **35**

Before embarking on any course of action, engage in some self-analysis. Chances are, no matter how difficult your boss is, you are also contributing to the conflict. "Talk to people who know you both, and get some honest feedback," suggests Mardy Grothe. "If you can fix the ways in which you're contributing to the problem, you'll be more likely to get your boss to change." **36**

Even if you can't, there's a silver lining: the worst bosses often have the most to teach you. Bullies, for example, are frequently masters at reaching difficult goals. Perfectionists can often prod you into exceeding your own expectations. **37**

---

[13]**tenure:** the period during which a job is held
[14]**intractable:** stubborn

As a young resident psychologist at the Menninger psychiatric hospital in Topeka, Kan., Harry Levinson was initially overwhelmed by the high standards of founder Karl Menninger. "I felt I was never going to be able to diagnose patients as well as he did or perform to such high academic requirements," Levinson recalls. He even considered quitting. But in the end, he rose to the challenge, and today believes he owes much of his success to what he learned during that critical juncture. 38

Dealing with a difficult boss forces you to set priorities, to overcome fears, to stay calm under the gun, and to negotiate for better working conditions. And the skills you sharpen to ease a tense relationship will stand you in good stead throughout your career. "Employees who are able to survive a trying boss often earn the respect of higher-ups for their ability to manage a situation," says Levinson. "And because a difficult boss can cause rapid turnover, those who stick it out often advance quickly." 39

Your bad boss can also teach you what *not* to do with subordinates as you move up—and one day enable you to be a better boss yourself. 40

Pair-or-Less Situation
Suzann Ledbetter

(See Reading as a Stimulus for Writing on page 430.)

Noah had the right idea when he loaded his ark with pairs of all the creatures on earth. Two by two, with future repopulation in mind, passengers loped, crawled, and flew aboard to weather the storm. 1

As a descendant of Noah, I therefore assume a pair of something to mean two of them. A pair of bunnies in the backyard means two animals grazing in the garden. A pair of wet socks left on the bed means two soggy spots, plus one son in a ton of trouble. 2

If a pair should equal two, then why do packages enumerating[1] undergarments as "three *pairs*" yield only three garments instead of six? Pantyhose are enveloped as pairs too, but surrender only one wad of tinted nylon. 3

Further investigation reveals more inconsistencies than answers. 4

If a man shops for new socks, he purchases a pair of two socks, not individual items of footwear. We wear pairs (two) of shoes, and pairs (two) of earrings, yet a pair of eyeglasses fit only one nose. 5

While mulling this revelation, I tried to figure out why clothing is thought of as paired whether the number of individual items would equal 6

[1]**enumerating:** listing

one or two. Could it be that underwear and slacks are "pairs" because of the number of appendages[2] inserted through openings?

This seemed a logical explanation until the same theory was applied to a shirt. If one counts armholes, shirts should be bought in singularly termed pairs, too. 7

A different Noah, the *Webster's Dictionary* daddy, defined a pair as "two corresponding things designed for use together," and the entry cites trousers to illustrate its meaning. 8

I'd ask wise Webster why his description is only accurate when referring to socks, underwear, slacks, and pantyhose, yet the same theory is not applicable to sweaters, shirts, and overcoats—but he cashed in his quill about a hundred and fifty years ago. 9

I find this tangle of terminology curious, but imagine what confusion it could cause an innocent immigrant. If Peter Piper, a new resident of our land, went into a department store to purchase some American clothing, I can only imagine the resulting conversation: 10

Clerk: "How may I help you, sir?"
Peter: "I want to buy jean, shirt, and a pair of socks."
Clerk: "Fine, let's start with the jeans. How many pairs do you need?"
Peter: "I do not want a pair, I just want one."
Clerk: "Er, one *what*, sir?"
Peter: "One jean."
Clerk: "You mean, one *pair* of jeans."
Peter: "No! I learned in English class that one pair equals two things. I cannot afford more than one jean today."
Clerk: "Ah, now I understand. You see, sir, in this country, we call them a *pair* of jeans because of the two legs. A *pair* of jeans is just one garment. Do you understand?"
Peter: "Yes, thank you. A pair of jeans is just one. Okay, then I also want two pairs of socks."
Clerk: "Two pairs of socks coming up."
Peter: "Wait! There are *four* socks in your hand. I have only two feet, so I only want two pairs."
Clerk: "But sir, this *is* two pairs. A pair of socks is one sock for each foot."
Peter: "I thought you said a pair was only one?"
Clerk: "Well, that's true for jeans because you cannot buy trousers of any kind with just one leg in them, but socks are just as you said earlier—a pair of socks is *two* socks."
Peter: "This is all very strange. I ask for socks as one pair of two socks. I ask for jean as one pair too, because they have two legs. Let me think just a minute, I want to get it correct this time. . . . For my final purchase I want a *pair* of shirts. One shirt, two arms; a pair, right?"

Noah or Noah Webster? Which pundit's principle should Peter Piper pick? 11

[2]**appendages:** limbs

No Books, No Brains, No Chance 〜〜〜〜〜〜〜〜
Sheryl McCarthy

(See Reading as a Stimulus for Writing on page 461.)

1   All over town yesterday, people were yelling about the cuts the mayor wants to make in the school budget.

2   At City Hall, some school superintendents yelled that the cuts were outrageous. In Queens, more than 100 parents yelled that they couldn't stomach the toll on schools in their district.

3   And at a hearing in an office building across from City Hall, students and alumni of New York's public schools said emphatically[1] that they had come to *praise* what the schools did for them, not to *bury* them.

4   Nobody yelled so eloquently as Dwight David Gregg, who limped into the hearing on the arm of his son, a high school junior. Gregg was in pain because he threw his back out last week, but he couldn't miss this, he said. It was too momentous.

5   Gregg is a parole officer who knows the school system through its back end. That is, he sees what happens when people *don't* get an education.

6   He works in the warrants section of parole, which means his job is to find people who have violated parole and lock them up. He and his fellow officers go looking for people every day. Sometimes they catch up with two or three, sometimes they get nobody.

7   The parole-breakers all have one thing in common. They are ignorant.

8   Gregg first became aware of this when he was a kid growing up in Philadelphia. "In the ninth grade I couldn't read. So I started to act out. I did everything I could to make people miserable. You treat people the way you want to be treated. I didn't like myself, so I treated myself terribly and I treated everyone else terribly."

9   In the 10th grade, he was kicked out of school. He wound up in the Job Corps in Tennessee, trying to learn a trade. Here he found lots of other young men—poor blacks and white hillbillies who, like himself, couldn't read.

10 He decided to try to educate himself.

11 Gregg joined the Marines and went to Vietnam. When he looked down the line of soldiers, he saw the same images he had seen in the Job Corps. "It was the same folks, guys with little education who couldn't read. Only now they were dying for it."

12 Two years in Vietnam shook him up sufficiently to make him go to college—and graduate—after he came home. He then became a drug counselor, worked in psychiatric hospitals, and finally became a parole officer.

13 Now when he sees the drug addicts and criminals who file past him, he sees in them a mirror image of himself as a young man. They have no edu-

---

[1]**emphatically:** firmly

cation, very little self-esteem—and like the guys in Vietnam, they, too, are dying.

A few months ago, Gregg was searching for a parole violator who was 22 years old. The fellow had shot five people, and finally somebody shot him. The bullet went through the back of his ear and came out his mouth. **14**

But he survived, which made him think he was really "bad." **15**

When Gregg looked at the shooter's file, what stood out was that he had no education. "He had dropped out in the ninth or tenth grade." **16**

The guy was finally caught. "On the surface he seemed like just a pleasant kid," Gregg said. But he was also ignorant, and he may die for it, too. **17**

"When you have a conversation with these men, you can see they don't know what's really going on in this world. They have no guidance. These are lost folks." **18**

In the jails of this city, only 10 percent of the inmates have finished high school. The state prisons are also pools of ignorance; 75 percent of the inmates have no high school diploma. **19**

Last month, a 17-year-old named Jerome Nisbett was sentenced to 25-years-to-life in prison for shooting a drama teacher in a Brooklyn park. During his trial, the most striking thing about Nisbett was his ignorance, and the feeling that he existed in a moral vacuum. When a police officer read Nisbett's confession in court, it sounded like something written by a fourth grader. **20**

So to Dwight David Gregg, the idea of cutting money for schools is preposterous. "In New York City, you have a *prop* called education, but you don't have the funds or the fortitude[2] to see that children get educated. It's a bone with no marrow in it." **21**

Yesterday, people in this city were yelling about the mayor's plan to cut out school antiviolence programs that have names like "mediation"[3] and "conflict resolution." These programs may all sound good, but there's no better way to short-circuit a life of crime than by teaching somebody to read. **22**

[2]**fortitude:** courage
[3]**mediation:** a process in which someone acts as a go-between to settle disputes

egy in which individuals should conform initially to the views of the source of influence. After doing so in order to establish themselves as competent and reasonable group members, they can behave more independently and espouse views that are contrary to the majority's views. Instead of remaining consistently adamant in a deviant position, as Moscovici's consistency approach suggests, Hollander's theory suggests that people should first conform—but that after establishing their "credentials," they should then press their minority views.

Experimental evidence supports both approaches (Maass & Clark, 1984; Wold, 1985). Consequently, it is clear that social influence is not a one-way street; when we are the targets of social influence, we have a fighting chance to remain independent.

Recap and Review I

Recap

- Social influence is concerned with situations in which the actions of one individual or group affect the behavior of another.
- The most important types of social influence are conformity and compliance. Conformity is a change in behavior due to a desire to follow the beliefs or standards of other people, while compliance reflects a change in behavior made in response to direct, explicit social pressure.
- Among the primary techniques for remaining independent from group pressure are inoculation, forewarning, and consistency.

Review

1. When social psychologists discuss _____ , they are referring to a change in behavior resulting from a desire to follow the beliefs or standards of others. However, when a change in behavior occurs in response to more direct social pressure, such as in the form of a direct order, the change is called _____.
2. List four of the most important variables producing conformity.

Liking and Loving: Interpersonal Attraction and the Development of Relationships
Robert S. Feldman

(See Assignment: Creating a Summary on page A 13)

LIKING AND LOVING: INTERPERSONAL ATTRACTION AND THE DEVELOPMENT OF RELATIONSHIPS

When nineteenth-century poet Elizabeth Barrett Browning wrote, "How do I love thee? Let me count the ways," she was expressing feelings about a topic that is central to most people's lives—and one that has developed into a major subject of investigation by social psychologists: loving and liking. Known more formally as the study of **interpersonal attraction** or **close relationships**, this topic encompasses the factors that lead to positive feelings for others.

Interpersonal attraction: *Positive feelings for others*
Close relationships: *See interpersonal attraction*

How Do I Like Thee? Let Me Count the Ways

By far the greatest amount of research has focused on liking, probably because it has always proved easier for investigators conducting short-term experiments

Love is a state of interpersonal attraction that can be clearly differentiated from mere liking. (*Edward L. Miller/Stock, Boston*)

to produce states of liking in strangers who have just met than to promote and observe loving relationships over long periods of time. Hence, traditional studies have given us a good deal of knowledge about the factors that attract two people to each other (Berscheid, 1985). Among the most important factors discovered are the following:

■ Proximity. If you live in a dormitory or an apartment, consider the friends you made when you first moved in. Chances are, you became friendliest with those who lived geographically closest to you. In fact, this is one of the best-established findings in the interpersonal attraction literature; **proximity** leads to liking (Festinger, Schachter, & Back, 1950; Nahome & Lawton, 1976).

Proximity (prox IM ih tee): *One's nearness to another, one cause for liking*

■ Mere exposure. Repeated exposure to a person is often sufficient to produce attraction. Interestingly, repeated exposure to *any* stimulus—be it a person, picture, record, or what have you—most frequently makes us like the stimulus more (Birnbaum & Mellers, 1979; Zajonc, 1968). Becoming familiar with a stimulus can evoke positive feelings; these positive feelings due to familiarity are then transferred to the stimulus itself. There are exceptions, though: In cases in which the initial interactions are strongly negative, repeated exposure is unlikely to cause us to like another person more; instead, we may end up disliking such an individual more the more we are exposed to him or her.

■ Similarity. We tend to like those who are similar to us; discovering that others are similar in terms of attitudes, values, or traits promotes liking for them (Byrne, 1969; Hill & Stull, 1981; Meyer & Pepper, 1971). Moreover, the more similar they are, the more we like them. There is also a strong **reciprocity-of-liking effect**, a tendency to like those who like us—as well as the converse: we assume that when we like someone else, they like us in return (Metee & Aronson, 1974; Tagiuri, 1958).

Reciprocity-of-liking effect: *A tendency to like those who like us*

■ Physical attractiveness. For most people, the equation "beautiful = good" is a very real one. As a result, people who are physically attractive are more popular than those who are physically unattractive, if all other factors are equal. This finding, which contradicts the values that most people would profess, is apparent even in childhood—with nursery-school-age children rating popularity

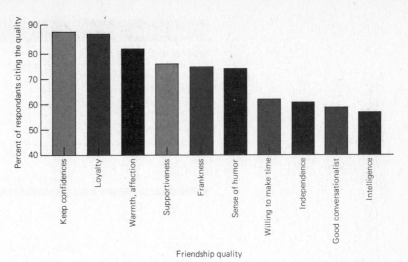

Figure 15-3
These are the key qualities people look for in a friend according to some 40,000 respondents to a questionnaire. (*Adapted from Parlee, 1979.*)

on the basis of attractiveness (Dion & Berscheid, 1974)—and continues into adulthood. Indeed, physical attractiveness may be the single most important element promoting initial liking in college dating situations, although its influence decreases when people get to know each other better (Berscheid & Walster, 1974). Moreover, there are some cases in which physical attractiveness is a drawback: Although good looks lead to more positive impressions of men in job-related situations, beauty can work against women in managerial positions, since a common (although totally unfounded) stereotype holds that attractive women attain their position due to looks rather than ability (Heilman & Stopek, 1985). Physical attractiveness, then, is generally a powerful factor in determining who people are attracted to and the kind of social life one has (Reis, Wheeler, Spiegel, Kerris, Nezlek, & Perri, 1982).

Proximity, mere exposure, similarity, and physical attractiveness are not, of course, the only factors that are important in liking. For example, survey research has sought to determine the factors that are critical in friendships. In one questionnaire that was answered by some 40,000 respondents, the qualities that were most valued in a friend were identified (Parlee, 1979). (See Figure 15-3.) The key factors were the ability to keep confidences, loyalty, and warmth and affection, followed closely by supportiveness, frankness, and a sense of humor.

How Do I Love Thee? Let Me Count the Ways

While our knowledge of what makes people like each other is extensive, our understanding of love is a more limited and relatively recent phenomenon. Many social psychologists believed for a long time that love represents a phenomenon too difficult to observe and study in a controlled, scientific way. However, love is such a central issue in most people's lives that, in time, social psychologists

TABLE 15-1

Loving and liking

Sample love items:
  I feel that I can confide in _____ about virtually everything.
  I would do almost anything for _____ .
  I feel responsible for _____ 's well-being.

Sample liking items:
  I think that _____ is unusually well-adjusted.
  I think that _____ is one of those people who quickly wins
    respect.
  _____ is one of the most likable people I know.

Source: Rubin, 1973

could not resist its allure and became infatuated with the topic (Sternberg & Grajek, 1984).

As a first step, researchers have tried to identify the distinguishing characteristics between mere liking and full-blown love. Using this approach, they have discovered that love is not simply liking of a greater quantity, but a qualitatively different psychological state (Walster & Walster, 1978). For instance, at least in its early stages, love includes relatively intense physiological arousal, an all-encompassing interest in another individual, fantasizing about the other, and relatively rapid swings of emotion. Similarly, Davis (1985) suggests that love has elements of fascination, exclusiveness, sexual desire, and intense caring that liking lacks.

Social psychologist Zick Rubin (1970, 1973) has tried to differentiate between love and liking using a paper-and-pencil scale. As can be seen from the sample items in Table 15-1, each question refers to the person to whom the individual is attracted.

Researchers have found that couples scoring high on the love scale differ considerably from those with low scores. They gaze at each other more, and their relationships are more likely to be intact six months later than are the relationships of those who score low on the scale.

Other experiments have found evidence suggesting that the heightened physiological arousal hypothesized to be characteristic of loving is indeed present when a person reports being in love. Interestingly, though, it may not be just arousal of a sexual nature. Berscheid & Walster (1974) have theorized that when we are exposed to *any* stimulus that increases physiological arousal—such as danger, fear, or anger—our feelings for another person present at the time of the arousal may be labeled as love, if there are situational cues that suggest that "love" is an appropriate label for the feelings being experienced. In sum, we say we are in love when general physiological arousal is coupled with the thought that the cause of the arousal is most likely love.

This theory explains, then, why a person who keeps being rejected or hurt by another could still feel "in love" with that person. If the rejection leads to physiological arousal, but the arousal still happens to be attributed to love—and not to rejection—then a person will still feel "in love".

Other researchers have theorized that there are actually several kinds of love (Hendrick & Hendrick, 1986). For example, Robert Sternberg (1986) suggests that love is made up of three components: an intimacy component, encompassing feelings of closeness and connectedness; a passion component made up of the

TABLE 15-2

The kinds of love

| | Component* | | |
	INTIMACY	PASSION	DECISION/COMMITMENT
Nonlove	−	−	−
Liking	+	−	−
Infatuated love	−	+	−
Empty love	−	−	+
Romantic love	+	+	−
Companionate love	+	−	+
Fatuous love	−	+	+
Consummate love	+	+	+

*+ = component present; − = component absent.
Source: Sternberg, 1986, Table 2.

motivational drives relating to sex, physical closeness, and romance; and a decision/commitment component encompassing the cognition that one loves someone (in the short term) and longer-term feelings of commitment to maintain love. As can be seen in Table 15-2, particular combinations of the three components produce several different kinds of love.

The Rise and Fall of Liking and Loving: Understanding the Course of Relationships

With one out of two marriages ending in divorce and broken love affairs a common phenomenon, it is not surprising that social psychologists have begun to turn their attention increasingly toward understanding what makes some relationships last and others fail (Hays, 1985; Ickes, 1984; Snyder, Berscheid, & Glick, 1985).

Social psychologist George Levinger (1983) has speculated on the reasons behind the deterioration of relationships. One important factor appears to be a change in judgments about the meaning of a partner's behavior. Behavior that was once viewed as "charming forgetfulness" comes to be seen as "boorish indifference," and the partner becomes less valued. In addition, communications may be disrupted; rather than listening to what the other person is saying, each partner becomes bent on justifying himself or herself, and communication deteriorates. Eventually, a partner may begin to invite and agree with criticism of the other partner from people outside of the relationship and look to others for the fulfillment of basic needs that were previously met by the partner.

Not all relationships deteriorate, of course. What characterizes successful ones? Some answers to this question come from a study by Jeanette and Robert Lauer (1985), who surveyed couples who reported being happily married for fifteen years or more. When asked to indicate what it was that had made their marriages last, both the husbands and wives gave remarkably similar responses. As you can see in Table 15-3, the most frequently named reason was perceiving one's spouse as one's best friend and liking him or her "as a person." There was also a strong belief in marriage as a commitment and a desire to make the relationship work, as well as agreement about aims and goals. On the other

TEXT CREDITS

CHAPTER 1   Excerpt from "Memoirs of a Non-Prom Queen" by Ellen Willis from *Rolling Stone*, August 26, 1976. By Straight Arrow Publishers, Inc. 1976. All Rights Reserved. Reprinted by Permission.   Excerpt from "The Future of Work" from *Harper's*, April 1989. Copyright © Robert B. Reich. Reprinted by permission of Raphael Sagalyn Literary Agency.

CHAPTER 2   "Don't Expect Me to Be Perfect" by Sun Park from *Newsweek*, Special Issue, Summer/Fall 1990, page 62. Every effort has been made to contact the author/rights holder.

CHAPTER 4   "The Little Store," excerpt from *The Eye of the Story* by Eudora Welty. Copyright © 1978 by Eudora Welty. Reprinted by permission of Random House, Inc.   Excerpt from *Blue Highways* by William Least Heat Moon. Copyright © 1982 by William Least Heat Moon. By permission of Little, Brown and Company.   Excerpt from *Wouldn't Take Nothin For My Journey Now* by Maya Angelou. Copyright © 1993 by Maya Angelou. Reprinted by permission of Random House, Inc.   "Easy Job, Good Wages" by Jesus Colon, from *A Puerto Rican in New York* (Mainstream, 1961). Reprinted by permission of International Publishers.

CHAPTER 5   Excerpt from *Wellsprings of Imagination* by Mark I. West. Copyright © 1992 by Mark I. West. Reprinted by permission of Neal-Schuman Publishers, Inc.   "Enough Bookshelves" by Anna Quindlen. Copyright © 1991 by The New York Times Company. Reprinted by permission.

CHAPTER 6   Excerpt from *The Years With Ross* by James Thurber. Copyright © 1959 by James Thurber. Copyright © 1987 by Rosemary A. Thurber. Published by Atlantic-Little Brown. Reprinted with permission.   "A Pothole from Hell" by Mark Goldblatt. *The New York Times*, April 26, 1989 (op ed). Copyright © 1989 by The New York Times Company. Reprinted by permission.

CHAPTER 7   Excerpt from "On Not Being a Victim" by Mary Gaitskill. Copyright © 1994 by *Harper's Magazine*. All rights reserved. Reprinted from the March 1994 issue by special permission.   "Only Daughter" by Sandra Cisneros, courtesy *Glamour*. Copyright © 1990 by the Conde Nast Publications.

CHAPTER 8   "Introductions to New York" by Bob Blaisdell. *The New York Times*, February 20, 1994. Copyright © 1994 by The New York Times Company. Reprinted by permission.

CHAPTER 9   "How Dictionaries Are Made" from *Language in Thought and Action, Fourth Edition*, by S.I. Hayakawa, copyright © 1978 by Harcourt Brace & Company, reprinted by permission of the publisher.

CHAPTER 10   "Probable Cause" by Keith Coffee, *Essence*, July 1991. Every effort has been made to contact the author/rights holder.

CHAPTER 11   "Watching China" by Amy Tan. Copyright © 1989 by Amy Tan. Reprinted by permission of the author and the Sandra Dijkstra Literary Agency.

CHAPTER 12   "How to Deal With a Difficult Boss" by Donna Brown Hogarty. Reprinted with permission from the July 1993 *Reader's Digest*.

CHAPTER 13   "Pair-or-Less Situation" from *The Toast Always Lands Jelly-Side Down* by Suzann Ledbetter. Copyright © 1993 by Suzann Ledbetter. Reprinted by permission of Crown Publishers, Inc.

CHAPTER 14   "No Books, No Brains, No Chance" by Sheryl McCarthy. *New York Newsday*, June 8, 1994. Reprinted by permission of the Los Angeles Times Syndicate.

ENRICHMENT CHAPTER E   Excerpt from The New York Public Library computerized card catalog.   Excerpt from computerized card catalog reprinted by permission of Bobst Library, New York University.   Excerpt from *Reader's Guide to Periodical Literature*. Copyright © 1992 by the H. W. Wilson Company. Used by permission.

WRITER'S GUIDE   By permission. From Merriam-Webster's Collegiate® Dictionary, Tenth Edition. © 1993 by Merriam-Webster Inc., publisher of the Merriam-Webster® dictionaries.

BACKMATTER   Excerpt from *Essentials of Understanding Psychology*, Robert S. Feldman. Copyright © 1989 by McGraw-Hill. Reprinted by permission of McGraw-Hill, Inc.

INDEX

content development and, 390

as content development strategy, 177-178

creating categories for, 388

for definition, 412-413

equal weight of categories for, 385

establishing purpose of, 387-388

oral, 383

parallel information for, 385

revising essays using, 396-403

setting tone for, 394-396

structure for, 390-393

thesis statement for, 388-390

transitions to link categories in, 385-386

writing tasks requiring, 386-387

Climax, 238

Coherence
in essays, 23-26
establishing during prewriting, 61-68
methods of achieving, 183
in paragraphs, 10-12
in writing process, 42

Coincidence, in cause/effect analysis, 326

Collaborative group, 6
guidelines for sharing in, 103

Collect-and-sort method for gathering support, 49-50

Comma splice, 158

Common features, for classification, 384-385

Compare. See Compare/contrast

Compare/contrast, as content development strategy, 171-173

Comparison/contrast
analogy, simile, and metaphor for, 180-181, 212-214

audience of, 363-364

block pattern for, 353

choosing topic for, 356

content development and, 357-358

establishing purpose for, 357

oral, 351

of parallel features, 352

point-by-point pattern for, 353-354

revising essays using, 367-375

setting tone for, 365-366

structure for, 358-363

thesis statement for, 357

transitions to link points in, 354

writing tasks requiring, 355

Computer catalog, A 30

Computers. See Word processing programs

Conceptual map. See mapping

Concluding sentence, 10

Conclusion, 22
body related to, 18-19
prewriting, 69-70

Conjunctions, 158, A 80, A 83

Connecting ideas and information, 192-196
pronouns for, 195
repeating key words for, 194-195
synonyms for, 195-196
transitions for. See Transitional words and phrases

Consistency, of point of view, 240

Content
development of. See Content development; Content development strategies; specific types of essays
evaluating, 89-92
organizing. See Chronological order; Order of importance or interest; Organization;

Spatial order; Structure of essay
planning approach to, 166
revising and editing and, 90, 153

Content development, 137-141. See also specific types of essays
choosing sources for, 138-139
in Writing Focus Chart, 131-132

Content development strategies, 167-183
analogy as, 180-181
cause/effect as, 178-179
choosing, 139-141, 182-183
classification as, 177-178
combining, 182
compare/contrast as, 171-173
definition as, 174-176
description as, 170
examples as, 169-170, 175
facts as, 168
narration as, 173-174
process as, 176-177
Strategies Box and, 167

Contrast. See Compare/contrast; Comparison/contrast

Convincing. See Arguments; Persuasive writing

Cross-reference, A 29

Dangling modifiers, 376-377, A 76-A 77

Definition(s), 411-431
audience for, 422
choosing topic for, 416-417
content development and, 418
as content development strategy, 174-176
establishing purpose for, 417
extended, 412, 414-415
identifying distinguishing features for, 413-414
oral, 411

Unfamiliar words, explaining, 99

Unity
creating during prewriting, 58-61
in essays, 23-26
in paragraphs, 10-12
in writing process, 42

Vague generalizations, 442
Vantage point, 188
Verbs, A 81, A 83, A 84-A 85
agreement with subject, 201-202, 230-231, A 71-A 72
helping, 288
irregular, 316-317, A 74-A 75
regular, 288-289, A 73
Verb tense, A 81
of irregular verbs, 316-317, A 74-A 75
of regular verbs, 288-289, A 73
unnecessary changes in, 404-405, A 77-78

Word(s)
choosing, 97, A 113-A 115
key, repeating, 194-195
proofreading for spelling of, 105

transitional. *See* Transition(s)
unfamiliar, explaining, 99
Word processing programs, 27
brainstorming using, 330, 448
for charting sequence of steps in a process, 305
for choosing categories for classification, 395
choosing strategies using, 183
creating time line using, 247
for developing comparison/contrast, 364
handling hard-to-spell words using, 108
outtakes files and, 278
for prewriting, 58
for structuring essays, 219
thesaurus feature of, 419
Word use, A 98-A 110
commonly confused words, A 107-A 110
dictionary use, A 98-A 101
evaluating, 90, 97-104
revising, 153
spelling, 105, 108, A 101-A 107
varying, 98
Writer's block, 42

Writer's Guide. *See Grammar fundamentals; Mechanics; Punctuation; Style; Word use*
Writing assignments, 27-31
Writing elements, 118-119
blending, 152
interdependence of, 132-136
Writing Focus Chart, 131-152
interdependence of elements in, 132-136
Writing process, 36-112. *See also* First draft; Prewriting; Proofreading; Revising
steps of, 40-70, 85-106
unity, support, and coherence in, 42
Writing purposes, 120-137. *See also specific types of essays*
choosing strategies and, 182
description as, 121-123
establishing, 136-137
informing as, 127-130
narration as, 123-125
number of, 130
persuasion as, 125-127
revising and editing and, 90, 153
in Writing Focus Chart, 131-132